KWAZULU/NATAL WILDLIFE DESTINATIONS

KWAZULU/NATAL WILDLIFE DESTINATIONS

A guide to the game reserves, resorts, private nature reserves, ranches and wildlife areas of KwaZulu/Natal

TONY POOLEY and IAN PLAYER

SOUTHERN
BOOK PUBLISHERS

Previous books by the authors:

TONY POOLEY
Discoveries of a crocodile man (1982) William Collins & Sons, London
Mashesha, the making of a game ranger (1992) Southern, Halfway House

IAN PLAYER
Men, rivers and canoes (1964) Simondium Publishers, Cape Town
The white rhino saga (1972) William Collins & Sons, London

ISBN 1 86812 487 8

First edition, first impression 1995

Published by
Southern Book Publishers (Pty) Ltd
PO Box 3103 Halfway House 1685

Cover design by Wim Reinders
Set in 9/11 pt Helvetica by 4-Ways DTP Services, Cape Town
Design by Wim Reinders & Associates, Cape Town
Reproduction by Hirt & Carter, Cape Town
Printed and bound by National Book Printers, Goodwood

CONTENTS

INTRODUCTION: HOW TO USE THIS BOOK

This compilation of information on the larger game reserves and resorts, private ranches, small nature reserves and other conserved areas in KwaZulu/Natal is intended to provide a portrait of what each has to offer. The province has been divided into regions based not on political or ecological grounds, but simply to advise the tourist of the number and nature of the reserves that can be visited in a particular area of KwaZulu/Natal. This list is by no means complete as some privately owned establishments did not respond to our requests for information and inclusion in this book. The marine reserves are not dealt with and neither are all of the state owned forestry reserves. Some of the smaller reserves are mentioned only briefly as limitations of space, and in some instances, a lack of information, present a problem. A few of the small conserved areas are included as they are valuable "witness" areas, preserving relict vegetation communities in now highly developed regions. It should be noted that some of the areas described as nature reserves have not been officially proclaimed. These are open-space areas designated for nature conservation and recreation by local authorities and categorised as nature reserves or parks.

This guide is presented in the following format:

1. **Name** of reserve, area in hectares and date of establishment.
2. **Location** and how to get there.
3. **Features:** the specific attractions of the reserve are highlighted for quick reference.
4. **Description:** a summary of the topography of the park and its natural features, e.g. geological formations, rivers, lakes, pans and habitat types such as grassland, dune forest, coastal forest, mistbelt forest, thornveld, bushveld or swamps, etc.
5. **Historical notes:** information on past land use of the area, important historical events and the development of the reserve is provided.
6. **Accommodation:** if applicable and booking procedures. The name, address and telephone number of each reserve is provided. Readers should note that some country telephone exchanges are to change over from manual to automatic systems and accordingly some of the numbers listed will change. **If difficulty is experienced in obtaining a number, dial 1023/5 for assistance.**

FLORA AND FAUNA

The selection of which species of plants, birds and mammals to include for each reserve was extremely difficult. For example, Ndumu Game Reserve harbours over 900 plant species, 420 bird, 62 mammal and primate, 76 reptile and chelonian, 45 amphibian and 43 fish species! Some of the typical or common examples which are most likely to be encountered in each reserve are listed. More particularly, the interesting, rare or endemic species have been mentioned.

The lists of fauna and flora were derived from publications, from the contributions of numerous individuals, from personal records as well as from information supplied by the owners and staff of the many private reserves, ranches and game lodges.

ZULU NAMES
The spelling and use of Zulu names can be confusing to people unfamiliar with the language. Some Zulu names have been anglicised as evident on road maps and road signs. Other old accepted names have been changed in accordance with current Zulu spelling. Examples are the Umkomaas river that flows into the sea at the upper Natal south coast resort of Umkomaas. In the catchment area the same river is known as the Mkhomazi river, sometimes spelt Mkomazi. The river from which Umfolozi Game Reserve derives its name is Mfolozi. Mkuzi Game Reserve derives its name from the Mkuze river as does Mkuze village. Ndumu Game Reserve signboards use the spelling Ndumu, Ndumo and Nduma. The Tugela river and the Thukela are one and the same. From older maps in the literature and in brochures one finds the area stretching northwards from the Mkuze river to the Mozambique border referred to as north-eastern Zululand, Thongaland, Tongaland and in more recent years as Maputaland. This accounts for the inconsistency in this book in the spelling of some names.

TARIFFS
Tariffs for reserves and parks have been omitted as these change quite frequently. Most establishments warn that tariffs are subject to alteration without notice. Some offer in-season and out-of-season rates. Some establishments offer package tours and group concession rates, depending on the number of persons in a group, their proposed length of stay and whether the in-season or out-of-season rates apply.

Finally, it must be mentioned that during the time between completion of the manuscript and final publication of this guide, changes in policy may occur that lead to the closure of a camp or the withdrawal of certain facilities or, conversely, the establishment of a new camp or provision of additional amenities. Game introductions or removals may alter species composition of the fauna within an area. Changing political influences may alter the status, size and boundaries of parks included in this book.

ADVICE FOR VISITORS
1. Visitors are advised to establish the full tariff, including entrance fees per vehicle and per person when making a reservation to visit a reserve, and to ascertain whether weekend or holiday rates apply to the tariffs quoted.

2. When making a reservation it is important to establish whether payment can be made by cheque, cash only or by bank credit card. Some remote camps cannot process credit cards and certain cards may not be accepted.

3. Establish the gate opening and closing times for each reserve. Natal Parks Board reserves generally allow entry between 5h00 to 19h00 in summer (1 October-31 March) and in winter between 6h00 to 18h00 (1 April-30 September). At some public resorts 24 hour access is permitted.

4. When making a reservation in a remote area, enquire whether petrol or diesel fuel is on sale in the reserve, and if not, establish the nearest source of supply to the reserve.

5. Visitors who regularly enter game reserves, nature reserves and resorts administered by the Natal Parks Board should be aware that a Golden Rhino Passport can be purchased from the reservations office in Pietermaritzburg and in most reserves and offices. These passports are good value and permit the owner, the passengers and vehicle, trailer, boat and caravan, multiple free entry into any reserve or public resort under the board's control. Passports are not transferable. They are valid for one calendar year and can be purchased at half price after 31 July each year.

6. Because of the increasing incidence of malaria in Zululand, visitors intending to visit this area are advised to consult a pharmacist, to take the prescribed medication before entering a malarial region and to continue the dosage recommended after returning from the area.

7. Before towing a boat to a distant inland or coastal resort establish what type of craft are permitted. Some types and sizes of craft are not permitted on certain dams, lakes and coastal estuaries. Obtain a free copy of the boating regulations that pertain to Natal Parks Board resorts (available from Natal Parks Board, Pietermaritzburg, and from resorts). These regulations specify the maximum length and width of craft, the number of persons permitted in the craft of each size class, and specify the safety equipment required before permission is given to launch it.

8. Anglers intending to visit Natal Parks Board inland resorts should be aware that licences are necessary for all inland fishing. Separate licences for trout and for other fishing are needed. Regulations controlling bag and size limits are in force. Trout dams are open throughout the year, trout rivers from 1 September to 1 June inclusive. General licences are obtainable from most magistrates' offices, sport dealers and Natal Parks Board reserves. A daily rod licence for fly fishing can be purchased in the reserve.

9. Although a licence to fish in the sea or in estuaries is not required, coastal fishing regulations specify which species of fish are protected and what fishing methods and gear may or may not be employed. Restrictions on the use of spear guns, bag limits and the minimum size limits for the various species that may be caught are given. Areas

closed to fishing are demarcated. The regulations detail the methods that can be used to gather or capture various types of bait. The coastal fishing regulations apply to line fishermen, spear fishermen, semi-commercial and commercial ski-boat operators. Copies of these regulations, and bait licences, are obtainable at Natal Parks Board resorts.

10. Anglers and visitors to coastal resorts should also ascertain the regulations controlling the types of vehicle that are permitted on the beaches, the permit requirements, and the areas where vehicles are prohibited.

11. On arrival in a game reserve, nature reserve or resort, visitors should request a map or general brochure, if available, and a copy of the rules and regulations if these have not been issued at the entrance gate. It is advisable, for your own safety and to assist the management staff, that you read these regulations. Remember also to take note of speed limits applicable and to be aware that the regulations of the Provincial Traffic Act are also applicable in nature and game reserves.

12. For your convenience, establish opening and closing times of camp offices, shops, camp kitchens, restaurants and petrol sales on arrival at a reserve. Enquire as to the departure times of guided vehicle or launch tours as these excursions usually have to be booked in advance. Bookings may be at a premium over holiday periods.

13. When camping in remote areas where security measures are difficult to enforce, visitors are strongly advised to hand in firearms, valuables and personal documents for safekeeping in the reserve office.

14. Remember that no pets of any description are allowed in game reserves, nature reserves and resorts or any protected wildlife area.

At the time of going to press, the administrative structures in KwaZulu/Natal were in a state of transition. Visitors should be aware that booking procedures and enquiry channels may change.

ACKNOWLEDGEMENTS

In researching and compiling the information for this guide, we were assisted by many individuals who willingly shared their knowledge and gave of their time to assist us. We take great pleasure in acknowledging this kind assistance. Staff and ex-staff members of the Natal Parks Board include: Barrie Barnes, Lynn Cairns, Jeff Gaisford, Johan and Annette Gerber, Pete Goodman, Garnet and Toni Jackson, David Johnson, Ron Physick, Dave Rowe-Rowe, Ray Scallan, Trevor Scheepers, Gilbert and Richard Schutte, Rob Scott Shaw, Tim Snow, Ricky Taylor, Johan Vermeulin, Rob Walters and Noel Wright. The former director, Col Jack Vincent MBE and the late Peter Potter, former deputy director of the Natal Parks Board, gave unstintingly of their time in discussions. Their advice was invaluable.

Nick Steele, head of the KwaZulu Department of Nature Conservation kindly arranged accommodation, facilities and the assistance of his staff, for which we are very grateful. We have pleasure in thanking the following individuals in this department: Sarah Allan, Sipho Buyisa, Mary King, Harry Lock, Patrick Mathe, Chris McBride, Vincent Ncgobo, Ed Ostrovsky, Graham Pollock and Robbie Roberts.

Mr Louis Loocke, director of the Natal Provincial Administration Department of Community Services and his staff enthusiastically provided data on the reserves under their control.

Keith Cooper, Conservation Director of the Wildlife Society of Southern Africa kindly provided reference material and advice on a number of queries, and Delise Coad is also thanked for researching material for us. Keith Cooper and Basil Harper, chairman of the Wildlife Society's Natal Branch Publications Committee are thanked for allowing us to use material from the society's handbook *Wild Places of Natal* by Olive Shepherd. Other Wildlife Society branch chairmen and members who rendered considerable assistance were Sue Swan (Umvoti Branch), Eddie du Plessis (Vryheid), Ken Gordon (Ladysmith), Adrian Riddle (Estcourt) and Pippa Rowlands (Empangeni).

For their kind hospitality, valuable discussions, reference material and advice, we thank Ian and Jean Garland, Tony and Maggie Abbott, Tony and Priscilla Henley, John and Meryn Turner, John Varty and Coby Bride (who also kindly put a Landrover station wagon at our disposal).

Others who provided assistance with information were Gina Baldo, Helen Bruigom, Hamish Campbell, Trevor Coleman, Bill Duthie, Graehame McCleod, Geoff Nichols, Hugh Nicholson, Terry Oatley, Michael Peters and Chris Wilkinson.

There are many others, too numerous to mention, including the owners, managers and staff of private and municipal game and nature reserves, who provided data or showed us over their properties. We extend our thanks to them all.

Jenny Roberts, Anne Player and Creina Alcock typed sections of the manuscript in its various stages for which we are very grateful. Special thanks are extended to Creina Alcock for helpful suggestions and for editing some material. Dr Nollie Zaloumis is thanked for allowing us to use his colour photographs and Helena Margeot for the map of KwaZulu/Natal.

Marina Pearson of Southern Book Publishers is thanked for editing the manuscript and we enjoyed working with Louise Grantham, commissioning editor, and thank her for compiling the table of facilities.

Finally we take pleasure in acknowledging Elsa Pooley for her advice on botanical names, and for producing the final draft of the manuscript.

HISTORY OF NATURE CONSERVATION IN KWAZULU/NATAL

The history of the conservation of game and nature reserves in KwaZulu/Natal would fill several volumes before the complete story could be told. Clearly it is impossible to give more than a quick sketch in this introduction.

Much of the material was drawn from JB Wright's *Bushmen raiders of the Drakensberg*, the unpublished *History of the Natal Parks Board* by J Vincent, *The struggle for wildlife protection in Zululand 1910-1930* by Shirley Brooks, *Game conservation in Zululand 1824-1947* by B Ellis, *Shaka's country* by TV Bulpin, the Magqubu Ntombela papers, official reports of the Natal Parks Board, *Take a horse to the wilderness* and *Bush life of a game warden* by Nick Steele, and the numerous books, articles, personal and official diaries of the authors. To reduce the mass of material to readable proportions became a nightmare. Many heroic men and women have devoted their lives to the conservation of game and the parks and nature reserves. In the early days they were poorly paid and ill equipped. Zulu game guards received a pittance, worked long hours and went everywhere almost entirely on foot. Their lives were always in danger.

The great South African ecologist, Professor John Phillips, at a game rangers' conference in Zimbabwe in the 1960s began his keynote address with a military metaphor. He said, "There will never be a Waterloo in wildlife conservation; only a long drawn out guerilla war."

Those who have spent their lives in the service of conservation know how true this is. Looking back over the turbulent past, there were times when all appeared lost. Then through what can only be described as supernatural intervention an apparently hopeless situation was resolved and conservation took another step forward. We can only hope that forces greater than ourselves continue to intervene at the critical moments that will certainly recur.

EARLY HISTORY

The game and nature reserves of KwaZulu/Natal as we know the region today are only remnants or witness areas of what was once vast and beautiful wilderness country. If we use our imagination and go back 3 000 years and imagine that we are an eagle soaring on the thermals and looking down on the landscape, we would see sights of extraordinary beauty stretching from what today is the Usutu river in the north to the Umtamvuna in the south. The Bushmen and even earlier inhabitants no doubt had their names for all the prominent features, most of which have vanished into the

7

mists of time, but with the eagle's eye, one would have seen the great rivers plunging in waterfalls and cascades from the huge mountain range on the west, now called Qahlamba or the Drakensberg, slowly gathering in strength and size as they made their way to the coast. Patches of highland mistbelt and coastal forests would glint in the morning sunlight. The whole landscape was breathtaking in its endless variety.

In the north-east was a chain of lakes with St Lucia one of the brightest gems in this necklace strung out across the land and glittering in the light. Reflections of the great green dune forests shimmered in the water and the islands, pans and inlets formed an intricate mosaic providing a habitat for an infinite variety of birds – storks, herons, waders, warblers, pinkbacked and white pelicans and greater and lesser flamingo. In the great ocean, beyond the dunes that separated it from the lake, massive shoals of mullet surged to the mouth of the lake, up into the narrows, leaping and jumping in bright silver flashes, while sharks and crocodiles, kingfish, salmon, fish eagles and goliath herons preyed upon the fish.

To the west, stretching north and south was a sea of *acacia*, green in summer and grey in winter, the home of elephant, black and white rhino, impala, duiker, nyala, reedbuck, wildebeest and zebra, lion, leopard and cheetah, all in their ecological niches.

In the riverine forests to the north, birdsong in spring welled up like a great symphony – Heuglin's and Natal robins, fishing owls and the kettle-drum calls of the crested guineafowl – but above all this vibrant sound from the birds and the animals there rose and fell like a great tenor the haunting, melodic cry of the fish eagle. There was the smell of the earth too, when it was dry and the dust swept before the north-east wind. After the first rains, sand and red earth sucked in the moisture and gave off the warm, heavy, exhilirating scent of Africa.

In the pans in the far north, surrounded by pale green fever trees and filled by the annual flooding and meeting of rivers, there were tiger fish, black and silver and red, stalking and streaking after their prey in the shallows. Barbel and tilapia moved in great shoals, providing food for the crocodiles and the pelicans. Swordfish and Zambezi shark came up from the ocean as far as the first rapids, and elephants swam and splashed across the rivers, feeding on the wide variety of trees, from the marula to the sycamore. Such would have been the eagle's view.

Throughout the game and nature reserves of today are artefacts of the very early humans who strode upright across the landscape, with primitive weapons in their hands; stones for bashing and for digging. Time passed and humans evolved; the weapons changed and humans grew more proficient. Plants, spiders and scorpions provided the basis for poisons, wood the material for bows and arrows, but who knows what manner of man and woman they were. Scientists collect and collate, label and examine the artefacts, but who really knows the ideas, the religions, the loves and hates of our human ancestors. This remains in the collective unconscious of mankind.

DH Lawrence, the English poet and novelist, wrote: "In the dust where we have buried the silent races and their abominations, we have buried so much of the delicate magic of life." In this sentence he captures the essence of the sense of loss, of a time gone by when humans lived and died in a landscape that was only slightly modified by human activity.

It can be truly said that KwaZulu/Natal was once a paradise, where before the coming of the white man, game, fish, birds and forests abounded. From oral and then written history we know that the Bushmen roamed the hills and valleys in small clans, living as hunter gatherers. Their impact, with the exception of fire, was minimal. They took what they needed and moved in a pattern dependent upon the seasons and the game migrations, although it is logical to believe they preferred the warmer areas. One anthropologist accurately described them as "the harmless people".

In KwaZulu/Natal they have vanished, after their clashes with the invading black and white cultures relentlessly pushed them into the mountains of the Drakensberg, where, despite their extraordinary bushcraft, by the 1890s only a few remained. But like all indigenous people, they fought back with ingenuity and great courage as they were being overwhelmed by vastly superior forces.

JB Wright in his *Bushman raiders of the Drakensberg 1840-1870* gives the most comprehensive historical review of the Bushmen of Natal and no one can read his book without feeling the terrible sense of loss so beautifully described by DH Lawrence.

One of the last raids into Natal by a Bushman band is recorded in the *Natal Mercury* of August 1872, and is described in JB Wright's book. It took place on the upper Pholela river in a snowstorm. The Bushmen stole 17 horses from Sakhayedwa's people, but the chief and his men tracked them into the mountains, came upon a group of five men, two women and a girl, and killed them. The *Natal Mercury* correspondent asks, "Could nothing be done to bring these unfortunate creatures, thorough outcasts of humanity, shot down as dogs whenever the opportunity offers, to live the quiet pastoral life ..."

But the plea was too late. The Bushmen of KwaZulu/Natal were finished. They remained a threat to the colonial government of Natal but the cattle, sheep and horse raiding bands were reduced to a few individuals by the 1890s, some of whom survived into the 1900s. The enormity of this genocide has been brought to modern man through the writings of Laurens van der Post, who movingly describes his childhood association with his Bushman nurse and then in later books his expeditions into the Kalahari to record what is left of their culture. The horror of the slaughter of these innocent people who for 8 000 years and more lived in a harmonious relationship with the natural world, will remain a festering sore in our psyches until we openly acknowledge the enormity of our crime and redress it in some practical way. We gave them nothing except smallpox, the common cold, the bullet and the assegai. They left us some of the most exquisite rock art the world has ever seen.

In the caves and overhangs their little artists painted human and animal forms and in the soft light of dawn and dusk the paintings glow luminously, a sad and constant reminder of a people who could have taught us how to live in greater peace. Psychics say that the spirits of the Bushmen can be experienced in the isolated caves and valleys of the Drakensberg. Children camping in the Ndedema cave have woken their parents, saying that they have heard voices in the dark.

Giant's Castle is today a reserve, an area where the Bushmen once lived, and their paintings are carefully protected in the main cave. From the camp one's eyes are drawn like a magnet to this cave which sits like the tip of a rifle sight aiming at the mountains. It is touched by the early morning sun and protected from the rain and cold of the south wind. A small forest in the kloof nearby would have provided fuel for the Bushman family. Today the Cape robin singing in the gloom of the trees is the only permanent resident.

A typical Bushman family is grouped at the east facing overhang. The realistic figures of fibre glass are a nostalgic reminder of the little people, and the paintings a glorious expression of the artist's sense of nature. Eland and lion, a snake and reedbuck-like antelope are delicately imprinted on the stone walls, the colour as good as anything modern man can produce. Despite thousands of people visiting the cave annually, there is still a strong sense of the presence of the Bushmen. Sitting quietly listening to the call of a soaring jackal buzzard or a baboon sentinel's bark ringing out on the sandstone cliffs takes one back into the timeless world the Bushmen once lived in. Shutting one's eyes and listening in a dream-like reverie, the sound of the Bushmans river drifts upwards. Above the sound of the rapids there is the rattle of sticks and clink of animal horns and hooves against the boulders. Is it fantasy, hallucination or imagination? Perhaps you can hear women laughing and children chattering and men with deeper voices calling out to each other in a rapid clicking language. Could this be a small Bushman band returning to their cave as they had done ever since they were driven into the mountains?

The whole Drakensberg with its caves and its paintings is a living art gallery. The atmosphere of the Giant's Castle Game Reserve is pregnant with the spirit of the harmless people and it is tragic beyond understanding how some modern humans will deface the paintings. What is it that makes some of our kind want to eradicate the last trace of these happy people? How poor we are without the physical presence of the Bushmen. As John Locke said, "Hell is truth learnt too late."

No historian is certain when the first Bantu-speaking people entered KwaZulu/Natal. Iron Age sites on the eastern shores of Lake St Lucia are estimated to be over 900 years old, but when the Iron Age people arrived the Bushmen had been there for more than 8 000 years. As the Bantu numbers increased it was inevitable that friction would arise with the Bushmen, but it is only with the coming of the white man that written recorded history gives us a clearer picture.

The interaction between the Nguni-speaking people must have been very profitable for the black invaders. The Bushmen were expert hunters and trackers and their knowledge of weather as well as of trees, plants, herbs and grasses made them natural conservationists. The information passed on to the Bantu speakers gave them a deep insight into what we today call ecology. There are stories passed down from generation to generation among the Zulus of young men who apprenticed themselves to Bushman hunters and learnt to stalk and kill elephant. The Bushmen were known as the *abatwa* and were considered to be magical people who could appear and disappear in the mist. It was said they could take cattle out of a kraal and no one would wake. Their knowledge of and ability to predict the weather is still strong in Bantu folklore.

Although the Bushmen have gone, parts of their language, philosophy and knowledge of the land were absorbed by invading Nguni people and continue to live on in this form. With the coming of the Iron Age the impact on the landscape was greater because the furnaces needed fuel and this meant the removal of trees and shrubs, but this in turn created a mosaic which favoured a mix of grazing and browsing animals.

RECENT HISTORY

If there is an emphasis on Zululand in the history of wildlife conservation, it is because it was in this region that the success or failure of conservation would be determined.

Wildlife conservation in KwaZulu/Natal as we know it today probably began in the late 1700s in the reign of the Mtetwa chief, Dingiswayo, son of Jobe. The centre of his kingdom was in what is today the Umfolozi Game Reserve, near the junction of the two Mfolozi rivers. Magqubu Ntombela, a game scout and wilderness guide who was born on the Ongeni hills in 1900 was shown the remnants of an extensive muzi of early inhabitants of the area on the slopes of Amatshemhlope, and subsequently he showed it to wilderness traillists. To this day after veld fires it is possible to see traces of the muzi and certainly grinding stones and other artefacts. Once some small blue beads were found half hidden in the soil. Dingiswayo had made contact with the Portuguese and began trading ivory and cattle for beads and other trinkets.

The elephant can be said to be the founder of the modern southern African conservation movement, and fittingly so because the elephant has always symbolised ambition, courage, sagacity and wit. The elephant in antiquity was the symbol of divine wisdom, endurance, gentleness, longevity, patience and modesty. The Chinese revered it as one of the four animals of power. In the Christian tradition its white ivory tusks represent firmness and purity. In some cultures it was the emblem of the sun. The root word is *elaphos* – the light of God everlasting. The Aryo Indians called it Hastin, meaning beast having a hand. It was known too as the bringer of fertilising rains. To the Zulus the elephant is *ndhlovu*, and forms part of the praise names of the king.

Elephants were common in the region and the Nguni people had devel-

11

oped sophisticated methods of hunting. Shaka Zulu served Dingiswayo and learnt about the passion of whites for ivory. When Dingiswayo was killed Shaka Zulu became king in 1818 and in 1823 the English arrived at Port Natal. Captain W Owen of the Royal Navy, on a voyage surveying the east coast, reported seeing a caravan with porters carrying ivory and driving cattle to Delagoa Bay. After sailing into the secluded Port Natal harbour, the first settlers soon made contact with Shaka at his kraal, Bulawayo, near modern-day Eshowe. Shaka liked the British, and was impressed with their guns and their stories of the power of their King George. He preferred their trading goods, believing that they were superior to those of the Portuguese.

Soon ivory grew to be of enormous importance to Shaka. He saw the power it had in the eyes of the white men. Some researchers suggest that Shaka was not a conservationist because he organised elephant hunts, but they miss an important point. Despite the heavy hunting of the elephant and other game by the Zulu people, it was only after the arrival of white settlers that wild animal numbers dwindled to pitiful remnants. Shaka understood the economic importance of wildlife long in advance of the whites who settled in Natal and who eventually smashed the Zulu kingdom.

The early Zulus through their king had an innate respect for wild animals, the elephant taking pride of place, and the hunter was a man who was looked up to. The kings were likened to the elephant and the lion and these animals formed part of the praise names. This was a form of conservation not recognised or understood by early white immigrants. Their own killing lust was epitomised in the words and actions of men like Cornwallis Harris, William Gordon Cumming and John Dunn who ruthlessly shot anything that crossed their path. The early Zulus killed too and enjoyed their hunting, but they had their own kind of game laws which were decreed by the king and the chiefs.

Certain animals such as the common duiker, warthog, guineafowl, francolin and canerat could be hunted at will. Larger game was the prerogative of the chiefs. Buffalo were regarded as the *inyonikapumuli* of the bush, the name given to the royal cattle because they were so numerous that tick birds had no time to settle. Buffalo meat was prized next to beef in excellence. Hippo and warthog were killed for their ivory and consequently had economic value too. The ivory and the hippo fat were much sought after for love potions and the hide was used to make whips from which the animals were given their Zulu name, *mvubu*. The warthog was respected and called *ndhlovudawane*, the diminutive elephant. Apart from the good ivory from the large tusks, the meat was valued, particularly that of a young sow.

The skins of leopard and lion were reserved for royal shoulders and their teeth and claws adorned the necks of kings and princes. The horns of the kudu were made into pipes and used in the smoking of *nsango* (cannabis) or as an instrument to summon men to war or a big hunt. The horns of the mountain and common reedbuck were inserted into red ivory wood to make elegant walking sticks, which could only be carried by indunas and other senior tribal men. The red ivory tree was much sought after too for its delicious fruit and the chiefs sent men in the fruiting season to keep the baboons away until the women had collected the berries.

Birds such as the bateleur eagle, vulture, secretarybird and purplecrested lourie were respected because their feathers were used as part of the head-dress. The blood red and black feathers of the purplecrested lourie were reserved for the heads of those important in the nation. The only picture we have of Shaka Zulu shows him standing with a long feather in his hair.

Crocodiles were protected. The teeth were used for ornaments. No croc-odile was killed without a report being given to a senior induna because a mixture of the brain and liver was said to be deadly poisonous. The chief would insist that four men were present at the killing to ensure that a big stone was tied to the liver before dropping it into the deepest pool in the river. So conservation in a form not properly understood by whites was widely practised.

In 1825 King Shaka was assassinated and Dingane became king. The Umfolozi valley had been regarded as a sacred place. Shaka had known it well and kept control of any excessive hunting.

The Voortrekkers came over the Drakensberg in search of their land of milk and honey. They clashed with the Zulus and a commando under Piet Retief was killed. Later, at the battle of Blood River the power of Dingane was broken and the Boers put Mpande on the throne, but at great cost of land to the Zulus. Vast areas were appropriated by the Boers. In Johannes Meintjes' book, *The Voortrekkers*, there is mention of Piet Retief's policy on game conservation: "There was to be no unnecessary shooting of game, and strict control was to be kept of veldburning. Rules and regulations were to be enforced by Retief's field-commandants, and offenders punished by fines."

Zulu traditions of game conservation continued where the dictates of the king and his indunas held sway, but the European numbers were increasing and in Natal were rapidly destroying the game. The Boer republic with Pietermaritzburg as its capital was short lived and in 1843 Natal fell under British control.

Mpande was benign, liked the whites and allowed hunters and traders onto the land he controlled. But as his son Ceteswayo who later became king remarked, "First comes the trader, then the missionary, then the red soldier."

The trader was also the hunter and by the late 1850s, after the Byrne set-tler immigration scheme, elephant were wiped out south of the Tugela river. Through the eyes of hunters like William Baldwin, Henry Drummond and the hunter-naturalist Adulphe Delegorgue, we peep through the keyhole of history and see the relentless pursuit of game for ivory, skins and fat. Mpande continued with the elephant hunts, conducting them from the slopes of Nqoloti hill that now lies within Umfolozi Game Reserve. He was following a tradition that Shaka began and Dingane continued. The ihlambo hunts after the death of an important individual were held to purify the mourners. But settlers, traders, hunters and adventure seekers came in ever-increasing numbers, asking the king's permission to enter his territory in pursuit of wild animals.

Nevertheless, when the early whites were hunting and trading they also took note of the way the Zulus lived in harmony with the land, which was another form of conservation based on a deep understanding of macro and micro climates.

The site of a muzi or kraal (home) was located on the slope or the crown of a hill, away from the uncomfortable conditions in the hot valley bottom. The cattle kraal was always in the centre of the muzi and on a gentle slope, enough to ensure a mild runoff, but not so steep as to cause soil erosion. The land was cultivated with primitive tools and the uncultivated land provided important sources of vitamins, protein, minerals and trace elements – from herbs, fruits, birds, insects and animals – which also provided a varied diet. With skills probably learnt from the Bushmen, many plants were used to maintain the health of the family. The knowledge of poisonous plants was also considerable and even modern scientists have not plumbed the secrets of some poisonous plants still known to the Zulus.

Everything for the building of the muzi came from plants and trees and grasses, each of which had a special function. For example, the bark of *Acacia karoo* as well as the nettle tree *Obetia tenax (Urera tenax)* was plaited into rope and used to tie the thin saplings for the beehive huts.

The Zulus cultivated a mosaic of fields and when they were left to lie fallow they provided food for wild animals. The Zulu system of cultivation ensured that indigenous plants and trees would survive. White cultivation on the other hand, showed little concern for the indigenous vegetation, everything being ripped out in the ploughing of large fields and in most instances the planting went right to the edge of the rivers.

Zulus had an innate understanding of the land. The early Zulus, like other indigenous people all over the world, knew that they were part of creation and not separate from it. Their lives were encompassed by the circle – the kraal, the beehive hut, the cattle kraal, and it represented an unconscious symbolism which modern European man, with the imposition of the square, has now changed beyond recognition. (Interestingly enough, in their beadwork and in decorative art, they often use angles.)

While it is true that the Zulus were primarily agriculturalists and pasturalists and had a psychic understanding of cattle, wild animal products such as skins were used for clothing and for drums, and were brayed for whips, while sinews were used for thread. Children from an early age learnt from older childen the names of animals, trees, birds, herbs, grasses and plants.

EJ Krige records, and this was confirmed by Magqubu Ntombela, that some animals were hunted to provide material for magic. The heart and the eyes of a lion or an elephant were eaten to overcome fear and nervousness.

In 1856 a great battle took place between two of Mpande's sons, Ceteswayo and Mbulazi. Estimates of the number of people killed are as high as 40 000, which included women and children as well as warriors.

John Dunn, a man who was to play an important role in the political affairs of Zululand, was an eyewitness to the battle and was himself involved. So many human bones were washed down the slopes of Ndondagasuka into one of the small tributaries of the Tugela that the little stream was renamed Mithambo (bones). Bodies were washed up onto beaches as far south as Durban. WC Baldwin, a well-known hunter returning from an expedition into Tongaland and Mozambique records how he suffered from the lack of food because so many kraals had been destroyed and the people killed. He mentions too a mass of vultures circling and feeding on the battlefield.

Mpande died in 1872 and Ceteswayo became king because he had defeated his main rival, Mbulazi, in 1856.

THE FIRST GAME LAWS

In 1866 the first game laws were promulgated in Natal, an indication that the government had become concerned about the decimation of wildlife in the colony. Hunters were still pouring into Zululand and a great killing of game was in progress. Records from the colony show that between 1861 and 1866 some £142 000 was received as revenue from 269 249 kg of ivory. In 1871, 2 470 rhino horns were exported. By this time there were no rhino south of the Tugela so the horns could only have come from Zululand. B Ellis in a paper entitled *Game Conservation in Zululand 1824-1947*, says that Mpande issued an edict protecting large mammals. Animal skins to the value of £90 068 from a total of 417 014 animals were exported in 1872. This represented "16,94 per cent of the total income from export of products and manufactures of the Colony". In 1875, 4 444 buffalo skins were exported.

ANGLO-ZULU WAR

Tension continued to grow between the Colony of Natal and the independent Zulu kingdom and in 1879 the British forced a war on the Zulus because they were obstructing imperial expansion. The British suffered a major defeat at the battle of Isandlwana, which has never been forgotten. The old Zulu order was practically destroyed and left an aftermath from which South Africa has never properly recovered. The final battle of the Zulu war was fought on the Ulundi plain on 4 July, 1879. The conquest and the crushing of the Zulu social order was not only to have severe political repercussions, but to cause profound ecological damage.

Sir Garnet Wolseley became Governor of Natal and the Transvaal, and High Commissioner for adjacent territories. He immediately split Zululand up into thirteen separate small kingdoms on the old British policy of divide and rule. Ceteswayo was exiled and a British Resident was appointed. Zululand was soon plunged into a civil war, the small kingdoms turning on each other with the weapons they had picked up on the Isandlwana battlefield after their victory.

Conservation of wildlife was far from anybody's mind, but when Zululand was annexed to the Crown in May 1887 the game laws of Natal became applicable to Zululand, but the slaughter continued.

THE NAGANA CAMPAIGN

In 1894 a severe drought decimated Zululand. At the same time the Zulus' cattle were dying of nagana, the disease carried by the tsetse fly (*Glossina pallidipes*). As a result of correspondence between the governor Sir Walter Heley-Hutchinson and Downing Street Surgeon Major David Bruce, Bruce came to South Africa and began working on nagana in the Ubombo district. By 1895 he was satisfied that nagana was carried by the tsetse fly. This was the beginning of a protracted struggle which led to the destruction of thousands upon thousands of head of game, and it continued until the 1950s.

The Zulus had coped with the tsetse fly and nagana in their own way, limiting exposure of the cattle to the disease and the king authorising big hunts to drive game away from settlements. The imposition of white conservation laws with a blanket restriction on killing undermined the way the Zulus conserved their game and ensured the survival of their cattle and settlements.

With more nagana outbreaks, game drives were held with the intention of controlling the testse fly, and in 1917 the tribal reserves in the Ubombo and Ingwavuma districts were thrown open to game destruction with the exception of nyala, hippo and rhino. Some 20 000 wildebeest were said to have been killed.

In 1919, after the First World War, the Ntambanana settlement was opened up for returned soldiers. They farmed cattle and cotton, but it was not long before the cattle began to die from nagana because no one had given them adequate warning of how devastating the tsetse fly could be. This outbreak of nagana led to the deproclamation of the 1907 southern section of the Umfolozi Game Reserve and in August of the same year the Umfolozi Game Reserve itself was abolished. One of the main protagonists for the removal of the reserve was JJ Muller, a member of the Provincial Council for Melmoth, who had told the Ntambanana Farmers Association that he would do his utmost to ensure the abolition of the reserve. He was but one of a long line of men who were determined to destroy the game reserves of Zululand.

In 1921 RHTP Harris arrived to study the life cycle of the tsetse fly and he established a camp overlooking the White Mfolozi river which became known as Makamisa, the Zulu name given to him because he stuttered badly. Both the Ntambanana farmers – who were suffering from the depredations of nagana – and the game preservationists, pinned their hopes on Harris. Through the work of DT Mitchell, a veterinary research officer, it had been proved conclusively that by injecting the blood from wild animals into cattle, nagana was induced.

Harris produced a fly trap which resembled a dummy animal and although he was to claim all the credit, Magqubu Ntombela said that the trap was actually made by William Foster, who was an assistant to Harris.

In 1919 the magistrate of the Lower Umfolozi district, Colonel Tanner, organised a game drive to move the game back from the Ntambanana settlement into the Umfolozi Game Reserve. Eyewitness accounts of this particular drive were given by the father of Ian Player and also by Magqubu Ntombela. Considerable butchery took place without much effect because when the drive was over the game went back to the farms.

In August 1920 another game drive was initiated, with the intention of exterminating all the game up to the White Mfolozi river. This drive was open to the general public and it was advertised as Zululand's "Monster Game Drive". The railways were asked to provide an extra train to take the "sportsmen" from Durban.

A big meeting was held in the Empangeni town hall prior to the drive and George Higgs, a notorious anti-game farmer, stated that he would not stop at the Mfolozi river, but would continue into the game reserve. In personal conversation, Magqubu Ntombela said that many of the farmers did go into the game reserve and some actually shot white rhino. Colonel Tanner, the magistrate, sympathised with the farmers. In this hunt some 3 000 head of game was killed. The Provincial Secretary described it as a farce, because nothing had been achieved.

Vaughan-Kirby, the game conservator, retired in 1928, an angry and disillusioned man, and in a letter to the then retired Provincial Secretary, Hershensohnn, he accused Harris of "broken faith, deceit, falsehood, dirty espionage and utter lack of organisation and of wanton and indiscriminate butchery".

Harris had fly traps established throughout Hluhluwe and Umfolozi game reserves, but to no avail. Although there was a lowering of the incidence of nagana, this could have been due to a parasitic wasp that preyed on the larvae of the tsetse fly.

Shortly after Harris retired there were severe outbreaks of nagana in 1939. This led to another game slaughter and between 1942 and 1950 approximately 100 000 animals were destroyed in the Umfolozi and Mkuzi game reserves, and it was only through the strength of character of Captain Potter that the animals in the Hluhluwe Game Reserve were saved. Only the white and the black rhino in Umfolozi Game Reserve were not shot.

In 1945, aerial spraying with DDT was carried out at Mkuzi Game Reserve and this was successful in eliminating the fly although it was costly. The aerial spraying was extended to Hluhluwe and Umfolozi game reserves and by 1952 *Glossina pallidipes* was eliminated. Aerial spraying was also used to control the locust invasions.

NATAL'S FIRST GAME RESERVES

In February 1895, CD Guise, an old hunter, was pressing hard for the establishment of game reserves to protect the big game. Guise suggested that the habitat of the white rhino be beaconed off as a game reserve. A precedent had already been established with the proclamation of the first game reserve in South Africa in 1894 in the Pongolo area of the Transvaal, although this was more of a political ploy by Kruger of the Transvaal Republic who had his eyes on Kosi Bay for a harbour. The clamour in Natal grew louder and finally five game reserves, St Lucia, Umfolozi junction, Hluhluwe valley, Umdhletshe (Hlabisa district), and Pongolo-Umkuzi area, were proclaimed in Zululand, in Government Notice No.12, gazetted on 30 April 1895. The conservation and the setting aside of proclaimed areas had at long last eventuated. It was the birth of the modern conservation movement, but it is doubtful if any other part of the world has seen so long and bitter a struggle to protect the remnants of once large herds of wild game.

From this time on, men with grit and determination were going to play a major part in the conservation of not only animals, birds, insects, plants and trees, but also in the protection of the landscape. It is perhaps a fitting tribute to the early Zulu kings, beginning with Dingiswayo, Senzagakona and Shaka, that it should have been in the sacred valleys of the Mfolozi rivers that this birth took place.

Perhaps the essence of the idea of the park was expressed in a letter to the *Natal Witness* by HL Carbutt who wrote that the strip of land between the Mfolozi rivers was a natural game reserve and needed only to be proclaimed. DW Montgomery wrote to the Governor of Natal on the same matter and said, "it is not as if a reserve had to be *made* here; it is ready made to our hands, and all we have to do is to preserve things in *status quo.*"

In June 1895, two game conservators were appointed in Zululand, D Tweedie who was in charge of the Ntonjaneni and Hlabisa districts, and S Silverton in the Lower Umfolozi district, at a salary of £10 a month each. (It is interesting to note that in April 1952, when Ian Player was appointed relief ranger in Zululand, he was paid £20 a month, and in 1957 when Tony Pooley was appointed, he was paid £22 6s 8d, an indication of the low inflation between 1895 and 1957.)

In addition to a bad drought at this time, huge swarms of locusts devastated crops and in the same year rinderpest decimated both game and cattle. The effect of the rinderpest, through the decimation of the big game and the cattle, was to cause great hunger and poverty among the Zulu people, but it did reduce the nagana outbreaks because the tsetse fly were deprived of a host. Regrettably this lesson of natural calamity was not fully understood by those in charge of game protection.

A few years after the rinderpest, game in the Umfolozi area began to increase. The game conservator of the Lower Umfolozi in a report made special mention of the white rhino, saying, "The white rhinoceros there are about the only specimens to be found anywhere in Africa, and have only been spared by timely preservation. There are about fifteen head of this kind in the reserve."

Two game conservators were now appointed in the Ubombo district but the resident magistrate, Oswald Fynney, wrote that the considerable distances to be covered, the shortage of police and conservators and sparse population, made effective enforcement of the game laws very difficult.

In 1905 a land delimitation commission with two commissioners, Charles Saunders and MM Dartnell, allocated approximately 3 887 000 acres "for permanent native occupation and one third, 2 613 000 for alienation by the

Natal government", but no mention is made of the game reserves, although in one report Charles Saunders talks about going into the Umfolozi Game Reserve. However, there is no doubt that Charles Saunders from the earliest days was a driving force for the establishment and protection of the parks.

In April two more game reserves were abolished after complaints by transport riders whose draught cattle were bitten by tsetse flies and died of nagana, but the Umfolozi Junction Reserve was extended to include about 58 000 acres south of the White Mfolozi river, eventually to be called the southern crown lands or southern buffer zone. It was Charles Saunders who pressed hard for this extension.

Nagana outbreaks were still occurring all over Zululand as both cattle and game built up in numbers after the rinderpest. In 1910 Sir Charles Saunders retired as Resident Commissioner and in one of his last letters urged the newly established Natal Provincial Administration to appoint a chief conservator for game in Zululand. In August 1911, Frederick Vaughan-Kirby was appointed. He was to fight tirelessly and with great courage for the game and the game reserves in Zululand. So much was going to depend on individuals as to whether the parks were going to survive or not and men like Vaughan-Kirby, the Provincial Secretary Hershensohnn, Ernest Warren and George Campbell, played a vital role until 1929-1930 when new men came on the scene.

Hershensohnn was tireless in his efforts to try to save the Umfolozi Game Reserve, but had a continuing struggle with the Minister of Agriculture who wanted all the game destroyed. This established a pattern that was to continue far into the future when the Natal Provincial Administration was pitted against the central government, and it is nothing short of a miracle that the game reserves survived.

In 1912 the Mkuzi Game Reserve that lay between the Mkuze and Msunduzi rivers was proclaimed. The earlier and bigger one north of the Mkuze river was deproclaimed. The proclamation of this reserve was due to the inspired efforts of the magistrate who had, through sheer personality alone, protected the area. It was known as the Magistrate's Mufti Reserve.

It was in Zululand that the main drama for the conservation of game reserves and game was being enacted. It continued to be this way in the authors' time and continues even now with the enormous struggle for the Greater St Lucia Wetland Park.

There are people, many of them in responsible leadership positions, who see no value in either the game reserves or the conservation of wild animals, and some destructive aspect of these people wants to eliminate all vestige of the wilderness. The clash between this mindset and of those who want to preserve and conserve wild animals and wild landscape has become a feature of our time and grows more pronounced as human populations increase.

Every generation of conservators has had a hard time and it would be difficult to say who had the hardest, but in 1919 when a large area of the

Ngwavuma magisterial district was thrown open to shooting, Vaughan-Kirby, the chief conservator, wrote to Ernest Warren, director of the Natal Museum, that he was an absolutely broken-spirited man. One can sympathise with him, but to his great credit he continued working for another ten years. Fortunately, Vaughan-Kirby did have some strong men helping him. JMNA Hershensohnn, the Provincial Secretary, was a great supporter, as were Ernest Warren and George and "Wac" Campbell, members of an old Natal sugar planting family.

Vaughan-Kirby's appointment in 1911 and the Game Ordinance of 1912 were both turning points in taking away control of wildlife from the Zululand magistrates, who had enormous power. The magistrates however, were very displeased and this led to continuing clashes over the next 50 years, with game conservation officers receiving little sympathy from the magistrates.

Shortly after Vaughan-Kirby retired he was appointed to a game advisory committee which was chaired by CF Clarkson, chairman of the Natal Executive Committee. Clarkson was to become a key figure and played a vital role in the saving of the game reserves from deproclamation. He was astute and diplomatic and those who knew him said he was never fazed. Vaughan-Kirby was sent by Clarkson to attend a conference in Pretoria and returned to say that a resolution had been passed to deproclaim the Hluhluwe Game Reserve. The Union government showed little sympathy, in fact hostility, for Natal's game conservation efforts.

Roden Symons took over from Vaughan-Kirby but he only lasted a year, and then RHTP Harris was put in charge of the reserves until the appointment of Captain HB Potter. This was a propitious time because Umfolozi Game Reserve was re-proclaimed and Captain Potter took up residence with ranger Edward Lightening inside Hluhluwe Game Reserve.

A new Provincial Secretary, AE Charter, had been appointed, a man who understood game conservation, and he and Captain Potter worked hard to establish tourist facilities within the Hluhluwe Game Reserve. This was another turning point in the history of game conservation because once the public began to visit the Hluhluwe Game Reserve they realised what a valuable asset Natal and Zululand had in its wildlife.

Captain Potter was a tactful man and made every effort to make friends with the farming community. Lake St Lucia, which had been deproclaimed in 1928, was re-proclaimed in 1938 and with Potter's drive and the appointing of lake rangers, it became a popular tourist attraction.

The first rest huts were built in Hluhluwe Game Reserve in 1934 and were able to accommodate 20 people, but the journey from Durban to Hluhluwe was not an easy one and it was only the adventuresome tourist who made the trip.

Mkuzi and Ndumu game reserves were visited by Captain Potter, but he had insufficient funds to appoint white rangers. Black game guards who were put in control carried out their work admirably despite hostility from both black and white neighbours. Like Vaughan-Kirby, Captain Potter realised the value of the white rhino and played heavily on their rarity.

In 1939 the Zululand Game Reserves and Parks Board was formed, and it represented agricultural, commercial and publicity interests.

BIRTH OF THE NATAL PARKS BOARD

In 1947 an ordinance was passed in the Natal Provincial Council due to the hard work of William Power and Douglas Mitchell. Ordinance 35, 1947 placed all parks and game reserves within Natal and Zululand under the control of the Natal Parks, Game and Fish Preservation Board. The board was to consist of nine members and to take "all measures deemed necessary to enforce the laws relating to game, fish and other fauna and flora of Natal."

The groundwork for the establishment of the parks had been done after the Zululand parks had been in the teeth of continual storms. Powerful forces contemptuous of any form of conservation were arrayed against a few men who were imbued with the ideal of ensuring that some wild country with its animals, birds and landscape would be passed on to the next generation.

The struggle had been so intense in Zululand that there had been little time or energy left to be concerned either about Natal or other aspects of conservation. Coastal fisheries, inland fisheries and the parks in Natal had been neglected and considered almost an appendage, because there had been little conflict and no real driving force to further their cause. This was now going to change with the new board which superseded the Zululand Parks and Game Board and took control of all conservation matters both in Zululand and Natal. Douglas Mitchell, who had been the Administrator of Natal and the instigator of the board along with WH Power, was appointed a member and Power became the chairman.

Douglas Mitchell was to play a crucial role from 1948 until he retired in 1974. In the central government in which he was a member of parliament, he was acknowledged as the opposition spokesman on conservation affairs and lost no opportunity during parliamentary recesses to take willing and sometimes unwilling MPs, departmental secretaries, cabinet ministers and on a number of occasions, prime ministers, to the parks.

The Zululand parks were still very much under threat, particularly Ndumu, Mkuzi and Umfolozi. Ndumu was eyed for tribal land, Mkuzi as ranching and agricultural land – this became even more critical after the building of the Jozini dam – and Umfolozi Game Reserve was coveted by cattle ranchers who were sympathetically supported by the majority in the government. Little had changed and with the exception of General JC Smuts and Deneys Reitz, the Union government would have preferred to abolish all the game reserves in Zululand, and in fact actively pursued this as a policy.

In October 1949 Colonel J Vincent MBE was appointed secretary to the board. No better man could have appeared at this critical time. Colonel Vincent had come to South Africa as a farm pupil with a deep interest in ornithology. He was selected by Admiral Lynes, an expert on the cisticola, to participate in collecting expeditions for the British Museum, for which Colonel Vincent himself later worked. He did his military service with the Royal Natal Carbineers and at the outbreak of war went north with the regiment as their adjutant to fight in Abyssinia. He was sent to the Staff College in Lebanon and was the only South African to get the staff corps dagger for passing.

Colonel Vincent's knowledge of administration and natural history enabled him to take a firm grasp of the conservation problems and initiate staff recruitment that would revolutionise conservation in Natal and Zululand. Captain HB Potter remained the chief conservator of Zululand and was succeeded by his son, Peter Potter, in 1950. From 1952 until he retired in 1963, Colonel Vincent continued to employ staff and expand the activities of the board.

The conservation areas were broadly broken up into two regions, Zululand north of the Tugela and Natal south of the Tugela, but in Natal officers were appointed to control coastal fisheries, inland fisheries and aviaries. Fisheries ordinances and game ordinances were updated. In April 1953 control over the Umfolozi Game Reserve reverted from the Department of Veterinary Services to the Natal Parks Board, and the first aerial count of the white rhinoceros was undertaken and 437 rhino were counted. The incorporation of Crown lands adjoining the Umfolozi Game Reserve dragged on and during the winter of 1955, white cattle farmers were granted grazing rights in the western Crown lands and passed through the Umfolozi Game Reserve with their cattle. Local tribesmen followed suit and illegal squatters began moving in and building settlements within the Crown lands which were regarded as a buffer zone. Rangers in the field battled to control the increase in poaching, the game guard force was expanded and serious confrontations took place, not only with the poachers but with the cattle ranchers who were bringing in their beasts.

In the latter part of 1955 the Department of Lands agreed that 25 000 acres should be excised from the corridor between Umfolozi and Hluhluwe for possible settlement of the coloureds, subject to the deproclamation of Mkuzi and Ndumu game reserves. Those in charge of the game reserves in Zululand at the time then understood what their predecessors, Tweedie, Vaughan-Kirby, Roden Symons and Captain Potter, had gone through. Potter had fought hard to have the once proclaimed and then deproclaimed corridor between Hluhluwe and Umfolozi game reserves secured. With Colonel Vincent's aggressive recruitment of new staff the scales were beginning to tip in favour of the parks but it was not until 1989 that the corridor actually became part of the Hluhluwe and Umfolozi game reserves.

In 1960 the first experiments in the capture and translocation of white rhino took place, and by 1962 what was to become known as Operation Rhino, the most successful capture and translocation of a species, was in full swing, with white rhino being taken to re-stock the Zululand game reserves, and then the Kruger National Park and other reserves in the Orange Free State, northern Cape, Zimbabwe and Botswana. At the same time the zoos of the world were being supplied and by 1969 groups of up to 20 rhino were being supplied to zoos such as Whipsnade in the UK and San Diego in the USA.

In 1955 the idea of having a wilderness area was mooted by Jim Feely

22

and Ian Player. The concept was backed by the director, Colonel Vincent, and became a reality despite some opposition in the Natal Parks Board from those members who wanted to establish hutted camps in the proposed wilderness area. In 1957 wilderness trails were conducted by the embryonic Wilderness Leadership School in Umfolozi and Lake St Lucia game reserves. In March 1959 the first official Natal Parks Board wilderness trail was led by Magqubu Ntombela and Ian Player. The popularity of the trails grew so rapidly that it became necessary to employ a full-time wilderness trails officer and Hugh Dent was employed for this task, and later ran the trails at Lake St Lucia.

In 1963, after the greatest achievements in the history of conservation in South Africa, Colonel Vincent accepted a post in Switzerland with the International Council for Bird Protection. Under his administration the Natal Parks Board had grown from a small group of men to well over a thousand, black and white, looking after game reserves, coastal patrols, inland patrols, public relations and administration. Colonel Vincent's position was taken by John Geddes Page who had been the secretary of the board. In 1964 Peter Potter became deputy director and was transferred to the Pietermaritzburg headquarters of the Natal Parks Board. Ian Player was promoted to chief conservator Zululand, and Eric von Puttkamer became the chief conservator of Natal. The inland fisheries section had been greatly expanded under the direction of the board's principal research officer, Bob Crass.

By now the Natal Parks Board had built up an enviable reputation in all fields of conservation, fisheries and game research, the provision of tourist facilities and game guard training schemes. There had also been a big increase in the proclamation of nature reserves. A new concept of conservancies was developed by Nick Steele, a senior Natal Parks Board officer. The farming community saw its value and within a few years conservancies were established all over Natal and Zululand, and wildlife outside the parks derived greater protection.

The conservation flame lit by the early Zulu kings had been fanned by Charles Saunders, Vaughan-Kirby, Hershensohnn, Captain HB Potter and AE Charter. The beauty of the royal and sacred valley of the Umfolozi had captured their imaginations and inspired their efforts to save the land and the game. Their struggles in the face of enormous anti-conservation forces had now borne fruit and like a relay race the baton has been handed from one generation to another. Inevitably, within the conservation ranks there were those who were leaders and those who followed, and those who fell by the wayside, unable to stand up to the pressure or attracted by material benefits. Fortunately there was always a core of distinguished Natalians, busy professional men, who gave of their time and expertise in many fields to serve on the Natal Parks Board as chairmen and board members. They provided backing to the efforts of dedicated administrators, researchers, maintenance staff, field men and their wives, who fought for the conservation cause.

With the increase in population and political changes, new problems and challenges constantly presented themselves. The demand for recreation grew rapidly and John Geddes Page enthusiastically accepted the challenge. Midmar, Albert Falls and other dams provided excellent opportunities for the provision of recreation amenities. The 1970s saw an enormous expansion in this regard.

Dering Stainbank, a descendant of early Natal settlers, became the new Natal Parks Board chairman after retiring as a member of the Provincial executive committee. Together with the director John Geddes Page, the Natal Parks Board coped with the building of new camps and the expansion of new reserves like Itala on the Pongolo river. Tourist numbers had risen beyond all expectations and the board's income had increased accordingly. The stage was set for a new generation to move in and on the retirement of John Geddes Page and Dering Stainbank, Dr George Hughes became the director and PM Goss the chairman. They follow a long line of men who fought valiantly for the wildlife of Natal and Zululand.

George Hughes, with a scientific background and Pat Goss, with accounting and business knowledge, are in charge when these skills are needed in the ever-growing complexity and sophistication of conservation administration. The problems of the number of staff, the huge budget, tourist facilities, expanding computerisation and diminishing government funding have become extremely demanding on all the staff.

The battle to stop the mining of the dunes of the eastern shores of St Lucia was in full swing when Pat Goss took the chair. He immediately proved to be a leader with diplomacy, courage and skill, and Natal can be thankful that so capable and sincere a man was available at so critical a time.

Many of the parks in Zululand were still in danger, but the Natal Parks Board was in a better position to counteract the threats. Visitors to the parks from all over South Africa and other parts of the world gave support to what was beginning to be called environmental protection. The worldwide plundering of natural resources quickened the conscience of the western world, making thoughtful people appreciate that natural resources were finite and not inexhaustible. Even in Zululand the descendants of families that had been violently opposed to game conservation began turning to game ranching, hunting and tourism. Economics and more practical land use motivated the changes.

KWAZULU DEPARTMENT OF NATURE CONSERVATION

In 1982 the KwaZulu government, under the leadership of the Chief Minister Dr Mangosuthu Buthelezi, established the KwaZulu Bureau of Natural Resources, recently renamed the KwaZulu Department of Nature Conservation. This gave the Zulu people a direct stake in the conservation affairs of the country that had historically been split up by the British and the Boers because the Zulus had physically resisted their invasions.

From a small beginning with a budget of half a million rand the department, guided and encouraged by the Chief Minister, began growing. In 1983 Nick Steele sought and was granted secondment from the Natal Parks Board to the KwaZulu Bureau of Natural Resources and together with the Chief Minister turned the department into a large, efficient organisation. In 1986 Nick Steele became the director and with the characteristic energy and courage he had displayed throughout his Natal Parks Board career, worked tirelessly to involve the rural Zulu people in conservation so that they would benefit economically. Kosi Bay and Ndumu Game Reserve came under the control of the bureau and some 26 areas have been proclaimed, making up 2,7 per cent of the total land area of KwaZulu. The reserves range from Amatikulu Nature Reserve to Ophathe Game Reserve and Lake Sibaya, a very creditable achievement. Conservation areas were established and regional chiefs were encouraged to make better use of their wildlife resources. By 1994 the staff had grown from the original 150 to 600 and the budget to 35 million rands.

For the Chief Minister and the King, descendants of the house of Shaka, and for Nicholas Arthur Steele who has a deep understanding of Zulu history and a profound love for the people, the achievements of the department were a matter of special pride. For far too long the Zulu people had been given insufficient say in wildlife conservation matters. They welcomed the scientific and administrative expertise brought by the whites and, together with their own deeply intuitive knowledge, a unique partnership has been established.

THE FUTURE

The history of wildlife conservation in Natal and Zululand and the saving of the game reserves has always depended on the resourcefulness, courage and vision of individuals. Professional men of calibre who were not prepared to be bullied have been the backbone of the conservation movement. It is unlikely to be different in the future and if the recent fight to stop the proposed mining on the dunes near St Lucia and the struggle to proclaim the Greater St Lucia Wetland Park is any guide, there are many men and women of courage fighting the same battles as their predecessors.

To predict the future is always hazardous, but since the release of Nelson Mandela from long incarceration in prison and the Nationalist government's reversal of apartheid legislation under the leadership of FW de Klerk, South Africa has embarked upon a new journey. It has the potential to be the most important country in Africa and could lead the continent into a new understanding of the importance of conservation. Much is going to depend upon professional men and women to help guide the new political leaders.

Nothing has ever been easy in wildlife conservation and in the next era it is imperative that the general public becomes more involved and knowledgeable about the multiplicity of issues. More non-governmental organisations need to be created so that help can be given to the authorities to ensure not only the survival but the expansion of reserves and parks, otherwise the population explosion could overwhelm everything that was achieved by earlier pioneers.

The authors hope that this guide book will inspire those who read it, and who travel to the wild areas of KwaZulu/Natal, to support the cause of wildlife conservation by becoming personally involved.

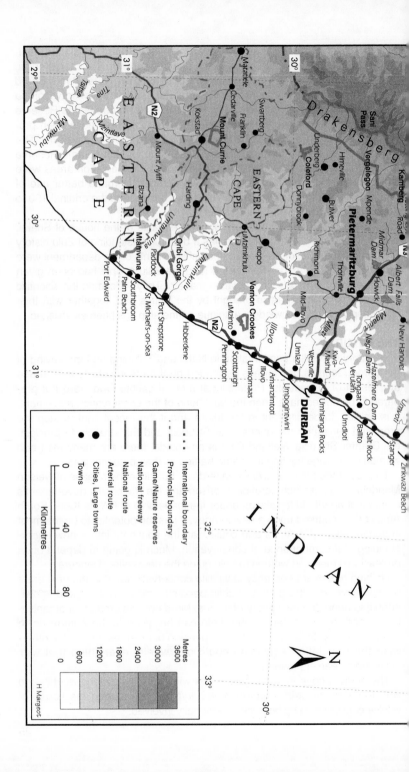

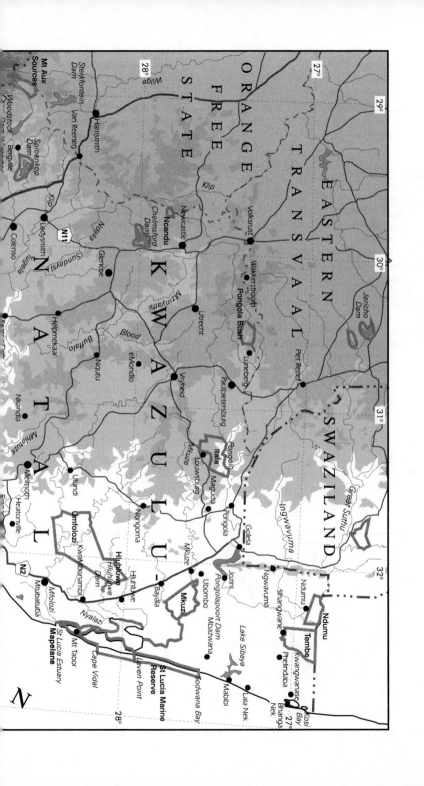

SOUTHERN NATAL COASTAL

1. ILLOVO LAGOON NATURE RESERVE
2. EMPISINI NATURE RESERVE
3. VERNON CROOKES NATURE RESERVE
4. TC ROBERTSON NATURE RESERVE
5. UMDONI PARK
6. ORIBI GORGE NATURE RESERVE
7. MBUMBAZI NATURE RESERVE
8. SKYLINE NATURE RESERVE
9. UVONGO RIVER NATURE RESERVE
10. FREDERIKA NATURE RESERVE
11. MPENJATI PUBLIC RESORT NATURE RESERVE
12. UMTAMVUNA NATURE RESERVE
13. TRAFALGAR MARINE RESERVE

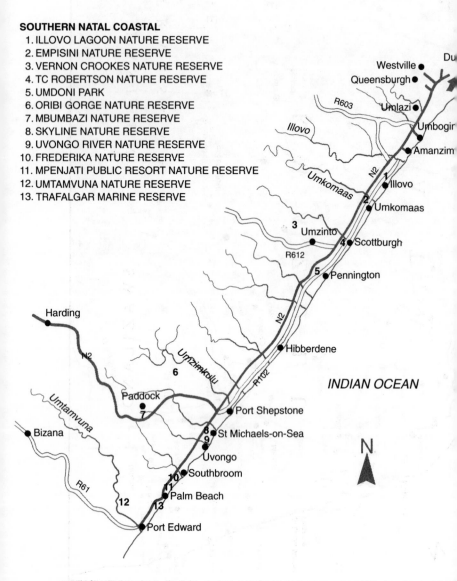

SOUTHERN NATAL COASTAL

The southern Natal coastal region in the 1850s must have been a garden of Eden with magnificent golden beaches, isolated rock formations and reefs richly carpeted with molluscs and seaweeds. A ribbon of green-clad, forested dunes, interrupted only by numerous clear rivers fringed the warm waters of the Indian Ocean. The high dunes formed a natural buffer between the sea and deep, clear, reed-fringed lagoons, tranquil estuaries and extensive swamp lands – the haunt of wildfowl and nursery areas for marine fishes, crustaceans and molluscs.

Inland, the gently sloping hillsides were covered by grasslands with a seasonal flush of wild flowers. There were woodlands, dense, hardwood forests in the valleys and deep gorges, and patches of scrub. These habitats supported an abundance and diversity of life forms. They were rapidly modified by the arrival of the first white settlers.

The forests were systematically stripped of timber for building houses, outbuildings, furniture and cattle kraals, for the construction of wagons – the only means of transport in those early years – for firewood and fuel for the first steam-driven sugar mills and coastal steamships that ferried goods between small south coast harbours and the developing port of Durban.

Timber was even exported to the Transvaal where the gold mines were being rapidly developed. It has been calculated that over the following 100 years about 90 per cent of the indigenous coastal and inland forests were destroyed.

The success of sugar cane as a commercial crop led to ploughing of grassy hillsides. Large areas of woodland were burned to provide grazing for cattle and fire encroached into the forest margins. Reeded swamps and marshlands were drained for agricultural purposes and siltation of rivers and estuaries occurred.

The warm coastal climate, the sea and magnificent beaches, with the recreational advantages and business opportunities that arose, attracted more and more permanent settlers to the South Coast region. Villages sprang up at the premier beaches offering a wide range of accommodation and the essential recreational amenities to cater for the needs of residents and the ever-increasing numbers of visitors attracted to one of the country's most popular tourist regions.

Despite the major impact that humans have had on the character of the coastal environment, there are still stretches of bush-clad dunes and unspoiled beaches, quiet estuaries and lagoons, rivers, forests, woodland and grassland. These habitats occur on private property and large estates or are owned by local municipalities. We are fortunate to retain some of the best examples in the small reserves. The true beauty of the former wild landscape, with its diversity of flora and fauna, is preserved in the Umtamvuna, Oribi Gorge and Vernon Crookes Nature Reserves and on some privately owned estates.

UMTAMVUNA NATURE RESERVE

Area: 3 257 ha
Established: 25 July 1971

LOCATION
South Coast, Natal-Transkei border. The reserve extends north-west upstream from the site of the old pontoon crossing south of Port Edward. Access is off the road to Izingolweni from Port Edward.

FEATURES
With magnificent views of the deep river gorge, Umtamvuna is a treasure house of rare and endemic trees and plant species in a diversity of habitats, with spectacular wild flower displays after the spring rains. The reserve has the best nature walks along the entire Natal coastline, with several marked trails to explore. A large colony of Cape vultures can be observed on their nesting sites. A small picnic site is situated above the office within the reserve, and a day visit is a most rewarding experience.

DESCRIPTION
The Umtamvuna river rises on the plateau of the Ingeli mountain range, at an altitude of over 2 000 m and flows eastwards. Streams join it from Natal and Transkei along its short course to the sea. The reserve lies along this river, the border between Natal and Transkei. It includes the section of river extending north-west and inland from the small coastal town of Port Edward about 19 km upriver. There is a tributary, the Bulolo river, within the reserve. The Umtamvuna changes its direction as it winds its way through the Mzikaba formation of the Natal Group sandstones and there are about 28 km of river frontage compressed into the 19 km length of the nature reserve.

There are breathtaking views from sites such as the Iron Crown in the western heights, both up and down the river gorges from forbidding weathered cliffs and straight down sheer rock faces some 240 m into forest to the river bed below. The steep gorges along the river, some deeply shaded, contain good stands of coastal scarp forest and some magnificent forest trees. There are patches of riverine forest, tangled thickets, small wooded kloofs and tiny waterfalls that cascade down to the boulder-strewn river bed. Sandstone krantzes are decorated with multi-hued lichens and trees bearing clumps of orchids. Banks of clivias and *Streptocarpus, Plectranthus*, begonias and ferns thrive in cool, damp forest patches.

The grassland flora above the krantzes is unusual in the preponderance of herbs, forbs and sedges and is a well-preserved relict community of typical Pondoland sourveld. The reserve is famous for its display of wild flowers in late spring, depending on rainfall and burns. Along the drier ridges and the small damp vleis overlying sheet rock, watsonias, ground orchids, agapanthus, scillas, numerous species of lilies, leucodendrons and three species of protea bloom. This creates an ever-changing carpet of colour as different species flower in succession amid the multi-hued pastel colours of numerous species of grasses and sedges. At this time of year, sunbirds and Gurney's sugarbirds – among the over 250 species of birds recorded locally – are much in evidence.

FLORA
The late Mr H Strey, pioneer botanist and former curator of the Natal Herbarium in Durban, Mr HB Nicholson and Mr Tony Abbott, collected and identified over 1 300 species of plants in this small reserve. They established an extremely valuable herbarium, open on request to visitors, at the Natal Parks Board's office within the park. Together with Professor Braam van Wyk, these botanists uncovered a fascinating community – the Pondoland/Natal sandstone endemics, with many species new to science and others extremely rare and endemic to this Natal Group sandstone habitat. One species, *Raspalia trigyna*, was thought to be extinct but was rediscovered and has now been successfully propagated and re-established with the help of Kirstenbosch National Botanical Gardens.

Trees of special interest in this reserve include:

Atalaya natalensis – Natal krantz ash
Cryptocarya wyliei – red quince
Dahlgrenodendron natalense – Natal quince
Encephalartos natalensis – Natal cycad
Eugenia verdoorniae – small-leaved myrtle
Eugenia erythrophylla – large-leaved myrtle
Manilkara nicholsonii – South Coast milkberry
Maytenus bachmannii – willow koko tree
Memecylon bachmannii – Pondo rose-apple
Pseudosalacia streyi – rock lemon
Rhynchocalyx lawsonioides – Natal privet
Rinorea domatiosa – bearded white violet bush
Syzygium pondoense – Pondo waterwood

BIRDS (258 species)
The reserve affords protection to a colony of Cape vultures estimated to be about 80-100 adult birds, and one of the few such colonies in the country that has increased in size. Other birds to be seen include:

black sparrowhawk
chorister robin
cuckoo hawk
eagles – African fish, crowned
green twinspot
grey waxbill
Gurney's sugarbird
hornbills – crowned, ground
Knysna woodpecker

Knysna lourie
lesser doublecollared sunbird
longtailed wagtail
mocking chat
nightjars – Natal, freckled
peregrine falcon
rock martin
spotted thrush
striped pipit

FAUNA

The reserve is not rich in animal life. Oribi have recently been reintroduced. The rare serval has occasionally been observed and leopard are said to occur in the forested gorges and ravines. The following animals occur:

black-backed jackal
blue duiker
bushbuck
Cape clawless otter
chacma baboon
common duiker
large-spotted genet

leopard
mongooses – large grey,
    slender, water, white-tailed
porcupine
reedbuck
samango monkey

MPENJATI PUBLIC RESORT NATURE RESERVE

Area: 80 ha
Proclamation: Pending

LOCATION

Lower South Coast. Palm Beach near Southbroom, about 18 km south of Margate.

FEATURES

A popular venue for board sailing, boating and canoeing. Fishing in the lagoon and surf angling are other popular recreational sports. Picnic sites with braai facilities are available and a short self-guided trail system has been laid out. Adjoins Trafalgar Marine Reserve.

DESCRIPTION

The resort includes a section of the Mpenjati river and lagoon, which probably derives its name from a reedy type of grass (mphenjati) growing in its vicinity, or from "the place of the warring buffalo". The interesting palmiet *Prionium serratum*, resembling a dwarf palm, is found in large communities

32

along the stream on the inland trail. It is close to the northern limit of its distribution. Pieces of the dry stem with unusual feathery black sheaths are found washed up along the lagoon and beach. There are examples of the *Scaevola* community on the beach, reed swamp, stands of *Juncus* sedge, grassland and coastal forest including coastal red milkwoods, Natal wild banana, lagoon hibiscus, coast silver oak, tassel berry, wild date palm, pigeon wood, amatungulu (big numnum), common turkey berry and many others. Of great interest is a well-preserved stand of dune forest (over 20 ha in extent), surrounding a small lake. This forest, the "Yengele", is poorly known.

BIRDS

African finfoot
African pied wagtail
blackbellied starling
blackcollared barbet
blackcrowned tchagra
bleating bushwarbler
bulbuls – sombre, terrestrial
Burchell's coucal
bush shrikes – greyheaded, olive
Cape white-eye
cardinal woodpecker
chinspot batis
cormorants – whitebreasted, reed
forktailed drongo
great white egret
green twinspot
kelp gull
kingfishers – brownhooded, pied
louries – Knysna, purplecrested
narina trogon
Natal robin
Natal thrush
paradise flycatcher
plumcoloured starling
redbacked mannikin
redfronted tinker barbet
sunbirds – collared, olive
water dikkop
whimbrel
whitefronted sandplover
yellowbilled duck

MAMMALS

Cape clawless otter
large grey mongoose
large-spotted genet
vervet monkey

TRAFALGAR MARINE RESERVE

Area: 1 500 ha
Established: 22 February 1979

LOCATION

Lower South Coast. Palm Beach, near Southbroom, about 18 km south of Margate (adjoins Mpenjati Public Resort).

FEATURES

Known as a good angling area, particularly for bronze bream. Trafalgar Point, within the marine reserve, is a favourite beach for board sailing. Parking is available in Trafalgar village and at the Mpenjati public resort.

DESCRIPTION

This small marine reserve extends from Centre Rocks in the north, to south of the Mpenjati river in the south. It adjoins Mpenjati Public Resort in its southern third and extends 500 m out to sea along its length. It was proclaimed to protect the unique marine cretaceous fossil beds found here. Within the boundaries of the sanctuary, bathing is permitted and so is rod and line angling, but there is a ban on collection of bait and shellfish.

BIRDS

African pied wagtail
common sandpiper
greenshank
kelp gull

kingfishers – giant, Natal, pied
turnstone
water dikkop
whitefronted plover

FREDERIKA NATURE RESERVE

Area: 7 ha
Established: 1976

LOCATION

South Coast, Southbroom, south of Margate; alongside the Southbroom golf course from the 17th tee to the 2nd green near Fairway Road.

FEATURES

A small pocket of unspoilt dune forest. No facilities. The land for this reserve was donated to the South African Conservation Centre (SANCO) by Mr Leo Dreisson and the reserve is administered by the Southbroom Health Committee.

UVONGO RIVER NATURE RESERVE

Area: Approximately 28 ha
Established: 1951

LOCATION
South Coast, near Margate, between Uvongo and Manaba Beach. Take the N2 to Uvongo, go over the bridge and take the first turn to the right.

FEATURES
A well-conserved area of coastal forest with a diversity of trees, shrubs, ferns and orchids, typical coastal bird species and a circular trail (about two hours) through the indigenous forest. More than 100 tree species have been labelled and a number of these only occur in the southern Natal region. A shaded parking area, picnic and braai sites are provided.

The Uvongo River Nature Reserve land was presented to the local borough of Uvongo in 1951 by Count Thure Lilliecrona as a gift. He was responsible for laying out the Uvongo township. The name Uvongo is an anglicised version of the Zulu "iVungu" – referring to the reverberating roar of the falls, found upstream along the course of the iVungu river.

SKYLINE NATURE RESERVE

Area: 15 ha
Proclamation: Pending

LOCATION
South Coast. At St Michaels-on-Sea, borough of Uvongo. Turn right at the second traffic light if coming from the north. The reserve is signposted from this point.

FEATURES
A fine collection of local and introduced South African indigenous flora and some exotic species, with a trail. A small herbarium and library is available to interested botanists and the public. A most pleasant venue for a morning or afternoon visit.

HISTORICAL NOTES
The arboretum was established by the well-known local botanist, Mr HB Nicholson in 1962, and donated to the borough of Uvongo in 1982. Prof HB Rycroft, retired director of Kirstenbosch Botanic Gardens, managed it for

some years. It was taken over by the Natal Parks Board in 1986. A valuable collection of pressed specimens of coastal plants is contained in a herbarium with an adjoining library which is frequently used by visiting botanists and interested members of the public.

DESCRIPTION

Better known as Skyline Arboretum, this small area preserves habitats that include grassland, swamp, dense bush clumps and small dams. These habitats contain many rare plants threatened with destruction due to the increasing and rapid development that is taking place on the South Coast. The reserve is subdivided into management blocks. Introduced exotic and indigenous species are propagated and maintained in the habitats that suit their specific requirements. There is, for example, a palm garden, containing 38 species of these spectacular plants.

BIRDS

barthroated apalis
blackcollared barbet
blackheaded oriole
bronze mannikin
brownhooded kingfisher
bulbuls – blackeyed, sombre
forest weaver
goldenrumped tinker barbet
goldentailed woodpecker

grey waxbill
gymnogene
Natal robin
speckled mousebird
squaretailed drongo
sunbirds – collared, grey, olive,
    black, scarletbreasted
trumpeter hornbill
yelloweyed canary

MBUMBAZI NATURE RESERVE

Area: 2 125 ha
Established: 25 April 1991

LOCATION

South Coast. Located on the farm Kranskloof 8100, 5 km from Paddock and 31 km from Port Shepstone. It borders on the former KwaZulu for the most part in the north-east and south-west and on sugar cane farms in the north-west and south-east.

FEATURES

This reserve contains between 600-800 ha of pristine coastal forest and Ngongoni veld. At present the collection and propagation of medicinal plants and bulbs is being undertaken in the reserve, although still on a small scale. Local people surrounding the reserve are permitted to remove thatching grass, firewood and building materials.

One of the aims of the reserve is to provide an environmental education centre for the estimated 110 000 school pupils who reside within a radius of 75 km around the reserve.

DESCRIPTION
The height above sea level varies from 200 m in the south to 400 m or more in the north. The terrain is undulating, with steep rolling land in the south contrasting with that in the north which rises to an escarpment, with steep slopes and buttresses of granite rock. A fault block outlier consisting of Natal Group sandstone occurs on the southern border. Overall the topography is rugged to undulating with well defined, steep and deep drainage lines. There are springs rising along the fault block outliers and many wetland areas in the southern part of the reserve. The main water supply, the iVungu or Uvongo river, divides the reserve into two separate areas, with many tributaries feeding into the system. The environment lends itself to a variety of different vegetation types: grasslands on the upper slopes leading down through woodlands where the vegetation changes to forest and riverine thickets.

HISTORICAL NOTES
Mr R Rossler was the first owner of the land and farmed sugar cane, livestock, eucalyptus plantations and wood lots. A portion of the present reserve, known as the Margate Corridor, was purchased by the Department of Development Aid in 1985 according to consolidation proposals, as compensatory land for people who moved from a portion of the area. The first proposals to develop the area for conservation purposes were made in 1980. The area was proclaimed as Ntubeni Nature Reserve on 25 April 1981. The name was changed to Mbumbazi Nature Reserve in 1988.

ACCOMMODATION
No accommodation is available for tourists or day visitors as yet. However, plans have been drawn up to build six luxury log cabins, as well as overnight facilities for school groups attending environmental educational programmes. The present infrastructure includes an office complex, stores and workshop, reserve manager's house, game guard housing and an environmental education centre. Enquiries can be directed to the Department of Community Services, NPA, Pietermaritzburg.

FLORA
Aloe arborescens – krantz aloe
Aloe barberae – tree aloe
Bridelia micrantha – mitzeeri
Ekebergia pterophylla – rock ash
Encephalartos natalensis – Natal cycad
Erythrina caffra – coast coral tree
Erythroxylum pictum – coast coca tree

Ficus craterostoma – forest fig
Ficus ingens – red-leaved fig
Ficus natalensis – Natal fig
Ficus sur – broom cluster fig
Grewia caffra – climbing raisin
Millettia grandis – umzimbeet
Mimusops obovata – red milkwood
Protea caffra – common sugarbush
Protea roupelliae – silver sugarbush
Protorus longifolia – red beech
Prunus africana – red stinkwood
Ptaeroxylon obliquum – sneezewood
Rauvolfia caffra – quinine tree
Rawsonia lucida – forest peach
Stangeria eriopus – stangeria
Syzygium cordatum – water berry
Syzygium gerrardii – forest waterwood
Tarchonanthus trilobus – camphor tree
Trichilia dregeana – forest Natal mahogany
Xymalos monospora – lemonwood

BIRDS (107 species recorded)

black saw-wing swallow
blackbellied glossy starling
blackheaded oriole
blackshouldered kite
Burchell's coucal
bushshrikes – greyheaded, orangebreasted
dusky flycatcher
halfcollared kingfisher
hornbills – ground, trumpeter
jackal buzzard

Klaas's cuckoo
Knysna lourie
lesser doublecollared sunbird
lesser honeyguide
longcrested eagle
narina trogon
neddicky
redbilled woodhoopoe
tawnyflanked prinia

MAMMALS

African wild cat
antbear (aardvark)
blue duiker
Burchell's zebra
bushbuck
Cape clawless otter
common duiker
dassies – rock, tree
greater canerat
large-spotted genet

mongooses – large grey,
   slender, water
monkeys – samango, vervet
Natal red rock rabbit
porcupine
scrub hare
serval
striped polecat
striped weasel

In addition there are smaller species such as shrews, bats and moles. In 1985 the skull and claws of a leopard caught in a snare were found in a gorge through which the Uvongo river flows, so this species may still be present in the reserve.

ORIBI GORGE NATURE RESERVE

Area: 1 837 ha
Established: 1 April 1950

LOCATION
South Coast, 21 km along the Harding road, west of Port Shepstone. The turn-off is marked "Nature Reserve".

FEATURES
Well known for its magnificent scenic views, a picturesque camp set amid an indigenous garden and a variety of day walks, hikes and climbs through several vegetation types. A pleasant circular drive takes visitors through the gorge and there is a quiet picnic and braai site on the river bank. Attractive veld flowers appear after the spring rains and some 250 bird, 40 mammal, 21 reptile, 14 amphibian and six fish species occur in this interesting area. It is ideal for a five day relaxed holiday, or a day of exploration and a picnic. Fishing is allowed in the river.

DESCRIPTION
The reserve is made up of a 24 km stretch of gorge cut by the Umzimkulwane river, through a plateau of Natal Group sandstone overlying granite. Altitudes vary from 120-680 m. The river, fed by numerous small, clear, permanent and semi-permanent streams from steeply sloped, thickly wooded forests, has a number of impressive waterfalls which are a feature along some of the trails. There are stretches of shallows and boulder beds, rapids and pools, quiet, deeper rock pools overhung by giant forest trees, reed-lined sections, sandspits and reaches of well-grassed banks providing pleasant picnic and fishing sites.

Towering sandstone cliffs, with sheer multicoloured faces, others broken by rock ledges and caves, the haunts of baboons, dassies and the nesting sites of birds of prey, cut out the sounds of civilisation. Without walking far up or downstream from the tourist road that passes through the reserve, one can enjoy the sounds of forest song birds. One hears the hoots of narina trogons, the braying of trumpeter hornbills, noisy Knysna louries and the staccato barks of baboons, samango monkeys and the extraordinary alarm calls of rock dassies. High above can be heard the hunting and communicating calls of black, crowned and longcrested eagles, jackal buzzards, lanner falcons and rock kestrels, as they soar and scan the rock faces and thickly wooded forests for prey. One can marvel too at the speed and precision of diving and wheeling black, Alpine and little swifts.

Good stands of both dry and moist coastal forest, small stretches of evergreen riverine forest, dense thickets, acacia-dominated valley bushveld, woodland and, on the plateau, attractive grassland are found in this reserve. Clumps of proteas and, after the spring burns, "fire-lilies" and a host of colourful veld flowers and ground orchids such as *Eulophia zehyeriana* and in the forest, the clivia *Clivia miniata*, are a botanist's and nature lover's delight. About 700 plant species, the majority of which are trees and shrubs, have been identified.

ACCOMMODATION
There are six three-bedded rest huts with a fully equipped kitchen and ablution block, and a self-contained cottage sleeping seven persons. Accommodation units are serviced. Visitors need to supply their own food and drink. A picnic site on the river bank, with picnic and braai facilities, has been established in the gorge. Reservations are made with the Natal Parks Board, Pietermaritzburg.

TREES
Some of the more attractive and unusual trees are:
Alberta magna – Natal flame bush
Cassine crocea – small-leaved saffron
Chrysophyllum viridifolium – fluted milkwood
Cryptocarya wyliei – red quince
Cussonia sphaerocephala – forest cabbage tree
Drypetes gerrardii – forest ironplum
Ekebergia pterophylla – rock ash
Encephalartos ghellinckii – Drakensberg cycad (unusual so near the coast)
Erythrina spp. – coral trees
Heywoodia lucens – Cape ebony
Loxostylis alata – wild pepper tree
Nuxia floribunda – forest elder
Ochna serrulata – small-leaved plane bush
Pseudobersama mossambicensis – false white ash
Pseudoscolopia polyantha – false red pear
Rhynchocalyx lawsonioides – Natal privet (family with only one genus and one species of this sandstone endemic)

BIRDS
For the birding enthusiast, some of the interesting species recorded include:
African black duck
African broadbill
African goshawk
black sparrowhawk

bluebilled firefinch
bluemantled flycatcher
cinnamon dove
cuckoo hawk

green twinspot
grey cuckoo shrike
grey waxbill
halfcollared kingfisher
honey buzzard
Knysna woodpecker
longtailed wagtail
olive bush shrike

robins – brown, chorister,
  Natal, starred
striped pipit
sunbirds – grey, olive, collared,
  lesser doublecollared
thrushes – Cape, spotted rock
yellowthroated warbler

MAMMALS

The following are the most likely species to be seen:

black-backed jackal
bushbuck
Cape clawless otter
chacma baboon
duiker – common, blue
large-spotted genet

mongooses – large grey,
  slender, water
reedbuck
rock dassie
monkeys – samango, vervet

There are three seldom seen and rare species, caracal, serval and aard-wolf, and unconfirmed reports of leopard occurring in the gorge.

UMDONI PARK

Area: Approximately 160 ha
Established: 1922

LOCATION

South Coast, south of Pennington. On the seaward side of the old South Coast main road. Turn off at Pennington and continue down Pennington drive until the sign indicating a turn-off to the right to Umdoni Park and golf course.

FEATURES

A magnificent area of coastal forest and grassland containing very fine examples of trees, shrubs and climbers. The very rare *Dahlgrenodendron natalense* (Natal quince) was first discovered along one of the trails in the park. The area is rich in bird species, and blue duiker, bushbuck and smaller mammals can be seen.

There are walking trails, picnic and braai sites at the beach, a tidal pool and the Umdoni Park golf course.

Umdoni is the Zulu name for the water berry tree *Syzygium caudatum*, and some particularly large, magnificent specimens are found in this park.

VERNON CROOKES NATURE RESERVE

Area: 2 189 ha
Established: 4 January 1973

LOCATION
South Coast. Turn off the South Coast freeway at the Park Rynie-Umzinto off-ramp and take the Highflats-Ixopo road. The reserve turn-off is approximately 3 km past Umzinto, 12,5 km from the freeway. The entrance gate is 6 km from this turn-off.

FEATURES
Open grassland, rolling hillsides, deep wooded gorges, thornveld, forests, vleis and a small dam where fishing is permitted. There are views over the terrain to the distant sea. Over 300 species of birds and 26 mammals have been recorded. After the spring rains, a wide variety of wild flowers are found around the small dam and in the grassland areas. About 12 km of tourist roads and some excellent walks are available. There are pleasant picnic sites with toilets.

DESCRIPTION
This small reserve preserves tracts of typical coastal forest with five subdivisions of forest types, mostly occurring in the lower lying valleys. There are extensive stands of sour grasslands on the undulating ridges and hills, thornveld and bush clumps, vleis of rank grasses and sedges. Permanent surface water is provided by artificial dams covered in waterlilies. Small stands of swamp forest and sponge areas occur on some forest margins. The altitude ranges from 150-610 m and from the upper plateau one has splendid views over the reserve down deep valleys, across the lower-lying farmlands to the distant sea. Three streams flow down well-wooded valleys through the reserve. The vegetation types provide an ideal niche for coastal, as well as inland bird species, which, at times, shelter here during seasonal movements to and from the lower coastal regions to higher altitudes. This diversity of habitats accounts for the over 300 species of birds recorded in this small reserve.

Previous land-use malpractices, such as denuding of forests, uncontrolled burning, cultivation and overgrazing over a period of many years, have altered the veld. Secondary grassland and scrub have appeared and invasive alien plant species, difficult and costly to eradicate, have encroached in places.

HISTORICAL NOTES
Like the other two South Coast reserves, this one, now almost totally surrounded by eucalyptus plantations, sugar cane fields and densely populated areas, is a valuable oasis of fauna and flora, and of relict habitats to

remind us of what the Natal South Coast must have been like before man encroached on the area after the mid-1850s. However, this land has had a chequered history. Parts of the present-day reserve featured in the Dumisa gold rush of 1887. The land was occupied, cultivated and grazed by local Zulus for a long period. It was later bought by sugar barons, the Reynolds brothers, and used mainly as a grazing area for cattle and mules in the early years of the sugar industry. Then Vernon Crookes, another sugar baron, acquired the land and, fortunately for future generations of South Africans, donated the area to the province in the early 1970s. Situated in the midst of what is today the South Coast sugar belt, the reserve is an extremely valuable asset to this area of Natal.

ACCOMMODATION
The Nyengelezi research camp, a rustic camp with 20 beds (five huts with four beds each), with kitchen block, ablution facilities and a small research laboratory, is available to the public and to study groups. Attractive picnic sites with all facilities are available within the reserve. Reservations are made with the Natal Parks Board officer-in-charge.

FLORA
Some of the interesting tree species are:
Bachmannia woodii – four-finger bush
Baphia racemosa – Natal camwood
Cassine crocea – small-leaved saffron
Combretum kraussii – forest bushwillow
Encephalartos natalensis – Natal cycad
Ficus glumosa – mountain fig
Grewia lasiocarpa – forest raisin
Halleria lucida – tree fuchsia
Xymalos monospora – lemonwood

The grasslands harbour a mass of flowers in early spring and after the rains. Noteworthy are the sore-eye flowers *Boophane disticha*, lobelias and watsonias. Orchids of the genera *Satyrium* and *Disa* are abundant. Within the bush clumps the dwarf, white-flowered snake lily *Haemanthus deformis* occurs and, in the mid-summer months, clivias *Clivia miniata* and swamp snake lily *Scadoxus multiflorus*.

BIRDS (over 300 species)
Vernon Crookes reserve is a mecca for ornithologists, with a number of special and interesting species for the enthusiast to search for. It is the ideal place for anyone interested in learning to identify or study cisticolas.

Some birds to be seen:
African broadbill   black sparrowhawk
black cuckoo   broadtailed warbler

Cape rock thrush
chats – familiar, mocking
cisticolas – Ayres', croaking,
  fantailed, lazy, Levaillant's,
  palecrowned
crowned cranes
  (they breed annually
  within this reserve)
eagles – crowned, longcrested,
  martial

flufftails – buffspotted, redchested
green coucal
lanner falcon
neddicky
pipits – longbilled, plainbacked, striped
quail finch
redbacked mannikin
starred robin
waxbills – orangebreasted, swee

MAMMALS

Reintroduced species include eland, zebra, blue wildebeest, reedbuck, impala, oribi and nyala. The rare caracal and serval have also been seen in this reserve. Other species include:

black-backed jackal
bushbuck
Cape clawless otter
chacma baboon
duiker – blue, common
greater canerat

large-spotted genet
mongooses – banded, large grey,
  slender, water, white-tailed
monkeys – samango, vervet
porcupine
striped weasel

TC ROBERTSON NATURE RESERVE

Area: Approximately 45 ha
Established: 1989

LOCATION

South Coast, Scottburgh. Off the old main South Coast road, turn into the reserve just north of the Mpambinyoni river bridge.

FEATURES

The reserve is situated along the eastern bank of the Mpambinyoni river, within easy walking distance of the village. It contains typical coastal forest, grassy hillsides, palmveld and riverine vegetation. A trail system traverses the five major habitats and picnic and braai sites, toilets and ample parking are provided. 200 species of bird, 96 species of tree, 15 mammal, 28 reptile and 20 fish species have been recorded.

The reserve was named in honour of the late Dr Thomas "TC" Chalmers Robertson, author, conservationist and ecologist, former director of the National Veld Trust and one of the most respected and acclaimed conservationists in South African history. TC Robertson spent the last 16 years of his life in Scottburgh. He died on 11 January 1989.

EMPISINI NATURE RESERVE

Area: 300 ha
Established: 1973

LOCATION
South Coast. From the N2 take the Umkomaas-Widenham off-ramp. At the stop street turn left, then travel a few hundred metres to the first left turn signposted SAPPI/SAICCOR. Continue down a steep hill for just over 1 km, turn left at the T-junction at the bottom of the hill and then left again through an unmarked gap in the fence. Follow the track for about 400 m to the parking and picnic area.

FEATURES
An attractive reserve, it is a good example of prime coastal forest with perennial small streams, a dam and swamp land. Over 100 species of birds have been recorded. There is a system of trails, a small resource centre, picnic and braai area and rustic toilet. A tree house and two rustic huts are available for overnight accommodation. Reservations should be made with the Umkomaas Town Board.

ILLOVO LAGOON NATURE RESERVE

Area: Approximately 13 ha
Established: 1977

LOCATION
South Coast. On the N2 travelling south from Durban take the Winkelspruit off-ramp, turn left then right at the traffic light, right at the next traffic light (past Pick 'n Pay on the left), then cross the river. The reserve is on the left via an entrance gate to a shooting range. It comprises the main lagoon and estuarine system of the iLlovo river.

DESCRIPTION
There are interesting estuarine systems of varying sizes and a stand of black and white mangroves with the fauna associated with this habitat. There are three trails. Picnicking is allowed but fires are not. It is a popular venue for fishermen.

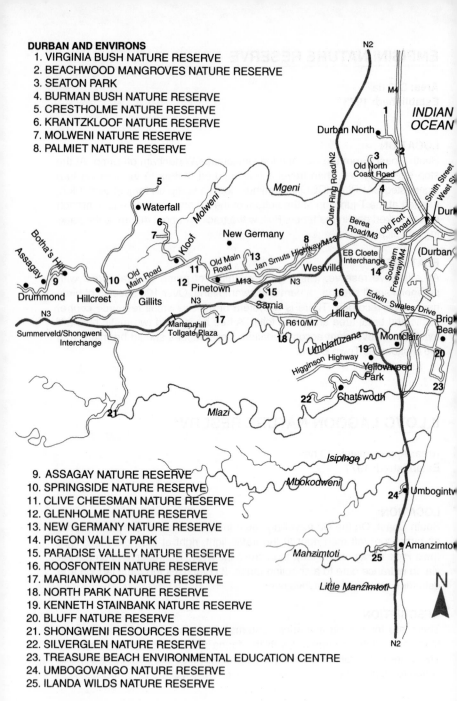

DURBAN AND ENVIRONS

1. VIRGINIA BUSH NATURE RESERVE
2. BEACHWOOD MANGROVES NATURE RESERVE
3. SEATON PARK
4. BURMAN BUSH NATURE RESERVE
5. CRESTHOLME NATURE RESERVE
6. KRANTZKLOOF NATURE RESERVE
7. MOLWENI NATURE RESERVE
8. PALMIET NATURE RESERVE

9. ASSAGAY NATURE RESERVE
10. SPRINGSIDE NATURE RESERVE
11. CLIVE CHEESMAN NATURE RESERVE
12. GLENHOLME NATURE RESERVE
13. NEW GERMANY NATURE RESERVE
14. PIGEON VALLEY PARK
15. PARADISE VALLEY NATURE RESERVE
16. ROOSFONTEIN NATURE RESERVE
17. MARIANNWOOD NATURE RESERVE
18. NORTH PARK NATURE RESERVE
19. KENNETH STAINBANK NATURE RESERVE
20. BLUFF NATURE RESERVE
21. SHONGWENI RESOURCES RESERVE
22. SILVERGLEN NATURE RESERVE
23. TREASURE BEACH ENVIRONMENTAL EDUCATION CENTRE
24. UMBOGOVANGO NATURE RESERVE
25. ILANDA WILDS NATURE RESERVE

46

DURBAN AND ENVIRONS

Over 150 years ago Durban was a large natural lagoon protected from the sea by the high, forested Bluff dune formation. Between the undulating sand dunes along the foreshore, northwards towards the Mgeni river and upstream to Sea Cow lake there was a vast depression, a wetland of reedbeds, swamp and pools reaching to the foot of the densely forested Berea hills overlooking the bay. The clear waters of the Mbilo and Mhlatuzana rivers emptied into the bay and swamplands extended as far south as the Isipingo river.

The subtropical coastal climate supported a wide variety of flora and fauna. Tropical mangrove islands dotted the shallows of the bay, supporting thriving nesting colonies of herons and egrets, numerous waders on sand-banks and pelicans, flamingoes and ibises in the shallows. Hippo and crocodiles basked on the mudflats. The swamps, grasslands and forests supported wildfowl, antelopes and even elephants in the forest-clad Berea ridge.

The settlement of the bay in 1824 and an ever-increasing number of set-tlers rapidly changed the landscape. Forest hardwoods were felled for build-ing purposes, the less valuable trees for fuel. Scrub and grasslands were cleared for housing and agriculture. Soon the elephants and hippos were exterminated for their valuable ivory and crocodiles and antelopes for their skins and hides. The lagoon was developed into a harbour. Around this busy port, commerce and industry flourished.

Durban provided a gateway to the interior of Natal and attracted increas-ing numbers of settlers.

Because of its favourable climate and wide beaches, Durban became a mecca for tourists, creating more business and employment opportunities. By the 1990s the urban sprawl and a vast industrial complex had spread as far as Amanzimtoti in the south and to Umhlanga Rocks in the north. The forested hills were ideal for housing development and gradually, as the human population increased, the inland grassy hillsides and forested val-leys were swallowed up by industry, agricultural development and suburban housing estates. Today Durban has one of the largest and busiest ports in Africa. It supports a rapidly burgeoning population of about 1,8 million peo-ple and attracts an estimated 350 000 visitors annually.

Durbanites and visitors to the city are fortunate in that there are about 23 small nature reserves and parks preserving the flora and fauna of this region. The Bluff Nature Reserve is an example of dune forest and wetland; Treasure Beach consists of grassland and a rocky seashore; Beachwood, a magnificent mangrove community; coastal lowland forest is found in Kenneth Stainbank, Burman Bush, Pigeon Valley and Virginia Bush;

riverine vegetation, forest, grasslands and steep wooded krantzes in Shongweni Valley, Palmiet and the scenic Krantzkloof nature reserves which all contain a prolific variety of bird and small mammal species; the Mgeni river mouth is noteworthy for seabirds and waders.

Many of these small reserves are linked up by the D'MOSS trails (Durban Metropolitan Open Space System which was initiated by the Wildlife Society and Regional Planning Commission in 1988). All of these small reserves are within 30 minutes drive of the city centre.

ILANDA WILDS NATURE RESERVE

Area: 20 ha
Established: 1965

LOCATION
South Coast, Amanzimtoti. On the N2 from Durban take the Amanzimtoti off-ramp. Turn right into Kingsway Drive. Travel about 50 m then turn right into Adams Drive. Cross the bridge then turn immediately left into Isundu Drive. Ilanda Wilds is about 1,5 km along this road and is next to the River Gardens Hotel.

FEATURES
A well-preserved area of coastal bush and thornveld with fine specimens of forest trees and over 100 species of birds recorded. There is a car park, toilets and picnic site, but no camping and braai facilities are provided.

The name of this reserve, "iLanda", is Zulu for cattle egret, which appears on the coat of arms of Amanzimtoti.

UMBOGOVANGO NATURE RESERVE

Area: 30 ha
Established: 10 March 1989

LOCATION
South Coast. Umbogintwini. From Durban on the N2, follow the directions from the Umbogintwini off-ramp just before Amanzimtoti, to the AECI factory.

48

FEATURES

There is a trail that circles the dams, four viewing hides along the water's edge and picnic and braai sites. A fully equipped environmental centre caters for 50 persons. This centre is extensively used by school groups and may be hired by other interested groups for seminars. Access to this private nature reserve is by appointment only. Telephone AECI Ltd on (031) 949081.

DESCRIPTION

It comprises large stormwater dams with reedbeds and grassed verges, largely surrounded by thick coastal bush in which 135 species of trees have been identified. It is a particularly good habitat for waterbirds – 182 species of aquatic and coastal bush birds have been recorded. Small mammals include banded mongoose, slender mongoose, water mongoose, Cape clawless otter, blue duiker and vervet monkey.

BLUFF NATURE RESERVE

Area: 45 ha
Established: 24 October 1974

LOCATION

Durban Bluff, east of Wentworth Hospital. Take the Edwin Swales VC off-ramp from the southern freeway and drive east. Turn left into Bluff Road, then right into Old Mission Road at the robot and continue along this road, then right into Tara Road. The nature reserve entrance is on the left.

FEATURES

A small natural vlei in an otherwise mainly industrial area, where numerous species of birds may be viewed from an attractive hide. Over 120 bird and 15 mammal species have been recorded from the vlei, open water, grassland, bracken fern, thornveld and dune forest. A pleasant venue for a morning's bird watching and photography.

DESCRIPTION

The area comprises a typical vlei of bulrushes *Typha latifolia* and an expanse of reed beds and mixed sedges fringing a large waterlily-covered pond. Aquatics, such as *Potamogeton* sp., *Nymphoides* and *Utricularia*, in among the sedges and grasses, provide an ideal food supply for resident and migratory birds. They also provide cover and food for a variety of aquatic insects, snails, eight species of frogs and toads and small fish – which in turn provide food for numerous species of water birds.

Cover for reptiles and amphibians, nesting birds and small mammals is available in the mixed grassland and thick clumps of bracken fern and a small area of thornveld and coastal forest. A small stand of Kosi palm *Raphia australis*, was introduced in the early 1970s.

HISTORICAL NOTES
Previously known as Happy Valley Swamp, the origins of this small "green lung" can be traced back to 1961 when Dennie McCulloch of the Natal Bird Club, Walter Lawson of the Durban Museum and Keith Cooper of the Wildlife Society – aided by Councillor Frank Cheeck – persuaded the Durban City Council that the area should be set aside as a bird sanctuary. This small swamp and several other vleis near Durban were scheduled to be drained because of complaints by residents that they were mosquito breeding areas. Each year the council spent large sums of money on labour and insecticides to deal with the problem. Fortunately the area was set aside for nature lovers. In an effort to combat mosquitos, the city's health department introduced mud bream, *Tilapia* species, which supposedly would feed on mosquito larvae. However, the species introduced fed on aquatic plants and over the ensuing years, had a profound and devastating effect on the indigenous vegetation.

In 1964 the Wildlife Society appointed a full-time patrol guard, Mr Ambrose Ncanana. Over the years he performed an invaluable role in both protecting and interpreting the area to the increasing number of Durban residents and visitors who now had access to the only major remaining wetland in the area. In 1974 the Natal Parks Board assumed control and the area was officially proclaimed a nature reserve.

BIRDS
Over 120 species of birds have been recorded, including 11 species of ducks and geese and eight herons and egrets (some are resident and breeding). Interesting species include:

African jacana

Baillon's crake

bittern

black crake

Caspian tern

cisticolas – blackbacked, fantailed

ducks – fulvous, knobbilled, whitebacked

gorgeous bush shrike

grey sunbird

grey waxbill

herons – black, squacco

little bittern

purple gallinule

pygmy goose

red bishop

sacred ibis

southern tchagra

spoonbill

thickbilled weaver

MAMMALS
The list of mammals numbers 15 species, with large-spotted genet, blue duiker, water mongoose, slender mongoose, banded mongoose and vervet monkey the most likely to be seen.

TREASURE BEACH ENVIRONMENTAL EDUCATION CENTRE

Area: 16 ha
Established: 1988

LOCATION
Durban Bluff. From Durban, on the southern freeway, take the Jacobs exit and turn left into Quality Street. Continue straight across Tara Road into Highbury Road. Approximately 150 m further on turn right into Nerissa Road. At the crest of the hill, turn left into Marine Drive, then first right and continue for about 70 m to the centre on the right.

FEATURES
This important small reserve contains a remnant patch of climax grassland, coastal forest, dune forest and a fine stretch of rocky shoreline. The Wildlife Society has established an environmental education centre. Qualified staff run courses for school children and interested groups on coastal ecology, particularly on the grasslands and marine life in the tidal pools. The centre is equipped for lectures, film and video shows, with limited catering facilities available for functions. Information on school courses, projects and lectures may be obtained from the Wildlife Society, 835 Marine Drive, Bluff 4052. Telephone: (031) 478507/8.

SILVERGLEN NATURE RESERVE

Area: 220 ha
Established: 1982

LOCATION
Durban, between Chatsworth and Umlazi. From the EB Cloete interchange follow the N2 south to the Chatsworth-Mobeni exit. At the traffic lights at the end of the off-ramp turn right into Higginson Highway and continue for 2 km before turning left into Havenside Drive. After 500 m turn left again into Silverglen Drive, travel another 3,7 km to just after the Caltex service station, then left again into Lakeview Road. Follow this narrow winding road for about 600 m to the reserve gates and a further 2 km to the visitor centre and plant nursery.

FEATURES
The reserve comprises a mosaic of coastal grassland and bush clumps and contains about 120 bird species. There is a medicinal plant and tree nursery, two trails (guided trails for school groups), a visitor centre, picnic and

braai sites, car park and public toilets. A trail guide is available at the visitor centre.

KENNETH STAINBANK NATURE RESERVE

Area: 214 ha
Established: 12 February 1963

LOCATION
Durban, in the south-western suburb of Yellowwood Park, 14 km from the city centre. From the southern freeway take the Montclair-Clairwood exit. At the traffic lights turn right into Blamey Road, go under the freeway, past the next set of lights, turning left at the third set of traffic lights into South Coast Road. After 2 km turn right into Kenyon Howden Road, and continue up the hill, over the freeway, to Yellowwood Park. At the circle bear left and go straight into Kingfisher Avenue, next right (still Kingfisher Avenue) and at the T-junction turn left into Coedmore Road. The reserve is well signposted along this road.

FEATURES
Some fine stands of woodland and forest trees interspersed with grassland, a small stream and dams, some well-defined nature trails (including one for the handicapped) and a variety of coastal birds and small mammals. It is a popular haunt of bird club members. The picnic sites are particularly attractive.

DESCRIPTION
This small but very important reserve lies in the midst of residential, agricultural and industrial areas. Adjacent to its boundaries are the huge Coedmore quarries, sugar cane fields, the modern suburb of Yellowwood Park, Chatsworth and Mhlatuzana township.

This reserve contains the largest area of climax forest remaining in the vicinity of Durban, and large areas of open grassland, woodland, scrub and riverine vegetation along the course of the Mhlatuzana river, the northern boundary of the reserve.

The area is low lying, with altitudes ranging from 30-150 m. It is fed by the Mhlatuzana river and a smaller stream which joins this river within the reserve. Above the junction, this stream has cut a kloof which forms the major physical feature of the reserve. A small dam has been built and this harbours a variety of water birds.

HISTORICAL NOTES
This area has a long and interesting history of past land use. In the time of King Shaka's reign a kraal known as "Ndabenkulu" was built here. Cattle

were kept for distribution to his various military kraals after their capture in raids down south.

In 1860 the Stainbank family, who arrived in Durban as settlers in 1857, established a farm and this land falls within the present reserve boundaries, as does the original homestead and farm buildings. Mr Dering Stainbank planted the original yellowwood and Cape chestnut trees, now forest giants, between 1875-1886, as well as various exotic species, such as pines, bamboo and guava. There is evidence that in some areas indigenous trees were felled, probably for building purposes.

Dairy farming was the main activity and this was continued right up until the late 1950s. To maintain grazing, forest clearing and burning was practised over a substantial portion of the reserve, including the woodland areas. Another disturbance was the opening up of a quarry to provide road building material. Over the years a number of alien plant species took hold in these disturbed areas, particularly *Lantana camara* and *Chromolaena odoratissima*.

Conservationists at heart, the Stainbank family presented this land to the province. In the early 1970s, Kenneth Stainbank also offered office accommodation to the Wilderness Leadership School, which now has its headquarters in this reserve. The Wilderness Leadership School was founded by Ian Player in 1957. In 1963 it became a trust and steadily grew in size and influence. It was the first non-governmental conservation organisation to be totally nonracial. The school now has branches in the Transvaal, Western Cape and Eastern Cape. Since its inception an estimated 40 000 people have been taken by its trails officers into the wilderness areas of St Lucia and Umfolozi game reserves.

A major threat to Kenneth Stainbank Nature Reserve occurred in 1970 when the city council of Durban proposed building a major access road through the reserve to service the suburb of Chatsworth. The Natal branch of the Wildlife Society, the Natal Parks Board and members of the public protested vigorously against this decision. The debate raged over a number of years. Eventually a commission of enquiry was appointed which found that there was no justification for such a route and the matter was dropped. In 1976 the Durban City Council again decided to investigate various routes through the reserve. Environmental impact studies were done and reports published. The decision was taken to reroute the planned access road. Nevertheless, there is still always the threat of such a development in the future.

TREES
Some interesting and fine specimens of forest and woodland trees and shrubs are found in this reserve. These include:
Cavacoa aurea – Natal hickory
Celtis mildbraedii – Natal white stinkwood
Chrysanthemoides monilifera – bush-tick berry
Oxyanthus pyriformis – Natal loquat

Podocarpus falcatus – common yellowwood
Podocarpus latifolius – real yellowwood
Trema orientalis – pigeonwood

Some species that have been introduced are the Zulu false thorn *Albizia suluensis*, Pondoland dwarf coconut *Jubaeopsis caffra* and Cape chestnut *Calodendron capense*.

BIRDS
The bird life is typical of low altitude coastal forest and grassland. Species to be looked for are:

African goshawk (breeds locally)
African jacana
barbets – blackcollared, white-eared
black crake
black saw-wing swallow
black sparrowhawk (breeds locally)
black tit
Cape batis
doves – cinnamon, tambourine
flycatchers – black, dusky
grey cuckoo shrike
greyheaded bush shrike
gymnogene
herons – greenbacked, grey, purple
kingfishers – brownhooded, giant, pied

little bee-eater
longcrested eagle
longtailed wagtail
Natal robin
purplecrested lourie
redbacked shrike (in summer)
redchested flufftail
squaretailed drongo
sunbirds – grey, whitebellied
woodpeckers – cardinal,
  goldentailed
yellowbellied bulbul
yellowbreasted apalis
yellowthroated longclaw

MAMMALS
Reintroduced mammals include impala, nyala, zebra and reedbuck. Indigenous species are:

bushbuck
duiker – blue, common, red
greater canerat
large-spotted genet

mongooses – banded, large
  grey, slender, water
vervet monkey

Small mammals such as rats, shrews, mice, moles and frugivorous and insect-eating bats occur.

BURMAN BUSH NATURE RESERVE

Area: 50 ha
Established: 1973

LOCATION
Durban, Morningside. Travel along Windermere Road, turn left into Goodwin Drive and left again into Burman Bush Drive, which leads to the reserve.

FEATURES
A valuable area of coastal bush considered to be virtually unchanged since early settlers arrived in Durban in the 1850s. In some parts, this bush is particularly dense and almost impenetrable and an ideal habitat for forest birds and blue duiker.

There are three short trails, picnic sites and braai facilities, parking and toilets, and a small resource centre.

PIGEON VALLEY PARK

Area: 10 ha
Established: 1965

LOCATION
Durban, Glenwood. From the city centre take Smith Street into Berea Road. Turn left into Manning Road and continue for about 2 km to Rhodes Avenue. Turn right to the entrance gate on the left.

FEATURES
This small park is listed as a Natural Heritage Site for its large population of the rare forest tree, Natal elm *Celtis mildbraedii* and other fine climax forest species. The bird life is particularly good. There is a short trail with numerous viewing points overlooking Durban bay and a parking and picnic area. Fires are not permitted.

This land was originally designated an Open Space area but was developed as a nature reserve in 1989.

PARADISE VALLEY NATURE RESERVE

Area: 50 ha
Established: 1965

LOCATION
From Durban on the N3 take the turn-off to Sarnia. Turn left immediately, then follow this road to its end.

FEATURES
A reserve that conserves coastal bush and grassland along the Mbilo river, it has a waterfall, rockfaces and steep valleys. Bushbuck, blue duiker, water mongoose, rock dassies and vervet monkeys are likely to be seen as well as some interesting birds and trees. Several trails have been laid out and a large picnic site with braai facilities overlooks the Mbilo river.

NORTH PARK NATURE RESERVE

Area: 53 ha
Established: 17 January 1968

LOCATION
Northdene, municipality of Queensburgh. From Durban take the N3 towards Pietermaritzburg. Take the N2 south exit, then the Edwin Swales-Queensburgh exit. Turn right at the traffic lights and travel towards Queensburgh on the M7 for 7,3 km. Take the North Park exit. Follow the M5 south (Main Road) under the railway bridge and up the hill. At the rhino sign, turn right into Anderson Road and drive to the entrance at the end of this road.

DESCRIPTION
A small tract of coastal forest, reed swamp, grassland and old settling ponds along the Mhlatuzana river, which, with its red sandstone cliffs, forms the border. There are interesting coastal vegetation and birds to be seen. Pleasant picnic sites, braai facilities and toilets are provided. A good venue for a day outing.

HISTORICAL NOTES
It was once the farm of the North family, early settlers who owned extensive property in the district and after whom the railway station and post office were named. Northdene is incorporated in the Queensburgh municipality.

SOUTHERN COASTAL AREAS

The grasslands, thicket and forests in the valleys of the Vernon Crookes Nature Reserve harbour over 300 species of birds.

The forest trails and bird life at Empisini Nature Reserve and several other South Coast reserves are popular with wildlife enthusiasts.

Previous page: The Umtamvuna Nature Reserve hiking trails allow walkers to enjoy vistas of deep forested gorges, the sandstone cliffs of the Umtamvuna river and to see rare endemic plant species.

SOUTHERN ZULULAND

Burchell's zebra are found in many of the game
reserves and private ranches in KwaZulu/Natal.

The Umlalazi Nature Reserve contains one of the finest stands of mangrove trees in South Africa.

Mapelane camp nestles between the sea and the high forest dunes near the mouth of the Mfolozi river.

CENTRAL ZULULAND

A wide range of waterbirds can be seen from the lounge/dining area of the camp in the Bonamanzi Game Park.

Granite outcrops, grassed hillsides and dense forest patches in the Ngoye Forest are the habitats for some extremely rare species of flora and fauna.

Guests at Bushlands Lodge are housed in colonial-style cottages sited at the edge of the dense bush.

The Hluhluwe river is an integral part of the Hluhluwe Game Reserve environment.

Elephants are now seen frequently in Hluhluwe Game Reserve.

Large numbers of nyala and other antelope are seen in the Umfolozi Game Reserve after the spring rains.

Umfolozi is the true home of the square-lipped or white rhinoceros. (Photo: Dr Nollie Zaloumis)

The land was donated to the Natal Parks Board and within the reserve is the old graveyard of the North family.

TREES

The vegetation is in most respects similar to that found in the nearby Krantzkloof and Kenneth Stainbank nature reserves. Interesting trees occur on the south-facing slope adjacent to the river.

Chrysophyllum viridifolium – fluted milkwood
Cryptocarya latifolia – broad-leaved laurel
Drypetes arguta – water ironplum
Englerophytum (Bequaertiodendron) natalense – Natal milkplum
Erythroxylum pictum – forest coca tree
Manilkara discolor – forest milkberry
Maytenus cordata – water silky bark
Mimusops obovata – red milkwood
Protea caffra – common sugarbush
Vepris lanceolata – white ironwood
Vitellariopsis marginata – Natal milkwood

BIRDS

African goshawk
African spoonbill
blackbellied glossy starling
bulbuls – terrestrial, yellowbellied
bush shrikes – gorgeous, greyheaded
Diederik cuckoo
greater honeyguide
green sandpiper

Knysna lourie
lanner falcon
longtailed wagtail
Natal robin
redfaced cisticola
sparrowhawks – black, little
squaretailed drongo
tambourine dove

MAMMALS

Recorded in the park are bushbuck, common duiker, blue duiker, water mongoose, slender mongoose and banded mongoose.

ROOSFONTEIN NATURE RESERVE

Area: 90 ha
Established: 1985

LOCATION

From Durban take the Westville off-ramp from the N3, then turn left and continue past Westville hospital. The reserve entrance is on the left.

FEATURES

The last unspoilt river valley, comprising grasslands along the river edge, with cliff community plants and riverine vegetation along the Mbilo river. There are three short trails of about one to three hours duration, a car park and two small braai areas.

NEW GERMANY NATURE RESERVE

Area: 110 ha
Established: 1986

LOCATION

New Germany-Westville. From the N3 take the off-ramp to enter St Johns Road. Cross the bridge over the freeway then take the first turn to the right into Old Main Road. Turn left into Escom Road, then right into Mountain Ridge Road and left into Gilbert Drive, which leads into the reserve.

FEATURES

A well-preserved area comprising remnant coastal bush, grassland and pro-tea communities. Red, common and blue duiker, samango and vervet monkeys, bushbuck, banded mongoose and porcupine occur. Reintroduced species include nyala, reedbuck, impala, steenbok and zebra. A bird hide has been built on a small dam and a wide variety of bird species occur in this reserve. There are four trails, picnic and braai sites, a rustic bush camp and an interpretation centre. Leaflets providing details of the trails are available.

This reserve has a history dating back to 1893 when Jonas Begtheir set aside the area as a commonage for the benefit of local residents.

PALMIET NATURE RESERVE

Area: 74 ha
Established: 1972

LOCATION

From Durban on the R613, take the Rockdale-Jan Hofmeyr Road turn-off, go left over the bridge, continuing along Jan Hofmeyr Road for about 1,5 km. Just before the Westville Hotel turn into David McClean Drive on the right. The reserve entrance is at the bottom of this road on the right.

FEATURES

Situated along the Palmiet river, this attractive reserve comprises riverine bush, overhanging cliffs, a small waterfall, reedbeds, scrub and grassland. These habitats support a variety of birds, bushbuck, vervet monkeys, blue duiker, water mongoose and smaller mammals. There is a system of trails, a picnic site and braai facilities. Conducted trails are periodically organised by members of the local Wildlife Society.

It was named after the palmiet *Prionium serratum*, which was reputed to have been found along the water courses.

KRANTZKLOOF NATURE RESERVE

Area: 535 ha
Established: 7 September 1950

LOCATION

Kloof, 26 km inland from Durban. Turn off the R613 at Kloof station turn-off, cross the railway bridge, turn immediately left, turn left again at the T-junction, then right into Kloof Falls Road and continue until after the eMolweni river is crossed, to the entrance.

FEATURES

There are impressive views of the gorge and waterfall and a variety of vegetation, birds and small mammals. Trails for hikers and nature lovers and pleasant picnic and braai sites are available. Worth a day's outing for a picnic in very pleasant surroundings.

DESCRIPTION

This popular small reserve, along the deep forested gorge of the eMolweni river, is known for its impressive scenery, particularly the 90 m high Kloof Falls and the small Iphithi and Nkufu waterfalls. There are many viewing sites, such as from the bridle path and over the Kloof Falls itself, affording impressive views of the gorge.

This is an important reserve, preserving good stands of coastal forest, mixed acacia veld, rolling "rooigras" *Themeda triandra* grasslands and small pockets of bush. The river bed, a stretch of some 6 km, with rock pools, sheer sandstone cliffs with crevices, hollows and ledges, based on a granite foundation, is most attractive, enhanced by many flowering plants.

This is the only remaining reserve in the Durban metropolitan area where forested gorges and spectacular waterfalls are protected and accessible to hikers, photographers and naturalists and those who enjoy a picnic amid scenically beautiful surroundings.

TREES

Interesting trees include fine specimens of the following:

Albizia adianthifolia – flat-crown
Celtis durandii – false white stinkwood
Cryptocarya latifolia – broad-leaved quince
Ficus natalensis – Natal fig
Ficus sur – Cape fig
Loxostylis alata – tarwood
Manilkara discolor – forest milkberry
Ochna arborea – Cape plane
Podocarpus latifolius – real yellowwood
Sclerocarya birrea – marula
Ximenia americana – sourplum

Numerous cycads and aloes occur in this reserve. There are also pockets of bush containing the silver sugarbush *Protea roupelliae*, which, when in flower, attract olive and malachite sunbirds and Gurney's sugarbird.

BIRDS (over 160 species listed)

cisticolas – croaking, rattling
eagles – crowned and Wahlberg's
   breed locally
forest canary
grey cuckooshrike
gymnogene
longtailed wagtail
mocking chat
neddicky
olive sunbird
puffback

redbacked shrike (in summer)
redchested cuckoo
rock kestrel
rock martin
rock pigeon
sombre bulbul
southern boubou
squaretailed drongo
trumpeter hornbill
willow warbler
yellowbilled kite

MAMMALS

Cape clawless otter inhabit the river and rockpools. Rock dassies can be seen on rock ledges and in the forested kloof.

bushbuck
bushpig
duiker – blue, common, red
large-spotted genet

mongooses – banded,
   slender, water
Natal red rock rabbit
serval
vervet monkey

GLENHOLME NATURE RESERVE

Area: 42 ha
Established: 1988

LOCATION

From the crest of Field's Hill on the old N3, take Village Road which runs parallel on the southern side of the N3 to where this meets the road leading from the bridge over the freeway. Turn left and continue a short distance to the reserve, which is adjacent to Kloof SPCA. This reserve is sited on land owned by the SPCA.

FEATURES

There are grassland and swamp forest patches along the river. A swamp with a dam at the lower end drains into a spectacular waterfall that cascades into a gorge. It has three self-guided trails. One of about an hour duration leads to the Clive Cheesman Nature Reserve. One of the trails caters for disabled persons including the blind. There is ample parking and toilets, picnic and braai sites.

CLIVE CHEESMAN NATURE RESERVE

Area: 5 ha
Established: 1979

LOCATION

Kloof. Take the Jerome Drive turn-off from the R613 at the foot of Field's Hill. Turn left into Edgecliff Drive and continue for about 2 km until the reserve is reached on the left.

FEATURES

A narrow belt of riverine forest and grassland. There are walks through the riverine forest and grassland, and the starting point of a trail leading to Glenholme Nature Reserve and the MOSS Ingweni Trail. There is an elevated hut with a toilet and accommodation for 10 persons and braai facilities. (No bedding provided.) For information and reservations contact the Wildlife Society, Durban.

This land was donated to the Wildlife Society by the Cheesman sisters, on condition it was managed as a nature reserve.

CRESTHOLME NATURE RESERVE

Area: 6 ha
Established: 1978

LOCATION
Hillcrest area. Approaching from the south, turn right into Inanda Road at the main traffic lights in Hillcrest. Go past Waterfall, then at Crestview turn left off the Inanda Road into Park Road which leads into the reserve.

FEATURES
One of the features of this little reserve is a spectacular cliff. There is a bush-clad ravine sweeping down into the valley and magnificent views across the Umgeni valley. A short trail is laid out through forest and grassland.

   This land was donated to the Wildlife Society by Mr Bob Mansfield and was formerly known as the Bob Mansfield Nature Reserve.

MOLWENI NATURE RESERVE

Area: 150 ha
Established: 1989

LOCATION
North-west of Durban in the Hillcrest area between Crestholme and Waterfall.

FEATURES
This small reserve contains interesting fauna and flora and will primarily function as an environmental education venue, mainly for black school children from the rural and urban areas of Durban. The reserve could be linked up with the Krantzkloof Nature Reserve, which is administered by the Natal Parks Board, to provide educational hiking trails, etc.

DESCRIPTION
This reserve is situated in a valley with gentle to steep slopes on either side of the eMolweni stream, which flows through the length of the reserve, draining in an easterly direction. There are some small patches of forest, grass veld and sparse riverine forest. The fauna and flora is similar to that of Krantzkloof Nature Reserve.

HISTORICAL NOTES
The land was previously occupied by small farm holders, who mainly farmed vegetables, fruit and to a lesser extent, livestock. In 1983 the land was expropriated by the state to incorporate it into KwaZulu.

ACCOMMODATION
None at present. Planned accommodation is to provide for up to 100 school children and teachers. A training centre exists but this needs upgrading.

FLORA
Typical plant species within this reserve include:
Acacia schweinfurthii – river climbing thorn
Albizia adianthifolia – flat-crown
Aloe arborescens – krantz aloe
Cussonia spicata – common cabbage tree
Dalbergia armata – thorny rope
Dalbergia obovata – climbing flat-bean
Ficus glumosa – mountain fig
Ficus natalensis – Natal Fig
Ficus sur – broom cluster fig
Halleria lucida – notsung
Protorhus longifolia – red beech
Syzygium cordatum – water berry
Ziziphus mucronata – buffalo thorn

Numerous small shrubs, lilies, orchids and other flowering plants occur in the grasslands and along the river banks.

BIRDS
African pied wagtail
blackcollared barbet
Burchell's coucal
common quail
common waxbill
falcons – lanner, peregrine
fantailed cisticola
forktailed drongo
great white egret
hadeda ibis
hamerkop
hornbills – trumpeter, crowned
pied kingfisher
purplecrested lourie
southern boubou
speckled mousebird
weavers – spectacled, spottedbacked

MAMMALS
common duiker
greater canerat
rock dassie
slender mongoose
vervet monkey

SPRINGSIDE NATURE RESERVE

Area: 21 ha
Established: 1973

LOCATION
Hillcrest, about 30 km north-west of Durban. From the N3 turn off to Hillcrest and follow the Old Main Road into Hillcrest. Turn right at the first traffic light, pass under the railway bridge, then right into Springside Road to the reserve entrance on the left.

FEATURES
This reserve is situated along both sides of a small stream which is swampy in parts, with some riverine forest. In the valley there are good stands of proteas. There is a trail system. A brochure can be obtained from the offices of the Hillcrest Town Board.

ASSAGAY NATURE RESERVE

Area: 7,5 ha
Established: 1979

LOCATION
Botha's Hill area. From the central traffic lights in Hillcrest travel about 4 km towards Botha's Hill, turning left just before Heidi's farm stall into Lello Road. Continue a further 11 km to a culvert over the Mhlatuzana river. The reserve extends on both sides of the road to Clement Stott Road.

FEATURES
Mainly low-lying marsh at the source of the Mhlatuzana river, with interesting indigenous trees and shrubs. There are no facilities as yet.

SHONGWENI RESOURCES RESERVE

Area: 1 700 ha
Established: 1993

LOCATION
Shongweni dam, 30 km from Durban. Take the N3 from Durban, past the toll plaza at Marianhill. Take the Shongweni-Assagay off-ramp (exit 32),

turn left towards Shongweni then left again at the sign to the dam. Take the first turn to the right along a gravel road for about 4 km to the Shongweni Dam Reserve. An approach can be made from Pinetown on the R613, and from the north, via Assagay and Botha's Hill.

FEATURES
The largest area of protected natural bush in the Greater Durban region, with an impressive dam wall impounding 51 ha of surface water, spectacular sandstone cliffs and the floodplain of the Mlazi river. It is known as a good birding spot (202 species recorded), contains interesting plants, small mammal species, and is noted for its butterflies. There are numerous braai and picnic sites and toilets. The area is popular for fishing. The rather sandy tracks within the area cover about 15 km of driving or walking trails. The trails cover 5 km, offering pleasant scenic views and an opportunity to enjoy the fauna and flora.

There are a few established sites for rock climbers of the Mountain Club of South Africa and affiliated organisations. Horse riding is offered but bookings must be made in advance by telephoning the reserve manager. Shongweni is also home to the Inzinyathi Canoe Club.

An entrance fee is payable at the gate.

DESCRIPTION
The Shongweni dam and the resources reserve is situated in a deep depression formed by the Mlazi, Sterkfontein and Ugede rivers. These rivers have cut their courses through the basement granites overlaid by Natal Group sandstone cliffs. The scenery of the area is dominated by these spectacularly high formations which are well weathered, colourful and characterised by numerous rock ledges and caves. Steep gorges and valleys of predominantly dry valley bushveld surround the dam. Numerous small streams are a feature of these valleys. There are small pockets of Zululand thornveld, palmveld, scrub and bush clumps and grassland on the lower-lying regions with small woodland communities. Large expanses of floodplain sands and grassland occur along the river banks. These grasslands have been heavily overgrazed by domestic stock in past years. Regrettably, lack of veld management has allowed the invasion of both indigenous and alien invasive woody plants of many species along the floodplain margins. Nevertheless, this reserve is very interesting botanically and some fine trees, notably *Euphorbia* species, occur.

HISTORICAL NOTES
Signs of human occupation of the area include Stone Age material. The caves have produced artefacts and some roof paintings from past civilisations. Some of the bone fragments of small animals include baboon and mountain reedbuck, species no longer recorded in the area.

The decision to develop the Shongweni dam was taken in 1920. The name probably should be Intshongweni, which means a column of smoke, referring to the spray from a waterfall on the Ugede stream, a tributary of the Mlazi river which the dam impounds. The dam is sited where the Sterkspruit and Ugede rivers join the Mlazi. The main concrete wall of the dam is 32 m high and 320 m long, with a tunnel running through its length. The wall, spillway and flood diversion works were completed in seven years and the dam was officially opened by the Administrator of Natal, Sir George Plowman KCMG, on 15 December 1927, to supply the growing city of Durban with a more than adequate water supply.

In the early 1990s the present water management controlling authority, Umgeni Water, decided to close the dam as other newer installations were more efficient. After consultation with various organisations including the Wilderness Leadership School, they decided to allow the dam and surrounding land to be used as a recreational area under the management of the Wilderness Leadership School and Msinsi Holdings.

TREES

Acacia robusta – ankle thorn
Aloe ferox – bitter aloe
Berchemia zeyheri – red ivory
Brachylaena elliptica – bitter-leaf
Burchellia bubalina – wild pomegranate
Coddia rudis – small bone-apple
Commiphora harveyi – bronze paperbark
Euphorbia ingens – candelabra tree
Euphorbia tirucallii – rubber hedge euphorbia
Faurea saligna – Transvaal beech
Ficus glumosa – mountain rock fig
Ficus natalensis – Natal fig
Manilkara discolor – forest milkberry
Mimusops obovata – red milkwood
Protorhus longifolia – red beech
Psydrax locuples – whipstick canthium
Sideroxylon inerme – white milkwood
Spirostachys africana – tamboti
Strychnos spinosa – spiny monkey orange
Tarchonanthus trilobus – camphor tree

BIRDS (202 species recorded)

African black duck
bat hawk
black cuckoo
black stork
bluebilled firefinch
brown robin
eagles – black, crowned,
  southern banded snake

giant kingfisher
grey cuckooshrike
ground hornbill
gymnogene
lanner falcon
longtailed wagtail
mocking chat
orangebreasted bush shrike

palm swift
redbacked mannikin
redthroated wryneck
snipes – African, painted
starlings – blackbellied
  glossy, plumcoloured

thrushes – Cape rock,
  kurrichane
wattled plover
whitebacked night heron
yellowthroated sparrow

MAMMALS
bushbuck
bushpig
Cape clawless otter
caracal
duiker – blue, red, common
large-spotted genet

mongooses – banded, water,
  white-tailed
porcupine
rock dassie
scrub hare
vervet monkey

REPTILES
Venomous species include:
black mamba
boomslang
common night adder

Mozambique spitting cobra
puff adder
vine snake

Protected species are African rock python and Nile monitor lizard.

BEACHWOOD MANGROVES NATURE RESERVE

Area: 76 ha
Established: 12 May 1977

LOCATION
Durban. On the north bank of the Mgeni river. From central Durban take the M4 north, cross the Ellis Brown bridge over the Mgeni river, then take the first left turn into Riverside Road, left again about 300 m along this road and then a short way to the entrance.

FEATURES
The last remaining mangrove swamp of any consequence south of the Tugela river. It is a marvellous venue, for school children in particular, to study mangroves and the rich fauna associated with this habitat, and pioneer dune plant succession. A resource centre has been established for this purpose and nature trails laid out. The bird life is interesting. Beachwood is well worth a morning or afternoon visit. It is a naturalist's and photographer's paradise. Recently a bird-viewing hide was built.
  Enquiries: Natal Parks Board, Durban office.

DESCRIPTION

Three species of subtropical mangrove trees occur, in a habitat of small, root-lined, muddy creeks and feeder channels that permit the inflow of salt water on the rising tides, leaving soft mud banks exposed when the tide goes out. There are small open clearings of soft and hard-baked mudflats. From the north, a small reed-lined freshwater stream enters the system. Beyond the mangrove swamp are the beach dunes supporting pioneer shrubs, sand-binding, fleshy-leaved plants and creepers, and the grasses that stabilise these windswept sand dunes.

HISTORICAL NOTES

Prior to its establishment as a nature reserve in May 1977, the Beachwood mangrove community was threatened by the building of a solid bridge across the main feeder creek. This would have prevented the tidal inflow of salt water vital to the health and survival of these trees. On the inland side to the north, an increase in freshwater from stormwater drains into this creek, which rises near the Beachwood golf course, dammed by the bridge, caused a dense growth of reeds, bulrushes, water hyacinths and the *Salvinia* Kariba weed to flourish and choke up this stream. The result was the dying off of a large number of white mangroves. Pollution and the activities of vehicles and machinery engaged in removal of builders' sand aggravated the situation.

Fortunately, the bridge was removed in late 1974 and a slow regeneration occurred. The reeds and other aquatic freshwater plants died back as salt water once again pushed in with the tide. Beachwood nearly suffered the same fate that has befallen the once notable communities of mangroves in Durban Bay and in the Isipingo river lagoon.

TREES

At Beachwood, the dominant components of this unique ecosystem are the white mangrove *Avicennia marina*, black mangrove *Bruguiera gymnorrhiza* and red mangrove *Rizophora mucronata*, the lagoon hibiscus *Hibiscus tiliaceus,* the powder-puff tree *Barringtonia racemosa* and the swamp reed *Phragmites communis.*

Three of the important sand dune plants are the sturdy fleshy-leaved plant *Scaevola thunbergii* that averages about 60 cm in height, the small, oval-shaped fleshy leaves of *Hydrophylax comosa*, which spreads like a carpet across the sand, and the almost indestructible pioneer grass *Sporobolus virginicus.*

BIRDS

A number of bird species are associated with mangrove swamps, notably the rare mangrove kingfisher. Other species are:
blackbacked cisticola
chinspot batis
common sandpiper

egrets – cattle, little
golden weaver
herons – blackheaded, greenbacked, grey, purple
kingfishers – malachite, pied
purplebanded sunbird
warblers – African marsh, great reed (in summer)
wattle-eyed flycatcher (breeds locally)
yellow white-eye
yelloweyed canary

Water dikkops, Mozambique nightjars and whitefronted plovers frequent, and nest in, the dune vegetation.

The beach, channels and the river are noted for many interesting resident, migrant and vagrant species that appear from time to time. These include:
greater frigatebird
gulls – lesser blackbacked, Sabine's
lesser noddy
pelicans – pinkbacked, white
plovers – crab, grey
terns – Arctic, common, crested, lesser, roseate, sandwich, sooty
woollynecked stork

MAMMALS
The swamps are visited by foraging vervet monkeys. Banded, slender and water mongooses occur. Their tracks, and the crushed shells of crabs they have eaten, are found along the creek edges.

ECOLOGICAL NOTES
The Beachwood mangrove community is an important area for many vertebrates and invertebrates that feed, shelter and breed in and among the dense profusion of roots lining the quiet, muddy creeks and channels. There are several small fish species, such as the "glassy" *Ambassis natalensis*, that are the prey of marine carnivores such as springer, rock salmon and kob – and of course, numerous fish-eating birds.

These nursery areas provide food and shelter for mullet, spotted grunter, bream and kingfish, shrimps, prawns and the large green swimming crab *Scylla serrata*, itself a major predatory species. Most of these species are important to our marine sport and fishing industry and are economically important.

The mudflats too harbour countless thousands of Sesarmid, Grapsid (mud) and fiddler crabs *Uca* species, and the prehistoric looking mud skippers *Periopthalmus kalolo*. Mangrove molluscs, whelks (three species), periwinkles, the Natal rock oyster and barnacles are also inhabitants of this mangrove community. Canopy dwellers include colourful spiders, tailor or weaver ants, and numerous insects that visit to feed.

69

SEATON PARK

Area: 6 ha
Established: 1934

LOCATION
Durban North. Take NMR Avenue travelling north out of Durban until it becomes Northway. Follow Northway to the bridge and after crossing it, turn immediately left into Lonsdale Road to a T-junction. Turn left, then immediately right into Lothian Road. The park is on the right.

FEATURES
A small stand of coastal forest containing a wide range of interesting plants and forest birds. It has a short trails system, parking, a playground and toilets.

The land for this park was donated to the Durban municipality by Mrs C Seaton in 1934.

VIRGINIA BUSH NATURE RESERVE

Area: 38 ha
Established: 1982

LOCATION
Durban North. Follow NMR Avenue north from the city until it becomes Northway. Follow Northway to a traffic circle, then turn right into Broadway. Take the second turn left into Kensington Drive and continue across Margaret Mayton Avenue to the reserve which is situated to the left.

FEATURES
An island of bush surrounded by suburbia. It contains some fine coastal trees and shrubs. It is considered to be the finest birding spot in the Durban area. Small mammals such as blue duiker, large-spotted genet and banded, slender and water mongooses may be seen. There are two short trails and 13 observation points, a visitor centre with an information board and brochures. There is also a regular monthly guided walk along the trails system.

This reserve was classified as Open Space land just after World War II, but only developed as a nature reserve in 1982.

MARIANNWOOD NATURE RESERVE

Area: 12,5 ha
Established: 1973

LOCATION
Drive north from Durban on the N3, then take the Mariannwood turn-off to the traffic lights. Continue a short distance, then turn left into 7th Avenue. Turn left, then first right, then second left to where the reserve is situated next to Brown's School.

FEATURES
A small reserve of grasslands and forest, rich in local flora. Common and blue duiker occur and impala have been reintroduced. There is a picnic site with braai facilities and parking.

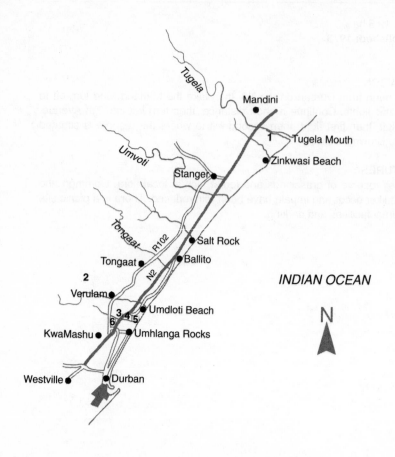

INDIAN OCEAN

N

NORTH COAST
1. HAROLD JOHNSON NATURE RESERVE
2. HAZELMERE PUBLIC RESORT NATURE RESERVE
3. HAWAAN FOREST RESERVE
4. UMHLANGA BUSH NATURE RESERVE
5. UMHLANGA LAGOON NATURE RESERVE
6. UMHLANGA PONDS

NORTH COAST

Visitors travelling from Durban on the N2 freeway towards the Tugela river might be forgiven for believing that the entire north coast is a never-ending succession of rolling sugar cane fields. Certainly this is also the impression gained if one follows the original old main road from Durban linking the small towns of Mt Edgecombe, Verulam and Tongaat to Stanger. These small towns are all business and commercial centres that have developed over the past 150 years because of intensive sugar cane, vegetable and other crop farming, the sugar mills and associated light industries.

The North Coast has far fewer rivers than the southern coastline. Before the advent of settlers and intensive agricultural development the landscape was attractive with extensive grassy hills and valleys, thickets, forests, streams and rivers. Today, the densely populated inland catchment areas have caused siltation of rivers, lagoons and coastal estuaries, attributed to overgrazing and trampling by domestic livestock, deforestation for timber and fuel, subsistence agricultural practices and injudicious burning. In more recent years, the use of herbicides, insecticides and the chemical composition of fertilisers used by the sugar industry has contributed to the impoverishment of the flora and fauna.

The coastal road, before it turns inland at La Mercy, affords glimpses of magnificent coastal dune and lowland forest, particularly the Umhlanga Bush and Lagoon nature reserves and Hawaan forest, and the lagoons, swamps and beaches at some of the river mouths. Along this coastline the attractive areas of beaches and coastal forests have been modified by residential and tourist development. Unlike the South Coast, this has not been as intensive. Intensively developed areas are at Umhlanga, Umdloti Beach, Ballito and Salt Rock and at smaller villages in between.

There are small but valuable habitats protected in nature reserves or by private landowners. Some of the lagoons and estuaries such as the Mdloti, Mvoti, Mdlotane and Zinkwazi areas conserve fine examples of coastal fauna and flora, especially for seabirds and waders and coastal forest species. The Harold Johnson Nature Reserve contains remnant patches of grassland, well-preserved coastal bush with steep cliffs and gullies. The flora and fauna is of great interest and there are some important historical monuments. The Hlogwane forest overlooking the Tugela river mouth is a most interesting area. Inland, near Tongaat, the Hazelmere dam, principally a resort for water sports and angling, also contains a small wildlife area. The township of Stanger cares for a small area of commonage.

HAWAAN FOREST RESERVE

Area: 118 ha
Established: 1860

LOCATION
North Coast, Umhlanga. From Durban take the M4, heading north along Stanger Street. After the first exit to Umhlanga take the Portland Drive exit. At the stop street turn right into Portland Drive, continue to a sharp left turn into Herald Drive. The entrance to Hawaan is on the right.

FEATURES
A well-preserved indigenous forest with magnificent coastal trees and birds typical of this forest type. Bushbuck, blue duiker, common duiker, red duiker, bushpig, banded and slender mongoose and vervet monkeys occur. There are trails through the forest. It is privately owned and permission is required to visit the reserve. Contact the Umhlanga centre of the Wildlife Society.

This property is jointly owned by Tongaat-Hulett and the Campbell family who first settled on the North Coast in 1859.

UMHLANGA LAGOON NATURE RESERVE

Area: 25 ha
Established: 10 July 1980

LOCATION
From Durban take the M4, heading north along Stanger Street. After the first exit to Umhlanga, take the Portland Drive exit. At the stop sign, turn right into Portland Drive, under the M4. Take the first left turn into Newlands Drive, to a yield sign. Turn left again, past Breakers holiday flats, to the entrance of the reserve on the right.

FEATURES
A fine, well-preserved example of coastal bush and lagoon. An interesting nature trail with boardwalks affords views of significant and rare trees and birds, with rich and varied invertebrate and insect fauna. A picnic site with toilet facilities is provided. A visit to this small reserve is recommended, particularly for children involved in nature study projects.

DESCRIPTION

A valuable area of pristine coastal forest on undulating dunes, with unspoilt dune and pioneer plants down to the beach. It has a small reed-lined stream and swamp, with stands of bulrushes *Typha latifolia*, favoured by nesting brownthroated, yellow and thickbilled weavers, red bishops and reed warblers. This area, and the lagoon, which opens to the sea after heavy rains, is most attractive. There are some fine specimens of the dune aloe *Aloe thraskii*. The lagoon hibiscus *Hibiscus tiliaceus* fringes the wetlands, its yellow to orange flowers contrasting with the blues of the flowering morning glory creepers that spread across the vleis and up into trees. The forest undergrowth is particularly dense and visibility is limited by stands of buckweed *Isoglossa woodii*, which provides cover for small animals and birds. On the forest floor, in the layers of leaf litter, damp, rank-smelling humus and beneath rotting logs, there is an astonishing variety of interesting life forms. Large black and vivid red millipedes, pill millipedes, *Peripatus* – a primitive small creature which is a "missing link" between worms and insects – centipedes, beetles, woodlice, spiders, several snail species including the large spiral-shelled *Achatina immaculata*, and a host of beautiful butterflies and insect species will delight both the naturalist and photographer.

A shell midden, said to date back to about AD 600, is conserved in this forest and is of historic value and interest.

TREES

Significant trees representing the dominant and most abundant as well as the rare species in the dune forest include:

Acokanthera oppositifolia – common poison-bush
Brachylaena discolor – coast silver oak
Cavacoa aurea – Natal hickory
Celtis africana – white stinkwood
Cola natalensis – coshwood
Diospyros natalensis – small-leaved jackal-berry
Euphorbia ingens – common tree euphorbia
Ficus natalensis – Natal fig
Mimusops caffra – red milkwood
Strelitzia nicolai – Natal wild banana
Vangueria randii subsp. *chartacea* – Natal bush medlar
Ziziphus mucronata – buffalo thorn

BIRDS

On the beach and at the lagoon mouth are:
greenshank
sandpipers – terek, wood

In the wetlands:
African fish eagle
African rail

herons – blackcrowned night, greenbacked, purple
redchested flufftail
warblers – African sedge, great reed

In the forest, there is an abundance of species, although many are difficult
to see because of the dense undergrowth:
bleating bush warbler
bulbuls – blackeyed, sombre, terrestrial, yellowbellied
crested guineafowl
flycatchers – dusky, bluegrey, black, fiscal, yellowthroated, wattle-eyed,
   fairy, paradise
forest weaver
grey waxbill
narina trogon
purplecrested lourie
robins – chorister, Natal, Cape, brown, whitebrowed
shrikes – boubou, puffback, olive bush, gorgeous, fiscal, orangebreasted
sunbirds – purplebanded, grey, olive, collared, black
tambourine dove
tinker barbets – goldenrumped, redfronted
trumpeter hornbill

Some species are seasonal migrants, e.g. Cape robin, chorister robin and
Natal thrush.

MAMMALS

blue duiker   mongooses – banded, slender, water
bushbuck   vervet monkey
bushpig

UMHLANGA BUSH NATURE RESERVE

Area: 28 ha
Established: 1936

LOCATION
On the north side of Umhlanga lagoon.

FEATURES
An attractive stand of dune forest known for a wealth of bird species and
fine trees. Bushbuck, red and blue duiker, banded mongoose and vervet
monkeys are found here. There is a trail system. Permission is required to
visit this reserve. Contact the borough of Umhlanga.

UMHLANGA PONDS

Area: 10 ha

LOCATION
North Coast, adjoining Hawaan Forest Nature Reserve. To reach this sewerage farm, continue up the hill past the entrance to Hawaan Forest to a stop street. Take a right turn and follow a gravel road for about 2,4 km. The ponds can be seen from the top of the hill, down on the right. Continue down the hill to the sign "Ponds" between sugar cane fields. Park on the lawn at a thatched shelter at the entrance to the sewerage works.

FEATURES
Open settlement ponds, some waterlily-covered, reeded at the water's edge. On the eastern side, the ponds are bordered by the Hawaan forest. It is a popular birding spot for local enthusiasts. Species recorded include:

African crake
black kite
blacknecked grebe
Cape shoveller
eagles – African fish, booted, crowned
grey cuckoo
herons – blackcrowned night,
   greenbacked, purple, squacco
Hottentot teal
lesser jacana

lesser moorhen
little bittern
Namaqua dove
painted snipe
purple gallinule
pygmy goose
terns – whiskered,
   whitewinged
woollynecked stork

HAZELMERE PUBLIC RESORT NATURE RESERVE

Area: 304 ha
Proclamation Pending

LOCATION
North Coast. From the N2, approximately 14 km north of Durban, take the Mount Edgecombe-Umhlanga off-ramp and turn left towards Mount Edgecombe. Ignore turn-offs to Mount Edgecombe, Ottawa and Verulam. After passing under a large, arched bridge, turn left at the Hazelmere dam sign. The dam is 10 km from this turn-off.

FEATURES
The dam is principally a resort area for aquatic sports – especially waterskiing competitions. It is a popular angling venue and picnic area. A small area has been set aside for nature walks and wildlife. Various bathing areas have been established.

DESCRIPTION
This resort, situated around a dam in the upper catchment area of the Mdhloti river, is largely an area of short grass and open woodland. The small nature reserve on the eastern side of the valley contains riverine thicket, patches of scrub and mixed grassland with some quite rocky sections and, on higher ground, valley bushveld.

ACCOMMODATION
There are camping sites and ablution facilities, with numerous braai and picnic sites, along the edge of the dam. Reservations can be made with the officer-in-charge, Hazelmere Public Resort.

FLORA
A few interesting trees occur which are not commonly found much further south:
Acacia nilotica – scented thorn
Acacia sieberiana – paperbark acacia
Dichrostachys cinerea – sickle bush
Erythrina lysistemon – common coral tree
Millettia grandis – umzimbeet
Ptaeroxylon obliquum – sneezewood

Some of the more common trees are:
Strychnos usambarensis – blue bitter-berry
Wrightia natalensis – saddlepod

The grasses, mainly *Paspalum* spp., *Eragrostis* spp., *Cynodon* and *Setaria* spp., are attractive to a variety of seed-eating birds. Flowering plants also attractive to birds include:
Crinum macowani – beautiful lily
Hibiscus trionum – bladder hibiscus
Leonotis leonorus – wild dagga
Plectranthus petiolaris – spurflower
Scadoxus membranaceus – snake lily

BIRDS
Common bushveld and scrub-dwelling birds occur and aquatic species of the coastal region may be seen along the shoreline. The grasses attract redbacked mannikin, common waxbill, grey waxbill, swee waxbill and blue-billed firefinch, among others.

FISH
The dam has been stocked with several species of fish, mostly bass, tilapia and scalies (yellowfish).

HAROLD JOHNSON NATURE RESERVE

Area: 104 ha
Established: 3 May 1967

LOCATION
North Coast, 24 km north of Stanger on the N2, near Newark. From the north the turn-off on the N2 is about 5 km south of the John Ross bridge over the Tugela river and is well signposted.

FEATURES
It has interesting vegetation, especially trees, epiphytic orchids and ferns. There are attractive views over the Tugela river. An interesting "Remedies and Rituals" trail is available. Incorporated within the reserve are the historical monuments of Fort Pearson, a military graveyard and the "Ultimatum Tree" which was of great significance to the commencement of the Anglo-Zulu war.

DESCRIPTION
Situated on the south bank of the Tugela river, the reserve comprises undulating hillsides covered by small patches of grassland, shrubs and dry bush. There are well-preserved stands of dense coastal bush extending down very steep cliffs and gullies. Typical coastal birds, a range of smaller mammals and a wide variety of seasonally abundant butterfly species can be observed. There are good views over the Tugela valley towards the sea from the camp site and picnic sites which are perched on the hilltop.

HISTORICAL NOTES
Within this small reserve are the remains of Fort Pearson, one of the launching points for the British invasion of Zululand in 1879 on the outbreak of the Anglo-Zulu war. Originally a large, stout, earthen wall on a high knoll overlooking the Tugela drift, it was named in honour of Colonel Charles Knight Pearson, commander of the first invasion of British soldiers into Zululand. At one stage about 5 000 men were garrisoned here. The reserve also contains the remnant of a huge old sycamore fig tree *Ficus sycomorus*, known as the "Ultimatum tree", under which the indunas (clan leaders) of King Ceteswayo sat, on 11 December 1878, to listen to the British ultimatum drafted by Sir Bartle Frere and read to them by John Wesley Shepstone. This ultimatum, among other conditions, defined boundaries for the Zulus and fines for cattle that had been rustled, demanded the immedi-

ate disbanding of the Zulu army and the re-admission of missionaries to Zululand. The speech took many hours to deliver as it had to be translated sentence by sentence by H. Bernard Fynney. The indunas were expected to memorise everything that was said and carry the information back to King Ceteswayo, who was not given time to implement the terms and conditions of the ultimatum. The war was forced on the Zulus. It ended in August 1879 with the capture of King Ceteswayo.

During this period Britain suffered one of the most severe defeats in its history at the battle of Isandlwana on January 22 1879. A column under Colonel Pearson was engaged in a major battle with the Zulus at Inhlezane on the same day as the battle of Isandlwana. Pearson's troops then moved on to Eshowe to establish a fort.

There is a small military cemetery just outside the nature reserve where men who died from wounds and diseases were buried. One man, Commandant Montgomery, died from the bite of a black mamba.

Below the bluff, which contains the outer perimeter redoubt of Fort Pearson, is the point where the men were transported across the Tugela river in pontoons. Currently, a new bridge has been built across the Tugela just below the pontoon launching jetty. The bridge and the new national road will impinge severely on the nature reserve. The new road was bitterly fought by conservationists, including the authors, because it is unlikely that the new bridge will survive a major flood such as caused by cyclone Demoina in 1984, which swept away the John Ross bridge over the Tugela river. The National Roads Transport Commission ignored warnings, prior to its construction, about the likelihood of the John Ross bridge being swept away and have once again done the same at Fort Pearson. The obvious site for a new bridge should have been where the rail and road bridge crosses the Tugela upstream. This old bridge is firmly anchored on a rock foundation and has withstood the floods of 1925, 1957, 1963 and 1984.

The land for this reserve, donated to the province by conservation-minded sugar farmer Mr Harold Johnson, was proclaimed a nature reserve on 3 May 1967. It was only officially opened to the public on 24 August 1976.

ACCOMMODATION
Limited camping facilities are available. Visitors must supply all their own camping equipment. Picnic sites are provided. Contact the Natal Parks Board officer-in-charge for bookings.

TREES
There are some fine examples of our local flora, particularly trees, epiphytic orchids and in spring, flowering shrubs and herbs associated with grasslands. Of the fern species, the dogs-ear fern, *Pyrrasia africana* is common. Interesting trees are:

Acacia robusta – splendid acacia
Acokanthera oppositifolia – common poison-bush
Apodytes dimidiata – white pear tree

Berchemia zeyheri – red ivory tree
Brachylaena discolor – coastal silver leaf
Chaetacme aristata – thorny elm tree
Combretum kraussii – forest bushwillow
Combretum molle – velvet bushwillow
Dovyalis caffra – Kei-apple
Euclea divinorum – magic guarri
Euphorbia ingens – candelabra tree
Euphorbia tirucalli – rubber hedge euphorbia
Harpephyllum caffrum – wild plum
Heteropyxis natalensis – lavender tree
Hippobromus pauciflorus – baster perdepis
Monanthotaxis caffra – dwaba-berry
Phoenix reclinata – wild date palm
Protorhus longifolia – red beech
Schotia brachypetala – weeping boer-bean
Sideroxylon inerme – white milkwood
Strychnos madagascariensis – black monkey orange
Uvaria caffra – cluster-pear
Vepris lanceolata – white ironwood
Zanthoxylum capense – small knobwood tree
Ziziphus mucronata – buffalo thorn tree

BIRDS
Typical coastal birds include:

blackbellied glossy starling
bluegrey flycatcher
Cape glossy starling
collared sunbird
forest weaver
narina trogon

Natal robin
purplecrested lourie
redfronted tinker barbet
redwinged starling
white-eared barbet
yellowbellied bulbul

MAMMALS
Mammals to be seen include blue duiker, common duiker, red duiker, bush-buck, bushpig, large-spotted genet, banded mongoose, slender mongoose and Cape clawless otter. Zebra and impala have been reintroduced.

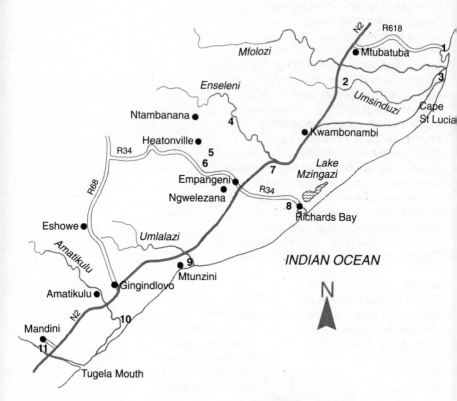

SOUTHERN ZULULAND
1. ST LUCIA ESTUARY
2. LAKE ETEZA NATURE RESERVE
3. MAPELANE NATURE RESERVE
4. WINDY RIDGE GAME PARK
5. NYALA GAME RANCH
6. FUNDIMVELO NATURE RESERVE
7. ENSELENI NATURE RESERVE
8. RICHARDS BAY GAME RESERVE
9. UMLALAZI NATURE RESERVE

SOUTHERN ZULULAND

From the Tugela, the largest river in Natal, northwards up the coastal belt to the Mfolozi river, the landscape of southern Zululand is dominated by extensive sugar cane and exotic timber plantations with crops such as maize, citrus, vegetables and cotton, and cattle ranches further inland.

Historically, the inland regions were well populated with a variety of game species but outbreaks of the tsetse fly-borne disease nagana and the resulting conflict between cattle ranchers and wildlife led to the subsequent eradication of almost all game. Today virtually the only remaining pockets of typical grassland, thornveld and thicket, well stocked with game – mostly reintroduced – are the privately owned Windy Ridge Game Park and Nyala Game Ranch.

This area has a long history of occupation by humans. The burgeoning human population has led to severe land degradation. Large areas of land have been intensively developed as residential and industrial centres by the several medium-sized towns that serve the agricultural communities. This region also contains the largest paper mill in Africa at Mandini. The gigantic port of Richards Bay is now almost surrounded by huge industrial complexes creating pollution problems and a rapidly expanding town and suburban sprawl. Strip-mining of the fragile coastal dunes north of the Richards Bay complex and the damming of the Nhlabane river by the mining company has left large scars on the landscape. Despite rehabilitation attempts, it is unlikely that the damaged areas will ever be restored to resemble the original vegetation and dune formations.

Along the coastline there are still some relatively undisturbed estuaries, lagoons, swamps, reedbeds, grassland and dunes remaining. Although unprotected, they preserve the floral and faunal characteristics of the southern Zululand coastal areas. From the south northwards, these include the Tugela river mouth, Nyoni estuary, Matigulu estuary, the Siyai river and lagoon, the Mhlatuze floodplain and Lake Mzingazi and river system.

The protected areas, small as they are, and subject to pressures from agricultural malpractices, include the newly established and important Amatikulu Nature Reserve. The Enseleni Nature Reserve is small in size but a "witness area" comprising relict coastal grassland, thicket, swamp and riverine forest vegetation and associated fauna. The Umlalazi Nature Reserve is exceptionally interesting and valuable, containing a magnificent mangrove community, stands of the rare Kosi palm, wetland, grassland, dune forest and a fine estuarine system. All of these habitats harbour a rich variety of subtropical species of fauna and flora. The Richards Bay Game Reserve, on the edge of enormous industrial developments, is of great significance. Through the combined efforts of industry, conservation officials of the Natal Parks Board and members of the Empangeni Wildlife Society, they have succeeded in preserving a vitally important sanctuary of mangroves, mudflats, tidal shallows and reedbeds, a refuge for waders uncommon to our shores as well as resident marsh-dwelling birds and other fauna.

The small Lake Eteza is another important oasis, feeding and sheltering waterfowl and aquatic birds in the midst of an area extensively planted to sugar cane and timber. The Mapelane Nature Reserve is particularly valuable for its papyrus filter beds, swamp forest communities, pristine dune forest, birds, small mammals and splendid offshore reefs. These reserves are remnants of what was once a magnificent coastal belt.

INGWENYA NATURE RESERVE

Area: 74 ha
Established: 1965

LOCATION

Southern Zululand, Mandini. From the N2 take the Mandini turn-off and turn left opposite the Nyoni turn-off. Follow the gravel road for about 1,5 km past Mandini township. Turn left at the Ngwenya signpost and drive 200 m to the top of Rock Ridge. Continue to the reserve entrance.

FEATURES

Situated alongside the north bank of the Tugela river, the reserve comprises coastal thornveld and scrub. A small stream flows through the reserve and a small waterhole has been built. Bushbuck and common duiker occur naturally. Small numbers of zebra, blue wildebeest and nyala have been reintroduced.

There is a trail and several footpaths, a lookout point over the Tugela river and a waterhole. Benches, tables, braai facilities and a toilet block are provided.

AMATIKULU NATURE RESERVE

Area: 1 476 ha
Established: 1987

LOCATION

Southern Zululand coast. Between the Tugela river and Mtunzini. Take the Amatikulu turn-off from the N2. The reserve is situated to the north of the Tugela river mouth.

DESCRIPTION

The reserve includes the estuarine area and the joint mouth of the Inyoni and Amatikulu rivers. It contains interesting vegetation zones from the beach, dunes, coastal dune forest, the vegetation along the river banks, swamp forest, acacia woodland and grasslands. It is a well-known fishing area for mullet, rock salmon, springer, kingfish and perch. Amatikulu Hatcheries, which exports live tropical fish and prawns, is located here.

There are proposals to link up this reserve with the adjoining Red Hill Nature Reserve to the south (proclaimed in 1992), thereby increasing the area to 1 712 ha. Canoe trails would be developed and existing walking trails extended, with a tented trail camp on the Inyoni river. To the north, the Talmaze pan area is also earmarked for inclusion in this complex and will add an additional 150 ha.

ACCOMMODATION

This reserve is undeveloped at present, but two tents for 12 persons are available for a small overnight party. Plans for future development include the building of a hotel, chalet complexes, camping sites, an interpretation centre, a golf course and clubhouse and a launch site for ski-boats. It is very popular with fishermen. Canoeists are attracted by the unspoiled nature of the rivers. Reservation enquiries should be made to the KwaZulu Department of Nature Conservation, Ulundi.

TREES

Acacia kraussiana – coast climbing thorn
Allophylus natalensis – dune false currant
Antidesma venosum – tassel berry
Canthium inerme – common turkey-berry
Deinbollia oblongifolia – dune soap-berry
Halleria lucida – notsung
Hyphaene coriacea – lala palm
Mimusops caffra – coastal red milkberry
Peddiea africana – poison olive
Phoenix reclinata – wild date palm
Psychotria capensis – blackbird berry
Rhoicissus digitata – baboon grape
Rhoicissus tridentata – bushman's grape
Tabernaemontana ventricosa – toad tree
Trimeria grandiflora – wild mulberry
Vangueria infausta – wild medlar

Swamp forest species include:
Barringtonia racemosa – powder-puff tree
Ficus sur – broom cluster fig
Ficus trichopoda – swamp fig
Hibiscus tiliaceus – lagoon hibiscus

Macaranga capensis – wild swamp poplar
Rauvolfia caffra – quinine tree
Voacanga thouarsii – wild frangipani

BIRDS

black cuckooshrike
blackbellied korhaan
bluebilled firefinch
chorister robin
dabchick
emerald cuckoo
fantailed cisticola
green twinspot

herons – goliath, squacco
lanner falcon
longcrested eagle
narina trogon
rameron pigeon
secretarybird
white pelican
woollynecked stork

MAMMALS

bushbuck
Cape clawless otter
common duiker
giraffe
impala
large-spotted genet
monkeys – samango, vervet

reedbuck
scrub hare
serval
striped polecat
water mongoose
waterbuck
zebra

REPTILES

forest cobra
Natal rock python
Nile crocodile

Nile or water monitor lizard
rhombic night adder

UMLALAZI NATURE RESERVE

Area: 1 028 ha
Established: 5 February 1948

LOCATION

Southern Zululand, coastal. Turn off from the N2 or the toll road to Mtunzini village. Take the left turn where the road forks, to the signpost about 600 m on the right along this road.

FEATURES

There is good lagoon and surf fishing, boating, beach bathing and wind surfing. It has nature walks through a wide variety of habitats, with interesting plants, birds, mammals and mangrove fauna. Well worth a day visit and preferably an extended stay. An extremely valuable outdoor classroom for school or university biology and ecology students is available.

DESCRIPTION

The Mlalazi river and lagoon, the northern boundary, contains one of the best preserved mangrove swamps remaining in South Africa, with red mangrove *Rizophora mucronata*, black mangrove *Bruguiera gymnorrhiza* and the white mangrove *Avicennia marina* in large stands. The swamp is home to the fascinating fauna of mud and fiddler crabs, mudskippers, various tree climbing whelks, snails and periwinkles, small eels and fish that shelter in the mangrove roots, along with shrimps and prawns. Hippo, crocodiles and sharks occur in the river and lagoon.

The estuary and beach areas are a refuge for a variety of resident as well as migrant seashore-estuarine birds. A transect up from the beach takes one through a remarkable succession of plant species and habitats in pristine condition: pioneer sand-binding dune creepers, with the shrubs and dune forest above these, clipped by the salt spray. The belt of the Siyayi dune forest is particularly wide with undulating dune ridges and steep-sided deep valleys lying parallel to the coastline. The undergrowth is mostly dense buckweed *Isoglossa woodii* hiding interesting birds, small mammals and molluscs, insects, arachnids and millipedes.

The dune forest opens out onto the mangroves along the south bank of the river. Along its eastern verges it opens onto swamps and drainage lines, with patches of matted grassland and sedges, reedbeds and open grassland on higher ground.

HISTORICAL NOTES

A magnificent grove of the Kosi palm *Raphia australis*, now declared a national monument, was planted from seed collected at Lake Amanzimnyana, Kosi Bay, by a magistrate, Mr CC Foxon, just after the turn of the century. The national monument was officially opened by Mr Foxon on 14 June 1986.

ACCOMMODATION

Comfortable five-bedded, fully equipped log cabins, a leisure home and camp sites with modern ablution facilities are available. In the Inkwazi camp site electric plug points are available for hire and there is a children's playground. A number of picnic tables and sites have been provided along the shoreline of the lagoon. A ski-boat launching site is available. Visitors must supply their own camping equipment. Reservations for the log cabins should be made with the Natal Parks Board, Pietermaritzburg.

TREES

Antidesma venosum – tassel berry
Brachylaena discolor – coast silver oak
Hibiscus tiliaceus – lagoon hibiscus
Hyphaene coriacea – lala palm

Mimusops caffra – coastal red milkwood
Phoenix reclinata – wild date palm
Sideroxylon inerme – white milkwood
Strelitzia nicolai – Natal wild banana
Syzygium cordatum – water berry
Trema orientalis – pigeonwood
Trichilia emetica – Natal mahogany
Ziziphus mucronata – buffalo thorn

A number of rare ground orchids occur in this area, including the first sapro-phytic orchid to be found in South Africa, *Dydymyoplexis verrucosa*. This was discovered in 1975 by Prof. van Steenis and over recent years has been found to be quite common at Umlalazi. (Saprophytic means that it is a species that lives and feeds on dead organic matter.)

BIRDS (310 species recorded)

African black oystercatcher
African finfoot
African goshawk
African marsh harrier
blackbellied glossy starling
bluebilled firefinch
bulbuls – sombre, terrestrial, yellowbellied
curlew sandpiper
doves – cinnamon, tambourine
eagles – African fish, southern
   banded snake, longcrested
European roller
flycatchers – bluemantled, wattle-eyed
forest weaver
goldentailed woodpecker
gorgeous bush shrike
green twinspot
grey waxbill
jackal buzzard
kingfishers – halfcollared, mangrove
little bittern

little stint
narina trogon
osprey
palmnut vulture
Pel's fishing owl
robins – brown, Natal
ruff
sanderling
scalythroated honeyguide
sooty falcon
sooty tern
sparrowhawk – black, little
spotted eagle owl
spotted thrush
sunbirds – grey, olive
trumpeter hornbill
turnstone
white-eared barbet
whitebacked night heron
yellowbreasted apalis

This area is noted for its resident breeding palmnut vultures and woolly-necked storks. Nesting palmnut vultures can be easily observed here. There is a large population of trumpeter hornbills that roost in a grove of gum trees on the perimeter of the village.

MAMMALS

bushbuck
bushpig

Cape clawless otter
duikers – blue, red

hippopotamus	thick-tailed bushbaby
large-spotted genet	vervet monkey
mongooses – banded, water	

AMPHIBIANS

About 32 species of subtropical frogs and toads inhabit the damp areas, many of them beautifully marked and brightly coloured, and worthy of a photographer's attention.

NYALA GAME RANCH

Area: 500 ha
Established: 1962

LOCATION

Southern Zululand. Turn off the N2 to Empangeni. Drive straight through the town on the R34, about 22 km towards Nkwalini. Just past the Jabulani Rehabilitation Centre turn right along the D130 (Game Ranch sign). Travel past two stores, cross the railway line and follow the signs to the entrance gate.

FEATURES

Visitor facilities and activities include a network of roads for game viewing and bird spotting drives and walks through the bush in search of game accompanied by a knowledgeable guide. Night safaris, either by vehicle or on foot, can be arranged. The large lounge at Mbondwe exhibits animal trophies, while a slide show with taped commentary on various aspects of wildlife can be arranged by the guard on duty. Horse trails with a guide are also offered.

This ranch is well known for its environmental courses for school children in groups from 15-60, which cover subjects such as ecology, game ranging, conservation (including field work) and hunting. These courses operate during term time as well as over holiday periods. Lectures for organised tour groups can be arranged, and catering and accommodation for small conferences can be pre-booked. A good bed and breakfast service is offered. A small tuckshop at Mbondwe stocks a limited supply of sweets and cold drinks.

DESCRIPTION

An attractive reserve of typical Zululand grassland, bushveld, thicket and large shade trees in the woodland areas.

HISTORICAL NOTES

Nyala Game Ranch, started in 1962 by Ian (deceased) and Richard Scott

Barnes, was the first privately-owned commercial ranch to be established in Natal. Previously one of the many cattle ranches in this area of Zululand, it had to be game-proof fenced before being stocked with various animals. There were still a few indigenous species to be found on the land, such as common duiker, bushbuck, warthog and the magnificent nyala, after which the ranch was named. An attempt was made to reintroduce white rhino in the early years but the idea was abandoned when these enormous beasts continually broke through the fences and headed back to Hluhluwe Game Reserve from where they had come.

The late Norman Deane, then officer-in-charge at Hluhluwe Game Reserve, played an important role in the development of this reserve. It became a model for the game ranching industry, pioneering many new concepts including rehabilitating disadvantaged local people, who were employed in fashioning curios from game products from the ranch.

ACCOMMODATION
There are three camps available. Mbondwe and Hlati provide comfortable rondavel accommodation, with a large lounge and swimming pool. Tents afford extra beds for larger parties or school groups. Electricity is provided at Mbondwe, but at Hlati, gas lamps are provided. Cooking is done by camp fire (around which meals are usually served) or electric and gas stoves in the kitchens, which have all the necessary equipment including fridges. Bedding, cutlery, crockery and cooking utensils and a cook-game guard is provided at all camps. Catering can be pre-booked but normally guests cater for themselves. The third camp, the Umvumvu bush camp, is for those who prefer camping in the bush. Rustic huts are provided with facilities as at the other camps. This camp is in the wilderness area of the reserve where no other tourists are permitted entry. Reservations are made with the reserve itself.

TREES
Acacia caffra – common hook-thorn
Acacia robusta – ankle thorn
Aloe marlothii – mountain aloe
Apodytes dimidiata – white pear
Berchemia zeyheri – red ivory
Cussonia zuluensis – Zulu cabbage tree
Euphorbia ingens – common tree euphorbia
Maytenus heterophylla – common spike-thorn
Rhoicissus tomentosa – common forest grape
Rhus natalensis – Natal karree
Schotia brachypetala – weeping boer-bean/tree fuschia
Sclerocarya birrea subsp. *caffra* – marula
Spirostachys africana – tamboti
Strychnos spinosa – green monkey orange
Trichilia emetica – Natal mahogany

Zanthoxylum capense – mall knobwood
Ziziphus mucronata – buffalo thorn

BIRDS

African goshawk
barthroated apalis
blackcollared barbet
blackcrowned tchagra
blackheaded oriole
brownhooded kingfisher
Burchell's coucal
cardinal woodpecker
chinspot batis
forktailed drongo
greater honeyguide
greyheaded bushshrike
Klaas's cuckoo

lilacbreasted roller
little bee-eater
plumcoloured starling
puffback
purplecrested lourie
redshouldered widow
sombre bulbul
spotted eagle owl
tawnyflanked prinia
thickbilled weaver
whitebellied sunbird
yelloweyed canary

MAMMALS

aardwolf
blesbok
blue wildebeest
bushbuck
bushpig
caracal
common duiker
impala
kudu
large-spotted genet

mongooses – slender,
    white-tailed
nyala
porcupine
reedbuck
steenbok
thick-tailed bushbaby
warthog
zebra

FUNDIMVELO NATURE RESERVE

Area: Approximately 600 ha
Established: February 1989

LOCATION
Southern Zululand, west of Empangeni, bordering on the Enseleni river valley.

FEATURES
It is planned to establish an environmental education centre for primary and secondary school children, particularly under-privileged children. Slide shows,

lectures and guided walks will be tailored to fit in with the relevant group's biology syllabus. The reserve is situated only 35 minutes drive from Empangeni and Ngwelezane and will service a huge urban and rural population.

DESCRIPTION
Altitude varies from 160 m in the low-lying areas to 350 m at the highest point – the Hlaza hill. The Mfaza river runs from north to south, creating small pools along its course and the Manzibomvu river rises on Hlaza hill. Micro-climates abound due to the undulating hills and valleys. The vegetation is mainly typical acacia-dominated Zululand thornveld. Dominant grasses are redgrass *Themeda triandra* and guinea grass *Panicum maximum*.

HISTORICAL NOTES
The reserve borders on the Enseleni river, once a part of the traditional hunting ground of Zulu royalty.

ACCOMMODATION
None at present. Accommodation is planned for 25-30 school children under teacher supervision.

TREES
Acacia caffra – common hook-thorn
Acacia gerrardii – red thorn
Acacia karroo – sweet thorn
Acacia nilotica – scented thorn
Acacia robusta – ankle thorn
Acacia sieberiana – paperbark thorn
Acacia tortilis – umbrella thorn
Cussonia spicata – common cabbage tree
Diospyros species
Dombeya rotundifolia – common wild pear
Erythrina lysystemon – common coral tree
Euclea species
Faidherbia albida – ana tree
Pappea capensis – jacket-plum
Sclerocarya birrea subsp. *caffra* – marula
Spirostachys africana – tamboti
Trema orientalis – pigeonwood
Trichilia emetica – Natal mahogany
Zanthoxylum capense – small knobwood

BIRDS
bat hawk
black stork
Cape robin
ducks – African black, yellowbilled

grey heron
hadeda ibis
hooded vulture
malachite kingfisher

masked weaver	sunbirds – grey, olive,
rock bunting	scarletchested
	tawny eagle

MAMMALS

bushbuck	nyala
chacma baboon	porcupine
common duiker	spotted hyaena
impala	vervet monkey
kudu	warthog

WINDY RIDGE GAME PARK

Area: 1 300 ha
Established: 1964

LOCATION

Southern Zululand, in the Heatonville area, west of Empangeni. Take the N2 to Empangeni, follow the R34 towards Melmoth for about 8 km. After the drive-in cinema, turn right and continue 9 km to Heatonville. Continue north-wards across a railway line. Thereafter the gravel road is well signposted for the last 10 km to the entrance gate. Day visitors are welcome.

There is a well grassed 678 m airstrip at 180 m above sea level in the reserve. Arrangements must be made for collection and transport prior to landing.

FEATURES

About 60 km of tourist roads have been laid out for game and bird spotting drives. Game viewing and night drives in open Landrovers with a knowledgeable guide can be booked. Special "game-on-the-spit" braais can also be arranged. Whether you are a serious hiker or simply enjoy walking, this park offers an opportunity to enjoy natural game trails, at your own pace, with an experienced guide, the ideal way to see some of the 200 bird and 29 mammal species. There are pleasant lookouts, as well as picnic sites, provided.

Self-catering cabins are available as well as accommodation for school groups. Full catering and secretarial services for a conference of up to 30 persons can be arranged. Depending on numbers and needs, accommodation can be provided. The park also caters for a limited number of trophy hunters and hunting for meat on a small scale. Game licences are available for purchase at the office. Skinners, a cool room and slaughtering facilities are provided.

DESCRIPTION

The park is located in the Enseleni valley and the river of the same name meanders through it. About two-thirds of the area comprises typical southern Zululand acacia-dominated thorn flats, mixed scrub, open woodland with riverine bush and thickets along the river banks. A third of the reserve consists of grasslands on the hillsides and flat savanna sweetveld. Situated close to the coast, the low-lying areas are about 120 m above sea level.

HISTORICAL NOTES

Windy Ridge was one of the first game ranches established in Natal and has now been operating for 30 years.

Originally settled in 1947, the present reserve was for many years a farm divided into cotton fields and natural grazing land for livestock. The area has been well frequented by game since the days before the Umfolozi Game Reserve was fenced. The decision to convert the farm into a commercial game ranch was taken in 1964.

ACCOMMODATION

There are three types of accommodation offered. In one camp there are six cabins with two to four beds each. For school children or larger groups, six cabins accommodate 48 persons. There is a fully furnished and equipped mobile home with two bedrooms, each with three beds. The camps are separately sited and are equipped with linen (except towels), a gas stove, pots, pans, cutlery, crockery, hot and cold showers and toilets. Guests bring their own food and drink and do their own cooking, but camp staff wash and tidy up. A traditional open-air boma-dining enclosure with braai facilities is available at each camp. Reservations are made with the game park itself.

TREES

Acacia caffra – common hook-thorn
Acacia karroo – sweet thorn
Berchemia zeyheri – red ivory
Erythrina lysistemon – common coral tree
Ficus thonningii – common wild fig
Harpephyllum caffrum – wild plum
Phoenix reclinata – wild date palm
Schotia brachypetala – weeping boer-bean/tree fuschia
Sclerocarya birrea subsp. *caffra* – marula
Spirostachys africana – tamboti

BIRDS (about 200 species recorded)

African finfoot
blackbellied korhaan
blackcrowned night heron
bushveld pipit

eagles – blackbreasted snake,
    lesser spotted,
    southern banded snake
flycatchers – bluegrey, wattle-eyed
grey penduline tit

hawks – bat, cuckoo
Heuglin's robin
melba finch
olive thrush
owls – giant eagle, Scops
plumcoloured starling
redbilled firefinch
redbreasted swallow

scalythroated honeyguide
threestreaked tchagra
vultures – hooded,
   lappetfaced
white helmetshrike
whitebacked duck
woollynecked stork
yellowthroated sparrow

MAMMALS (29 species)
antbear (aardvark)
blesbok
bushbuck
bushpig
chacma baboon
civet
duiker – common, red
giraffe
greater canerat
honey badger
impala
kudu
leopard

mongooses – banded,
   slender, water, white-tailed
mountain reedbuck
nyala
porcupine
reedbuck
spotted hyaena
steenbok
thick-tailed bushbaby
vervet monkey
warthog
waterbuck
white rhino

ENSELENI NATURE RESERVE

Area: 293 ha
Established: 22 January 1948

LOCATION
Southern Zululand, between Empangeni and Mtubatuba, about 13 km north of Empangeni on the N2, which goes through the reserve.

FEATURES
An attractive area of coastal grassland and luxuriant subtropical riverine forest on a bend of the Enseleni river. Several interesting trees and birds occur and it is noted for a seasonal proliferation of butterflies. A number of mammal species have been reintroduced. A 5 km swamp trail, including a ramped boardwalk section, passes over the swamplands permitting good views of the vegetation and bird species. Picnic sites and toilet facilities are provided. The reserve is worth visiting for a morning or afternoon ramble, or an all-day picnic.

DESCRIPTION

An attractive area of coastal grassland and scattered Ilala palms *Hyphaena coriacea*, with coastal forest and scrub on the higher lying sandy hills. The ground slopes down to dense and luxuriant subtropical swamp forest and riverine forest dominated by powder-puff trees *Barringtonia racemosa*, with Cape beech *Rapanea melanophloeos*, swamp fig *Ficus trichopoda*, sycamore fig *Ficus sycomorus* and the sandpaper fig *Ficus capreifolia* along parts of the river bank.

On the forest margin there is a wide, dense bed of papyrus *Cyprus papyrus*, interspersed with swamp reeds *Phragmites australis*, with ferns, the broad, ridged-leaved sword grass *Setaria chevalieri* and the trees, lagoon hibiscus *Hibiscus tiliaceus*, the broom cluster fig *Ficus sur* and wild date palm *Phoenix reclinata* on damp, black, clay soils.

The reserve, bisected by the national road, is totally surrounded by sugar cane fields and timber plantations. The perennially flowing Enseleni river becomes periodically choked by rafts of the exotic water hyacinth which probably originated from an ornamental pond on private property upstream but unfortunately flourishes in the river.

HISTORICAL NOTES

One of the largest crocodiles ever recorded in Zululand was found dead in the Enseleni river. It measured 5,40 m. There used to be a ferry boat at the site of the present N2 bridge across the river. William Foster, a pioneer in Zululand and former game supervisor of the Umfolozi Game Reserve, told one of the authors that people would arrive drunk at the ferry boat, having imbibed marula wine. They would lounge back and, despite the warnings of the ferry-man, allow their hands to droop over the side. Many was the person who was reputedly pulled out of the boat by the crocodiles that lurked in the still river.

TREES

There are a number of tree species of interest:
Acacia burkei – black monkey thorn
Acacia nilotica – scented thorn
Acacia robusta – ankle thorn
Aloe rupestris – bottlebrush aloe
Bersama lucens – glossy white ash
Celtis durandii – false white stinkwood
Ficus sur – broom cluster fig
Nuxia oppositifolia – water elder
Salix woodii – Natal willow
Strelitzia nicolai – Natal wild banana
Teclea gerrardii – Zulu cherry-orange
Teclea natalensis – Natal cherry-orange
In the deep shade of the forest the dominant undergrowth is buckweed *Isoglossa woodii* and the carpet-like soft grass *Oplismenus hirtellus*. Water berry *Syzygium cordatum* occur on the swamp margins.

BIRDS

Along the river greenbacked heron and African finfoot should be looked for in and under the low overhanging branches.

In the riverine forest:

blackbellied glossy starling	grey sunbird
blackcollared barbet	Natal robin
cinnamon dove	scalythroated honeyguide
forest weaver	wattle-eyed flycatcher
green coucal	white-eared barbet

MAMMALS

A number of mammal species such as nyala, impala, waterbuck, wildebeest and zebra have been reintroduced in small numbers. Visitors may also see:

bushbuck	red duiker
bushpig	reedbuck
Cape clawless otter	serval
large-spotted genet	striped polecat
mongooses – banded, slender, water	

Hippo occur in the river in small numbers and seasonally move in and out of the system, depending on water levels.

REPTILES

Crocodiles and Nile or water monitor lizards occur in and along the river banks in small numbers.

RICHARDS BAY GAME RESERVE

Area: 700 ha
Established: 5 September 1935

LOCATION

Southern Zululand, coastal. The turn-off to Richards Bay is well signposted from the N2, about 18 km east of Empangeni. Proceed through Richards Bay towards the harbour mouth. Follow the Natal Parks Board bait house signs. At this office, ask for directions to the three areas that can be visited.

FEATURES

The reserve has remnant stands of swamp forest, the Thulazihleka bird viewing hide in a small swamp and the tidal mudflats and shallows south of the Mhlatuzi river. 300 species of birds have been recorded in these habitats including several rare migrant species new to the list of Natal birds. It is a popular angling venue.

DESCRIPTION

Despite the reduction in size of the original conservation area, Richards Bay is still a reserve of major importance. There are stands of swamp forest along the banks of the Mzingazi stream and inland of Mzingazi lake, such as the one where the Thulazihleka hide has been built. The tidal shallows and mudflats and the stands of mangrove species have increased in size over recent years. In the bay, small numbers of hippo and crocodiles still occur but the area is most important for its bird life.

HISTORICAL NOTES

Richards Bay was named after Frederick William Richards RN of HMS Forrester, who surveyed the coastline in 1879. In those days the bay must have been a wildlife paradise with hippos, crocodiles, a great variety and large concentrations of birds, lush mangrove communities and many game mammal species in the dune forests, swamps and grasslands. Up until the late 1960s, this was still the case and the waters of the bay, as well as the surf zone, yielded excellent catches of game fish. Richards Bay was a favourite haunt of fishermen. However, the entire area has been greatly modified by the building of the huge harbour. The dredging of this commenced in 1971 to enable ore carriers to enter and load coal exported from the giant coal terminal. Enormous industrial complexes and a small town have been established adjacent to the harbour. Fishermen maintain that pollution, the stirring up of the harbour bed and dumping of sand offshore have had adverse effects on angling results. Much of the original habitat has disappeared along the shoreline.

BIRDS

The list for the area includes many uncommon species:

avocet
Baillon's crake
bartailed godwit
Basra reedwarbler
bittern
bluecheeked bee-eater
brownthroated weaver
European oystercatcher
knot
lesser blackbacked gull
lesser jacana
mangrove kingfisher
Mongolian sandplover
osprey
pinkbacked pelican

plovers – crab, grey, ringed
pygmy goose
redshank
redwinged pratincole
sandpipers – buffbreasted,
  broadbilled, curlew, terek
stints – little, Temminck's
terns – common, gullbilled,
  lesser crested, little,
  sandwich, swift,
  whitecheeked
wattle-eyed flycatcher
yellow wagtail
yellowbilled stork

MAMMALS

Mammals are scarce but the following occur in the area:

bushbuck
Cape clawless otter
greater canerat
hippopotamus

large-spotted genet
mongooses – slender, water
vervet monkey

LAKE ETEZA NATURE RESERVE

Area: 350 ha
Established: 3 June 1976

LOCATION
Southern Zululand. On the N2 beyond the Kwambonambi turn-off, continue northwards until crossing the Msinduzi river bridge. The lake will be seen on the right-hand side of the road and about 1 km distant. From the north it can be seen from the next bridge beyond the Mfolozi river.

FEATURES
A shallow lake about 3 km long which, over some seasons, may dry out and become overgrown with grasses and reeds. It is a valuable sanctuary for wildfowl when filled with water. At present it is not open to the public.

DESCRIPTION
Lake Eteza is filled by the floodwaters of the Msinduzi river and, after extremely high floods, by water backing up from the Mfolozi river. It becomes a shallow pan some 3 km long, 1 km wide and up to 2 m in depth. However, during severe drought periods it may dry out completely to hard-baked mudflats.

The lake is surrounded by undulating land almost wholly planted with sugar cane and timber. There are isolated patches of sycamore figs *Ficus sycomorus*, powder-puff trees *Barringtonia racemosa*, wild date palm *Phoenix reclinata* and weeping boer-bean *Schotia brachypetala* trees at the water's edge.

Along the shore line and in the shallows are dense reed beds, papyrus and buffalo grass *Echinochloa pyramidalus* with mats of water lilies *Nymphaea capensis* and *Nymphaea lotus* across the surface. The lake is particularly rich in its abundance and diversity of aquatic plants. These include water chestnuts *Trapa natans*, four species of bladderworts *Utricularia* spp., duckweed *Lemna gibba*, hornwort *Aratrophyllum demersum*, four species of *Potamogeton* and the bulrush *Typha latifolia*.

Although not yet open to the public, this small oasis deserves protection for the important role it plays in the ecology of the greater St Lucia wetland complex.

BIRDS

The rich food supply available in the form of aquatic vegetation, frogs, fish and water insects attracts large concentrations of birds. This small lake is not only a valuable feeding ground in an area almost covered in timber and sugar cane, but it is also a protected roosting and breeding site.

Birds recorded include:
egrets – black, cattle, little
geese – Egyptian, pygmy, spurwinged
herons – Goliath, purple, squacco, black, little egret
ibis – sacred, glossy
jacanas – African, lesser
kingfishers – giant, pied, mangrove
little bittern
moorhen
storks – marabou, yellowbilled, white, openbill

White pelicans occur at times in large flocks, as do whitewinged terns. Redwinged pratincoles breed nearby. Over the summer months blue-cheeked bee-eaters may be seen.

MAMMALS AND REPTILES

Cape clawless otter, large-spotted genet, slender mongoose and water mongoose occur. Hippo and crocodile move in and out of the system depending on water levels.

FISH

Fourteen fish species have been recorded, including five euryhaline species (tolerant of both fresh and salty water), which reflect the lake's connection to the sea via the Mfolozi river. They are oxeye tarpon, bulldog, flathead mullet, tank goby and eels. It is likely that more species remain to be discovered. The freshwater fish include two species of catfish, three tilapia and southern mouth brooder. This accounts for the occasional concentrations of pelicans.

MAPELANE NATURE RESERVE

Area: 900 ha
Established: 1897

LOCATION

Southern Zululand, coastal. South of Lake St Lucia estuary, on the south bank and at the mouth of the Mfolozi river. Turn off the N2 at Kwambonambi at the St Lucia lighthouse signboard. Follow this gravel, and in parts, very sandy road, for about 40 km to the camp. The road is not recommended for saloon cars, or for vehicles with a low clearance. Caravans, with single-axle only, towed by a 4x4 vehicle are allowed. Boats must not exceed 5,79 m (19 ft) and vehicles must not exceed 1,5 tonnes.

FEATURES
Mapelane provides excellent ski-boat and surf fishing, a sheltered bathing beach and an attractive offshore reef, popular because of its interesting marine life and for crayfish, mussels and oyster beds. There are dense coastal forests, beach walks and a varied bird life including marine, estuarine, swamp and swamp forest species. It is recommended for a relaxing camping holiday. Log cabins and camp sites are available.

DESCRIPTION
Mapelane is situated on the south bank of the Mfolozi river, where the river enters the sea. It was originally a favourite haunt of fishermen, who, in the 1950s, built wooden shacks at the base of the high forest-clad Mjakaja hill that rises steeply from the beach.

There are three distinct vegetation types. Firstly, the narrow belt of dune forest, varying in width and canopy height, dense and tangled in parts with a thick understorey of buckweed *Isoglossa woodii*. This forest extends about 9 km southwards from the river mouth and separates the inland floodplain and the sea. Secondly, the river bank and true swamplands upstream from where the Mzsinduzi river joins the Mfolozi river. The floodplain flora consists of dense papyrus *Cyperus papyrus* swamps interspersed with *Cyperus immensis*, the common reed *Phragmites* sp. and buffalo grass *Echinochloa* sp. Thirdly, there are scattered patches of swamp forest dominated by swamp figs, broom cluster figs, wild rubber figs, sycamore fig, blue sweetberry, mitzeeri, wild poplars, lagoon hibiscus, quinine trees and the powder-puff tree. This type of vegetation is an example of a unique habitat which serves to trap the silt-laden floodwaters of these two rivers. This type of natural filter bed is rapidly disappearing from the mouths of Zululand rivers.

HISTORICAL NOTES
The potential of the Mapelane area was first recognised in 1897 when it was proclaimed as part of the St Lucia Game Reserve but it was subsequently deproclaimed and administered by the Department of Forestry.

In the late 1940s fishermen discovered that the beach afforded excellent fishing. They forged a road through the dense, tangled dune forest to reach Mapelane and erected numerous permanent holiday shacks at the base of the dunes.

The discovery of rich deposits of titanium by General Mining and their success in obtaining prospecting rights and a concession to strip mine the dunes threatened the future of the area. In 1968 Gavin Wiseman and Ian Garland of the Natal branch of the Wildlife Society of Southern Africa prepared a report on the fauna and flora of Mapelane, describing it as one of our best examples of coastal dune forest. Representations by the Wildlife Society and Natal Parks Board officials to the minister for mining affairs, for the setting aside of Mapelane as a nature reserve continued over a protracted period, ending happily with the mining company relinquishing their rights in return for a similar strip of dune forest further south.

Mapelane is the Zulu name for the bush cockroach.

ACCOMMODATION

This comprises ten five-bedded, fully equipped and serviced log cabins, each with two bedrooms, a bathroom, fully equipped kitchenette and a small lounge cum dining room area. There are 44 camping and caravan sites serviced with ablution blocks. No more than six persons per camp site are permitted. Visitors need to provide all their own camping equipment. Reservations for log cabins are made with the Natal Parks Board, Pietermaritzburg and for camp sites with the officer-in-charge, Mapelane.

TREES

Acacia karroo – sweet thorn
Barringtonia racemosa – powder-puff tree
Bridelia cathartica – blue sweet-berry
Bridelia micrantha – mitzeeri
Chionanthus peglerae – giant pock ironwood
Diospyros inhacaensis – Zulu jackal-berry
Diospyros natalensis – small-leaved jackal-berry
Englerophytum (Bequaertiodendron) natalensis – Natal milkplum
Ficus polita – wild rubber fig
Ficus surn – broom cluster fig
Ficus sycomorus – sycamore fig
Ficus trichopoda – swamp fig
Hibiscus tiliaceus – lagoon hibiscus
Inhambanella henriquesii – milk pear
Macaranga capensis – wild poplar
Mimusops caffra – coastal red milkwood
Mimusops obovata – red milkwood
Rauvolfia caffra – quinine tree
Teclea gerrardii – Zulu cherry-orange
Zizyphus mucronata – buffalo thorn

BIRDS

Access to the swamps is difficult for the keen bird watcher and visibility in the dune forest equally difficult. It is highly likely that the present list of 170 species of birds may be increased to over 200. Forest birds are best found along the verges of the entrance road through the dense forest, and along the edges of camp sites. For those visitors unfamiliar with the bird calls of coastal species, it would be helpful to take a tape recorder plus tapes of calls to play back in this type of habitat. In this manner some of the shy, difficult to see species can be enticed out to the forest verges where they can be seen and enjoyed.

Typical dune forest species in this area include:

bleating bush warbler	green pigeon
bulbuls – sombre, terrestrial, yellowbellied	louries – Knysna, purplecrested
	Natal robin
flycatchers – bluegrey, bluemantled, dusky, paradise	squaretailed drongo
	sunbirds – collared, grey, olive
forest weaver	tambourine dove
goldenrumped tinker barbet	white-eared barbet
goldentailed woodpecker	yellowbreasted apalis
green twinspot	

At times when the build-up of a sandbar at the mouth forms a large shallow lagoon, many waders, herons, ibises, storks and sea birds are attracted. Cape gannet, whitebreasted cormorant, kelp gull, greyheaded gull, Caspian, swift and little terns, among others, appear. White pelicans, sometimes in large groups, can be seen.

MAMMALS

A number of mammals inhabit the dense dune forest undergrowth, including blue duiker, bushpig, bushbuck, white-tailed and banded mongoose and large-spotted genet with red squirrels and vervet monkeys in the canopy. Along the reed fringes, water mongoose and greater canerat occur. Hippo are normally found in the Mfolozi river and the papyrus swamps of Mapelane are an important refuge for them during drought periods.

REPTILES (31 species recorded)

In the winter months of low water levels, large numbers of crocodiles congregate along the banks of the Mfolozi river. Visitors are strongly advised not to take chances by allowing children to play in the shallows and along the river banks. Bathing too, is strictly forbidden in the river.

Poisonous species:

cobras – forest, Mozambique spitting	green mamba
common puff adder	sea snakes – black, yellow
gaboon adder	southern vine snake

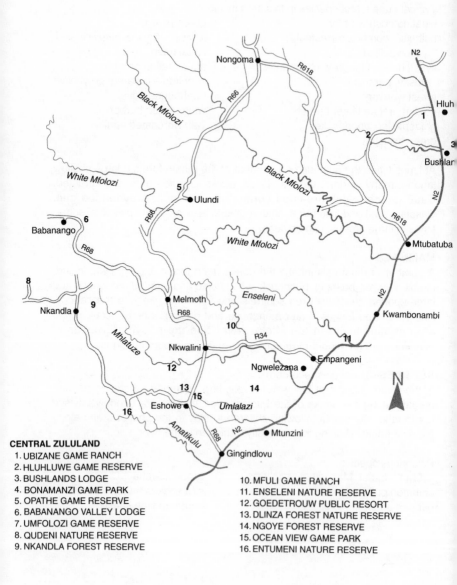

CENTRAL ZULULAND

1. UBIZANE GAME RANCH
2. HLUHLUWE GAME RESERVE
3. BUSHLANDS LODGE
4. BONAMANZI GAME PARK
5. OPATHE GAME RESERVE
6. BABANANGO VALLEY LODGE
7. UMFOLOZI GAME RESERVE
8. QUDENI NATURE RESERVE
9. NKANDLA FOREST RESERVE

10. MFULI GAME RANCH
11. ENSELENI NATURE RESERVE
12. GOEDETROUW PUBLIC RESORT
13. DLINZA FOREST NATURE RESERVE
14. NGOYE FOREST RESERVE
15. OCEAN VIEW GAME PARK
16. ENTUMENI NATURE RESERVE

CENTRAL ZULULAND

Historians may one day record that the fight for conservation in Natal largely centred around the scenic wooded valleys, grassy hillsides and forests of the Umfolozi and Hluhluwe game reserves. These reserves and the wildlife, flora and land in and around them, have been subjected to great pressures over the years. Umfolozi was, for a long period, settled by people. Shaka, when still an induna serving under the Mtetwa chieftain Dingiswayo, led an army against the Ndwandwe people, defeating them in a battle within the area of the game reserve. Later during his reign, Shaka conducted one of the biggest game hunts in Zululand's history in this reserve.

The Anglo-Zulu wars and the Zulu-Boer battles were waged around this region. Soldiers with firearms, living off the land, must have taken a toll on wildlife as did the early white hunters, traders and adventurers who ventured into the interior.

Although proclaimed as game reserves in 1897, Umfolozi and Hluhluwe, along with St Lucia, the oldest in Africa, did not benefit from protection at all for a great number of years. In fact, parts of Umfolozi were more than once deproclaimed then later reproclaimed during the controversial nagana campaign, when over 90 000 head of game, with the exception of rhinos, were shot to eradicate tsetse flies. The veterinary department administered the reserve for many years and their research eventually led to the aerial spraying of Hluhluwe and Umfolozi with insecticides. This programme, while successful, must also have exacted a toll on a myriad other life forms with unknown long-term effects on the fauna and flora. In addition to this damage, a large area of Hluhluwe was cleared of vegetation as part of the tsetse fly campaign and large-scale slaughter of game was carried out here as well.

Umfolozi was only handed over to the Natal Parks Board in 1953 and the first white resident ranger appointed. Umfolozi was then largely unfenced and the staff had to contend with squatters, who had settled within the boundaries, and with large bands of armed poachers who frequently invaded the reserve on organised hunting drives. The fencing of the reserve and the education of land hungry people to the value of a conservation area was a lengthy process. The fight for the "Corridor", a strip of unallocated state-owned land linking the two reserves and a natural game migration route between them, was negotiated over a period of more than 40 years. The area was only finally secured as recently as 1989.

The first camp was constructed in Hluhluwe Game Reserve in 1934, opening up this wildlife sanctuary to the outside world. It was here that the first herbarium and field laboratory was established in later years. Conservation management planning concepts, veterinary research and game capture techniques, the latter nowadays practised all over Africa, were developed here. The capture and translocation of white rhinos to destinations all over Africa and to zoos worldwide commenced in Umfolozi in 1960. It was one of the most successful exercises ever in the saving of a species from extinction. The deployment of horses in this programme, and to provide greater mobility for the anti-poaching forces in the ceaseless battle against poachers, was initiated in Umfolozi. Today these reserves, now a single complex, form the third largest reserve in South Africa. They are well stocked with game and are immensely popular as tourist destinations, thanks to the tireless and dedicated efforts of many fine conservationists.

The central Zululand region also contains some magnificent forest reserves – Qudeni, Entumeni, Dlinza, Nkandla and Ngoye, the latter unique for its endemic fauna and flora. There are privately-owned game ranches and lodges which offer a high standard of accommodation and facilities where the fauna and flora typical of the region can be enjoyed. An exciting new development is the recently proclaimed Opathe Game Reserve near Ulundi, in close proximity to many famous historical battlefields, monuments and graves. When established and stocked with game Opathe will undoubtedly become a reserve of major importance.

With the burgeoning human population and the rapid growth of towns like Empangeni, Ngwelezana, Melmoth, Eshowe, Ulundi, Nongoma and Hluhluwe, our existing game reserves may be inadequate to cope with the demands of local and international tourism in the not too distant future.

NGOYE (UNGOYE) FOREST RESERVE

Area: 3 903 ha
Established: 1913

LOCATION
Central Zululand, Mtunzini district. From the south, take the N2 straight past the turn-off to Mtunzini. Continue until 4-5 km past the Forest Motel complex, then turn off to the left. Follow this gravel road to the entrance gate. A four-wheel drive vehicle is needed to travel the rough tracks to this reserve. (A permit is required from the KwaZulu Department of Nature Conservation, Ulundi.)

FEATURES
Magnificent forest with rare and endemic plants, birds, mammals and invertebrates, with superb views over the surrounding country. Well worth a day's visit. No overnight facilities are provided.

DESCRIPTION

First described by the Woodward brothers in 1895, Ngoye is well known as probably the most impressive indigenous forest in Natal and famous for its unique flora and fauna.

Described as moist, evergreen, coastal scarp forest, Ngoye is about 11 km from the coast at an average altitude of 400 m. It covers an area about 10 km in length, running parallel to the coast along the tops of a low ridge of hills. The forest is not continuous. In the steep gullies there are small, fast-flowing streams. Many isolated granite outcrops, with lichen-covered rock domes, afford superb panoramic views over the forest canopy and the valleys to the distant coast. These clearings, as well as short-grassed natural open glades, are extremely attractive in the otherwise dense forest with its wealth of fern life. There are numerous attractive flowering species, such as *Haemanthus, Scadoxus, Pelargonium, Leonotis, Lobelia, Clivia, Watsonia, Plectranthus, Hibiscus, Ochna, Streptocarpus* and many orchid species.

The importance of Ngoye is that it is an extraordinary, isolated link between the tropical forests of Tanzania, Malawi, Kenya and northern Mozambique, and the southern Natal-Transkei forests and the temperate Tsitsikamma to Knysna forests even further south.

Many rare and endemic animal and plant species occur at Ngoye. Perhaps the most famous is Wood's cycad *Encephalartos woodii*, extinct in the wild since the early 1900s. Only one small group of male plants was ever found. One can still see specimens of this magnificent plant in Durban's Botanic Gardens. The forest supports some magnificent butterflies including the Forest Green *Euryphera achlyus*, and the Ngoye centipede *Cormocephalus granulosis*, both of which are found nowhere else in South Africa.

HISTORICAL NOTES

The Ngoye forest was first protected by the Zulu royal household under King Mpande because of the valuable medicinal plants to be found within it. From 1840 to 1872 Ceteswayo, King Mpande's son, had his kraal in the vicinity of the forest. In 1857 King Mpande granted occupational rights over a large part of the area to the white chief, John Dunn. At that stage Dunn was his advisor and supplier of firearms. Dunn decimated much of the game found in the area, but was not allowed to exploit the forest while the king was alive. Ceteswayo moved his kraal to Ulundi on the death of his father and control over the forest diminished.

Ngoye was proclaimed a forest reserve by the Department of Forestry (Section V, of Act No 16 of 1913) but by then, exploitation of valuable timber from this forest, especially by John Dunn, had occurred and hardwoods had been extracted and shipped from Port Durnford to a boat-building industry in Durban. In 1909 the Ngoye Forest Company established a mill alongside the forest and constructed the few forest roads still in existence. As far as can be ascertained, approximately 250 000 cubic metres of timber were removed, a good deal of which was used for pit props for the

Transvaal mines. No further extraction of timber has been legally undertaken since 1924. The illegal removal of timber by an expanding local population and the practice of burning along the forest margins to provide grazing for cattle, has reduced the size of this unique forest.

In 1968 the Department of Forestry handed the area over to the South African Bantu Trust, whose control was minimal. Finally, in 1992, the area was handed over to the KwaZulu Department of Nature Conservation to administer under Government Notice No 36 of 1992. A new proposal seeks to include the adjoining Ezigwayini, Impeleshu and nearby Denguvini forest reserves, which would bring the combined protected area to 4 283 ha.

FLORA

Rare species include:
Alchornea hirtella var. *glabrata* – Zulu bead-string tree
Asplenium sandersonii – an epiphytic fern
Bolusiella mandae – an epiphytic orchid
Corymborchis welwitschii – a ground orchid
Loranthus woodii – a hemiparasite
Nectaropetalum zuluense – Natal coca tree
Olyra latifolia – a forest grass
Pseudobersama mossambicensis – false white ash
Stictocardia woodii – a forest climber
24 other members of the orchid family

Notable trees are:
Cavacoa aurea – Natal hickory
Celtis africana – white stinkwood
Celtis durandii – false white stinkwood
Chrysophyllum viridifolium – fluted milkwood
Clerodendrum myricoides – blue-flowered tinderwood
Eugenia zeyheri – wild myrtle
Faurea macnaughtonii – terblanz beech
Ficus bizanae – Pondo fig
Garcinia gerrardii – forest mangosteen
Homalium dentatum – brown ironwood
Millettia sutherlandii – giant umzimbeet
Olinia radiata – Natal hard pear
Phyllanthus cedrelifolius – forest potato bush
Podocarpus latifolius – real yellowwood

BIRDS

For the serious ornithologist and keen amateur birder, Ngoye is well worth a visit. The green or Woodwards' barbet, not uncommon here, is found in no other forest in South Africa. Among other interesting and uncommon species are:

banded goshawk
buffspotted flufftail
Cape batis
crowned eagle
Delegorgue's pigeon
green coucal
green twinspot
honeyguides – lesser, scalythroated
longtailed wagtail
Mozambique nightjar
narina trogon
Natal francolin

olive bush shrike
olive woodpecker
redbacked mannikin
robins – brown, chorister, starred
striped pipit
thrushes – kurrichane, olive, spotted
tinker barbets – golden-rumped, redfronted
wood owl
yellowstreaked bulbul

Ngoye is unique in that of the 85 species of forest birds in Natal, 73 occur in this small area.

MAMMALS
Ngoye is also home to the endemic red squirrel, separated from its nearest relative, a smaller subspecies that occurs in the dune and sand forests further north, about 100 km away. Other species of mammals recorded are:

bushbuck
bushpig
duiker – blue, common, red
Hottentot golden mole
large-spotted genet
molerat

mongooses – banded, slender, water, white-tailed
monkeys – samango, vervet
mountain reedbuck
porcupine
thick-tailed bushbaby
tree dassie

Chacma baboons are common and the leopard is their major predator.

REPTILES
common puff adder
green mamba
green water snake
Mozambique spitting cobra

Natal rock python
rhombic night adder
southern vine snake

MFULI GAME RANCH

Area: 280 ha
Established: 1990

LOCATION
Central Zululand, in the Nkwalini valley. From Melmoth take district road R68, then onto the R34 to the signposted turn-off. From Empangeni take the road to Nkwalini and the Mfuli turn-off.

FEATURES

Mfuli has comfortable, fully serviced log cabins in sight of game on the opposite slope of a small valley which makes the view from the elevated veranda rewarding. Landrover drives, a walking trail as well as a bush braai in the heart of the property can be arranged. Hunting with a rifle or bow can be organised and amenities include a swimming pool, snooker, pool, darts and table tennis, as well as a curio shop.

The reserve is well positioned for visits to other attractions in the vicinity, e.g. Zulu dancing. It is a 45 minute drive to the coast, 90 minutes to game reserves, and historic sites are within short travelling distance.

DESCRIPTION

The steeply sloped Mfuli, catchment valley of the Nkwalini valley, stretches from the Mhlatuzi river southwards to the top of the property, with views from Nkwenkwe hill, haunt of the snake god Mningi, according to local Zulu legend. The south-eastern slopes are rich with Natal wild banana clumps among the sandstone rocks and dense woodland. The dominant trees in the valley below are acacia species, silver cluster leaf and tamboti in woodland communities. The mountain aloe is abundant in this reserve and most attractive during the winter flowering season.

ACCOMMODATION

The ranch provides six log cabins with elevated balconies, each with two bedrooms, one with a double bed and the other with two bunk beds, a full bathroom (bath and shower) and an open-plan, air-conditioned lounge leading onto a kitchen, with electric stove, oven and fridge freezer. The cabins are fully equipped and are serviced. A small restaurant and a bar are available for meals for those who do not wish to cater for themselves. Reservations are made with the game ranch manager.

TREES

Typical species include:

Acacia karroo – sweet thorn
Acacia nigrescens – knobthorn
Acacia tortilis – umbrella thorn
Aloe marlothii – mountain aloe
Carissa bispinosa – forest num-num
Gardenia species
Grewia species
Hyphaene coriacea – lala palm
Peltophorum africanum – African wattle
Phoenix reclinata – wild date palm
Schotia brachypetala – weeping boer-bean/tree fuschia
Sclerocarya birrea subsp. *caffra* – marula
Spirostachys africana – tamboti
Strelitzia nicolai – Natal wild banana

Strychnos spinosa – green monkey orange
Terminalia sericea – silver cluster leaf
Ziziphus mucronata – buffalo thorn

BIRDS

blackshouldered kite
bluebilled firefinch
bronzewinged courser
Burchell's coucal
eagles – bateleur, booted, brown snake,
   crowned, longcrested
giant kingfisher
goldenbreasted bunting
green pigeon
gymnogene
hornbills – crowned, ground
kurrichane thrush
lanner falcon

narina trogon
orangebreasted bush shrike
purplecrested lourie
redbacked mannikin
redfaced mousebird
Richard's pipit
scimitarbilled wood hoopoe
threestreaked tchagra
whitebrowed robin
whitenecked raven
yellowthroated apalis
yellowthroated longclaw

MAMMALS

blue wildebeest
bushpig
common duiker
impala
large-spotted genet
mongooses – banded, slender,
   water, white-tailed

nyala
scrub hare
thick-tailed bushbaby
vervet monkey
zebra

REPTILES

Venomous species include common puff adder, vine snake, Mozambique
spitting cobra, boomslang and black mamba. The harmless and protected
African rock python also occurs.

BABANANGO VALLEY LODGE

Area: 1 945 ha
Established: August 1986

LOCATION

Central Zululand. Take the R68 from Babanango towards Dundee, then the
D139 turn-off 4 km from Babanango and proceed for 12 km to the lodge.
The road is well signposted from Babanango. From Durban, the lodge can

be reached via Eshowe, Melmoth and Babanango. From Pietermaritzburg use the Durban route or inland via Ladysmith and Dundee. From Johannesburg travel via Standerton, Volksrust and Dundee.

FEATURES

An exclusive small resort, where guests are comfortably accommodated and enjoy outstanding meals and the personal attention of their hosts. For those keen on botany or birds, hikes through the countryside are most rewarding in this peaceful landscape. Dr John Turner, the host, is happy to lead morning and afternoon walks. He has made the study of the Anglo-Zulu wars and nearby battlefields his speciality and conducts guided tours on request. The lodge is ideally situated close to a number of these sites, including Emakhosini "the Valley of the Kings", Qokli Hill, (the first major battlefield of King Shaka), emGungundhlovu (Dingaan's kraal), Ondini (Ceteswayo's kraal) and the KwaZulu Cultural Museum.

Important places from the Zulu-Boer conflicts of 1838, including Blood river, Piet Retief's grave, Opathe gorge and, nearby, the big seven major battlefields of the 1879 Anglo-Zulu War – Nyezane, Isandlwana, Rorke's Drift, Hlobane, Khambula, Ginginhlovu and Ulundi and many fortifications erected by the British, are all within easy reach of the lodge. Private or charter fly-in tours can be arranged with flights over the battlefields. Umfolozi Game Reserve is within easy reach for a day's tour which may be combined with visits to Zulu historical sites en route.

The farm Goudhoek was proclaimed a Natural Heritage Site and forms the core of this private nature reserve. A game reintroduction programme has been embarked on, starting with impala. It is planned to introduce several other antelope species.

DESCRIPTION

The nature reserve is located on the transition between lowveld and highveld, with a difference in altitude of 550 m from the valley floor to the mountain tops. The topography is varied, as is the flora, with the valley bottoms dominated by broad-leaf woodland, extending up the dry mountain slopes. The area is well watered by streams, with well-vegetated granite koppies, quartzite ridges, sandstone cliffs and exposed glacial pavements. Lowveld and southern tall grassveld is varied because of the different geology and soils and more than 75 grass and 135 tree species have been identified. The trees include nine species of *Acacia* and seven species of fig. It is this rich variety of habitats that contribute to the scenic beauty of this small reserve.

HISTORICAL NOTES

Artefacts from the Early, Middle and Late Stone Age have been discovered on the property. More recently, the area formed part of the traditional Buthelezi tribal area of the old Zulu kingdom. There are caves in the sandstone cliffs which appear to have been inhabited circa 1800-1860 by fugitives from the Zulu kings. Shards of pottery found in the caves confirm this.

A relatively rare feature is an isiVivane, a pile of stones growing out of a superstition or tradition of Zulu travellers – each adding a stone to the pile as they passed that way.

In 1886 the land was settled by Boers of the Vryheid Republic in return for services to King Dinizulu. The farms were first sold under freehold title in October 1898. There is a disused copper mine with several shafts which was mined in about 1905. The old wagon route between Babanango and Vryheid passed through the property and wagon tracks carved into the granite are still visible.

Portions of land comprising "Goudhoek" changed hands several times. In the 1950s it was used as a labour farm. This system involved the exchange of accommodation and the use of land in the low potential farming areas by black families for their labour on the more arable land of the white owner. During this period the land was heavily settled, overgrazed and ploughed for crop planting.

The farm was then purchased by Mr Wilfred Thole in 1961, who changed the farming practice and dismissed the labour. The present farm, now a nature reserve, was purchased by the Turner family in 1964 and rehabilitation and conservation measures were implemented.

ACCOMMODATION
Part of the original old farmhouse has been converted into four two-bedded fully furnished en suite rooms to accommodate eight guests. From each room there is a magnificent view over the valley. There is a swimming pool for guests. School and youth groups interested in Zulu history and the Anglo-Zulu wars and natural history, are accommodated in tents. Excellent meals are provided. Reservations should be made with the lodge itself.

TREES
Acacia karroo – sweet thorn
Acacia nilotica – scented thorn
Acacia tortilis – umbrella thorn
Combretum apiculatum – hairy red bushwillow
Combretum erythrophyllum – river bushwillow
Combretum molle – velvet bushwillow
Cussonia natalensis – rock cabbage tree
Ekebergia pterophylla – rock ash
Erythrina humeana – dwarf coral tree
Erythrina latissima – broad-leaved coral tree
Erythrina lysistemon – common coral tree
Ficus abutilifolia – large-leaved rock fig
Ficus burtt-davyi – veld fig
Ficus cordata subsp. *salicifolia* – wonderboom fig
Ficus glumosa – mountain fig
Ficus ingens – red-leaved fig
Ficus natalensis – Natal fig

Ficus sur – broom cluster fig
Greyia sutherlandii – Natal bottlebrush
Lopholaena platyphylla
Olea capensis – false ironwood
Pappea capensis – jacket-plum
Protea caffra – common sugarbush
Protea roupelliae – silver sugarbush
Rapanea melanophloeos – Cape beech
Tarchonanthus trilobus – trident camphor bush

BIRDS

bald ibis
bat hawk
black stork
blackcrowned tchagra
blue crane
chats – buffstreaked, mocking
eagles – African fish, African hawk, bateleur, black, blackbreasted snake, brown snake, crowned, martial, tawny, Wahlberg's
fierynecked nightjar
goshawks – gabar, little banded

greater doublecollared sunbird
grey lourie
ground hornbill
lanner falcon
rameron pigeon
secretarybird
Shelley's francolin
thrushes – groundscraper, kurrichane
vultures – Cape, lappetfaced, whitebacked
whitewinged widow
yellowthroated longclaw

MAMMALS

aardwolf
African civet
African wild cat
antbear (aardvark)
black-backed jackal
blesbok
bushbuck
bushpig
Cape clawless otter
caracal
chacma baboon
common duiker
impala

large-spotted genet
mongooses – slender, water, white-tailed
mountain reedbuck
Natal red rock rabbit
porcupine
rock dassie
scrub hare
steenbok
striped polecat
thick-tailed bushbaby
vervet monkey

OCEAN VIEW GAME PARK

Area: 25 ha
Established: 1970

LOCATION
Central Zululand, Eshowe. At the entrance to Eshowe take the sign "Businesses" to the left. The Ocean View Park sign is on the right just before entering the town.

FEATURES
An area comprising about 10 ha of forest and 15 ha of grassland and scrub with trails. Mammals reintroduced include zebra, blue wildebeest, blesbok and impala. Bushbuck and blue duiker are indigenous to the area. Picnic and braai sites and toilets are provided.

GOEDETROUW PUBLIC RESORT

Area: Unknown
Established: 1976

LOCATION
Central Zululand, Eshowe area, in the Nkwalini valley. Take the Melmoth road north of Eshowe and travel about 13 km. The resort is clearly signposted.

FEATURES
The vegetation consists mainly of acacia woodland and grassland. A number of birds are attracted to the dam, but few mammals occur. There are picnic sites and fishing is popular. A fishing licence is required.

ENTUMENI NATURE RESERVE

Area: 564 ha
Established: 9 July 1970

LOCATION
Central Zululand, Eshowe district, 16 km west of Eshowe on the road to Nkandla.

FEATURES
Coastal scarp forest, containing many rare trees and interesting birds. No facilities are provided as yet. Well worth a day's visit for the interested botanist or birding enthusiast. Permits are obtainable from the KwaZulu Department of Nature Conservation, Ulundi.

DESCRIPTION
A little-known and as yet undeveloped small forest reserve at an altitude of about 650 m. Many magnificent and rare tree species. In parts the undergrowth is dense, with ferns of several species, many ground orchids and shrubs providing good cover for birds. Situated in a sugar cane growing region, it is an important wildlife sanctuary.

HISTORICAL NOTES
It was administered by the Department of Forestry until handed over to the KwaZulu Department of Nature Conservation in 1970.

TREES
Some of the rare and interesting trees and plants are:
Alchornea hirtella var. *glabrata* – Zulu bead-string
Bersama swinnyi – coastal white ash
Brachylaena uniflora – Natal silver oak
Cassipourea gerrardii (*C. malosana*) – common onionwood
Cola natalensis – coshwood
Cryptocarya myrtifolia – myrtle quince
Cryptocarya wyliei – red quince
Cyathea dregei – common tree fern
Drypetes gerrardii – forest ironplum
Encephalartos villosus
Eugenia woodii – mountain myrtle
Garcinia gerrardii – forest mangosteen
Margaritaria discoidea – common pheasant berry
Millettia sutherlandii – giant umzimbeet
Oricia bachmannii – twinberry tree
Rawsonia lucida – forest peach
Rinorea angustifolia – white violet bush
Teclea natalensis – Natal cherry-orange

BIRDS
Delegorgue's pigeon is common in this forest but elsewhere quite rare and poorly known. In the cool, damp forest patches, notable species are:

African broadbill	grey cuckooshrike
black cuckoo	ground hornbill
crowned eagle	Knysna lourie
green coucal	lesser doublecollared sunbird
green twinspot	narina trogon

olive woodpecker
rameron pigeon
redbacked mannikin

spotted thrush
starred robin
yellowstreaked bulbul

MAMMALS

bushbuck
bushpig
Cape clawless otter
duiker – blue, red
large-spotted genet

leopard
mongooses – slender,
   water, white-tailed
vervet monkey

DLINZA FOREST NATURE RESERVE

Area: 200 ha
Established: 8 July 1972

LOCATION
Central Zululand. This reserve borders the Eshowe municipal caravan park, with an entrance next to the Eshowe High School.

FEATURES
A small but interesting patch of indigenous forest, containing magnificent trees, some uncommon bird species and a wealth of insect life. There are trails and picnic sites. Well worth a day visit.

DESCRIPTION
This dense forest contains many species of hardwoods, forest climbers, and dense undergrowth, especially fern species. For this reason it is difficult to find birds that dwell in the lower strata or on the ground. The use of a tape recorder and tapes of calls of coastal forest species is recommended in order to flush them out. There are small grassy glades in and around the forest margins.

HISTORICAL NOTES
The Zulu name has been interpreted by some to mean "the grave-like place of meditation". The main road through a part of the forest was originally cut by British soldiers before the first Anglo-Boer war in 1880-1881. A clearing known as "Bishops Seat" was made by a Bishop Carter for annual children's picnics.

TREES
Some of the trees worth looking for are:
Alchornea hirtella var. *glabrata* – Zulu bead-string
Brachylaena uniflora – Natal silver oak
Bridelia micrantha – mitzeeri
Chaetachme aristata – thorny elm
Chrysophyllum viridifolium – fluted milkwood
Cryptocarya wyliei – red quince
Cussonia sphaerocephala – Natal forest cabbage tree
Cussonia spicata – common cabbage tree
Drypetes gerrardii – forest ironplum
Ficus natalensis – Natal fig
Ficus sur – broom cluster fig
Harpephyllum caffrum – wild plum
Maesa lanceolata – false assegai
Millettia sutherlandii – giant umzimbeet
Oricia bachmannii – twinberry tree
Oxyanthus speciosus – wild loquat
Protorhus longifolia – red beech
Rawsonia lucida – forest peach
Trimeria grandiflora – wild mulberry
Xymalos monospora – lemonwood
Zanthoxylum davyi – knobwood

BIRDS
This forest is a major breeding locality for the spotted thrush, one of our rarest birds, and the yellowstreaked bulbul, also a rare and little-known species. Other birds found locally are:

African broadbill
black sparrowhawk
bush blackcap
cinnamon dove
crowned eagle
crowned hornbill
Delegorgue's pigeon
emerald cuckoo
grassbird
green coucal
green twinspot
grey cuckooshrike
narina trogon
Natal francolin
olive bushshrike
olive woodpecker
plainbacked pipit
redbacked mannikin
robins – brown, chorister
scalythroated honeyguide
thrushes – groundscraper,
    spotted

MAMMALS
As with many forests in Natal, the mammalian fauna has been poorly documented. Although scarce and difficult to see, bushbuck, blue duiker, red duiker, bushpig, large-spotted genet, white-tailed mongoose, water mongoose, slender mongoose and vervet monkeys inhabit this forest.

QUDENI NATURE RESERVE

Area: 2 356 ha
Established: Early 1900s

LOCATION
Central Zululand, Nkandla district. From Eshowe take the Nkandla road through the village. Take the first left turn and continue for 29 km. Turn right at a junction and after 5 km the road enters Qudeni forest.

FEATURES
There are magnificent forest trees, including some uncommon species, and a number of rare forest birds. The forest and its fauna is poorly known and this makes a visit more exciting. At present there are no plans to develop the reserve for tourism.

DESCRIPTION
This large forest is almost at the northernmost limit of the midland mistbelt region of Natal and varies in altitude from the lower regions of semi-coastal forest at 1 100 m to nearly 1 700 m where mostly mixed *Podocarpus* forest predominates. The topography is steep with a number of sloping terraces separated by krantzes. There are many small streams. The forest contains a number of grassland patches of red grass, *Themeda triandra* and Ngongoni bristlegrass *Aristida junciformis*. In the moister parts the ground layer is luxuriant with mosses, liverworts, lichens, ferns and *Streptocarpus* species. In drier areas, ground cover is absent or sparse. Epiphytes are abundant but climbers are less evident. There are thick bramble tangles on the edges of some parts of the forest.

Qudeni means "the place of the rooster". It is so named because of its height – like a rooster towering above hens. It is Zululand's highest range and is occasionally snow clad.

HISTORICAL NOTES
Like other forests in this region, Qudeni has a long history of exploitation. As far back as 1880 there was considerable trade in timber with Natal and the forest was heavily worked. The Qudeni Saw Mill Company established a steam saw mill in about 1897, which was eventually dismantled in 1918. Prior to that, sawyers felled the giant yellowwoods in particular. Many other trees were exploited for their medicinal properties by local Zulus.

The reserve was originally the responsibility of the Department of Forestry, followed by the SA Bantu Trust, before being handed over to the KwaZulu Department of Nature Conservation under Government Notice No 55 of 1992.

TREES

The species diversity in this forest is impressive. Predominant species are:

Apodytes dimidiata subsp. *dimidiata* – wild pear
Burchellia bubalina – wild pomegranate
Calodendrum capense – Cape chestnut
Celtis africana – white stinkwood
Chionanthus peglerae – giant pock ironwood
Combretum kraussii – forest bushwillow
Croton sylvaticus – forest fever-berry
Cryptocarya latifolia – broad-leaved quince
Cryptocarya woodii – Cape quince
Curtisia dentata – assegai
Cussonia sphaerocephala – Natal forest cabbage tree
Faurea macnaughtonii – terblanz beech
Ficus natalensis – strangler fig
Halleria lucida – notsung
Homalium dentatum – brown ironwood
Kiggelaria africana – wild peach
Maytenus penduncularis – Cape blackwood
Ocotea bullata – stinkwood
Olea capensis subsp. *macrocarpa* – black ironwood
Podocarpus falcatus – common yellowwood
Podocarpus latifolius – real yellowwood
Prunus africana – red stinkwood
Ptaeroxylon obliquum – sneezewood
Rapanea melanophloeos – Cape beech
Xymalos monospora – lemonwood
Zanthoxylum davyi – knobwood

BIRDS

Species to be found include:

African goshawk
doves – cinnamon, tambourine
eagles – crowned, martial
green twinspot
Knysna lourie
lesser doublecollared sunbird
narina trogon
olive bush shrike
orange thrush
pigeons – Delegorgue's, rameron
robins – chorister, starred
scrub warbler
sparrowhawks – black, little
yellowthroated warbler

MAMMALS

blue duiker
bushbuck
bushpig
large-spotted genet
monkeys – samango, vervet
tree dassie

NKANDLA FOREST RESERVE

Area: Approximately 2 787 ha
Established: 1992

LOCATION
Central Zululand, Nkandla district. From Eshowe about 50 km along the Nkandla road. The reserve is signposted on the right.

FEATURES
A magnificent tract of indigenous forest, with rare birds. Well worth a day visit for tree and bird enthusiasts. There are no facilities at present.

DESCRIPTION
Situated in the Tugela basin at altitudes from 400-1 300 m, Nkandla, a large tract of coastal scarp forest, shows transitional features to mistbelt mixed *Podocarpus* forest. It consists mostly of steeply undulating country. Soils on the ridges where rock outcrops occur are shallow, with fairly deep soils at the bottom of some of the well-watered valleys. The upper tree canopy is more or less contiguous, but the ground layer, except on the steeper slopes, is poor due in part to the browsing, grazing and trampling by live-stock over decades. The retreating margins of the forest verges and their replacement by grassland and low scrub is due to recurrent hot fires and the depredations of humans and their livestock. The forest is patchy, with glades up to several hectares in extent which are also regularly burned to provide grazing for cattle. In parts where steep cliffs prevent the advance of fire, the undergrowth and forest is dense and inaccessible, with the tree ferns *Cyathea dregei* and *Cyathea capensis* occurring quite commonly. In the moister parts, ground cover includes liverworts, lichens, ferns, *Plectranthus* and *Streptocarpus* species. There are at least 15 species of forest climbers.

HISTORICAL NOTES
Originally protected by the Department of Forestry, this forest was handed to the KwaZulu Department of Nature Conservation and reproclaimed under Government Notice No 37 of 1992. Recent proposals are to combine Nkandla with neighbouring proclaimed areas (Mome, Vungwini, Edodweni, Mndunduzeli, Dlabe and Sibhudeni nature reserves) to give a combined area of 3 792 ha. The whole will probably still be called Nkandla.

Nkandla is one of the traditional forests of the Zulu nation and has significance in their culture. It was here, in the Mome gorge, that Bambatha took refuge from the British in 1906. The forest was frequently used as a refuge in times of trouble. The grave of King Ceteswayo, who died in 1884, can be seen in the Mome gorge.

TREES

Some of the larger trees are:

Brachylaena discolor subsp. *transvaalensis* – forest silver oak
Calodendrum capense – Cape chestnut
Celtis africana – white stinkwood
Combretum kraussii – forest bushwillow
Cryptocarya latifolia – broad-leaved quince
Cussonia sphaerocephala – Natal forest cabbage tree
Faurea macnaughtonii – terblanz beech
Ficus craterostoma – forest fig
Harpephyllum caffrum – wild plum
Homalium dentatum – brown ironwood
Kiggelaria africana – wild peach
Nuxia floribunda – forest elder
Olea capensis subsp. *macrocarpa* – false ironwood
Olinea radiata – Natal hard pear
Podocarpus latifolius – real yellowwood
Ptaeroxylon obliquum – sneezewood
Rapanea melanophloeos – Cape beech
Syzygium gerrardii – forest waterwood
Vepris lanceolata – white ironwood
Zanthoxylum davyi – knobwood

BIRDS

Bird life is typical of this altitude and forest type. For the keen ornithologist, a visit to Nkandla will be a rewarding experience. Species to be found include:

African goshawk
black sparrowhawk
cinnamon dove
eagles – crowned, martial
green twinspot
lesser doublecollared sunbird
narina trogon
olive bush shrike

orange thrush
pigeons – Delegorgue's, rameron
robins – brown, chorister, starred
scrub warbler
yellowthroated warbler

UMFOLOZI GAME RESERVE

Area: 47 753 ha
Established: 27 April 1897

LOCATION

Central Zululand. From the N2 a few kilometres from Mtubatuba take the road signposted Nongoma-Umfolozi Game Reserve. The game reserve turn-off is 27 km along this road on the left.

FEATURES
Umfolozi is best known for its abundance of animals, for game viewing (84 mammal species), birdlife (347 species), its interesting flora, as well as for the stunning views from the comfortable camps over grassed hillsides, bushveld and wooded valleys.

There are many activities for visitors to this prime reserve. These include self-guided walking trails affording excellent views, day walks into the reserve with an experienced guide, and an auto trail traversing 60 km of tourist roads with the aid of a map and explanatory booklet obtainable from the well-appointed curio shop. Night drives with an experienced guide offer a unique opportunity of seeing a variety of animals by spotlight, including seldom seen nocturnal species. With the recently opened road linking Umfolozi via the Corridor to Hluhluwe Game Reserve, it is now easier to explore the whole complex and see a greater variety of scenery and habitat types.

There are game viewing hides at waterholes – ideal for the enthusiastic photographer where many hours can be spent in studying nature. Picnic and braai facilities are located at secluded spots where one can relax and observe the comings and goings of animals to the river below. For the more adventurous, a four day trail through the wilderness area, camping in the tented trail camps, can be enjoyed. During school holidays children's educational camps are offered. For the tourist seeking relaxation and solitude, bush camps are the ideal retreat.

DESCRIPTION
Umfolozi is a reserve of wide, deep valleys and steep hilly country, occupying the foothills of the first escarpment rising from the coastal plain. Altitudes range from 60 m in the river beds and low-lying areas, to over 650 m in the western hills. A number of streams and the two main rivers, the Black and White Mfolozi, drain the hills, the two drainage basins separated by a wedge-shaped watershed, diminishing from about 20 km in width in the west until the two rivers meet at their confluence on the eastern boundary. Both rivers are wide and shallow, the Black Mfolozi having short stretches of sandy bed and numerous outcrops of rock, deep pools and a muddy substrate in comparison to the generally sandy bed of the White Mfolozi. Gradients are gentle and, except in the summer floods when they flow to fill the uDadethu and eMquisweni pans, both rivers are slow flowing. Except for a few impressive krantzes, they have sandy banks.

In May 1957 and July 1963, serious floods changed the character of the Black Mfolozi river and in March 1984 almost all of the huge, magnificent fig trees and other riverine forest species that lined the river banks, were scoured away by the floodwaters of cyclone Demoina. The scars left by the floods can still be seen today.

The main vegetation types comprise riverine vegetation, broadleaf wood-

123

land, acacia woodland, more open acacia savanna, with low-lying thickets and both short and tall grassed areas. A diversity of soil types is responsible for these vegetation changes.

The name "Umfolozi" is a corruption of "mfulawozi", which means "rivers of fibre". This name is derived from the Zulu for *Obetia tenax (Urera tenax)*, a fibrous bush of the nettle family which grows along the banks and is used by the Zulus in mat making.

HISTORICAL NOTES

It is thought that Iron Age communities settled along the coast and in the lower river valleys about 1 500 years ago. Sites in the reserve indicate iron smelting and metal working activities, as well as farming.

The area was later occupied by people of the Mthethwa clan under the Zulu king Dingiswayo until he was killed in 1818. King Shaka, who ruled from 1818 to 1828, conducted one of the biggest hunts in Zululand's history between the two rivers near their junction at iYembene. Game pits dating back to his reign are still visible.

The whole reserve is rich in Zulu history, preserved in the names of the hills and streams. The late Qumbu Magqubu Ntombela worked from the age of 14 in the Umfolozi Game Reserve. He learnt its history orally from his father, his grandparents and the older famous game guards, men like Mali and Mankentshane Mdhletshe. It is on Nqolothi hill that all the Zulu kings from Shaka to Mpande directed the massive elephant hunts.

The discovery of white rhino at the junction of the two Mfolozi rivers in the 1890s, when they were thought to be extinct, led the colonial authorities to proclaim Umfolozi and four other areas the first game reserves in Natal.

Tortuous years lay ahead and the lot of the game conservators was never an easy one. The first game conservator, D Tweedie, was appointed to look after the Ntonjaneni and Hlabisa districts in June 1895. In August 1911 Frederick Vaughan-Kirby was appointed chief conservator. He was known to the Zulus as Mfohloza because he used to wear long khaki trousers which, when he walked through the long grass and heavy dew, made a sound of "fohla-fohla", hence the onomatopoeic Mfohloza. He and his two Zulu guards were assisted in their duties by the Natal police. Stationed at Nongoma, he used to ride out on a motorcycle to visit the as yet unfenced Umfolozi and Hluhluwe reserves.

Thereafter a turbulent period in the history of the reserve began. Neighbouring farmers petitioned the Natal Provincial Administration for the deproclamation of a portion of the reserve. The reason was that an outbreak of nagana, a disease harboured by game and transmitted by tsetse flies, was causing large losses of domestic stock in the area. The farmers were successful and the entire area adjacent to the reserve was opened up in 1916. By 1918 the nearby Ntambanana settlement was opened up for soldiers who had returned from World War I. Any game wandering up to 20 km from the still unfenced reserve were shot. Further outbreaks of nagana occurred among the stock farmers. The Provincial Administration handed the reserve over to the Department of Veterinary Services in 1932, and between then and 1939, the reserve was actually deproclaimed, then reproclaimed and administered by the veterinary authorities until 1952. Records show 26 539 head of game, representing 13 species, destroyed between 1929 and 1950, in the game reserve and to the south. Between 1942 and 1950 a further 70 332 head of game of some 16 species were killed in Umfolozi Game Reserve and on the adjoining state lands. Only rhino were spared. Between 1945 and 1947, Umfolozi Game Reserve was again deproclaimed, then reproclaimed. It was not until 1952 that the veterinary department handed control of the reserve to the relatively new Natal Parks Board (established in 1947). By then there were few animals remaining. Thereafter the intensity of game extermination, as a means of eradicating the remainder of the disease, decreased. Instead, aerial spraying with the insecticides DDT and BHC commenced. This continued till August 1951 and was effective in eliminating tsetse flies and nagana.

It was not until 1953 that the first Natal Parks Board ranger was appointed. The first permanent house in the reserve was only built in 1957 and occupied by Ian Player and his family. The first huts at Mpila camp were opened to the public in 1958. The camp superintendent was John Kinloch and the ranger in charge of the southern crownlands was Nick Steele. The senior game guard was Magqubu Ntombela.

The wilderness area was set aside by regulation and on 19 March 1959 the first wilderness trail took place, led by Magqubu Ntombela and Ian Player. This was the beginning of a new era in wildlife conservation in Zululand. Soon people were being taken out by selected, experienced staff who could impart their knowledge over the three days and nights spent roaming the reserve on foot, sleeping out under the stars and experiencing the value of true wilderness. This concept grew and spread to other regions. It led eventually to the formation of the Wilderness Leadership School. The movement spread to other countries and culminated in World Wilderness Congresses being held in several countries over the following years.

Umfolozi Game Reserve was not yet allowed to remain in peace though, for over the following years large bands of poachers, armed with assegais, knobsticks, pangas, and some with firearms, made poaching forays into the reserve with their dogs. There were only two or three guards in remote areas. Numerous skirmishes with the small bands of patrolling game rangers and game guards occurred and some guards paid the supreme sacrifice in the cause of conservation.

Until 1962, there was no fence of any kind around Umfolozi Game Reserve. The allocation of parts of the state-owned land to the reserve in that year allowed a start to be made in rectifying this problem. Over the preceding years, squatters had moved into certain game reserve areas and, without a fence, there had been nothing to stop them. Game was still able to move out of the reserve and bands of poachers continued coming in. The erection of fences, as well as diplomatic negotiations by parks board staff with local chiefs, gradually resolved these problems to a large extent. Once a sufficient area of the reserve had been fenced, a number of game species were reintroduced, among them lion, cheetah and giraffe. Elephant were reintroduced from 1981 onwards.

In 1960, the Natal Parks Board decided that it was unwise to risk maintaining all its white rhino – an animal once on the very brink of extinction in southern Africa but now increasing in numbers – in Umfolozi and Hluhluwe game reserves. "Operation Rhino" was born. Under the dynamic leadership of Ian Player and with a dedicated team of workers, backed by Col Jack Vincent, director of the Natal Parks Board, and with the assistance of Dr Toni Harthoorn, a veterinary researcher, one of the most successful and dramatic conservation exercises of all time commenced in the Umfolozi Game Reserve. Up to 1988 more than 3 300 white rhino were successfully translocated to other game reserves and zoos all over the world, thus ensuring the survival of the species. In recent years, as populations of black rhino have come under pressure from poachers all over Africa, the Natal Parks Board has stepped up its efforts to distribute these animals to ensure the survival of this species as well.

ACCOMMODATION
There are two main camps. Mpila consists of twelve fully serviced, three-bedded huts in two groups of six. Each group of huts is serviced by a communal kitchen, in which meals are prepared by experienced cooks, and has a communal ablution block. There are six, five-bedded chalets, each with two bedrooms, lounge-diningroom, bathroom, toilet and kitchenette. Linen is provided. These are self-contained and serviced but visitors do their own cooking. (Cutlery, crockery, stove and a refrigerator are provided.)

A second hutted camp, Masinda, is situated 7 km from the Mambeni entrance gate. There are six, three-bedded huts and one six-bedded lodge. This has three bedrooms, two bathrooms, one of them en suite, and sleeps six persons. It also has a two-bedded flatlet, which can serve as accommodation for couriers or drivers. The services of a cook are provided and the lodge is sited in a secluded spot well away from the main camp. There are also two seven-bedded cottages, similarly fully furnished and equipped, with cooks in attendance.

Two bush camps, Sontuli and Nselweni, are situated on the banks of the Black Mfolozi river. Built of poles, reeds and thatch, these offer the tourist a more intimate experience of the bush. They are fully equipped, although visitors do their own cooking.

The Mdindini trails camp is also available as a bush camp between December and February.

Visitors supply their own food and drink. Reservations are made with the Natal Parks Board, Pietermaritzburg.

TREES
Acacia caffra – common hook-thorn
Acacia gerrardii – red thorn

Acacia karroo – sweet thorn
Acacia nigrescens – knobthorn
Acacia nilotica – scented thorn
Acacia robusta – ankle thorn
Acacia tortilis – umbrella thorn
Acalypha glabrata – forest false-nettle
Azima tetracantha – needle bush
Brachylaena ilicifolia – small bitter-leaf
Cadaba natalensis – Natal worm bush
Cassine transvaalensis – Transvaal saffron berry
Combretum hereroense – russet bushwillow
Croton gratissimus – lavender fever-berry
Cussonia zuluensis – Zulu cabbage tree
Diospyros lycioides – Karoo bluebush
Ehretia rigida – puzzle bush
Euphorbia grandidens – valley-bush euphorbia
Ficus abutilifolia – large-leaved rock fig
Ficus glumosa – mountain fig
Ficus ingens – red-leaved fig
Ficus stuhlmannii – lowveld fig
Galpinia transvaalica – Transvaal privet
Gardenia volkensii – Transvaal gardenia
Manilkara concolor – Zulu milkberry
Ochna natalitia – Natal plane
Ormocarpum trichocarpum – curled caterpillar bush
Schotia brachypetala – weeping boer-bean/tree fuschia
Schotia capitata – dwarf boer-bean
Sideroxylon inerme – white milkwood
Strychnos madagascariensis – black monkey orange
Terminalia phanerophlebia – Lebombo cluster-leaf
Ziziphus mucronata – buffalo thorn

BIRDS (347 species recorded)

bald ibis
bearded robin
bronzewinged courser
brownheaded parrot
Cape vulture
corncrake
cranes – blue, crowned
cuckoos – great spotted, Jacobin
dwarf bittern
finches – cutthroat, melba
francolins – Shelley's, Swainson's
gabar goshawk
ground hornbill

hawks – bat, cuckoo
herons – rufousbellied,
   whitebacked night
honey buzzard
Jameson's firefinch
knobbilled duck
larks – chestnutbacked, sabota
lemonbreasted canary
olive thrush
owls – giant eagle, Pel's fishing
oxpeckers – redbilled, yellowbilled
purple roller
pygmy goose

sharpbilled honeyguide
sooty falcon
South African shelduck
sparrowhawks – black, little
Stanley's bustard

storks – black, openbilled,
    saddlebilled, woollynecked
vultures – lappetfaced, white-
    backed, whiteheaded
white helmetshrike

There are a large number of eagles:
African fish, African hawk, bateleur, black, blackbreasted snake, booted, brown snake, crowned, lesserspotted, longcrested, martial, southern banded snake, steppe, tawny, Wahlberg's.

MAMMALS (84 species)
The species likely to be seen, excluding small mice, rats, shrews and bats are:

antbear (aardvark)
aardwolf
black-backed jackal
blue wildebeest
buffalo
bushbuck
chacma baboon
cheetah
clawless otter
duiker – common, red
elephant
giraffe
greater canerat
hippo
honey badger
impala
klipspringer
kudu
large-spotted genet
leopard

lion
mongooses – banded, slender, water,
    white-tailed
mountain reedbuck
nyala
porcupine
reedbuck
rhinoceros – black, white
scrub hare
serval
spotted hyaena
steenbok
striped polecat
thick-tailed bushbaby
vervet monkey
warthog
waterbuck
wild dog
zebra

HLUHLUWE GAME RESERVE

Area: 23 067 ha
Established: 27 April 1897

LOCATION
Central Zululand. From the north, leave the N2 at the Hluhluwe off-ramp. At the stop street turn right and cross over the freeway, follow this tar road for about 14 km to the Memorial Gate, the northern entrance to the reserve.

From the south, turn left off the N2 about 3,4 km past the first Mtubatuba exit, at a roadsign which reads Nongoma-Umfolozi Game Reserve. Turn off to Hluhluwe Game Reserve to the right about 17 km along this road, onto a gravel road leading to the Gunjaneni southern entrance gate. It is well sign-posted. A new entrance road, turning off further on in the "Corridor" is presently under construction.

FEATURES

Not only is Hluhluwe one of the three oldest proclaimed game reserves in Africa, but it is also the most famous of Natal's reserves. Hluhluwe is noted for its scenic views. From the Hilltop camp on a clear day one can see across grassy hillsides and deep wooded valleys to the distant coastal dunes of Lake St Lucia's eastern shores.

Hluhluwe is home to a wide variety of trees and one of the finest examples of coastal scarp forest in Natal covers the higher hilly slopes. It is an area rich in fauna, with 86 mammals, including elephant, black and white rhino, lion, buffalo, leopard, cheetah and wild dogs. There are about 340 bird, 55 reptile, 4 chelonian, 26 amphibian and 21 fish species occurring within its boundaries. Visitors can cover some 96 km of tourist roads on game viewing drives. Auto trails can be followed with the aid of information booklets (obtainable at the reception centre), detailing numerous points of interest dealing with geology, ecology, fauna and flora. A ranger-naturalist is also available to provide information. Film and slide shows are periodically shown. Short self-guided walks are available and longer walks guided by a game guard may be booked at certain times of the year. There are attractive picnic sites with benches, tables, braai grids and ablution facilities. An attractive game viewing hide overlooking a waterhole can also be visited as a break from game viewing drives.

In the Hilltop camp the new "Mpunyane Restaurant", with spectacular views over the game reserve, caters for all tastes and offers unusual game dishes. A comfortable bar/lounge provides a pleasant and relaxing venue for sundowners after a day's game viewing. A well-stocked curio shop is also available. New luxurious units offer spacious, comfortable bedrooms and wide, cool verandas. An exciting part of staying at the Hilltop camp is the night sounds of lion, zebra, owls, nightjars, the distant barks of a pack of jackals on the hunt, or the eerie howl of a prowling hyaena passing close by.

DESCRIPTION

Hluhluwe is notable in that it contains within its boundaries most of the rock series found in Natal. The subsequent erosion of these over millions of years has produced a great variety of soils and allowed the growth of many plant species. The topography is rugged in parts and altitudes range from below 80 m to 540 m on the high ridges. These ridges support tall semi-deciduous trees in coastal scarp forests, in parts quite rich in ferns, mosses, lichens and orchid species. In general the reserve is well watered. Numerous tiny streams originate from the steep slopes. The principal river is the Hluhluwe which rises in the Nongoma district, flows through the game reserve, and then runs into False Bay in the Lake St Lucia complex. Its main tributaries are the smaller, seasonal Nzimane and the Manzimbomvo.

The Hluhluwe is a narrow river consisting of a series of deep, elongated rock pools, separated by sandbanks and rock beds and outcrops, with some quite steep krantzes on the upper reaches. Along much of its course it is overhung by riparian forest vegetation. It ceases flowing during the dry season but the succession of pools retain water. The deep, wide water at the picnic site is caused by backing up from the Hluhluwe dam outside the reserve's eastern boundary.

The lower-lying valleys comprise thickets of mixed scrub and woodland where acacia species, such as black monkey thorn *Acacia burkei*, common hook-thorn *A. caffra*, sweet thorn *A. karroo*, knobthorn *A. nigrescens*, scented thorn *A. nilotica*, ankle thorn *A. robusta* and umbrella thorn *A. tortilis* dominate. Small, shallow pans which hold water for short periods are scattered throughout the reserve on the low-lying flats.

On the higher ground there are tracts of bushveld. The slopes and crests of the many hills are mostly well grassed and sparsely vegetated. The principal grass species found from the deep valleys up to the hilltops include redgrass *Themeda*, lovegrass *Eragrostis* species, panic grass *Panicum* species, fingergrass *Digitaria* species, thatchgrass *Hyparrhenia* species and turpentine grass *Cymbopogon* species.

The reserve derives its name from the thorny rope liana *Dalbergia armata*, or "iHluhluwe", as it is known to the Zulus.

HISTORICAL NOTES

Nowadays, few visitors arriving in their air-conditioned vehicles on a good tar road ever stop to read the brass plaque at Hluhluwe's northern Memorial Gate entrance. This plaque commemorates Captain HB Potter, Mr William M Power and Mr AE Charter, three outstanding personalities in Natal's conservation history.

William Power, a former member of the Provincial Executive Committee, along with Mr Douglas Mitchell, also an MEC and later an administrator of the province, were the architects behind the formation of the Natal Parks Board in 1947. Mr AE Charter was a former provincial secretary who also did much for conservation in the early years. (Charter's Creek camp was named after him.) Capt HB Potter was appointed Zululand's Conservator of Game in 1929 and was the father of Hluhluwe Game Reserve.

The first resident white ranger appointed to this reserve was Mr Edward Lightening, who took up residence at the site of the present Hilltop camp in 1927. He later moved to the Gontshi area. Next was Capt Harold B Potter, also appointed by the Natal Provincial Administration to care for Zululand's game reserves. After a month with RHTP Harris, who invented the famous "Harris fly trap" for eradicating tsetse flies and resided in the Umfolozi Game Reserve, Capt Potter moved to pitch his tent at Hilltop in August 1929. The provincial authorities wanted him to reside at Nongoma, where game conservator Vaughan-Kirby had lived. However, Potter was adamant that to be able to effectively control poaching, as well as develop and manage Hluhluwe, he had to live there.

In those early years the only access to the reserve was along footpaths made by the many Zulus who lived there and along game trails. By 1930, Potter had built a four-bedroomed house from local timber and thatch grass bound on with bark. The floors were of mud, stones and cowdung, highly polished with leaves. He used some materials scrounged from discarded Harris fly traps and a total of fifty pounds was spent on nails and window panes. To his dismay, the provincial authorities were aghast that he had built this structure on provincial land without official permission. He eventually had to procure invoices from Holmes' store in distant Mtubatuba before they would recompense him for this unlawful expenditure. The authorities apparently expected him to live indefinitely in a flimsy tent, through all kinds of weather conditions, often surrounded by buffalo and with rhino at times uprooting the tent pegs. By the end of 1930, the house was completed and his wife and children joined him. It had been a lonely year with only Edward Lightening and four locally recruited Zulus, whom he trained as game guards, as occasional company. The arrival of his wife and children was a pioneering event as well. They were driven up by the Mtubatuba store owner Mr Eric Holmes in the first motor vehicle ever to enter the game reserve.

Potter, who was christened "Mtwazi" by the locals after a type of monkey-rope or liana, because he was tall, lean and wiry, set to work to lay out a network of roads in the reserve. He and his small but dedicated staff fought a relentless battle against poachers, camping out at night in all parts of the reserve in order to intercept and apprehend the culprits entering at daybreak. He would light a fire at night wherever he was camped so that his wife could look out from her lonely house on the hilltop, scan the blackness, and know that all was well when she saw his fire.

Visitors started pouring into Hluhluwe in the early 1930s and between 1935-6, when the first cottages were completed, many famous visitors, both local and overseas, journeyed to see this magnificent reserve and to meet the legendary Capt Potter, who, with his charming wife, acted as host to many of them.

In 1942, because of the threat of nagana, the disease that killed cattle and was transmitted by tsetse flies, it was decided to eradicate thousands of head of game, except rhinoceroses, in order to eliminate this threat to an ever increasing number of stock farmers in Zululand. While game species harboured the parasites, they were immune to the disease. "Abolish the game reserves and exterminate all the animals within them", was the demand voiced by the Zululand farmers. Commencing in 1942, it was decided to clear a tract of bush and scrub from 500 m to 8 km in width along the eastern and northern boundaries of Hluhluwe Game Reserve as a fly-free buffer zone between the reserve and white farming settlements. Thousands of head of game were slaughtered to eliminate the harbourers of the parasite. This measure, along with the use of Harris fly traps, and even "bait cattle", with attendants who hand-captured the dreaded flies as they alighted on the beasts for a blood meal, were methods employed to exterminate the tsetse flies.

In 1945, the large-scale aerial spraying of the reserve with the deadly insecticides DDT and BHC commenced and this was continued until the flies had been eradicated by 1952.

Capt HB Potter retired from his post on 1 August 1950. He died on 17 January 1956. Today's visitors can thank him for his tenacity and determination in developing this world-famous reserve. He was succeeded by his son Peter, born and brought up at Hilltop, who continued in his father's footsteps in further developing Hluhluwe. As Chief Conservator for game in Zululand, he was instrumental in developing many other reserves. He retired as Deputy-Director of the Natal Parks Board after 38 years of unbroken service. He died on 10 December 1993.

Hluhluwe is the birthplace of conservation in Natal. The first rest camp, still in existence, was built in this reserve. The first herbarium and field laboratory was established under the direction of the ecologist CJ "Roddy" Ward. Wildlife research and game management techniques were initiated in Hluhluwe, and the present Game Capture Unit pioneered many of their successful techniques in Hluhluwe.

We have scant knowledge of human's past occupation of the area. Recent evidence suggests that parts of the reserve were settled by man about 1 500 years ago. Iron Age sites and fragments of pottery indicate that in the distant past the principal activity was iron smelting.

There is a notable "isivivane" on the southern entrance road into the reserve. This cairn of stones is believed to have marked the territorial boundaries of early tribes. It was believed that for good luck passing travellers should add a stone to the cairn as they passed. The exact origin of this custom is uncertain.

ACCOMMODATION

Mtwazi Lodge consists of three bedrooms, each with an en suite bathroom and can accommodate six persons. An annexe provides an additional three beds. This lodge is fully furnished and equipped and fully serviced. There is also a cook.

The original camp contains four six-bedded (two bedroomed) entirely self-contained cottages, and 20 two-bedded rest huts. Separate kitchens and ablution blocks are provided for them.

There are new luxurious units in the Hilltop camp. Seven two-bedded chalets and 22 four-bedded chalets have recently been opened. Each has a pullout bed for an extra guest. Full catering is provided.

Tour groups are catered for with 20 exclusive units, each offering tea and coffee facilities and a bar fridge. The conveniences of a restaurant, superette, curio shop, interpretation centre and petrol station have also been provided. Reservations should be made with the Natal Parks Board, Pietermaritzburg.

TREES

Acacia karroo – sweet thorn
Albizia suluensis – Zulu false thorn
Aloe barberiae (*A. bainesii*) – tree aloe
Berchemia zeyheri – red ivory
Calodendrum capense – Cape chestnut
Combretum molle – velvet bushwillow
Commiphora harveyi – red-stem corkwood
Croton sylvaticus – forest fever-berry
Cussonia natalensis – rock cabbage tree
Dalbergia armata – thorny rope
Dichrostachys cinerea – sickle bush
Englerophytum natalense (Bequaertiodendron natalense) – Natal milkplum
Erythrina lysystemon – common coral tree
Euclea racemosa subsp. *zuluensis (E. schimperi)* – bush guarri
Ficus natalensis – Natal fig
Gardenia cornuta – Natal gardenia
Harpephyllum caffrum – wild plum
Kigelia africana – sausage tree
Pancovia golungensis – false soap-berry
Rauvolfia caffra – quinine tree
Schotia brachypetala – weeping boer-bean
Sideroxylon inerme – white milkwood
Strychnos spinosa – green monkey orange
Trichilia dregeana – forest mahogany
Warburgia salutaris – pepperbark tree
Ximenia caffra – Natal sourplum

BIRDS (340 species)

African finfoot
African marsh harrier
black crake
blackbellied korhaan
blue quail
bluemantled flycatcher
buffspotted flufftail
bully canary
chestnutbacked finchlark
coucals – black, Burchell's
cutthroat finch
eagles – blackbreasted snake, tawny
European roller
fantailed cisticola
freckled nightjar
gorgeous bush shrike

grass owl
great spotted cuckoo
greenbacked heron
grey penduline tit
ground hornbill
malachite kingfisher
marico sunbird
orangebreasted waxbill
peregrine falcon
pigeons – Delegorgue's, green, rameron, rock
plumcoloured starling
redfaced cisticola
redthroated wryneck
redwinged starling
rock martin

starred robin
tchagra
trumpeter hornbill

vultures – lappetfaced,
   whiteheaded
whitebacked night heron
whitefronted bee-eater

MAMMALS (84 species)

antbear (aardvark)
blue wildebeest
buffalo
bushbuck
bushpig
chacma baboon
cheetah
duiker – blue, common, red
elephant
giraffe
greater canerat
hippo
honey badger
impala
kudu
large-spotted genet
leopard
lion

mongooses – banded, slender,
   water, white-tailed
monkeys – samango, vervet
mountain reedbuck
nyala
pangolin
porcupine
reedbuck
rhinoceros – black, white
scrub hare
serval
spotted hyaena
steenbok
thick-tailed bushbaby
warthog
waterbuck
wild dog
zebra

REPTILES (67 species)

The venomous reptiles are: forest cobra, blacknecked cobra, black mamba, puff adder, boomslang and vine snake. Nile crocodiles occur in the Hluhluwe river and both species of monitor lizards may be encountered.

OPATHE GAME RESERVE

Area: 8 825 ha
Established: 1991

LOCATION

Central Zululand, near Ulundi on the Ulundi-Melmoth road.

FEATURES

This is a new reserve, not yet open to the public. (See under historical notes and description.) Future plans include building a lodge, bush camps, a camping-caravan site, trail camps and facilities for day visitors who will be able to go on game viewing drives. Enquiries to KwaZulu Department of Nature Conservation, Ulundi.

DESCRIPTION
It is very rugged country, stretching from the White Mfolozi river to the upper regions of the Mtonjaneni Heights. The vegetation varies from bushveld dominated by acacia species, to mistbelt and highveld, including many spectacular krantzes with orchid and cycad colonies.

The reserve has only recently been fenced and a full inventory of the vegetation and habitat types has not yet been completed.

HISTORICAL NOTES
The new reserve was one of the major projects of the KwaZulu Department of Nature Conservation, and is situated only a few kilometres from Ulundi. It is located in the heartland of Zulu history, at the north-eastern end of the Valley of the Kings (eMakosini). Opathe means "where an ambush has occurred". It is extraordinarily well positioned for anyone who wishes to visit Zulu historical sites. Four wars were fought in this area and more than 68 battlefields lie between Eshowe and Vryheid. The land was, until recently, five separate cattle ranches.

BIRDS
A preliminary list includes:

blackcollared barbet
blue waxbill
buzzards – jackal, steppe
Cape vulture
dark chanting goshawk
eagles – African hawk, bateleur,
   black, crowned, longcrested,
   martial, tawny
francolins – coqui, crested
glossy ibis

ground hornbill
gymnogene
kingfishers – giant, pygmy,
   woodland
orangethroated longclaw
plumcoloured starling
purplecrested lourie
secretarybird
storks – black, white
trumpeter hornbill

MAMMALS
Recorded to date:

antbear (aardvark)
bushbuck
bushpig
chacma baboon
common duiker
impala
klipspringer
leopard
mongooses – banded, slender,
   white-tailed

mountain reedbuck
nyala
porcupine
reedbuck
spotted hyaena
steenbok
thick-tailed bushbaby
vervet monkey

There are plans to reintroduce major species such as white and black rhino, giraffe, kudu and other species suited to these habitats.

REPTILES
Interesting reptiles recorded are:

black mamba	Mozambique spitting cobra
boomslang	Natal rock python
eastern tiger snake	rinkhals
monitor lizards – Nile or water, rock	southern vine snake

UBIZANE GAME RANCH

Area: 1 200 ha
Established: 1964

LOCATION
Central Zululand, Hluhluwe district. From the N2 take the road signposted Hluhluwe Game Reserve. Follow this road for about 6 km to the game ranch. The route is clearly signposted.

FEATURES
There are open vehicle game and bird spotting drives within the reserve and night spotlight drives. Ubizane is well stocked with game and visitors generally see a number of species. Day visitors are welcome to participate in the game viewing drives when light lunches are served. Daily walking trails with an experienced guide can be arranged as well as "bush braais". There are also closed vehicle trips in a microbus to either Hluhluwe, Umfolozi or Mkuzi game reserves, or open vehicle drives (4x4 landcruiser) into Hluhluwe Game Reserve.

DESCRIPTION
The terrain ranges from open savanna to bushveld with some large trees and rocky hills. There are a number of small natural pans and smaller water holes. The Mzinene river flows through the property and a large dam has been built. A dense forest of fever trees lines the banks of this river.

HISTORICAL NOTES
Ubizane was originally a cattle ranch but was converted to a game ranch in 1964. It is one of two in Natal which have been operating for 30 years. It is named after a prominent hill within the reserve, from which the Zulus called the surrounding community to meetings in earlier times. The translation of "Ubizane" is "a place from which to call the people".

ACCOMMODATION
Ubizane offers two types of accommodation. One is a traditional Zulu beehive-hutted camp, which can hold 40 persons. Visitors must bring their

own food and drink and cook for themselves. The other is an exclusive luxury forest lodge, consisting of six twin-bedded log cabins with en suite shower, toilets and basins. Each cabin is built on stilts with its own private veranda and overlooks a dense fever tree forest, which is floodlit at night. The maximum number of guests that can be accommodated at the lodge is 14 per night. All meals are provided but guests must bring their own drinks. A small boma offers braai (barbecue) facilities and an open-sided catering and recreation cabin, also on stilts, completes the camp. From the camp it is possible to see a variety of game grazing on the lawns. Reservations should be made with the game ranch.

TREES
Acacia burkei – black monkey thorn
Acacia nigrescens – knobthorn
Acacia nilotica – scented thorn
Acacia robusta – brack thorn
Acacia tortilis – umbrella thorn
Acacia xanthophloea – fever tree
Dichrostachys cinerea – sickle bush
Euphorbia ingens – common tree euphorbia
Ficus sur – broom cluster fig
Hyphaene coriacea – lala palm
Sclerocarya birrea subsp. *caffra* – marula
Trichelia emetica – Natal mahogany
Ziziphus mucronata – buffalo thorn

BIRDS
blackbellied korhaan
blackshouldered kite
blue waxbill
Burchell's coucal
crested guineafowl
eagles – brown snake, crowned, martial
European bee-eater
European roller
giant kingfisher
gymnogene
narina trogon
openbilled stork
purplecrested lourie
redbilled woodhoopoe
secretarybird
spotted dikkop
spotted eagle owl
trumpeter hornbill
vultures – Cape, whitebacked

MAMMALS
antbear (aardvark)
black-backed jackal
blesbok
blue wildebeest
bushpig
duiker – common, red
giraffe
hippo
hyaena
impala
kudu
large-spotted genet
leopard
mongooses – banded, white-tailed

nyala	warthog
reedbuck	waterbuck
suni	white rhino
thick-tailed bushbaby	zebra
vervet monkey	

REPTILES

African rock python	Nile crocodile
boomslang	puff adder
cobras – forest, Mozambique spitting	small lizards, geckoes and
mambas – black, green	skinks
monitor lizard	vine snake

BUSHLANDS LODGE – ZULULAND SAFARIS

Area: 300 ha
Established: 1967

LOCATION

Central Zululand, Bushlands. From the N2 north of Mtubatuba and south of Hluhluwe, take the Bushlands off-ramp from where the route is signposted. It is 4 km to the entrance gate.

FEATURES

The accommodation complex is situated in sand forest containing game and a variety of birds. There is a restaurant, serving four-course meals including venison dishes, a bar and a swimming pool. All units are fully serviced. It is the only lodge in the country owned by a touring company (Zululand Safaris), who offer transportation from all the main centres to the area. They arrange pick-ups in Kruger Park, Swaziland, Durban and Ulundi. Guests are also taken on game drives by experienced guides to the surrounding game reserves of Hluhluwe, Umfolozi, Mkuzi and Lake St Lucia. This park caters almost exclusively for overseas guests and offers luxury accommodation inclusive of meals.

DESCRIPTION

An area comprising typical Zululand savanna, acacia veld, woodland and sand forest, with a number of interesting trees and shrubs.

ACCOMMODATION

A lodge on stilts high above the ground. Each unit is inter-connected by raised wooden walkways. Accommodation units comprise 20 chalets, each with two beds and en suite bathrooms, luxuriously furnished to cater for the international market. Reservations are made with the game lodge manager.

BIRDS
Over 120 species recorded.

FAUNA
All plains game and antelope species occurring in Zululand. None of the "big five".

BONAMANZI GAME PARK

Area: 4 000 ha
Established: 1971

LOCATION
Central Zululand, Hluhluwe. From the N2 take the Hluhluwe village off-ramp. Cross the bridge and drive down through Hluhluwe village towards the railway station. Turn right and drive about 5 km to the Bonamanzi sign-post on the left. It is a further 5 km to the entrance gate.

FEATURES
Attractive luxury treehouses, a tree lodge, a game lodge used by hunting parties and 10 units for accommodating larger groups. A fully equipped conference centre is available for 20 guests with accommodation and dining facilities catering for all meals. All accommodation is sited amid shade trees and giant lala palms.

The reserve is zoned for recreational activities. There are a number of trails and guests may explore Bonamanzi day and night by car or on foot. There is a "walking only" wilderness area.

Hunting is catered for in a designated area for 21 species of game and certain bird species. The nature of the terrain lends itself to different methods of hunting. The use of crossbows and handguns is permitted in the northern hunting area of Mkuzi as well, with top class trophies being regularly taken. The services of an experienced professional hunter, tracker and skinners are offered and the skinning and field preparation of trophies is undertaken. Photographic safaris for up to four persons over a minimum of four days are offered and tariffs, as for hunters, include transport to and from Richards Bay airport, daily transport, accommodation, full catering and entrance fees to all reserves visited.

Bonamanzi is ideally situated within an hour's drive of Mkuzi, Hluhluwe and Umfolozi game reserves and the coastal and lake resorts of St Lucia.

DESCRIPTION

Grassland with stands of lala palms, open woodland with large shade trees, thicket and acacia-dominated veld are the main habitats of this park. The area is low lying and water is limited to three large pans. There are good views over Hell's Gates, False Bay and Lake St Lucia proper, east of the park. The name "Bona Manzi" means "see the water".

ACCOMMODATION

Bonamanzi offers treehouses nestling high in the foliage of coastal sand forest. Each isolated unit has two double bedrooms that lead off a viewing veranda with a private view. Beneath the treehouse platform is a kitchenette, braai area, toilet and shower with hot and cold water. The treehouses are equipped with electric lights, gas cooker and fridge and supplied with linen, crockery, cutlery and cooking utensils. Guests bring their own food and drinks. Reservations should be made with the game park itself.

The Tree Lodge has wonderful views of Lake St Lucia and accommodates up to 8 persons. It has three luxury, air-conditioned bedrooms en suite, each with its own balcony. An open walkway leads to the air-conditioned lounge which is comfortably furnished and has a pull-out sleeper couch for two. Sliding doors open onto the treetop veranda and the view of the lake. The fully equipped modern kitchen includes a coffee machine, toaster and two fridges. A maid or cook can be hired at a reasonable charge.

The Game Lodge offers accommodation for up to six guests. It has two air-conditioned double bedrooms with en suite showers, as well as two single rooms and a bathroom and shower, a fully equipped modern kitchen and an open plan dining and lounge area. The lodge overlooks a waterhole with good views of various animal and bird species coming down to drink in the early mornings and afternoons. There is also a private swimming pool. Lodge visitors have the option of self-catering, as all crockery, cutlery, cooking utensils and kitchen appliances are provided, or they can arrange to have a full service provided.

The Lalapanzi camp is a complex of thatched huts that provides for families or groups. All the huts offer double bedroom comfort with en suite bathroom and electricity. These huts face onto a picturesque dam and are served by a communal dining area that towers over the water's edge. Each unit has its own fridge and grocery cupboard. The dining area is fully equipped with cookers, utensils, cutlery and crockery. Braai facilities are provided. These are self-catering units and guests bring their own food and drinks. The camp has its own swimming pool surrounded by lawns, lala palms and shade trees.

TREES

Acacia burkei – black monkey thorn
Acacia nilotica – scented thorn
Acacia robusta – ankle thorn

Acacia tortilis – umbrella thorn
Acacia xanthophloea – fever tree
Albizia adianthifolia – flat-crown
Antidesma venosum – tassel berry
Balanites maughamii – torchwood
Brachylaena discolor – coast silver oak
Cassine aethiopica – koo-boo berry
Chaetachme aristata – thorny elm
Dialium schlechteri – Zulu podberry
Euphorbia ingens – common tree euphorbia
Ficus stuhlmannii – lowveld fig
Hyphaene coriacea – lala palm
Kigelia africana – sausage tree
Rhus queinzii – thorny karree
Schotia brachypetala – weeping boer-bean/tree fuschia
Sclerocarya birrea subsp. *caffra* – marula
Spirostachys africana – tamboti
Tabernaemontana elegans – toad tree
Trichilia emetica – Natal mahogany
Vepris lanceolata – white ironwood
Zanthoxylum capense – small knobwood
Ziziphus mucronata – buffalo thorn

BIRDS (over 300 species)

black crake
black cuckooshrike
blackbellied korhaan
brownheaded parrot
crested guineafowl
crowned hornbill
eagles – African fish, Ayres',
    bateleur, longcrested, tawny,
    Wahlberg's
fiscal flycatcher
giant kingfisher
lemonbreasted canary
lesser honeyguide
little bee-eater
narina trogon

nightjars – fierynecked, Natal
orangebreasted bush shrike
palm swift
purplebanded sunbird
pygmy goose
redbilled quelea
scimitarbilled woodhoopoe
wattled plover
white helmetshrike
whiteheaded vulture
whitethroated robin
woollynecked stork
yellowspotted nicator
yellowthroated longclaw

FAUNA

antbear (aardvark)
banded mongoose
blesbok
blue wildebeest
bushbuck

bushpig
duiker – common, red
giraffe
hippo
impala

kudu
large-spotted genet
leopard
nyala
red hartebeest
red squirrel
reedbuck
serval
slender mongoose

steenbok
suni
thick-tailed bushbaby
vervet monkey
warthog
waterbuck
white rhino
zebra

THE GREATER ST LUCIA WETLAND PARK

Area: 259 644 ha
Established: 27 April 1897, with several additional areas from 1897-1992

LOCATION
Central Zululand coastal, extending from the St Lucia estuary for over 60 km northwards. Access is via the N2, past Mtubatuba and 29 kilometres to St Lucia village, or off the N2 to Charter's Creek, Fanie's Island and False Bay Park, all well signposted.

FEATURES
For the full range of facilities and features of the St Lucia complex, see the following headings: False Bay Park, Fanie's Island, Charters' Creek, St Lucia Public Resort, St Lucia Crocodile Centre-Game Park, Mission Rocks, Cape Vidal-Bhangazi South and Eastern Shores State Forest and Nature Reserve.

DESCRIPTION
Lake St Lucia is the largest estuarine lake system in Africa. It is approximately 40 km long, on average 3-8 km wide, with a maximum width of about 21 km. It is made up of several self-contained but adjoining compartments of water, dotted with small to large grassed or reeded islands. The average depth is little more than 1 m, with the deeper zones less than 3 m.

The system is fed by the Mkuze river in the north, the Mzinene, Nyalazi and Hluhluwe rivers and some smaller rivers and streams, such as the Mbazwane, Nkazama and the Mpate.

Seepage from the high vegetated dune forests, vleis and wetlands along its eastern shores is an important addition to the water supply of the system. The lake forms a rough H shape, the western limb of which is False Bay and the imaginary crossbar, a strait known as Hell's Gates, generally quite deep. The main body of the lake is divided by a large expanse of reeded islands (Fanie's islands) resulting in a northern and southern body

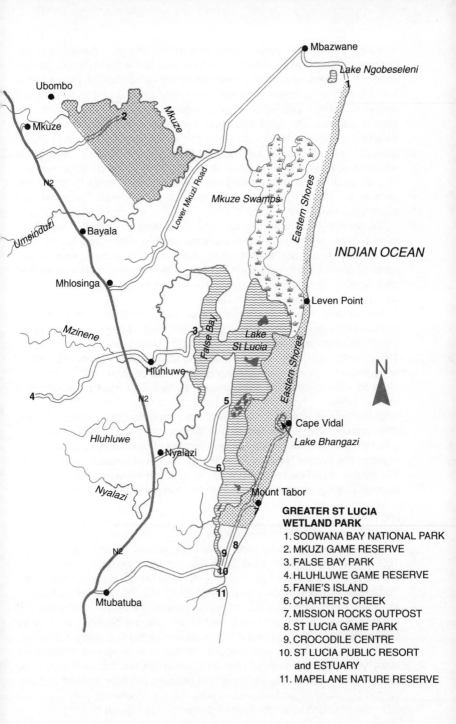

**GREATER ST LUCIA
WETLAND PARK**
1. SODWANA BAY NATIONAL PARK
2. MKUZI GAME RESERVE
3. FALSE BAY PARK
4. HLUHLUWE GAME RESERVE
5. FANIE'S ISLAND
6. CHARTER'S CREEK
7. MISSION ROCKS OUTPOST
8. ST LUCIA GAME PARK
9. CROCODILE CENTRE
10. ST LUCIA PUBLIC RESORT
    and ESTUARY
11. MAPELANE NATURE RESERVE

of water, the whole system connected to the sea by a narrow winding channel 21 km in length. The total surface area of the lake is about 300 sq. km, but this varies considerably between low (drought) and high (flood) levels.

Much of the shoreline is fringed with reed beds, in parts by grassed areas, mud and sandbanks, forested regions, and in the north, by a vast natural papyrus and reed swamp at the delta of the Mkuze river. This extends northwards to include some fair sized pans and wetland areas. Most of the lake bottom is soft mud but there are sandbanks in parts of the southern compartment. The entire area was once covered by the sea and in areas such as False Bay, along the steeper banks in Hell's Gates and on parts of the western shore, cretaceous fossils are found. There are also submerged reefs.

The hydrology of the lake is complex, depending on rainfall in the catchment regions, seepage of water from the eastern shores, the condition of the estuary mouth and tidal rhythms. Wind too is important, moving volumes of water from the southern through to the northern compartment and back again. The health of the system, to a large extent, depends on salinity levels reliant on some of these factors.

The lake and its environs support a diverse flora and fauna. There are mangrove communities, dune forests, papyrus and reed swamps, swamp forests, thornveld, grasslands and bogs, protea communities, orchids and mosses. The islands support important breeding sites of colonially nesting birds – white pelicans, greyheaded gulls, spoonbills, Caspian terns, and during some seasons – flamingoes. The area contains the largest protected populations of the Nile crocodile, hippos and reedbuck in the country. Some 420 species of birds inhabit and visit the system, and 105 *Red Data Book* species of mammals, reptiles, amphibians, birds, butterflies and fish occur in these habitats.

In fact, the area contains a greater diversity of fauna and flora than found in either the Kruger National Park or the Okavango swamps of Botswana. The region qualifies for recognition as a World Heritage Site, the most important recognition which may be given to areas of natural heritage.

HISTORICAL NOTES

Lake St Lucia, and the eastern shores of the lake in particular, are known to have been populated by humans as far back as the Early Iron Age (AD 250-1000). To the Thongas and the Zulus who inhabited the region the lake was known as "Cwebeni las Entlengeni" – "the lagoon of rafts". But it was the Portuguese explorer and navigator Manuel Perestrello, who, when passing the area in 1575, named it Santa Lucia in honour of the saint. Today Lake St Lucia is known world wide as a wildlife and angling paradise and for its scenic beauty. It is listed by SATOUR as one of the five major ecosystem destinations for tourism and outdoor recreation, a reputation enjoyed for many years. But the story of Lake St Lucia reads like that of a child's rag doll. To start with, clean, attractive and unspoilt, but later abused and discarded by uncaring and insensitive playmates – chiefly the politicians and other greedy individuals who both neglected and plundered its riches.

In the 1850s the Lake St Lucia complex attracted hunters out to make their fortunes from the sale of ivory taken from the teeming wildlife in and around the lake. The famous William Charles Baldwin recorded that one party of hunters killed 150 hippo and 91 elephant at the lake in 1853. John Dunn, another notable, is quoted as saying "that season I killed to my own gun, 203 seacows and a lot of other game and was away only three months". His notes record that "the finest day I ever made was one morning before 10 o'clock – 23 seacows". These hunters exterminated many species no longer found in Zululand. The last elephant was shot in the Dukuduku forest as recently as 1916.

After the Zulu War, the Boers of the New Republic (Vryheid) acquired St Lucia and other areas, in recognition of assisting King Dinizulu in his battles against opposing chiefs. They decided they needed a trade outlet for this area and that a town be built at the estuary. A German trading company called Lüderitz claimed in November 1884 that they had bought the lake and the land adjoining the estuary. The British, not to be outdone, despatched HMS Goshawk to St Lucia and control of the land was recovered in December 1884. Small plots of land were sold at St Lucia estuary thereafter.

In April 1897, the Natal government proclaimed the water surface area of the lake and its islands – an area of 36 826 hectares – as a game reserve, along with Umfolozi and Hluhluwe. They are three of the oldest game reserves in Africa.

In 1911 the Umfolozi settlement was established and the Umfolozi Flats cleared for planting sugar cane. Canals were dug in much of the area and swamps were drained to increase agricultural land. As a result, sediment from the catchment areas silted up the Umfolozi-St Lucia mouth. By 1936, Warners Drain had been built right through the dense papyrus and reedbeds that acted as a natural silt trap. The intention was that during flood times, the flow of the river would not be impeded or back up to inundate the farmlands. Instead, water with a huge silt load flowed directly to the estuary and river mouth where the silt was deposited.

In 1939, the St Lucia Park was proclaimed, adding an 800 m wide strip of land around most of the lake shore. In early 1943, part of a Royal Air Force squadron was based on the eastern shores to carry out anti-submarine patrols with Catalina flying boats. When returning from maritime patrols, these aircraft would, at times, swoop low over the Mkuze swamps and strafe basking crocodiles with machine-gun fire. Buildings, a jetty, roads and observation buildings sprung up on the lake edge and on Mount Tabor. Fortunately the base was abandoned in February 1945.

In the previous year, 1944, False Bay Park, an area of 2 247 ha, had been added to the complex.

By the early 1950s, the silting up of the estuary had become a serious problem and there were fears that the lake would become permanently blocked with a mass die-off of plant and animal life. It was decided to divert the Umfolozi river, one of the main sources of fresh water, to south of the estuary. This was accomplished in 1952, in the face of much criticism, as many feared there would be insufficient water flowing into the system. Eighty per cent of the lake water flowed from the Umfolozi, Mkuze, Mzinene, Hluhluwe and Nyalazi rivers and 20 per cent from seepage off the eastern shores. Already heavy demands for water were being made by farmers upstream along the banks of these rivers. The denuding of riverine forest and poor agricultural practices were bringing more silt into the system.

Also in 1952, the Department of Forestry proclaimed three major state forests around the lake. These were Sodwana State Forest (47 127 ha), Cape Vidal State Forest (11 313 ha) and Eastern Shores State Forest (12 873 ha). The planting of commercial timber, *Pinus elliotti* commenced, with 5 244 ha planted over the ensuing years. At the same time, the local people, about 5 000 or so, were removed from their lands and homes and resettled to the north and south to make way for tree planting. This tree planting was to have a major effect on the inflow of fresh water from the eastern shores of the lake. Thirsty trees dried up the seepage veins, the vleis and the marshes, adding to the steady rise in salinity levels in the lake. The diversion of the Umfolozi river had not helped. A full scale dredging unit was installed near the estuary mouth and day and night two large, noisy machines sucked up silt and pumped it out of the estuary mouth area to maintain a lifeline to the sea.

In the early 1960s the government proposed damming the Hluhluwe river. This provoked a public outcry which led to the tabling in parliament of a commission of enquiry to investigate the alleged threat to animal and plant life in the Lake St Lucia system (the Kriel Commission). This commission comprised some of South Africa's top scientists of the time.

In 1966, having completed their investigations, the Kriel Commission pronounced that "St Lucia was a unique environment" with great potential for tourism. It recommended an increase in the size of the conservation area as a matter of extreme importance. The commission recommended that existing commercial pine plantations be phased out, that no new plantations be established, and that water quotas vital to the survival and well-being of the lake be implemented.

Their recommendations were ignored. Afforestation continued. More people were relocated. The Hluhluwe dam was built. In 1968, the Minister of Defence announced the building of the country's first missile testing range in the wilderness area of the lake – one of only two such wilderness areas proclaimed in Zululand. Operations were undertaken by Kentron and only terminated in 1990. This area of the lake was subjected to the disturbance of missile blasts, low-flying jet aircraft, helicopters and boats to retrieve missile heads, etc.

By the late 1960s, demands on the water supply of the rivers flowing into the lake had increased to such an extent that during drought periods salinity levels soared to over twice that of the sea water (35 parts per 1 000). There was a steady die-off of plant and animal life. In September 1970, the position was so bad that a large-scale operation was launched to capture and translocate the remaining adult crocodiles. By now salinity levels had risen to over 100 parts per 1 000 salt, exacerbated by a prolonged drought, with a massive die-off of plant life, shellfish, fish, crocodiles, crabs and other invertebrates. The crocodiles were translocated some 40 km to the only source of fresh water entering the lake – the tiny Nkazama stream, flowing from rainwater captured by the high forested dunes and slowly percolating down through the soil along the eastern shores of the lake (the area where Richards Bay Minerals propose to mine titanium with a prospecting license granted to them by the government in the early 1970s).

In 1975, the South African government signified its approval of the RAMSAR Convention, which was founded by UNESCO to preserve wetlands of international importance. South Africa was one of the original contracting parties which brought the convention into force on 21 December of that year, registering the Greater St Lucia Wetland region as a designated site. It was later a signatory to the Bonn Convention, which protects such wetlands of importance for the conservation of migratory reptile, fish, turtle, mammal and bird species.

Another significant administrative and legislative event was the handing over of the Eastern Shores State Forest area to the Natal Parks Board by the Department of Forestry in 1987. This enabled the conservation authority to commence restocking this area with game, and to introduce tourist facilities.

A major event in the history of the lake occurred in March 1984, when cyclone Demoina caused widespread devastation in Zululand. The effect of the abnormally heavy rainfall and flooding of the rivers was to flush out the system, scouring out a wide, deep channel at the estuary mouth. There was an improvement to the health and productivity of the system which by September 1993, began to deteriorate again when the mouth blocked up after a two-year drought and had to be opened by heavy machinery.

On 9 February 1990, the Minister of Environmental Affairs announced the government's intention to assist the Natal Parks Board in establishing a major protected area to be called "The Greater St Lucia Wetland Park", an area that would become the third largest protected area in South Africa. Unfortunately, despite these intentions, Richards Bay Minerals intended to strip-mine an area 17 km in length for titanium and other minerals that would destroy the forested dunes of the eastern shores of the lake. A public outcry resulted in the commissioning of the most comprehensive environmental impact study of an area yet to be undertaken in South Africa. The results of this, published in May 1993, with two additional volumes in August 1993, have drawn widespread condemnation from scientists, conservationists and the general public, both locally and overseas. A review panel under the chairmanship of Mr Justice Leon was appointed by the government to consider the environmental impact assessment. On 10 December 1993 the review panel announced that it had come to a unanimous decision that no mining should be allowed. They recommended that the area should be proclaimed a national park and should acquire World Heritage Status.

The proposed Greater St Lucia Wetland Park has still not officially come into being, adding to the turbulent history of conservation of this magnificent region of southern Africa.

The existing and proposed components to be incorporated into this park are:

Area	Approximate size: ha	Date proclaimed
Cape Vidal State Forest	11 313	1956
Dukuduku	10 125	1956
Eastern Shores State Forest	12 873	1956
False Bay Park	2 247	1954
Makasa Nature Reserve	1 700	1992
Mapelane Nature Reserve	1 103	1953
Maputaland Marine Reserve	39 740	1987
Mkuzi Game Reserve	37 985	1912
Nyalazi State Forest	1 367	1956
Sodwana Bay National Park	413	1950
Sodwana State Forest	47 127	1956
St Lucia Game Reserve	36 826	1895
St Lucia Marine Reserve	44 280	1979
St Lucia Park	12 545	1939
Total	**259 644**	

ACCOMMODATION
Described under St Lucia Public Resort, Cape Vidal-Lake Bhangazi South, Charter's Creek, Fanie's Island and False Bay headings.

FAUNA AND FLORA
Described in the sections that follow.

FALSE BAY PARK

Area: 2 247 ha
Established: 27 April 1944

LOCATION
Central Zululand, on the western shore of Lake St Lucia. Turn off the N2 to Hluhluwe village and travel straight through the village, towards the railway station. Turn left at the T-junction, travel past the shopping complex and follow the well-signposted route 15 km to the entrance gate.

FEATURES

Guided launch tours are available for those who do not have their own boats. There is good fishing, boating, game viewing, bird watching, hiking and a self-guided trail. It has interesting habitat and trees, some 280 species of birds and attractive, comfortable camping and caravan sites, each with a superb view over the lake. A most pleasant reserve to visit for a day's outing or to camp at for several days.

DESCRIPTION

The bay itself forms the north-western arm of the H-shaped Lake St Lucia complex. The eastern boundary follows the shoreline of the Nibela peninsula, the well-known Hell's Gates, the narrow, steep-sided connecting entrance to the main lake, with the eastern shoreline continuing southwards from Ndhlozi Point to the southern boundary, the Hluhluwe river. The park's northern boundary is the Mzinene river and the game park and tourist camping area lies along the western shores. The area is some 22 km in length but only 3,5 km in width at its widest point.

False Bay is a famous fishing resort and has been popular for angling, boating, camping and caravanning for 50 years. It slowly developed into a significant park as land was acquired and added to the original small area proclaimed. Local Zulu inhabitants, who had occupied the land prior to 1946, moved out, making it possible to fence the western boundary. It has become increasingly popular for game viewing, bird watching, photography and hiking.

The vegetation comprises open woodland, dominated by black monkey thorn, buffalo thorn, spineless monkey orange, tamboti, marula and silver cluster leaf and thicket which includes species found in woodland as well as in sand forest. False Bay Park has fine examples of closed canopy sand forest. Many of the sand forest species are more commonly found further north through Maputaland and into southern Mozambique.

There are no extensive grassland areas in False Bay Park but there are numerous small, clay-lined vleis and pans scattered throughout the veld, which are utilised by game and birds for fresh water when the salinity levels of the lake are high.

False Bay Park contains some significant fossil deposits and, just off Lister's Point, a popular camping site, a quite extensive coral bed. There are various mollusc fossils in the shoreline cliffs, and in the steep cretaceous strata cliffs on either side of Hell's Gates, giant ammonite fossils have been discovered.

ACCOMMODATION

At the Dugandlovu rustic camp, there are four huts with four beds each. Only basic requirements are provided, i.e. cold-water shower, toilet, gas cookers, braai places, paraffin lamps, drinking water, wood and a deep-freeze. Visitors need to supply their own provisions and sleeping bags. Reservations for this camp can be made with the Natal Parks Board, Pietermaritzburg.

There are 40 camping and caravan sites along the shoreline of the lake, with ablution blocks and water points. Visitors supply their own camping equipment. Picnic sites with attractive views have also been provided. Bait can be purchased from the office.

Camp site bookings are made with the officer-in-charge.

TREES

Acacia burkei – black monkey thorn
Balanites maughamii – green thorn
Brachylaena huillensis – lowveld silver oak
Cladostemon kirkii – three-finger bush
Cleistanthus schlechteri – false tamboti
Coffea racemosa – Mozambique coffee
Craibia zimmermanii – peawood
Croton steenkampianus – marsh fever-berry
Dialium schlechteri – Zulu podberry
Drypetes arguta – water ironplum
Drypetes natalensis – Natal ironplum
Erythrophleum lasianthum – Swazi ordeal tree
Grewia flavescens – rough-leaved lemon
Hymenocardia ulmoides – red-heart tree
Monodora junodii – green apple
Newtonia hildebrandtii – Lebombo wattle
Pteleopsis myrtifolia – stink bushwillow
Salacia leptoclada – lemon rope
Sclerocarya birrea subsp. *caffra* – marula
Spirostachys africana – tamboti
Strychnos madagascariensis – black monkey orange
Suregada zanzibariensis – sand canary-berry
Tarchonanthus camphoratus – wild camphor bush
Terminalia sericea – silver cluster leaf
Uvaria caffra – small cluster-pear
Uvaria lucida – large cluster-pear
Ziziphus mucronata – buffalo thorn

BIRDS

The bird list numbers over 280 species. At times, the floodplains of the Hluhluwe river attract spectacular large flocks of ducks and geese. Aquatic species that appear seasonally in large numbers are greater and lesser flamingoes, pinkbacked pelicans and, more commonly, white pelicans, which breed in the main lake nearby. Many species may be seen in the shallows and along the shoreline, as well as at some of the small clay-lined vleis and pans scattered through the veld. Some of the interesting birds to be enjoyed in this park are:

African broadbill
black egret

crested guineafowl
goliath heron

green coucal
grey sunbird
lesser jacana
little bittern
lizard buzzard
narina trogon
Neergard's sunbird
painted snipe
pinkthroated longclaw
pinkthroated twinspot

robins – bearded, whitethroated
Rudd's apalis
snake eagles – black-
   breasted, southern banded
storks – yellowbilled,
   woollynecked
white helmetshrike
yellowbellied bulbul
yellowspotted nicator

MAMMALS

Mammals to be seen along the roads and during walks along the trails include:

black-backed jackal
Burchell's zebra
bushbuck
cheetah
duiker – common, red
elephant shrew
greater canerat
honey badger
impala
kudu
mongooses – slender, water,
   white-tailed

nyala
red squirrel
reedbuck
scrub hare
serval
small-spotted genet
suni or Livingstone's antelope –
   found in the sand forest, South
   Africa's rarest small antelope
vervet monkey
warthog
waterbuck

Hippo occur in several regions of the lake, some herds appearing just off-shore of the camp sites at times. Visitors should be aware that they come ashore to graze the lawn grasses along the lake shore after dark. They sometimes meander right into tented camps, so care should be exercised when walking around after dark.

Because of the scarcity of good grazing areas, the number of ungulate species stocked has been limited, and these herds are maintained in small numbers. There are also shy or nocturnal animals – not likely to be seen by tourists, such as leopard, aardwolf, pangolin, spotted hyaena, thick-tailed bushbaby, antbear (aardvark), bushpig, porcupine and various bats and rodents.

FISH

Fishermen are able to angle for freshwater barbel and tilapia near the inflow of the river systems. Saltwater species include: yellowfin bream, mini kob, oxeye tarpon, springer, flathead mullet and milk shark, as well as many other species including large green crabs. False Bay is noted for the annual runs of succulent kob (Cape salmon) and spotted grunter.

151

REPTILES

Some 26 species of reptiles have been recorded. Venomous snakes that occur are: boomslang, Egyptian cobra, forest cobra, Mozambique spitting cobra, black mamba and puff adder. Natal rock python, Nile or water monitor and rock or tree monitor lizards are quite common. There are also Natal hingeback and leopard tortoises and two terrapin species.

FANIE'S ISLAND: ST LUCIA PARK

Area: Part of St Lucia Park
Established: 31 August 1939

LOCATION

Central Zululand, on the western shore of Lake St Lucia. Turn off the N2 about 30 km south of Hluhluwe, or 25 km north of Mtubatuba and follow the signs to Charter's Creek via Nyalazi river halt. Turn left at the Fanie's Island sign.

FEATURES

A popular, secluded camp, well known by fishermen, with a camping and caravan site overlooking the lake. There is a short trail through open parkland, coastal bush and forest, where a rich variety of bird life and plants can be enjoyed. Recommended for a five day stay for its pleasant views of the lake, and to enjoy the fauna and flora in a peaceful setting. Boats can be hired, but motors are not supplied. A resource centre has recently been completed.

DESCRIPTION

This camp, set in parklike surroundings with wonderful scenic views, is not in fact an island but is situated on the western shore of Lake St Lucia overlooking a maze of reeded islands. These are formed by numerous hippo channels, extending almost right across to the opposite shoreline. Beyond that are the grasslands, forests and finally the distant, forested Cape Vidal coastal dunes in the east.

The beautiful scenery, the sense of peace and tranquillity and the rich variety of wildlife add to the enjoyment of fishermen and wildlife enthusiasts.

Within a small radius of the camp one can view the open waters of the lake, reedbeds and grass areas close-cropped by hippo, open woodland, coastal bush, forest and stands of tall grassland on the forest margins. Many interesting trees are to be found in these habitats.

ST LUCIA

The view from Fanie's Island camp stretches across
the islands of reeds to the coastal dunes on the
eastern shore of Lake St Lucia.

Charter's Creek is a premier fishing resort on Lake St Lucia.

The Bats' Caves, situated a few kilometres north of Mission Rocks, are home to thousands of migratory and resident bats.

The beach at Cape Vidal, protected by an outer reef, is a favourite with surf fishermen and underwater enthusiasts.

The camp sites at False Bay Park are set into the edge of the bush overlooking Lake St Lucia.

Lake Bhangazi, a tranquil lake undisturbed by boats. A trail through the dune forest and along the shores of this lake allows one to view interesting birds and trees. (Photo: Dr Nollie Zaloumis)

Crocodiles basking on the eastern shores of Lake St Lucia near the Mkizi Trail.

A large adult male crocodile feeding on a reedbuck haunch at the St Lucia Crocodile Centre.

The numerous vleis on the eastern shores of Lake St Lucia are a haven for aquatic birds.

The St Lucia estuary is one of South Africa's premier holiday resorts.

NORTHERN ZULULAND

Nsumu pan in Mkuzi Game Reserve attracts thousands of waterbirds during the winter months. (Photo: Dr Nollie Zaloumis)

The luxury glass-walled suites of the Forest Lodge in the Phinda Resource Reserve are built into the forest.

The bushveld and woodland of the Pongolapoort Public Resort Nature Reserve overlook the Jozini dam and the Lebombo mountains.

The Nhlonhlela bush camp in the Mkuzi Game Reserve looks out over the Nhlonhlela pan.

MAPUTALAND

The quiet reaches of the Sodwana stream, fed by inland lakes.

The Mabibi camp is set in dense coastal forest.

Lake Sibaya is the largest body of fresh water in South Africa.

The Sileza Forest Nature Reserve contains sand forest, deep and shallow waterlily-covered pans, open woodlands and grassland and hosts a rich variety of bird species.

An early morning Landrover trip along the shores of Lake Inyamiti is often the highlight of a stay at Ndumu Game Reserve.

Visitors to the exclusive, remote Rocktail Bay camp are housed in luxurious tree houses.

Black Rock, a well-known landmark on the Maputaland coastline, is a prime fishing spot.

The open woodland and palmveld of Tembe Elephant Park.

Kosi Bay has the only forest of raffia palms (*Raphia australis*) in South Africa.

The Thonga tribe have used traditional fish traps in the Kosi estuary for centuries.

The African rock python is found in the warmer parts of KwaZulu/Natal.

The Tongaland cycad (*Encephalartos ferox*) is found on the dunes of Maputaland.

MIDLANDS

The historical village at Midmar dam has many authentic exhibits showing the early culture of Natal, including a railway station and steam locomotive.

Roan antelope have been reintroduced to Weenen Nature Reserve.
(Photo: Dr Nollie Zaloumis)

Weenen Nature Reserve has magnificent examples of valley bushveld,
easily visible from tourist loop roads.

Lush grassland and bushveld provide grazing and browsing for a wide range of game in the Spioenkop Nature Reserve.

The yellow pansy is a fairly common butterfly in KwaZulu/Natal.

HISTORICAL NOTES
Originally named after a local Zulu headman Chief Fanie, the present-day fishing and camping area was discovered by pioneer farmers from Mtubatuba, although it was not until 1949 that the first rest huts and camp sites were developed.

ACCOMMODATION
This consists of one seven-bedded cottage and 12 two-bedded rondavels, which are fully equipped. Two centrally situated kitchens and an ablution block serve the camp. Each hut is equipped with a refrigerator. There are more than 20 attractive shaded camp sites, most large enough for caravans. Two ablution blocks with hot and cold water service these sites. Reservations for hutted accommodation are made with the Natal Parks Board, Pietermaritzburg. For reservations for camp sites contact the Natal Parks Board, Fanie's Island camp.

TREES
Acacia robusta – brack thorn
Bauhinia tomentosa – bush neat's foot
Bersama lucens – glossy white ash
Brachylaena discolor – coast silver oak
Catunaregam spinosa – thorny bone-apple
Commiphora neglecta – green-stem corkwood
Cordia caffra – septee tree
Croton sylvaticus – forest fever-berry
Erythrina lysistemon – common coral tree
Ficus lutea – giant-leaved fig
Ficus thonningii – common wild fig
Hippobromus pauciflorus – false horsewood
Rhus chirindensis – red currant
Rothmannia globosa – bell gardenia
Sapium integerrimum – duiker berry
Tabernaemontana elegans – lowveld toad tree
Trichilia dregeana – forest mahogany
Vepris lanceolata – white ironwood

BIRDS
Birdlife is prolific and at times one can view large skeins of lesser and greater flamingo from the camp. Among the numerous shoreline aquatic birds, the following are of interest: whitewinged, whiskered, lesser crested, swift and sandwich terns as well as Caspian terns which breed nearby. Other species are:

black saw-wing swallow
crested francolin
crested guineafowl
flycatchers – bluegrey, bluemantled,
dusky, paradise,
wattle-eyed
gorgeous bush shrike
narina trogon

olive sunbird
pigeons – green, rameron
squaretailed drongo
tambourine dove

whitebrowed robin
woodpeckers – cardinal,
  goldentailed
yellowbreasted apalis

Birds of prey are well represented by:

African goshawk
blackshouldered kite
eagles – African fish, blackbreasted
  snake, brown snake, crowned,
  longcrested

eastern redfooted kestrel
gymnogene
steppe buzzard

MAMMALS
Mammals include:

bushbuck
bushpig
duiker – common, red
reedbuck

vervet monkey
warthog
waterbuck

The usually shy red duikers are both abundant and used to the presence of humans. They are readily seen in and around the camp.

FISH
Fanie's Island is noted as a prime fishing resort. Seasonally good catches of spotted grunter, yellowfin bream, springer and kob (salmon) are taken, as well as many other species.

CHARTER'S CREEK: ST LUCIA PARK

Area: 12 545 ha
Established: 1939

LOCATION
Central Zululand, within St Lucia Park, on the western shore of Lake St Lucia. Turn off the N2, about 30 km south of Hluhluwe, or 25 km north of Mtubatuba. It is clearly signposted from the N2, and it is 13 km to the camp via Nyalazi river halt.

FEATURES
This camp, with wonderful views over the lake, has long been a favourite among fishermen and bird lovers and for those in search of relaxation and interesting nature walks. One of these walks is the Isikhova trail (about 7 km) which meanders through coastal forest and along the Isikhoveni stream. There are two picnic sites along the trail. Charter's Creek is ideally

154

situated within easy reach of a day trip to almost every game and nature reserve in Zululand.

DESCRIPTION
This scenically attractive camp in a tree-shaded setting is perched on the edge of a steep cliff right on the edge of the lake. It commands panoramic views both to the north and to the south, as well as across the lake to the distant forested dunes of the eastern shores. From the camp one may often view lesser and greater flamingo, as well as rafts of white pelicans feeding in the shallows. Along the shoreline, fish eagles and numerous species of gulls, terns, waders, herons and ibises can be seen. Crocodiles and hippo occur offshore and in the evenings hippo are usually heard grunting before they come ashore to graze below and around the camp grounds.

A number of habitat types are within walking distance of the camp. They include lake-shore, reedbeds, moist and dry grasslands, the small creek lined with swamp forest species, grassland and scrub, woodland and coastal forest.

Apart from being popular and well known for its well-appointed camp, Charter's Creek is loved for its tranquil setting, trails through the forest and along the lake shore and spectacular sunrises. For the fishermen there is the chance of hooking a succulent kob, a fine grunter or perch while enjoying the rhythm of the waves and the tang of salt-laden air.

HISTORICAL NOTES
Charter's Creek camp was named in honour of AE Charter, a provincial secretary who did much to further the cause of wild life in Natal's early conservation history. The small tree-lined creek below and to the north of the camp also bears his name.

ACCOMMODATION
An attractive shaded camp overlooks the lake, consisting of a cottage with seven beds, fourteen three-bedded huts and one with two beds, all fully furnished and serviced. A communal lounge and two centrally situated kitchen blocks serve the camp. All cleaning and cooking is undertaken by the camp staff. There is a swimming pool in the camp grounds. A boat launching area and braai and picnic sites are available along the lake shore. Reservations should be made with the Natal Parks Board, Pietermaritzburg.

TREES
For tree enthusiasts, some of the trees and shrubs to be seen are:
Acacia karroo – sweet thorn
Acacia nilotica – scented thorn
Acacia robusta – brack thorn
Acacia schweinfurthii – river climbing thorn
Annona senegalensis – wild custard-apple
Azima tetracantha – needle bush

Celtis africana – white stinkwood
Chaetachme aristata – thorny elm
Combretum molle – velvet bushwillow
Cussonia sphaerocephala – Natal forest cabbage tree
Cussonia zuluensis – Zulu cabbage tree
Dichrostachys cinerea – sickle bush
Euphorbia ingens – common tree euphorbia
Ficus lutea – giant-leaved fig
Ficus trichopoda – swamp fig
Harpephyllum caffrum – wild plum
Monanthotaxis caffra – dwaba-berry
Strychnos spinosa – green monkey orange
Uvaria caffra – small cluster-pear

BIRDS

The Charter's Creek area supports a good selection of birds:

blackcrowned tchagra	lilacbreasted roller
bulbuls – blackeyed, sombre, terrestrial, yellowbellied	narina trogon
	pinkthroated twinspot
bush shrikes – gorgeous, orangebreasted	puffback
	robins – bearded, brown, Natal
drongos – forktailed, squaretailed	southern boubou
fiscal shrike	starlings – blackbellied
green coucal	glossy, plumcoloured
lesser honeyguide	yellow white-eye

In the reedbeds and moist grassland areas:

African sedge warbler	longbilled crombec
apalis – Rudd's, yellowbreasted	marsh warblers – African,
bleating warbler	European
Cape reed warbler	willow warbler
cisticolas – blackbacked, croaking, fantailed, rattling	

Occasional sightings include woollynecked stork, saddlebilled stork, yellow-billed stork and southern banded snake eagle. A few of the aquatic species are: ringed plover, grey plover, turnstone and avocet.

MAMMALS

Red duiker are especially common in the forest areas, particularly along the entrance road to the park. Some other species are:

black-backed jackal	mongooses – banded,
bushbuck	slender, white-tailed
bushpig	reedbuck
common duiker	thick-tailed bushbaby
large-spotted genet	vervet monkey

ST LUCIA PUBLIC RESORT and ESTUARY

Area: Part of the 12 545 ha St Lucia Park
Established: 1939

LOCATION
Zululand coast. From the N2 take the turn-off to Mtubatuba, and follow the signs to St Lucia Estuary, a distance of 29 km. After crossing the bridge near the entrance to the village, take the first turn right and continue for 2 km through the main street of St Lucia to the Natal Parks Board reception centre.

FEATURES
The St Lucia resort has for many years enjoyed a reputation as one of the country's premier fishing resorts. Ski-boat owners and surf anglers are drawn by the diversity of desirable marine and estuarine fish species which enter the lake system.

Boats can be hired locally, and the St Lucia Ski-boat Club offers deep sea fishing excursions. A Natal Parks Board bait shop is open 24 hours a day. The estuary mouth is a well-known shark fishing beach where many competitions are held annually.

This resort is known for pleasant, sheltered camp sites in lush, subtropical coastal forest, wide but unprotected beaches, and the scenic beauty of a unique estuarine system which entices visitors back again and again.

Local amenities include: guided launch tours up the lake which provide close-up views of hippo, crocodile and many of the 350 bird species; the Crocodile Interpretation Centre, where hundreds of live reptiles can be viewed in open-air ponds; nature trails through various habitats, which allow bird watching, game viewing, and tree identification; First Rocks – a short drive northwards up the beach – with reefs and pothole pools which are rich in marine plants and animals and where numerous species of snails, crabs, shrimps, colourful fish, anemones, sea urchins, beds of mussels, oysters, barnacles and periwinkles can be observed.

St Lucia Resort is the gateway to the eastern shores of the lake, with attractions which include Mission Rocks with its rock ledges, pools and beaches; Cape Vidal, popular for fishing and camping; Lake Bhangazi-south with its high, forested dunes, extensive wetlands, grasslands and associated fauna. The resort is also within reach of Zululand's major game reserves.

For those holidaymakers who do not want the bother of preparing and cooking food, meals can be obtained from a variety of takeaway outlets, restaurants, cafés and a hotel in the village.

DESCRIPTION
There are a number of habitat types which may be explored. These include the beaches with pioneer dune plants and the dense, tangled, almost

impenetrable dune forest. The climax dune forest has a canopy of up to 20 m, with lianas dangling from the upper branches and a dense understorey of buckweed. The mangrove communities along the banks of the estuary and the lake itself are a major breeding ground for penaeid prawns, crabs and numerous fish species that find shelter and food among the mangrove roots. There are reedbeds, mudflats, vleis and grassland communities.

ACCOMMODATION
There are three Natal Parks Board camping and caravan parks:

Sugarloaf Camp (92 sites), near the lake edge and estuary mouth; Eden Park (20 sites), east of the village; and Iphiva (70 sites), about 3 km from the beach, north of the village. Ablution blocks with hot and cold running water are provided in each camp, as well as children's playgrounds. There is a swimming pool at the Sugarloaf camp. Make bookings for camp sites with the Natal Parks Board, St Lucia Resort.

In the Iphiva camp there is a large timber lodge designed for use by educational groups. Kitchen and ablution facilities are provided. Reservations can be made with the Natal Parks Board, Pietermaritzburg.

In addition to Natal Parks Board facilities, St Lucia village offers a wide variety of visitor accommodation in the form of camp sites, caravan parks, rondavels, fishing lodges, duplexes, holiday flats, timeshare complexes and a hotel. The village is well equipped and provisioned to provide for virtually all the needs of the large volume of tourists who visit this resort annually.

TREES
The following trees occur:
Avicennia marina – white mangrove
Bruguiera gymnorrhiza – black mangrove
Celtis africana – white stinkwood
Chaetacme aristata – thorny elm
Cussonia sphaerocephala – forest cabbage tree
Dracaena aletriformis (D. hookeriana) – dragon tree
Ekebergia capensis – Cape ash
Erythrococca barberidea – prickly red-berry
Ficus lutea – giant-leaved fig
Grewia caffra – climbing raisin
Hyperacanthus amoenus – thorny gardenia
Inhambanella henriquesii – milk pear
Olea woodiana – forest olive
Peddiea africana – poison olive
Psychotria capensis – blackbird-berry
Scolopia zeyheri – thorn pear
Scutia myrtina – cat thorn
Strychnos decussata – Cape teak
Vepris lanceolata – white ironwood
Xylotheca kraussiana – African dog-rose

The orchids *Cyrtorchis arcuata*, *Microcoelia exilis*, *Mystacidium venosum* and *Aerangis mystacidii* are common forest species.

A number of trees on the local Gwalagwala Trail have been labelled for the information of visitors. The trees planted along and behind the dunes towards the mouth are beefwoods, *Casuarina equisetifolia*, an exotic species that is an excellent sand binder.

BIRDS
For the birding enthusiast the estuary and environs has much to offer. On the beach and in the estuary mouth area lesser crested, swift, Caspian, sandwich, whitewinged and whiskered terns, as well as greyheaded gulls should be looked for. During the winter months seabirds such as Cape gannets, Cape cormorants, petrels, prions, skuas and albatrosses may be seen off the beaches.

Other interesting species recorded from various habitats include:

avocet	robins – bearded, brown
bluecheeked bee-eater	Rudd's apalis
flamingoes – greater, lesser	ruff
Knysna lourie	sand martin
mangrove kingfisher	short-tailed pipit
Natal nightjar	southern banded snake eagle
Neergard's sunbird	storks – saddlebilled,
pelicans – pinkbacked, white	woollynecked, yellowbilled
pinkthroated twinspot	turnstone
plovers – grey, ringed	yellow white-eye
plumcoloured starling	yellowspotted nicator
redchested flufftail	

MAMMALS
Hippo are readily seen and heard in the estuary region, while smaller diurnal and nocturnal mammals which may be encountered are:

bushpig	red squirrel
Cape clawless otter	serval
large-spotted genet	thick-tailed bushbaby
mongooses – banded, large grey, slender, water, white-tailed	vervet monkey

Several other species occur in the nearby game park.

FISH
Edible fish commonly caught in the estuary include blacktail, sandfish, rock cod, snapper salmon, kob (Cape salmon), perch, silver and yellowfin bream, spotted grunter, stumpnose, springer and eels. Some very large sawfish enter the lake to drop their young, and the seasonal migrations of mullet in and out of the lake system can be a spectacular sight. Other

159

marine species enter the lake system to feed on the rich variety of shell life and worms to be found on the lake bottom, as well as to scavenge or prey on smaller fish, prawns, crabs, plankton, detritus and vegetable matter.

In addition to five species of shark, honeycomb stingrays also enter the estuary. The annual runs of shad (elf) off the beaches are usually excellent.

REPTILES

Crocodiles are frequently seen in the estuary, and visitors are warned of the real danger of attack from both crocodiles and sharks. Warning signs placed along the shores should be obeyed.

The Nile monitor lizard or water leguaan is another large reptile often seen along the lake shores. It is harmless to humans, and a protected species. Other reptiles of the region include:

boomslang	Natal green snake
brown slug-eater	Natal rock python
brown water snake	olive grass snake
East African egg-eater	red-lipped herald snake
forest cobra	rhombic night adder
gaboon adder	sea snakes – black, yellow
green mamba	southern cross-barred snake
Mozambique shovel snout	

ST LUCIA CROCODILE CENTRE and GAME PARK

Area: Part of Lake St Lucia Park
Established: 1974

LOCATION

Zululand coast. From the N2 take the turn-off to Mtubatuba and follow the signs to St Lucia Estuary, a distance of 29 km. After crossing the bridge near the entrance to St Lucia village, take the first turn to the left, signposted Cape Vidal. The Crocodile Centre, the airstrip and the southern boundary of the game park are located at the control gate 3 km along this road.

FEATURES

The Crocodile Centre, a large, thatched building, contains a series of displays that provide information on the breeding, feeding, anatomy, general ecology and distribution of this prehistoric and now protected reptile. There are also displays, photographs, maps and diagrams of the Lake St Lucia system covering the sea, beach, dune forests, grasslands and lake shore. Aquaria hold examples of living organisms which are found in the various habitats. There is an interesting and varied collection of traps, weapons and equipment used by poachers. Open-air ponds afford visitors an opportunity to view and photograph at close range about 200 Nile crocodiles of all sizes, as well as two other African species, the longsnouted and dwarf crocodiles. There are also American alligators for comparison. Feeding of the adult crocodiles takes place at 15h00 on Saturdays and Sundays. There is an entrance fee to the Crocodile Centre.

The trails through the game park start at the Crocodile Centre car park and a map showing the several routes (3-9 km) is available from the Crocodile Centre curio shop. Traillists normally have good views of blue wildebeest, zebra, impala, waterbuck and especially reedbuck which are common in the area. Game is best seen in the early mornings and late afternoons. Hippo occasionally lie up in the small bush clumps and entering one of these, away from the trails, could be hazardous.

DESCRIPTION
The Crocodile Centre contains large open ponds with sandbanks for nesting. Indigenous trees and shrubs have been planted in the spacious enclosures and gardens. An interesting feature is the colony of spottedbacked weavers that seasonally build their nests in trees overhanging the ponds, and the thickbilled weavers that nest in the bulrushes. An unusual cycad garden which will display every species found in Natal is presently being established.

The game park has many varied habitats within a small area, stretching from the beach, up through the coastal dune forest, onto open, rolling grassland with occasional clumps of thicket and coastal forest. There are seasonal vleis, quite deep pans, marshland, reed and sedge beds, swamp forest, bush thickets, and along the lake shore, mangroves.

HISTORICAL NOTES
The opening of the Crocodile Centre was a milestone in the conservation of crocodiles in Africa. The Nile crocodile had been all but exterminated in many countries for its valuable belly hide, for medicinal purposes and because it competed with man and his livestock, and posed a threat in recreational areas. In 1957 a young white boy was killed by a crocodile in False Bay Park. This led to a public outcry and the subsequent shooting of a large number of crocodiles in the St Lucia system. Still classed as vermin in Natal up to 1969, professional hunters from countries to the north came to Zululand and continued slaughtering these reptiles for profit. This exploitation caused our stocks to decline rapidly.

In 1958, one of the authors, Tony Pooley, commenced what was to become a life-long study of these maligned creatures. His observations, together with those of colleagues and researchers in neighbouring countries, proved that as a master predator in the aquatic food chain, the crocodile was of great ecological significance and deserved protection. By 1966 the decline in numbers was so dramatic that the Natal Parks Board financed a major Experimental Crocodile Rearing Station in the Ndumu Game Reserve. Here the problems of egg incubation, hatchery management, diet and diseases of crocodiles were studied and overcome. It was possible to release young crocodiles back into the lakes, pans and river systems and, on request from private landowners, onto private game ranches.

This project was recognised by the International Union for Conservation of Nature and Natural Resources (IUCN) as one of the best of its kind in the world. The project received considerable media coverage, particularly after new discoveries into the fascinating and complex parental care exercised by these survivors of the dinosaur era were documented for the first time.

Realising the possibilities of earning revenue from a public display of crocodiles, and the conservation education potential for interpreting the role of crocodiles in the environment, the Natal Parks Board decided to expand the crocodile research and conservation programme. The Lake St Lucia estuary area with its large annual visitor numbers was the logical site for this programme.

TREES

The trees to be seen in the game park include:

Acacia karroo – sweet thorn
Albizia adianthifolia – flat-crown
Antidesma venosum – tassel berry
Apodytes dimidiata – white pear
Avicennia marina – white mangrove
Barringtonia racemosa – powder-puff tree
Brachylaena discolor – coastal silver leaf
Bruguiera gymnorrhiza – black mangrove
Erythrina lysistemon – common coral tree
Euclea natalensis – large-leaved guarri
Garcinia livingstonei – African mangosteen
Harpephyllum caffrum – wild plum
Hibiscus tiliaceus – lagoon hibiscus
Maytenus heterophylla – common spike thorn
Mimusops caffra – coastal red milkwood
Ozoroa obovata – broad-leaved resin tree
Phoenix reclinata – wild date palm
Sclerocarya birrea subsp. *caffra* – marula
Scutia myrtina – cat thorn
Sideroxylon inerme – white milkwood
Strelitzia nicolai – wild banana
Strychnos madagascariensis – black monkey orange
Syzygium cordatum – water berry
Tabernaemontana elegans – toad tree
Trema orientalis – pigeonwood

After the spring rains the magnificent *Crinum delagoensis* and colourful ground orchids bloom in the damp areas. Clumps of *Protea caffra* occur here too. When out hiking, beware of the thorny *Smilax* creeper. It can be avoided by keeping to the marked trails.

BIRDS
In addition to the common coastal dune forest birds, visitors should look out for the following species, some of which only occur seasonally:

bee-eaters – bluecheeked, little
cisticolas – blackbacked,
   croaking, fantailed
European roller
grassveld pipit
pygmy goose

redwinged pratincole
storks – saddlebilled,
   woollynecked
tawnyflanked prinia
yellowthroated longclaw

In the dune forest there are brown robin, yellowbreasted and Rudd's apalis, green twinspot and Woodwards' batis.

MAMMALS
Indigenous mammals which may be encountered include:

duiker – common, red
hippo
large-spotted genet
mongooses – banded, slender,
   water, white-tailed

red squirrel
reedbuck
side-striped jackal
thick-tailed bushbaby
vervet monkey

Reintroduced species include impala, waterbuck, blue wildebeest and Burchell's zebra. The strictly nocturnal antbear (aardvark) occurs in the park, and evidence of its deep burrows can be seen along trail routes.

The game park is home to some very large pythons, and on a warm day one may be lucky enough to see one sunbathing close to its retreat, usually a disused antbear (aardvark) burrow.

EASTERN SHORES STATE FOREST and NATURE RESERVE: MFABENI SECTION

Area: 12,874 ha
Established: 1956 and 1964

LOCATION
Zululand coast. From the N2 take the turn-off to Mtubatuba and follow the signs to St Lucia Estuary, a distance of 29 km. After crossing the bridge near the entrance to the village, take the first turn to the left, signposted Cape Vidal. Continue for 3 km to the Natal Parks Board control gate

between the Crocodile Centre and the airstrip. The Mfabeni section is the land lying north of the game park.

DESCRIPTION

If one were to do a transect from the open sea, right across the eastern shores to the lake shoreline, it would reveal an area comprising one of the most diverse habitat types in the province and an area exceptionally rich in fauna and flora. Moving shorewards from the deep open water of the Indian ocean, there are coral reefs of the littoral zone supporting an incredible assortment of life forms. There are the outer rock platforms, the intertidal pools rich in marine plants and animals and shelves covered by mussel, oyster and barnacle communities. Barnacles and periwinkles cling to the saltspray-lashed higher rocks, and in damp crevices. There are vast stretches of sandy beaches, where the sand is so clean it squeaks under the foot of the beach explorer. Brightly patterned shells of many shapes and colours and the carcasses of victims of undersea battles can be found along the high tide mark.

The beach rises to the foothills of the dunes, where fleshy-leaved creepers and shrubs trap the wind-blown sand, and help shape and stabilise the dunes. Then, rising steeply, are some of the tallest forested dunes in the world, towering almost 200 m above the ribbons of beach. On the seaward side they have a curiously clipped appearance from the constant wind action and effects of the salt-laden air. These forests, with their spreading canopy, shelter a thickly wooded understorey of small trees and shrubs and a dense ground layer of ferns, shade-loving grasses in the deeper troughs between the dune formations, and numerous lianas reaching up for the light past epiphytic orchids and lichen-bedecked tree trunks.

The dune forest opens abruptly onto steeply sloping grass and *Helichrysum* carpeted hillsides that roll down to meet the plains. There is a mosaic of habitats, including small, shallow, lily-covered vleis, extensive areas of shallow water wetlands and clumps of coastal forest comprising a greater variety of plant species than the dune forest, on knolls of higher ground. There are patches of water berry and wild date palms, deep semi-permanent open pans, stands of swamp forest, hygrophilous (water-loving) grassland and large expanses of dry grassland and mixed woody plant species down to the lake edge with its community of sedges and reedbeds along the shores. There are also stands of white mangroves in places. In the north is Lake Bhangazi South, a large permanent body of water.

In terms of its biodiversity, this is one of the most valuable conservation areas in South Africa and it is the core of the Greater St Lucia Wetland Park.

HISTORICAL NOTES

The Eastern Shores area is rich in the remains of Early Iron Age (AD 250-1000) and Late Iron Age (AD 1000-1840) settlements. To date, 50 Iron Age middens and 94 remains of such settlements have been discovered by archaeologists. The early inhabitants subsisted principally on the basis of

164

shifting cultivation, at the same time exploiting marine resources such as oysters and the mussel *Perna perna* found in abundance along the rocky coastline. They developed a specialised iron smelting industry. This industry required a great deal of charcoal and wood which was abundant in the indigenous forests. It is believed that the present-day grassy dunes were cleared of their forests by these early iron workers and maintained by frequent burning. Only later did livestock play an important role in their lifestyle and economy. Clearly, humans have had a major influence on this area over a very long period of time.

We have scant knowledge of the former abundance and species of wildlife that occurred along the eastern shores. There are records that giraffe, kudu, buffalo, eland, wild dog, red hartebeest, cheetah and lion were shot in the area north of the lake. Tsessebe, zebra, warthog, blue wildebeest and nyala were also recorded as having occurred in the environs of the lake and very probably on the eastern shores. It is well known that elephant migrated down the eastern shores to cross the lake by way of what is today called Brodie's Crossing. The last elephant to fall to a hunter's rifle, in the Dukuduku forest area, was shot as recently as 1916, having crossed this shallow area of the lake. To the early Nguni migrants moving north or south, this crossing was well known as "Indlelayendhlovu" – "the elephants' path" – and had probably been used for centuries.

Many big game hunters concentrated their efforts around Lake St Lucia in the mid-1850s, particularly because of the hippo and elephant populations to be found there. The arrival of the white man in the area was of great significance. Mission stations were established in the late 1880s at Cape Vidal, Ozabeni near Ochre Hill and on Mount Tabor, to minister to the quite large population of Tongas and Zulus resident on the eastern shores.

In 1943, during World War II, part of the Royal Air Force's 262 squadron was based on the eastern shores to carry out anti-submarine patrols along the coastline with Catalina flying boats. They erected observation buildings on Mount Tabor, which are today used as overnight huts for wilderness traillists. The disturbance from their take-offs and landings to the wildlife on the eastern shores (Catalina Bay) must have been considerable. Regrettably, it is known that at times, when returning from patrols, they would fly low over the Mkuze swamps and shoot up crocodiles basking on the mudflats. Fortunately, this base was abandoned in February 1945.

In the early 1950s, a major impact on the environment occurred. The Department of Forestry evicted some 5 000 Zulus and Tongas from the region in order to establish commercial forest plantations. The species planted was the Elliot pine *Pinus elliottii*. This development had a major impact on the hydrology of the entire area, drying out pans, vleis and seepage veins of fresh water captured from the heavy rainfall experienced along the coastal dunes. This rainfall percolates down to feed the lake. In times of severe drought, the supply of fresh water is vital to the survival of many organisms in the lake. The pine plantations deprived the system of this freshwater inflow. Fortunately, in 1992, the decision was made to cease planting and to remove every last tree. It will take about 15 years to eradicate 5 224 ha of pine plantations.

The conservation history of the eastern shores and the development of tourism commenced in the mid-1940s, when anglers discovered Cape Vidal to be a prime fishing spot and potential resort area. The Eastern Shores State Forest of 12 873 ha and the Cape Vidal State Forest of 11 313 ha were proclaimed in 1950. The Eastern Shores Reserve, now known as the Mfabeni Section, stretches from St Lucia Game Park, just north of St Lucia township boundary, to Cape Vidal. The area is state land and prior to 1978, was managed by the Department of Forestry. Since then, all conservation responsibilities have been taken over by the Natal Parks Board.

ACCOMMODATION
See entries under Mission Rocks Outpost, Mount Tabor and Cape Vidal and Lake Bhangazi South Complex.

TREES
Acacia karroo – sweet thorn
Acacia kraussiana – coast climbing thorn
Albizia adianthifolia – flat-crown
Allophylus natalensis – dune false currant
Antidesma venosum – tassel berry
Brachylaena discolor – coast silver oak
Bridelia micrantha – mitzeeri
Celtis africana – white stinkwood
Drypetes natalensis – Natal ironplum
Ekebergia capensis – Cape ash
Ficus burtt-davyi – veld fig
Ficus lutea – giant-leaved fig
Ficus natalensis – Natal fig
Ficus trichopoda – swamp fig
Garcinia livingstonei – lowveld mangosteen
Macaranga capensis – wild poplar
Mimusops obovata – coastal red milkwood
Peddiea africana – poison olive
Protea caffra – common sugarbush
Sclerocarya birrea subsp. *caffra* – marula
Sideroxylon inerme – white milkwood
Strelitzia nicolai – Natal wild banana
Syzygium cordatum – water berry
Trema orientalis – pigeonwood
Vangueria infausta – wild medlar
Voacanga thouarsii – wild frangipani
Xylotheca kraussiana – African dog-rose
Stenochlaena tenuifolia is an attractive epiphytic fern, common in swamp forest.

BIRDS

African goshawk
African marsh harrier
apalises – Rudd's, yellowbreasted
black egret
blackcrowned tchagra
bluemantled flycatcher
bluecheeked bee-eater
broadbilled roller
brown robin
crested guineafowl
ducks – fulvous, knobbilled, yellowbilled
eagles – blackbreasted snake, brown
    snake, crowned, longcrested
goldenrumped tinker barbet
gorgeous bush shrike
green coucal
green twinspot
greenbacked heron

grey sunbird
grey waxbill
gulls – greyheaded, kelp
Knysna lourie
narina trogon
Natal nightjar
pygmy goose
rufousnaped lark
steppe buzzard
storks – saddlebilled,
    woollynecked
terns – common, sandwich,
    swift
wattle-eyed flycatcher
white-eared barbet
wood owl
Woodwards' batis
yellowspotted nicator

MAMMALS (about 49 species)

aardwolf
black rhino
blue wildebeest
brown hyaena
buffalo
bushbuck
bushpig
Cape clawless otter
cheetah
duiker – common, red
greater canerat
hippo
impala
kudu
large-spotted genet
leopard

mongooses – banded, large
    grey, water, white-tailed
monkeys – samango, vervet
porcupine
red squirrel
reedbuck
scrub hare
serval
side-striped jackal
spotted hyaena
steenbok
thick-tailed bushbaby
warthog
waterbuck
zebra

Three shrews, two moles, four bats, one molerat, one gerbil and three mice species are found.

Many of these species were hunted to extinction in historical times and have been reintroduced.

REPTILES (41 species)

There are 41 species of reptile occurring along the eastern shores, as well as two tortoise and one terrapin species. Venomous snakes include:

boomslang
cobras – blacknecked, spitting
gaboon adder

mambas – black, green
puff adder
vine snake

MISSION ROCKS OUTPOST and MOUNT TABOR

Area: Part of the Eastern Shores State Forest
Established: 1956

LOCATION
Zululand coast. From the N2 take the turn-off to Mtubatuba and follow the signs to St Lucia Estuary, a distance of 29 km. After crossing the bridge near the entrance to the village, take the first turn left signposted Cape Vidal. Travel 3 km to the Natal Parks Board control gate between the Crocodile Centre and the airstrip. Proceed for about 14 km beyond the gate then take the well signposted turn-off on the right.

FEATURES
From the Mission Rocks Outpost, atop very high dunes, a track winds down towards the beach to a small car park and shaded picnic area. A short path through the dunes leads to a long series of rock platforms and outcrops. The flat, potholed ledges have shallow and deep pools with fascinating marine fauna and flora, including extensive oyster beds and mussel colonies.

This is a popular venue for school and other groups, who, under the guidance of a Natal Parks Board interpretation officer, are able to study marine ecology as well as plant succession on the dunes and in the coastal forest.

It is a popular angling site as one can cast off into deep water, especially at low tide.

To the north the beach is wide and clean against a backdrop of very steep, vegetated dunes. There are small bays and offshore reefs where crayfish are plentiful. There are few suitable bathing areas. About 5 km north of the car park along the beach is a well known local landmark, Bats' Caves. A large colony of resident as well as migratory, mainly fruit-eating bats are to be found in a series of small caves almost at the water's edge.

There are picnic sites on the top of the very high dunes at Mission Rocks Outpost. A lookout offers panoramic views over Lake St Lucia from the Narrows, across Mitchell Island and Catalina Bay, towards Charter's Creek on the distant western shore. The views are best in the early morning or towards sunset.

The Mziki Trail system operates from an old radar station site on the ridge of Mt Tabor, 2 km from Mission Rocks. Over three days, traillists traverse three different routes 10-l8 km in length. They experience the extensive grasslands, open hillsides, ridges and valleys; the Mfazana pan, home to hippo, crocodile, waterfowl, waders and aquatic birds in the wet season; numerous vleis and bush clumps, the eastern shores lake-edge communities and dune forest, pine plantations and the beach zone.

For visitors staying at St Lucia Estuary it is less than an hour's drive to Mission Rocks Outpost, and well worth the trip. (For details of the local fauna and flora, see entry under Eastern Shores.)

HISTORICAL NOTES
The mission station on Mt Tabor was started in 1898 by a Norwegian missionary, Reverend LO Feyling, to minister to the Zulu and Tonga people who were resident on the eastern shores. However, in the mid-1950s, the forestry department moved these people out to develop huge timber plantations, and the mission station closed down.

Of interest is an old brick kiln – the only one of its kind in South Africa, which should be designated a national monument. It was apparently used for baking bread as well as for firing bricks. Behind, hidden in the dense bush, are two remaining tombstones of what was a small cemetery. The original church has been demolished.

ACCOMMODATION
There is one eight-bedded hut for persons booked on the Mziki Trail. Make trail bookings with the Natal Parks Board, Pietermaritzburg.

CAPE VIDAL and LAKE BHANGAZI SOUTH COMPLEX

Area: Part of the Cape Vidal State Forest
Established: 1950

LOCATION
Zululand coast. From the N2 take the turn-off to Mtubatuba and follow the signs to St Lucia Estuary, a distance of 29 km. After crossing the bridge near the entrance to the village, take the first turn to the left, signposted Cape Vidal. Travel 3 km to the Natal Parks Board control gate between the Crocodile Centre and the airstrip. Cape Vidal camp is about 32 km beyond this gate. The existing gravel road is very rough, and for those towing ski-boats, great care should be taken.

FEATURES
This resort has rapidly gained in popularity in recent years with a reputation for ski-boat fishing and surf angling. There are wide beaches and a safe but unprotected bathing area which is sheltered from the open sea by a reef. The scuba diver and keen spearfisherman are drawn by a large variety of

game fish. For those keen on snorkelling, there are colourful tropical reef fish and invertebrates, with oyster beds, mussels and crayfish in the clear water.

Many ski-boat and angling clubs have regular competitions off these shores with catches of barracuda, dorado, garrick, kob, king mackerel, kingfish, potato bass, queenfish, bluefin tuna, yellowfin tuna, bonito, wahoo, black marlin and sailfish as the prizes. Off some of the outer reefs congregations of sharks are found.

The shad (elf) runs are usually very good, and surf angling is also notable for the variety of inshore species that may be hooked. For those with four-wheel drive vehicles, rock and surf angling is possible all the way up to Leven Point, the boundary of the marine sanctuary.

Three species of ghost crabs inhabit these beaches, living in underground burrows and emerging at night to feed. It is a remarkable sight to see them by torchlight, in waves of pink, scuttling across the sand at night. There are also two species of mole-crabs or "sea-lice" inhabiting the wetter shoreline zone.

There is a wealth of birdlife and small mammal fauna in the dune forests sheltering the camp sites and along the self-guided Umvubu Trail through the forest down to the shores of Lake Bhangazi. For visitors staying in the camp, walks into the wilderness area under the guidance of a game guard are interesting.

For the less energetic in search of relaxation, there are the night sounds of eagle owl hoots, bushbaby calls, tree frogs and crickets, the dawn chorus of forest birds punctuated by the occasional staccato barks and calls of samango monkeys, and the ever-present sound of the surf. This is a pleasant place to spend an idle day.

For visitors staying at St Lucia, a trip to Cape Vidal takes less than two hours, passing through habitats which include commercial pine plantations, vast open grasslands and, during the summer months, wetland areas and vleis. There is the chance of seeing a variety of game, especially reedbuck, before reaching the spectacular dune forest, the lovely Lake Bhangazi, and following the dune forest drive to the beach.

Visitors should try to reach Cape Vidal before low tide in order to enjoy swimming or snorkelling, scuba diving, a beach drive, or a picnic in the numerous sheltered hollows between the steep beach dunes.

(See entry under Eastern Shores for details of the fauna and flora.)

HISTORICAL NOTES

Cape Vidal was named after Lieutenant Alexander Vidal RN, captain of the *Barracouta*, which, with two other survey ships, the *Leven* and the *Cockburn*, were sent by the Royal Navy to survey this coastline in 1822. Leven Point, north of the resort, was named after the sloop *HMS Leven*.

This rocky coastline has been the scene of some remarkable shipwrecks and salvage operations, such as that of the *Dorothea*, which developed a leak after sailing from Durban. It ran aground during the night of 31 January 1898, a few kilometres east of Cape Vidal. The crew abandoned ship, taking to the lifeboats, and were picked up by passing steamships. A rumour circulated that she had been carrying a cargo of illicit gold bought on the Witwatersrand and smuggled out via Lourenco Marques (Maputo) harbour. Different syndicates made attempts to salvage this treasure the same year, and again in 1899, 1901, 1903 and 1904. All attempts ended in failure, or bankruptcy, and with some loss of life. Finally, in 1908, a salvage operation recovered some anchor chains and poles which were left on the rocks.

Another wreck was the Italian steamship *Timavo*, which beached just north of Leven Point in June 1940. It was forced ashore by the air force after slipping out of Durban harbour when Italy declared war on the Allies. The remains of this wreck can be seen on the beach at low tide.

The present Cape Vidal camping area was first discovered in the mid-1940s when keen Mtubatuba fishermen forced their way through the tangled coastal forest to come upon a fishing paradise. The Dunns were the first to build a shack there, and in 1951 the Bangazi Angling Club of ten members built another. After the war the Van Rooyens, Ozzie Jackson and others cut a road down to the beach, and the advent of 4x4 jeeps enabled more and more keen fishermen to reach Vidal. At one stage, prior to the Department of Forestry handing control of the area to the Natal Parks Board, 15 different angling and ski-boat clubs had shacks and cabins at Cape Vidal.

ACCOMMODATION

There are log cabins, fishing cabins, a bushcamp and 50 camp sites. At Vidal there are 18 five-bedded log cabins and 12 eight-bedded cabins. These units have two bedrooms, a bathroom, shower, fully equipped kitchen, and a dinette cum lounge.

There are five fishing cabins on the shore of Bhangazi lake. They have eight, 12, 14 and 20 beds respectively, and are fully equipped.

The Bhangazi bush camp, 7 km from the hutted camp, sleeps eight people in four two-bedded, self-contained and serviced units. A fully equipped kitchen is provided.

Reservations for hutted accommodation should be made with the Natal Parks Board, Pietermaritzburg and camp site bookings with the officer-in-charge, Cape Vidal.

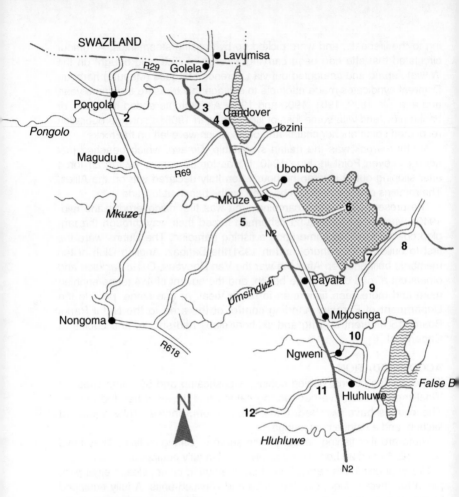

NORTHERN ZULULAND

1. LEEUKOP GAME RANCH
2. UMZIKI GAME RANCH
3. PONGOLWANE PRIVATE NATURE RESERVE
4. PONGOLAPOORT PUBLIC RESORT NATURE RESERVE
5. ABU MADI GAME RANCH
6. MKUZI GAME RESERVE
7. PUMALANGA NATURE RESERVE
8. ZULU NYALA SAFARIS
9. PHINDA RESOURCE RESERVE
10. SUNGULWANE GAME LODGE
11. UBIZANE GAME RANCH
12. HLUHLUWE GAME RESERVE

NORTHERN ZULULAND

Northwards from Hluhluwe to Pongola on the Eatern Transvaal border and Gollel on the Swaziland border, the terrain is rather flat, with gently undulating hills in some areas, while to the east of the N2 motorway the Lebombo mountain range gradually rises into prominence. It increases steadily in height to Ubombo village which towers 465 m over the flat country of Mkuzi below. It is typical lowveld country. The climate is hot to very hot and humid in summer. The vegetation is predominantly mixed acacia scrub, grassland, woodland and seasonally filled depressions after the summer rains. There are few rivers and streams – the Msinduze, Mzinene, Mkuze and Pongolo, fringed with narrow belts of riverine forest, are the only watercourses of note. Overall this is a somewhat arid region and as a result sparsely populated. The south is not an intensely developed agricultural region and the lack of small villages, apart from Hluhluwe and Mkuze, reflects this lack of development. In the mid-1950s the large-scale production of pineapples was initiated but eventually the majority of these smallholdings were phased out as uneconomical. Sisal too was a major crop. A large processing plant just outside Hluhluwe village still operates, but due to a fall in prices of the by-products, the extensive areas originally planted have been greatly reduced in size. Other crops include cotton, vegetables, timber and sugar cane in the Mkuze area. The greater part of this area of bushveld is comprised of large cattle ranches, private game ranches mainly for trophy and meat hunting, as well as game ranches and lodges catering for tourists. The Jozini dam, east of the Lebombo range in the gorge incised by the Pongolo river, impounds this river, pushing water back to flood former grasslands, past the Candover area and northwards to the Swaziland border. West of the mountains the dam is scarcely utilised for agricultural purposes. However around Pongola, bordering the Eastern Transvaal, is an area of intensive agricultural development. It is a major sugar cane, citrus, tropical fruit and cotton producing district centred around an extensive irrigation system from the Pongolo river. A major sugar mill, a cotton gin and fruit packing plants are established in Pongola.

Northern Zululand historically was an area rich in species and with an abundance of game. It attracted many hunters from the mid-1850s. The programme of slaughtering game when the nagana tsetse fly eradication programme commenced in the early 1940s also contributed to the extermination of game in this region. Today Mkuzi Game Reserve's rich mammal, bird and reptile fauna, with its diversity of vegetation and habitat types, survives as a reminder of what the northern Zululand lowveld had to offer before and just after the turn of the century.

ZULU NYALA SAFARIS

Area: 650 ha
Established: 1981

LOCATION
Northern Zululand. From the Eastern Transvaal on the N2, take the Ngweni-Sodwana turn-off left, 102 km south of Pongola. At the T-junction turn right, travel 4,4 km and turn left over the railway line (look out for the Zulu Nyala sign); travel a further 3,2 km to Zulu Nyala Safaris on the left.

From the south, on the N2, pass the Hluhluwe sign until reaching the Ngweni-Sodwana turn-off. Follow the above directions to reach the reserve. A private airstrip on the property allows access to small planes. Visitors flying into Richards Bay can arrange to be met.

FEATURES
There are game viewing drives in an open Landrover, night drives, game viewing hides for photographers, horse riding, clay pigeon shooting, excellent freshwater fishing in the dam and walks with an experienced guide. Excursions for big game fishing and scuba diving at Sodwana Bay, launch cruises on Lake St Lucia or game viewing trips to neighbouring game reserves can be organised. There is an outdoor boma for evening meals if preferred, and Zulu dancing can be arranged for guests' entertainment. Amenities include a floodlit tennis court, swimming pool and a full-sized snooker table in the bar area. Conferences can be arranged on request. Bush braais for private groups can be arranged out in the reserve.

DESCRIPTION
Situated in the Ngweni region of northern Zululand, the area is one of steep hills, rocky in parts, in the foothills of the Lebombo mountains. It comprises rolling grassy hillsides, valley bushveld, open acacia savanna, woodland, riverine thicket and fever tree forest along the banks of the Mhlosinga river. Dams and waterholes have been provided for game in the low-lying clay soil regions.

ACCOMMODATION
A luxurious 24 bed lodge, fully equipped and serviced. It comprises one master suite which has a luxury spa bath, seven luxury suites and four twin family rooms with extra sleeper couches, all with en suite bathrooms. All meals are provided, it is licensed and has a fully stocked bar. Reservations must be made with the lodge itself.

TREES
Acacia xanthophloea – fever tree
Aloe arborescens – krantz aloe

Aloe marlothii – mountain aloe
Berchemia zeyheri – red ivory
Hyphaene coriacea – lala palm
Maytenus senegalensis – red spike-thorn
Ozoroa sphaerocarpa – currant resin tree
Pappea capensis – jacket-plum
Schotia brachypetala – weeping boer-bean/tree fuschia
Sclerocarya birrea subsp. *caffra* – marula
Sideroxylon inerme – white milkwood
Spirostachys africana – tamboti
Strychnos spinosa – green monkey orange
Terminalia sericea – silver cluster leaf
Trichilia emetica – Natal mahogany
Ziziphus mucronata – buffalo thorn

BIRDS (about 400 species)

barbets – pied, redfronted tinker
brownheaded parrot
eagles –
   bateleur, martial,
   southern banded snake
European bee-eater
European golden oriole
green coucal
green pigeon
grey lourie
Heuglin's robin
hornbills – crowned, yellowbilled
narina trogon
pearlspotted owl

redbacked mannikin
redcrested korhaan
redfaced mousebird
rollers – European,
   lilacbreasted, purple
roseringed parakeet
rufousnaped lark
secretarybird
spotted dikkop
striped kingfisher
tambourine dove
whitebacked vulture
whitenecked raven

MAMMALS

blue wildebeest
bushpig
duiker – common, red
elephant
giraffe
impala
kudu
large-spotted genet
leopard
mongooses –
   banded, white-tailed

mountain reedbuck
nyala
reedbuck
steenbok
suni
warthog
waterbuck
white rhino
zebra

PHINDA RESOURCE RESERVE

Area: 15 000 ha
Established: 1990

LOCATION

Northern Zululand. From the south, turn off the N2 at the Ngweni-Sodwana Bay signpost. Cross over the N2, turn left at the stop sign, go 4 km down the road and turn right at the "Sodwana Bay" signboard and continue to the Phinda Nyala gate on the right. From the north, travel about 40 km past Mkuze, take the Ngweni-Sodwana Bay off-ramp to the left and continue as above.

There are regular commercial flights from Durban and Johannesburg to Empangeni, Richards Bay and Mkuze. Transfers to the lodge can be arranged. There is a private, serviceable 1 500 m grass strip. The co-ordinates are 27° 52 mins S. 32° 18 mins E. Prior arrangements to land and to be collected must be made.

FEATURES

Phinda Nyala lodge offers the ultimate in luxury, fine facilities and excellent service. The main lodge and reception centre feature spacious, comfortable lounges, a large curio shop, an executive meeting room and spacious verandas with views towards the Lebombo mountains in the west, and over typical Zululand bushveld and the coastal plains to the east. The dining room is spacious and in the evenings guests enjoy a sumptuous dinner beneath the stars in a large, lantern-lit open-air boma. The entire complex is built into the mountainside. From a large swimming pool and viewing deck, guests can look out over the bushveld and rock outcrops. The chalets are landscaped into the trees and boulder formations.

The Forest Lodge, set in the sand forest, has a central lounge, bar and covered diningroom with views over a natural pan. Guests may enjoy game and bird viewing while sampling the excellent cuisine. An unusual outdoor dining area is set into the forest.

Game drives in open safari vehicles are available with an experienced ranger who can answer questions concerning the local fauna and flora and the overall ecology of the area, and who can explain the conservation problems of game reserve management. Game drives are undertaken in the early morning and late afternoon. A 20 km river cruise can be undertaken up the Mzinene river, which is flanked by fever trees, giant figs and reedbeds where a large variety of bird species, as well as crocodiles, will be seen. The return trip at sunset is spectacular, with snacks and drinks served as the double-decker launch cruises slowly back. This can be followed by a night drive searching for game and birds. Some of the nocturnal, unusual mammals and reptiles may be encountered.

Daily walks accompanied by Zulu trackers are popular and on game drives or walks a variety of vegetation types are explored, including the sand forest, wetland, riverine forest, rolling grassland, bushveld, woodland and rock outcrops.

In addition to the fascinating terrain in Phinda, trips can be arranged to nearby Mkuzi Game Reserve; for scuba diving or swimming in the warm tropical sea on the Maputaland coast, and between November and February, night drives to watch the nesting of giant leatherback and loggerhead sea turtles along the beaches. Flights over the huge lakes, riverine systems, swamp forests, lala palmveld, right up to the Mozambique border, are a major feature of the services offered.

Phinda has a wide range of trees and plants. Tourists may encounter many of the over 350 species of birds and over 50 species of mammals and predators, as well as many smaller rodents and bats. After the summer rains, the various calls of over 20 species of frogs and toads and the night sounds of the bush can be enjoyed.

For a true wilderness experience, a day spent paddling down-river by canoe, a bush picnic, or even a private bush dinner can be arranged.

DESCRIPTION

The geology and soil types of Phinda, typical of this southern region of the vast Makatini flats, are similar in some respects to the nearby Mkuzi Game Reserve and sections of the Lebombo foothills. On the lower lying ground are the white to grey leached soils with sand forest and drier vegetation types along the Mzinene river. In the vlei areas the heavy clay soils support riverine forest trees and thickets, with sedges, dense reedbeds and aquatic species along the riverbanks.

There are tall grassed zones, open woodland and large tracts of *Acacia* (seven species) dominated bushveld, in parts almost impenetrable. The soil types change from heavy, dark clay soils, to the red sands with savanna vegetation. As the terrain rises to the higher elevations of the Lebombo foothills, shales, boulder outcrops, bare rock faces and koppies are visible. The terrain comprises rolling valleys, drainage lines and woodland covered hills. It is this diversity of habitat types that accounts for the rich and diverse fauna and flora found in Phinda. As a result it is a scenically attractive environment for browsers, grazers, predators and scavengers.

HISTORICAL NOTES

This area of Maputaland has undergone many changes. It was originally settled by the Thembe-Tonga tribe, who practised shifting agriculture, fishing, hunting and the gathering of indigenous fruits. They later farmed with cattle and goats. In the mid-1850s there was an influx of white hunters who decimated the vast herds of game, especially elephant for their ivory and hippo for their ivory, meat, fat and tough hides for the making of sjamboks. Vast herds of buffalo, eland, waterbuck, wildebeest, zebra, kudu and predators such as lion and leopard were virtually exterminated for the export of their skins. Only the dwellers of thick forest, such

177

as nyala, were left, with remnant herds of wildebeest and zebra remaining in Mkuzi Game Reserve when this reserve was proclaimed in 1912. An outbreak of rinderpest later caused a die-off of wild and domestic animals and the vegetation was effected by a tremendous locust plague across the Makatini flats.

In 1917 an outbreak of nagana (sleeping sickness), carried from game to domestic stock by tsetse flies, set the authorities on a systematic slaughter of game in an effort to get rid of the carriers of the disease. It was only between 1943 and 1952 that the aerial spraying of the deadly insecticides DDT and BHC put an end to the tsetse threat. The long-term effect of these chemicals on the insect life, bird life, animals and flora was sadly never researched.

In 1948, after World War II, the area was subdivided into economic farming plots for returned soldiers. This led to widespread bush and woodland destruction to create grazing areas for cattle. Phinda was one of the areas selected and even today the scars of erosion are still visible as a result of poor management practices in some regions.

It was not until 1990 that a group of farmers and conservationists acquired the land comprising the present Phinda Resource Reserve, between the Sodwana State Forest Reserve and the Mkuzi Game Reserve. They founded the Conservation Corporation which has developed this large park, with the luxurious camp which was opened in October 1991, and have systematically restocked this region to create a major tourist attraction, "Phinda Izilwane – the return of the wildlife". Unhampered by government and provincial red tape and administrative restraints, they have responded to the needs of the local tribal people by creating 300 jobs. Training has allowed their staff to acquire a variety of skills. The reserve also provides natural resources such as firewood for the neighbouring communities.

ACCOMMODATION

The Phinda Nyala Lodge consists of six two-bed luxury chalets and 15 two-bed bush suites, each with a separate lounge area, a private balcony, a fully equipped bathroom en suite and a second toilet. There is a top of the range two-bed suite called "The Lookout". The standards of decor and furnishing are superb and each unit enjoys privacy as well as wonderful views over the terrain. A maximum of 46 guests can be accommodated in the main camp.

The new Forest Lodge has 17 luxurious glass-fronted suites, elevated above the ground, each with views of giant trees, built and landscaped into the sand forest habitat. This lodge was opened in November 1993.

Reservations are made with the reserve or Phinda Holdings, Johannesburg.

TREES

A number of interesting sand forest species occur in Phinda. A few of these are:

Albizia forbesii – broad-pod false thorn
Cleistanthus schlechteri – false tamboti
Coddia rudis – small bone-apple
Combretum zeyheri – large fruited bushwillow
Croton gratissimus – lavender fever-berry
Croton steenkampianus – marsh fever-berry
Dialum schlechteri – Zulu podberry
Erythrophleum lasianthum – Swazi ordeal tree
Hymenocardia ulmoides – red-heart tree
Newtonia hildebrandtii – Lebombo wattle
Salacia leptoclada – lemon rope

Other attractive species are:
Acacia xanthophloea – fever tree
Aloe arborescens – krantz aloe
Aloe marlothii – mountain aloe
Balanites maughamii – green torchwood
Euphorbia ingens – candelabra tree
Ficus sycomorus – sycamore fig
Gardenia volkensii – Transvaal gardenia
Schotia brachypetala – weeping boer-bean/tree fuchsia
Strychnos madagascariensis – black monkey orange
Strychnos spinosa – green monkey orange
Tabernaemontana elegans – toad tree
Terminalia sericea – silver cluster leaf

BIRDS (350-400 species)

African broadbill
African finfoot
African rail
arrowmarked babbler
avocet
black egret
brown robin
brownheaded parrot
coucals – black, green
crowned crane
cuckoos – black, Jacobin
eagles – African hawk, bateleur,
   blackbreasted snake
gorgeous bush shrike
grey waxbill
ground hornbill
honey buzzard
kingfishers – greyhooded, pygmy

knobbilled duck
Knysna lourie
lemonbreasted canary
lesser jacana
lilacbreasted roller
melba finch
narina trogon
Natal nightjar
openbilled stork
owls – giant eagle, Pel's fishing
peregrine falcon
pinkbacked pelican
pinkthroated longclaw
rameron pigeon
redbilled oxpecker
redcrested korhaan
redwinged pratincole
rock pipit

179

Rudd's apalis
wattle-eyed flycatcher

Woodwards' batis
yellowspotted nicator

MAMMALS
Those most likely to be seen are:

aardwolf
antbear (aardvark)
black-backed jackal
blesbok
blue wildebeest
buffalo
bushbuck
bushpig
chacma baboon
cheetah
duiker – common, red
elephant
giraffe
greater canerat
hippo
honey badger
impala
klipspringer
kudu
large-spotted genet
leopard
lion

mongooses – banded, dwarf,
   slender, water, white-tailed
monkeys – samango, vervet
mountain reedbuck
Natal red rock rabbit
nyala
otters – Cape clawless,
   spotted-necked
porcupine
red hartebeest
red squirrel
reedbuck
scrub hare
serval
spotted hyaena
steenbok
striped polecat
suni
thick-tailed bushbaby
warthog
white rhino
zebra

PUMALANGA NATURE RESERVE

Area: About 3 500 ha
Established: 1974

LOCATION
Northern Zululand, in the southern foothills of the Lebombo mountain range, bordering Mkuzi Game Reserve in the north and the Phinda Resource Reserve in the south. From the N2 take the Ngweni-Sodwana Bay off-ramp. Turn left at the stop sign, travel 4 km, cross a railway line and then follow the Sodwana Bay sign along this gravel road to the Pumalanga gate.

FEATURES
This is an attractive area combining typical game country of high open grasslands, lower bushveld on the plains and riverine forest along the banks of the Munywana river. Game viewing drives and walks, bird watching, freshwater fishing and night drives with spotlights are available. Hunting can be arranged for local and overseas clients. On request, diving and fishing excursions can be organised to Sodwana bay, about an hour's drive away. The reserve is also situated within easy driving distance for a day trip to either Ndumu, Mkuzi, Hluhluwe or Umfolozi game reserves.

DESCRIPTION
Situated between the Mkuzi Game Reserve and the Phinda Resource Reserve, the topography, fauna and flora is very similar. For a description of habitats and a listing of the plant species to be found, consult these two reserve descriptions.

HISTORICAL NOTES
The land now known as the Pumalanga Nature Reserve was purchased and settled by the Van Rooyen family in 1943, and used for cattle ranching. In 1974, the livestock was sold off and a start made on erecting game-proof fencing and introducing the numerous species now in abundance in this attractive reserve. It was not until 1989 that the reserve was opened to the public. It offers exclusive facilities to the visitor in search of a wilderness experience. The name "Pumalanga" means "the place where the sun rises".

ACCOMMODATION
The Mfula Lodge offers luxurious but rustic accommodation, ideal for a large family or party. It accommodates 15 persons, in three separate five-bedded units. It is fully furnished and equipped with crockery, cutlery, cooking utensils, bedding and towels. Visitors provide their own food and drink and cook for themselves. A swimming pool and open-air modern braai facilities are provided. Reservations should be made with the reserve.

BIRDS (about 234 species)

bearded robin	grey penduline tit
Bennett's woodpecker	Jacobin cuckoo
blackbellied korhaan	Jameson's firefinch
blackcrowned tchagra	lemonbreasted canary
crested guineafowl	melba finch
dark chanting goshawk	narina trogon
eagles – brown snake, lesser	night herons – blackcrowned,
spotted, Wahlberg's	whitebacked
European roller	openbilled stork
golden weaver	pallid flycatcher
grey hornbill	purplebanded sunbird

vultures – Cape, whiteheaded
redbilled oxpecker

wiretailed swallow
yellowbellied eremomela

MAMMALS

antbear (aardvark)
black-backed jackal
blue wildebeest
chacma baboon
civet
common duiker
elephant
giraffe
impala
kudu
large-spotted genet
leopard
mongooses – banded, white-tailed

nyala
porcupine
reedbuck
scrub hare
spotted hyaena
steenbok
suni
thick-tailed bushbaby
vervet monkey
warthog
waterbuck
white rhino
zebra

SUNGULWANE GAME LODGE

Area: 2 600 ha
Established: 1990

LOCATION

Northern Zululand, at the foot of the Lebombo mountain range. From the N2 south, the distance to the Bayala off-ramp is 30 km from Hluhluwe, and from the north 20 km south of Mkuze. Take the Bayala turn-off, cross the railway line and take the road signposted Sodwana. Follow this road for 1 km, then turn off at the Sungulwane turn-off. A further 3 km will bring you to the lodge.

FEATURES

Guests may go on early morning guided walks, or an early morning game drive in an open vehicle to watch the sun rise over the Lebombo mountains. After breakfast they may go swimming or visit the hide overlooking the waterhole and watch or photograph animals and birds coming to drink. In the late afternoon there is a sundowner drive in an open vehicle to watch the sunset from the top of the Lebombo mountain range, returning after dark to see how many animals can be picked out by spotlight. One of the features is good home cooking, including many traditional South African venison dishes.

From Sungulwane, half-day and full-day safaris can be arranged to Kosi Bay and Mkuzi, Umfolozi, Hluhluwe game reserves, or to Lake St Lucia and a launch tour on this wonderful estuarine system. Excursions can be arranged to Ndumu Game Reserve, South Africa's premier bird area. There are many other trips, such as to Sodwana bay for deepsea fishing, scuba diving and snorkelling over the coral reefs and fishing trips to catch the magnificent fighting tiger fish.

Hunting on a small scale is permitted either for venison, biltong or trophies. Trackers, skinners and slaughtering and coolroom facilities are available and hunting licences can be purchased from the office.

DESCRIPTION
Nestling at the foot of the Lebombo range, the area is one of boulder-strewn mountain slopes, bushveld and grassed plains with woodland. The vegetation is similar to that of Mkuzi Game Reserve, with the animal and bird species favouring these habitats.

ACCOMMODATION
There is a camp comprising eight two-bed rondavels, with a spacious lounge, diningroom, bar and a swimming pool. Each rondavel is serviced and equipped with en suite shower with hot and cold running water. Reservations are made with the lodge.

BIRDS
barbets – blackcollared, crested, pied
eagles – bateleur, brown snake, crowned, longcrested, martial
green twinspot
kingfishers – pygmy, woodland
korhaans – blackbellied, redcrested

louries – grey, purplecrested
melba finch
Neergard's sunbird
vultures – lappetfaced, whitebacked

MAMMALS
antbear (aardvark)
black-backed jackal
bushpig
caracal
civet
duiker – common, red
giraffe
honey badger
impala
kudu
large-spotted genet

leopard
mongooses – banded, slender, white-tailed
nyala
red hartebeest
reedbuck
suni
thick-tailed bushbaby
vervet monkey
warthog
waterbuck

MKUZI GAME RESERVE

Area: 37 985 ha
Established: 15 February 1912

LOCATION
Northern Zululand, east of the Lebombo mountains, about 335 km from Durban along the N2. From the south the turn-off to the reserve is signposted 35 km north of Hluhluwe. Follow this gravel road for about 15 km to the next signpost, and continue on a gravel road up and over the Lebombo range. It is a further 10 km to the reserve entrance. Visitors from the north may follow the same route off the N2, but a shorter route is through Mkuze village, a distance of 28 km to the reserve's entrance gate.

FEATURES
Mkuzi is a favourite with regular visitors to Natal's game reserves. The scenery is attractive and the diverse soil and vegetation types (over 700 plant species), support a variety and an abundance of wildlife with 78 mammal, 430 bird and 64 reptile species recorded. For the birding enthusiast it ranks with the Ndumu Game Reserve as one of the top bird-viewing areas in South Africa. In addition to its natural attractions, there are four game-viewing hides at Kubube, Kumasinga, Kwamalibala and Kumahlala. These are artificial waterholes where visitors may relax in comfort and enjoy photographing small and large game coming to drink, especially over the drier winter months. They can also see a wide variety of bushveld bird species.

At the Nsumu pan, two hides have been erected to view the large concentrations of wildfowl, pelicans, other aquatic species and hippo and crocodiles that assemble there over the dry season.

Within Mkuzi an 84 km network of tourist roads allows the visitor to traverse the habitat types of almost every section of the reserve. For the more energetic, a self-guided trail through the magnificent fig forest, a walk with an experienced Zulu guide and overnight camping and wilderness trails are available in season. Guided night drives have recently been introduced.

Future developments include building a cultural village in the Gwambane area of the reserve and the creation of natural resource areas adjoining the reserve in cooperation with the local Kwa Jobe tribal people. The cultural village will be of great interest to visitors. Guided tours of the complex will enhance their understanding of the culture and history of the local people.

For the keen sports hunter, Mkuzi offers limited hunting in an area set aside for this purpose. Clients are accommodated in the Umkumbi bush camp in season.

Whatever your preference may be – Mkuzi main camp, bush camp or rustic huts – the accommodation is comfortable, the hides superb. The atmosphere of this reserve attracts many thousands of tourists who return annually to this splendid park with its beautiful game herds, prolific bird life, diverse vegetation and the myriad sounds and scents of the bush.

DESCRIPTION

Mkuzi Game Reserve lies at the southernmost limit of the coastal plain that extends southwards from Mozambique. It is situated between the Mkuze river, the northern and eastern border, the Umsinduzi river in the south, and the Lebombo mountain range, which rises to over 400 m, on the west. The topography and wide variety of soil types support a diverse vegetation. There are seasonally filled floodplain pans. These may dry out during severe drought periods, but, during good rainfall seasons, may be water-lily covered on the surface, containing a wealth of submerged plant species. There are large areas of reedbeds and swamp, the Mkuze river itself and the spectacular riverine forest with giant fig, fever and mahogany trees, along its banks. The sand forest, with many unusual subtropical species, is found on the pallid sands. On the lower-lying areas are large tracts of umbrella thorn dominated acacia-veld and scrub. There are dense thickets of mixed vegetation, open woodland of knobthorns and tree wisterias, short and tall savanna country and grasslands ranging from the short grass species of the open plains to the tall grasses up the slopes of the Lebombo mountains.

In the south, in what was formerly the Nxwala state lands, the country is more hilly, as is the western section of the reserve. There are isolated rock outcrops, volcanic in origin, and numerous small streams that rise in the Lebombo foothills. Throughout the lower-lying area of clay soils, there are numerous shallow depressions that hold water for short periods after heavy summer rains. The area is rich in fossils, particularly the Nhlonhlela hill, where fossilised tree trunks and ammonite specimens may still be discovered. These date back to the Cretaceous era, when shallow seas covered the entire area.

HISTORICAL NOTES

Occupation of what is now Mkuzi Game Reserve goes back thousands of years, evidenced by the finding by archaeologists of implements such as hand axes used by early Stone Age man. Much more recently, old Arab encampments, the finding of trade goods such as beads on the Kundunakazi foothills, and the presence of old grave sites, still visible, indicate the presence of modern man well over a hundred years ago. People were still resident along the river floodplain, where they cultivated the Nhlonhlela valley, as recently as 1943, the year they were moved out of what is now the game reserve.

In the late 1880s, game hides were in great demand for export and fetched good prices. Farmers and hunters, mainly from the Transvaal, came down in the winter months and hunted especially for buffalo, eland and kudu. Fortunately the presence of tsetse flies and malaria allowed them to hunt only during the cooler winter months, but they were responsible for exterminating buffalo, eland and waterbuck from this region.

Mkuzi was officially proclaimed a game reserve on 15 February 1912. For several years prior to 1912, the area enjoyed the unofficial protection of the wildlife-conscious resident magistrate at Ubombo, Mr O Finney. He kept a careful watch on illegal hunting in the area which, at that stage, was unfenced and a reserve in name only.

A major setback occurred in 1939. Farmers in the northern area of Zululand had suffered severe stock losses from the disease known as nagana, transmitted by tsetse flies, to which game mammals were immune but which were hosts to this parasite. General Kemp, then Minister of Agriculture, acting in response to the outcry from the farmers, stated that Mkuzi Game Reserve was to be abolished. The reserve was in fact deproclaimed and taken over by the Department of Veterinary Services.

The pioneers of this reserve were the late LC "Singie" Denyer and his wife Dawn, who took up residence in a small wattle and daub cottage in 1943. In those days access from the south was via the lower Mkuze road from Hluhluwe, across the Msinduzi river, the Nxwala state lands, entering the reserve via the Mlambamude stream crossing. From the north it was via the mountain-top village of Ubombo, down across the Makatini flats, to the Mkuze river at Denyer's Drift where the river was crossed, if water levels permitted, just below where the present reception centre is sited. At that stage Singie Denyer was employed by the veterinary department.

The next major development occurred in 1944. The policy of destroying all the game in Mkuzi Game Reserve commenced with eliminating the hosts of the dreaded nagana and by doing so, eliminating the tsetse fly. Mkuzi echoed to the shots of rifle fire as teams of hunters systematically sought out and shot every animal they could find, with the exception of black rhino. This led to the slaughter of over 38 000 head of game over the following years.

The next programme to eliminate the dreaded flies then commenced. This involved the aerial spraying of the flies and their suspected breeding grounds. The game reserve airstrip was constructed in 1945 and Avro Anson aircraft, flying in formation, sprayed out a billowing cloud of DDT and BHC insecticide mixed with diesel fuel and atomised through the aircraft's exhaust pipes. These aircraft flew day after day discharging their deadly poison. This method, together with the chopping out of large tracts of dense scrub where the tsetse flies deposited their eggs and pupae developed, proved to be successful, but expensive. The campaign terminated in 1949 and control of Mkuzi reverted to the Natal Parks Board in September 1954.

A further serious threat to the well-being of the reserve occurred in the late 1950s. Increased farming development, involving overhead irrigation of crops and the building of storage dams and weirs across the Mkuze river at and around Mkuze village, caused the river to cease flowing along the reserve's boundary. With the drying out of the river and the Nhlonhlela and

Nsumu pans, there was no surface water at all for game to drink. Singie Denyer conceived the idea of laying a pipeline from the river to the Kubube pan, and later to Kumasiga. Water was pumped to these small pans by means of well-points sunk deep beneath the dry river bed. This measure prevented a large-scale exodus of animals out of the game reserve.

Added to this threat was the ceaseless war against poachers. The reserve was, and still is, surrounded by a large population of peasant farmers. Over lean seasons and when crops failed they would resort to hunting with dogs, spears and knobsticks, or to setting snares and traps to obtain meat. Many men, both past and present, have spent countless hours, often under extremely trying conditions and in dangerous situations, in an effort to combat this threat to Mkuzi's wildlife.

One of the rewards of their efforts was that between 1959-1962, under the direction of Mr Peter Potter, then Chief Conservator for Zululand, 2 495 impala were captured and distributed to farmers in the Transvaal, Natal and Zululand, as well as to Ndumu and False Bay game reserves, to establish new breeding herds of these graceful antelope.

Up to 1958, Mkuzi was not open to the public and hardly known. The building of three small rustic huts in that year attracted many curious visitors and from then on the reserve grew in popularity. This was just as well, for in the early 1960s, the Natal Parks Board approached the Department of Lands to transfer a portion of land to the west of the Umfolozi Game Reserve, into which a large number of white rhino had moved. The department agreed, on condition it received an equivalent area in return. It was agreed to exchange a portion of Mkuzi Game Reserve.

The Natal branch of the Wildlife Society of Southern Africa contested this decision and in 1965 appealed to the public to help save Mkuzi. They produced numerous press releases, magazine articles, public addresses and a film entitled "Save Mkuzi", produced by a keen conservationist and businessman, the late Ian Hepburn, which was widely shown. A petition was organised and 44 000 signatures were collected in support of this move against deproclamation of a portion of the reserve. The petition, together with a memorandum, was handed to the Department of Lands by the president of the society, Mr WE Pearse. No further announcements were made by the Department of Lands after these actions and the boundaries remained intact.

Over subsequent years there was further talk that once the Jozini dam was completed, a portion of Mkuzi should be allocated to farmers for irrigated agricultural plots, but happily this has not happened.

A more positive note in the chequered history of the reserve occurred on 1 March 1972, when the Department of Agricultural Credit and Land Tenure invited the Natal Parks Board to take over control of the Nxwala state lands adjoining the game reserve in the south, an area of 5 774 ha. A pearlite mine had operated there, local farmers had grazed their cattle and it had been a favourite poaching haunt of farmers. This land is now a part of the reserve.

The origin of the name "Umkhuze" or "Mkuze" is not clear. One explanation is that in early years, during times of severe drought when the river dried up, the locals would resort to digging deep pits in the river bed in order to obtain drinking water. In the event of a flash flood, it would be dangerous for anyone below the surface when floodwaters arrived and for this reason persons positioned on the river bank could "khuze" or shout a warning to those below. So it became known as Mkuze, or the river where they call or warn you. Another theory is that the river was named after the aromatic wild lavender trees *Heteropyxis natalensis*, which grew in profusion along the river banks in earlier years.

ACCOMMODATION

The Mantuma camp comprises six two-bedded rest huts in one locality, served by communal ablution facilities and a communal kitchen, where a cook prepares meals. Another locality has five five-bedded bungalows and four three-bedded bungalows with communal kitchen facilities. There are also two seven-bedded self-contained cottages. All of these units are equipped with refrigerators and all are serviced.

There is a rustic camp of four four-bedded huts. Visitors supply their own bedding. Cutlery and crockery is supplied. There are no refrigerators at this camp. Communal ablution facilities are available. At this camp visitors cook over open braai grids and, as with all the other types of accommodation, visitors supply their own food and drink. Future plans for the rustic camp are the provision of 17 two-person tents to replace the wooden huts. A feature of the Mantuma camp complex is the large, secluded, floodlit swimming pool which is available to all the occupants of this complex.

The Umkumbi bush camp is situated in the controlled hunting area and is used only from October to March. It consists of four large two-bedded safari tents with wardrobe, bedside tables and small refrigerator. An en suite shower, washbasin and toilet ensure complete privacy for visitors. A thatched wood and reed lounge, diningroom and bar have been built opposite a natural pan to give visitors the enjoyment of a typical bush camp in a traditional African setting.

The Nhlonhlela bush camp comprises four reed and thatch roof two-bedded huts with toilet and shower en suite. They are connected by boardwalks to a communal lounge and diningroom complex sited on a clifftop overlooking the pan. The scenery is magnificent, from the fever tree and sycamore fig forest on the floodplain of the Mkuze river to the Lebombo mountains in the west. The sunsets are stunning. Visitors have the entire north-western area of the reserve to themselves.

At the entrance to Mkuzi, the Emshopi camping and caravan park can accommodate about 60 persons. It is fully equipped.

Reservations for the hutted camps are made with the Natal Parks Board, Pietermaritzburg; camp sites with the officer-in-charge, Mkuzi Game Reserve.

TREES
Acacia burkei – black monkey thorn
Acacia luederitzii – bastard umbrella thorn
Acacia nigrescens – knobthorn
Acacia nilotica – scented thorn
Acacia tortilis – umbrella thorn
Acacia xanthophloea – fever tree
Albizia forbesii – broad-pod false thorn
Aloe barberiae (*A. bainesii*) – tree aloe
Ancylanthos monteiroi – dune false medlar
Balanites maughamii – green thorn
Berchemia zeyheri – red ivory
Bolusanthus speciosus – tree wisteria
Boscia albitrunca – shepherd's tree
Cassine aethiopica – koo-boo berry
Cleistanthus schlechteri – bastard tamboti
Combretum molle – velvet bushwillow
Combretum zeyheri – large fruited bushwillow
Commiphora neglecta – green-stem corkwood
Craibia zimmermannii – peawood
Dialium schlechteri – Zulu podberry
Dombeya rotundifolia – common wild pear
Dovyalis caffra – Kei-apple
Encephalartos lebomboensis – Lebombo cycad
Euclea divinorum – magic guarri
Euclea natalensis – Natal guarri
Gardenia volkensii – Transvaal gardenia
Haplocoelum gallense – galla plum
Kigelia africana – sausage tree
Manilkara concolor – Zulu milkberry
Peltophorum africanum – weeping wattle
Phoenix reclinata – wild date palm
Pteleopsis myrtifolia – myrtle bushwillow
Rhus gueinzii – thorny karree
Schotia brachypetala – weeping boer-bean/tree fuchsia
Sclerocarya birrea subsp. *caffra* – marula
Sideroxylon inerme – white milkwood
Strychnos madagascariensis – black monkey orange
Strychnos spinosa – green monkey orange
Terminalia sericea – silver cluster leaf
Ziziphus mucronata – buffalo thorn

BIRDS (430 species recorded)
bluegrey flycatcher
broadbilled roller
brownheaded parrot
burntnecked eremomela
bushveld pipit
desert cisticola

dwarf bittern
eagles – Ayres', lesser spotted,
   southern banded snake, steppe
fantailed flycatcher
gorgeous bush shrike
green coucal
grey waxbill
hawks – bat, cuckoo
honey buzzard
hooded vulture
lesser jacana
Neergard's sunbird
oxpeckers – redbilled,
   yellowbilled

Pel's fishing owl
pinkbacked pelican
pinkthroated twinspot
pygmy goose
robins – bearded, Heuglin's,
   whitethroated
Rudd's apalis
scalythroated honeyguide
warblers – olivetree,
   Stierling's barred
white-eared barbet
whitefronted bee-eater
woodland kingfisher
yellowspotted nicator

MAMMALS
antbear (aardvark)
black-backed jackal
blue wildebeest
bushbuck
bushpig
Cape clawless otter
caracal
chacma baboon
cheetah
duiker – common, red
eland
four-toed elephant shrew
giraffe
greater canerat
hippo
honey badger
impala
kudu
large-spotted genet
leopard

mongooses – banded, slender,
   water, white-tailed
mountain reedbuck
Natal red hare
nyala
pangolin
porcupine
red squirrel
reedbuck
rhino – black, white
scrub hare
steenbok
striped polecat
suni
thick-tailed bushbaby
vervet monkey
warthog
waterbuck
zebra

REPTILES
Of the venomous species, boomslang, vine snake, puff adder, Egyptian cobra, Mozambique spitting cobra and black mamba occur. Pythons, both species of monitor lizards and Nile crocodiles occur in small numbers.

ABU MADI GAME RANCH

Area: 475 ha
Established: 1992

LOCATION
Northern Zululand, 10 km south-west of Mkuze village on the D240. From the N2 turn off at the Nongoma-Mkuze intersection. The Nongoma road has a good gravel surface leading to the D240.

FEATURES
The lodge has a pleasant view overlooking thousands of hectares of typical Zululand bushveld, with a spectacular view of Ghost mountain and the Lebombo range in the east. The accommodation is comfortable. There is a swimming pool on the terrace overlooking the bush. An attractive reed boma is a feature, where guests enjoy their evening meal and swap stories round a log fire.

Tree hides have been built for game and bird viewing over pools in the river and guests can spend the night in them. For the energetic walker, marked trails meander through demarcated areas. A professional guide is available for those who wish to learn about the bush, fauna and flora. Much of the ranch can be traversed in an ordinary saloon car but a 4x4 vehicle is preferable. Game drives by day in an open vehicle, or night drives with a spotlight in search of the more uncommon creatures, can be arranged with the manager.

The lodge is ideally placed for the 30 minute drive to Mkuzi Game Reserve or to the Jozini dam, with a spectacular drive up over the Lebombo mountains and views over the vast Makatini flats, stretching northwards to the Mozambique border; or for a day trip to Ndumu Game Reserve.

DESCRIPTION
The lodge is situated on the highest point to the south of the property. The land slopes away from the hillsides to valleys of thick riverine bush and fever tree forests. The Msegane river winds its way through the ranch and although it doesn't flow most of the year, pools in the riverbed retain water. There are large areas of tall grass and acacia-dominated savanna, open woodland and dense thickets on the low-lying ground. With a range of palatable grasses, the area is ideal for many species of game.

HISTORICAL NOTES
The early occupation of land in this area is evidenced by the number of Stone Age implements found on the ranch. In recent historical times it is said that the nearby Ghost mountain, or, to give it its correct Zulu name "eTshaneni – the place of the small stone", was used as a burial ground for chiefs in the 1800s.

Since earliest times game herds have inhabited this area and despite man's occasional, and usually unsuccessful attempts at agriculture, the game has survived and thrived alongside commercial cattle ventures. It was for this reason that Mr Mike Balcomb decided in 1992 to change what was a cattle ranch into a game ranch.

ACCOMMODATION
The lodge is a cluster of stone and thatched cottages which can sleep 15 in five rooms, all fully furnished and serviced. The main rondavel comprises lounge-diningroom, a modern kitchen with stove, microwave, deep-freeze and refrigerators, as well as three bedrooms and a bathroom. An additional outside ablution block with two toilets and a shower serves the rondavel.

A few metres from the main living area are two additional rondavels en suite, one with three beds and the other with four beds. Bed linen is provided but guests are requested to bring their own towels.

Camping is permitted in specified areas. Day visitors are welcome, but prior arrangement must be made for the gate to be opened.

Abu Madi is self-catering. Cooking utensils, crockery and cutlery are provided. Guests need to bring their own food and drink. A maid services the cottages and lights the boma fire in the evenings. Reservations should be made with the lodge.

TREES
Acacia caffra – common hook-thorn
Acacia karroo – sweet thorn
Acacia xanthophloea – fever tree
Bolusanthus speciosus – tree wisteria
Commiphora neglecta – green-stem corkwood
Euclea undulata – common guarri
Ficus sycomorus – sycamore fig
Maytenus species
Schotia brachypetala – weeping boer-bean/tree fuschia
Schotia capitata – dwarf boer-bean
Sclerocarya birrea subsp. *caffra* – marula

BIRDS (311 species recorded)
bee-eaters – European, little
blue waxbill
Cape vulture
crowned plover
eagles – brown snake, martial
francolins – crested, Natal,
   Swainson's
guineafowls – crowned, helmeted
harlequin quail

kingfishers – brownhooded,
   striped
melba finch
pinkthroated twinspot
plumcoloured starling
purplecrested lourie
redcrested korhaan
rollers – European,
   lilacbreasted
whitebellied sunbird

MAMMALS

antbear (aardvark)
black-backed jackal
bushbuck
bushpig
civet
duiker – common, red
impala
kudu
large-spotted genet

mongooses – banded,
  slender, white-tailed
nyala
porcupine
reedbuck
serval
steenbok
suni
warthog

Zebra were reintroduced in 1992, and blue wildebeest and mountain reedbuck in 1993. Giraffe are also to be reintroduced.

PONGOLAPOORT PUBLIC RESORT NATURE RESERVE

Area: 11 693 ha
Proclamation: Pending

LOCATION
Northern Zululand. The turn-off to the resort is 8 km off the N2, north of Mkuze village. Turn right at the Jozini sign. The resort is signposted on the left of this road. From the north, take the Jozini turn-off from the N2.

FEATURES
At present no facilities are provided. The reserve is open to day visitors. Tiger fishing in the Jozini dam is popular. This is a scenically attractive area, with grasslands and acacia scrub surrounding the dam against the backdrop of the Lebombo mountains. It is about an hour's drive from the Mkuzi Game Reserve and ten minutes from the Ghost Mountain Inn in Mkuze village. A good birding locality, 228 species have been recorded. This area is best visited during the winter months when tracks are passable.

This reserve has been linked up with neighbouring private game ranches and Provincial Nature Conservation areas to establish a biosphere reserve in this corner of northern Zululand, bordering on the Eastern Transvaal. It encompasses approximately 31 000 ha surrounding the Jozini dam. The area can support viable populations of larger herbivores and predators including black and white rhino, elephant and wild dog.

DESCRIPTION
In the western region there are patches of dense acacia-dominated thorn scrub, open savanna woodland and grasslands to the water's edge. On

the eastern side is a stretch of higher ground with krantzes, deep wooded gullies and forest patches on the Lebombo mountains. Seasonal fluctuations in water levels of the dam cause the clay-like soils to become waterlogged and some of the tracks used by vehicles are submerged when the dam is filled to capacity.

HISTORICAL NOTES
The Jozini dam's construction was started in 1958. The present reserve was previously owned by cattle farmers whose land was expropriated in the mid-1960s as the waters of the dam flooded the flat grassland, tree savanna and thorn scrub – originally prime cattle grazing country.

TREES
Acacia karroo – sweet thorn
Acacia nigrescens – knobthorn
Acacia nilotica – scented thorn
Acacia tortilis – umbrella thorn
Dichrostachys cinerea – sickle bush
Encephalartos lebomboensis – Lebombo cycad
Encephalartos ngoyanus – Ngoye cycad
Euclea species
Maytenus species
Schotia brachypetala – weeping boer-bean/tree fuchsia
Spirostachys africana – tamboti

BIRDS (228 species recorded)
arrowmarked babbler
bearded woodpecker
bluecheeked bee-eater
burntnecked eremomela
Cape shoveller
cuckoos – great spotted, Jacobin, striped
ducks – African black, fulvous, knobbilled, yellowbilled
eagles – African fish, African hawk, bateleur, brown snake, longcrested, tawny, Wahlberg's
fairy flycatcher
goldenbreasted bunting
grey lourie
grey penduline tit
guineafowls – crested, helmeted
Heuglin's robin

hornbills – crowned, grey, redbilled, trumpeter, yellowbilled
korhaans – blackbellied, redcrested
lemonbreasted canary
little bittern
little stint
lizard buzzard
melba finch
Namaqua dove
orangebreasted waxbill
osprey
owls – grass, whitefaced
painted snipe
pallid harrier
pinkbacked pelican
pinkthroated twinspot
plumcoloured starling
redbreasted swallow

rollers – European, lilacbreasted,
  purple
Rudd's apalis
ruff
sabota lark
secretarybird
shrikes – gorgeous bush,
  longtailed

storks – black, yellowbilled
sunbirds – marico, Neergard's
teals – Hottentot, redbilled
vultures – lappetfaced,
  whitebacked, whiteheaded
wattled plover
white helmetshrike

MAMMALS

bushbuck
common duiker
large-spotted genet
mongooses – banded, slender,
  water, white-tailed

porcupine
scrub hare
thick-tailed bushbaby
vervet monkey

PONGOLWANE PRIVATE NATURE RESERVE

Area: Unknown
Established: 1986

LOCATION

Northern Zululand, at the foot of the Lebombo mountains on the western shoreline of the Jozini (Pongolapoort) dam, adjoining Leeukop game ranch. This nature reserve and the Nkwazi Lodge fall within the recently established Pongolapoort Biosphere Reserve (31 000 ha). Entrance to this reserve is 24 km from Mkuze off the N2.

FEATURES

Situated at the foot of the Lebombo mountains on the western shore of the Jozini dam, there are fine views across the water into the Pongola Nature Reserve. From the lodges there is good game viewing with white rhino, giraffe, kudu and plains game coming to the water's edge to drink. Bird life is prolific, especially aquatic species. Over the winter months a count may reveal over 5 000 whitefaced ducks, about 1 000 moulting spurwinged geese, several other wildfowl species, and at least a dozen or more wader species on the *Cynodon* lawns, along the banks and in the shallows. There is an established nesting colony of yellowbilled storks in the north-eastern region of the dam and on boat rides hippo and crocodiles are usually seen.

During the summer months, fishing is very popular. Good-sized barbel (catfish) and bream may be caught. It is one of the few areas in Zululand where the highly prized tiger fish, a species renowned for putting up a spectacular fight, can be angled for. Two game viewing drives from an open 4x4 vehicle are conducted daily, as well as boat trips. These excursions are included in the overall tariff.

There is accommodation for 19 people in total privacy at the two lodges.

DESCRIPTION

The reserve is characterised by typical northern Zululand acacia-dominated grassveld, with thickets, woodland and bush clumps. The terrain is mainly flat and similar in topography and habitat to areas in Mkuzi Game Reserve, the Pongalopoort Public Resort Nature Reserve and Leeukop Game Ranch.

ACCOMMODATION

The Nkwazi luxury lodge is fully equipped with Eskom power and air-conditioning or ceiling fans in all the rooms. It accommodates a maximum of 14 persons. A boma with modern braai facilities is provided and an unfenced swimming pool is available.

The Igababa Lodge, which is similar, is situated about 100 m away and accommodates five persons. At both lodges guests supply their own food and drink and cook their own meals, but a daily cleaning service is provided. Reservations are made with the nature reserve.

MAMMALS

The reserve has similar plains game species to Mkuzi Game Reserve but black rhino are absent.

BIRDS

Cape shoveller
ducks – African black, fulvous,
   knobbilled, whitefaced, yellowbilled
fish eagle
geese – Egyptian, spurwinged
glossy ibis
sandpipers – marsh, wood
secretarybird
vultures – lappetfaced

greenshank
helmeted guineafowl
herons – goliath, squacco
little stint
osprey
redbilled teal
   whitebacked
wattled plover
yellowbilled stork

LEEUKOP GAME RANCH

Area: 6 000 ha
Established: 1992

LOCATION
Northern Zululand, bordering on the Pongolo river and Jozini (Pongolapoort) dam. Entrance is off the N2 between Mkuze and Gollel, about 1 km from the Pongolo river.

FEATURES
Bordering on the Pongolo river and Jozini dam, Leeukop's 6 000 ha contains a rich flora with a large variety of game and bird species. The area is classed as a Natural Heritage Site (Site No 127) and the Mvubu camp falls within the recently formed Pongolapoort biosphere reserve (31 000 ha). Two game viewing drives per day are available with a guide in an open 4x4 vehicle. Guests may arrange their own programmes regarding times of departure and return from drives. Alternatively, the game drives, which are included in the accommodation costs, can be exchanged for boat rides. There are two eight-seater double-hull boats and motors available. Mhlozi and Sondaba camps are situated about 15 km from the boat launching site.

It is also possible to request night spotlight game viewing drives. There are no restricted areas and long walks can be undertaken, with or without a guide.

Although guests provide their own food and drink, venison, braai-sausage, sosaties (kebabs), cheese-sausage, biltong and dry wors can be purchased.

As with the nearby Pongolapoort Public Resort Nature Reserve and Pongolwane Private Nature Reserve, excellent angling for tiger fish, as well as bream and barbel, can be enjoyed during the summer months. In winter, the large concentrations of wildfowl and waders add to the pleasure of bird watching.

DESCRIPTION
Situated in the northern Zululand bushveld on the Pongolo river and Jozini dam, this reserve contains riverine trees, thicket and scrub and acacia-dominated grassveld with open woodland and bush clumps. The topography and vegetation types are similar to the low-lying flats in Mkuzi Game Reserve and adjoining Pongola Public Resort Nature Reserve and Pongolwane Private Nature Reserve.

ACCOMMODATION
There are three separate camps in the reserve. Mhlozi camp accommodates 14 persons in three two-bedded rondavels with shower and toilet en suite, three two-bedded huts and one two-bedded rondavel sharing an

ablution block. Mvubu Camp accommodates 12 persons in six two-bedded huts. Sondaba camp houses 10 persons in five two-bedded huts sharing an ablution block. The Mhlozi and Sondaba Camps operate off a 12 volt power system but gas fridges, freezers and geysers are provided. Mvubu Camp has Eskom power and each hut is fitted with a ceiling fan.

Facilities include a large, fully equipped kitchen and lounge containing gas stove, fridge, freezer and a boma with full braai facilities. There is a swimming pool with a thatch roof over the shallow end. All bedding, towels, crockery, cutlery, etc. are provided. Visitors cater for themselves but there is a daily cleaning service.

Reservations are made with the ranch.

MAMMALS

The reserve contains most of the mammals (except black rhino) to be found in Mkuzi Game Reserve.

UMZIKI GAME RANCH

Area: Unknown
Established: 1984

LOCATION

Northern Zululand, approximately 20 km from Magudu. The turn-off to the ranch is off the Pongola-Vryheid tar road. Take district road D496 and continue to the steel entrance gates, then follow the road until approximately 75 m from the Mkuze river, turn to the right and continue to the lodge. The ranch is situated within 20 km of an airstrip.

FEATURES

For non-hunting parties, there is a network of roads for game viewing drives. A bakkie is recommended. Walks with a guide can be undertaken anywhere in the reserve. The river, with a clean sandy bed and pools, is completely safe for swimming. Fishing for catfish (barbel) and yellowfish (scalies) is available. Guests must bring their own tackle.

This ranch is mainly used by hunting parties. The facilities provided include vehicles for hire, trackers, and a butchery with full slaughtering services, i.e. skinner, fly-screened working area and hanging space, electric bandsaw, walk-in coldroom and large deep-freeze room. Skinners will cut and prepare biltong if required but clients must provide their own salt. Only certain calibre rifles may be used. Handguns, shotguns and crossbows are not permitted to be used unless prior arrangements have been made with the owners. The ranch is situated within 20 km of a resident taxidermist.

"Umziki" is the Zulu name for the reedbuck.

DESCRIPTION
The ranch comprises typical north-eastern Natal bushveld with the Mkuze river flowing through it. There are some fine riverine forest trees along the river banks, thicket with flat grass plains and densely bushed hillsides rising above to some mountainous areas.

ACCOMMODATION
There is a 12-bedded, fully furnished, thatched lodge, with all bedding and towels provided, and a fully equipped kitchen including stove, deep-freeze, fridge and all cutlery, pots and pans, etc. The lodge has Eskom power, hot and cold running water and separate bath, shower and toilet. Braai facilities are provided, with servants in attendance. Guests need only bring food, drink and toiletries. Extra camp beds can be added if required.

Reservations should be made with the ranch.

BIRDS
There is no list available but species would be similar to those found in Mkuzi Game Reserve.

MAMMALS
bushbuck
duiker – common, red
giraffe
impala
kudu
mountain reedbuck
nyala

reedbuck
steenbok
warthog
waterbuck
white rhino
zebra

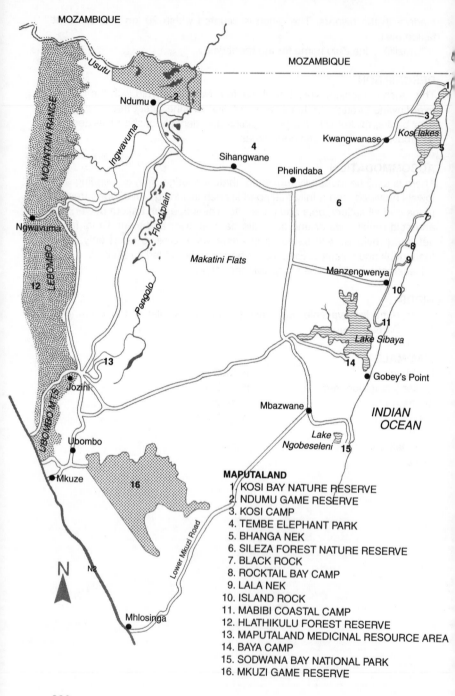

MAPUTALAND

1. KOSI BAY NATURE RESERVE
2. NDUMU GAME RESERVE
3. KOSI CAMP
4. TEMBE ELEPHANT PARK
5. BHANGA NEK
6. SILEZA FOREST NATURE RESERVE
7. BLACK ROCK
8. ROCKTAIL BAY CAMP
9. LALA NEK
10. ISLAND ROCK
11. MABIBI COASTAL CAMP
12. HLATHIKULU FOREST RESERVE
13. MAPUTALAND MEDICINAL RESOURCE AREA
14. BAYA CAMP
15. SODWANA BAY NATIONAL PARK
16. MKUZI GAME RESERVE

MAPUTALAND

Maputaland is generally defined as the area bounded by the Mozambique border in the north, by the Lebombo mountain range in the west, the Mkuze river and across the upper Lake St Lucia swamps intersecting the coast just north of St Mary's Hill in the south, and by the Indian Ocean in the east. It covers an area of about 8 000 sq km, incorporating the Ingwavuma and Ubombo magisterial districts. This north-eastern corner of Natal was for many years known as Tongaland, after the Thonga tribe who settled this region about three centuries ago, having moved south from Mozambique. In historical times it was also known for a short while as Maputaland and in recent years the KwaZulu government authorities requested that this name be reinstated.

There is evidence that Early Stone Age humans settled the area about 130 000 years ago and lived in caves in the Lebombo mountains.

This region, one of the most beautiful but least-known areas of South Africa, only became accessible to tourists from the mid-1960s. The roads had previously been in too poor a condition.

Historically the area teemed with game and attracted hunters in large numbers as far back as the 1850s. Elephant and hippo were the main targets as well as the enormous herds of plains game and predators such as lion, leopard, cheetah and hyaena recorded by the early hunters and traders. In addition to the hunters who exterminated many species of game and predators in Maputaland, an outbreak of rinderpest took a heavy toll of game and livestock between 1895-1903. Then between 1917-1919 both magisterial districts were thrown open to hunters because of an outbreak of nagana and the policy of exterminating wildlife to eradicate the tsetse fly. Over the following years many thousands more animals were slaughtered, including predatory species that were a nuisance to livestock and for which bounties were paid.

Maputaland is unique in many respects. It incorporates a wide diversity of ecosystems. There are magnificent offshore coral reefs, wide beaches, lush dune forests, coastal lakes including Lake Sibaya, the largest freshwater lake in South Africa, and the spectacular Kosi lakes and estuarine system with raffia palms, swamp forests and tropical mangrove species. Moving inland along the 60 km coastal plain, the topography seldom rises more than 100 m above sea level to the Lebombo mountains, parts of which rise to 700 m above sea level. There are areas of coastal grass and palmveld, the Mosi swamp, small papyrus-lined pans, bushveld, thicket, the unusual sand forest and forested gorges in the mountains. Along the Usutu and Pongolo rivers there is impressive riverine forest as well as a

201

chain of natural lakes and pans along the floodplain of the Pongolo river between the mountains and Ndumu Game Reserve.

Development in Maputaland has been minimal, and includes commercial timber plantations along the sandy coastal regions and the failed Jozini dam irrigation scheme. It is a poor agricultural area and tourism is likely to be the major industry of the future. The attractions are the magnificent coral reefs and about 1 200 colourful tropical and other fish species in the clean warm waters of the Indian Ocean, excellent lake, surf and big game fishing, scuba diving and unspoiled beaches, attractive camps, wilderness trails, splendid game parks and an outstanding bird and plant life in an area of great scenic beauty.

SODWANA BAY NATIONAL PARK

Area: 413 ha
Established: 7 December 1950

LOCATION
Maputaland coast. From the north, Sodwana is approached by turning off the N2 at Candover to Jozini, from where the route is clearly signposted via Tshongwe and Mbazwana. From the south, turn off the N2 at Mhlosinga, north of Hluhluwe, from where Sodwana is well signposted on the direct lower Mkuze road to Mbazwana and then to the park.

FEATURES
Sodwana is renowned for its sport fishing. Record billfish and sailfish have been landed. It is probably South Africa's most famous ski-boating and angling resort and has become the largest open camping ground in the southern hemisphere. The diversity of fish and invertebrates on the tropical coral reefs attracts thousands of scuba divers and underwater photographers. During the summer months night tours to observe the nesting of loggerhead and leatherback turtles may be booked. There is a short self-guided trail through the coastal dunes and a longer nature trail to the near-by Ngoboseleni lake, one of the last unspoilt coastal lakes in Zululand. The vegetation, bird and mammalian fauna are also very interesting, as are the colourful butterflies and a myriad other insect species.

DESCRIPTION
The popularity of Sodwana stems from its incredible angling potential for ski-boat, rock and shore fishermen. The warm water of the Agulhas current comes in very close to shore, the continental shelf reaches to within a kilometre of the beach, and the very deep trenches, with near vertical sides,

provide for exceptionally deep water very near to land, which is ideal for game fish.

Sodwana is famous too for the extensive coral reefs just offshore, with colourful soft corals of various shades and hues, and large formations of the hard but delicate, staghorn, flat, plate-shaped and brain corals. In these warm, tropical, silt-free waters, plant life thrives and the reefs support an endless variety of colourful sea creatures from worms to sea cucumbers, anemones, clams, cowries, octopus and crayfish. Several hundred species of fish, in a multitude of colours, shapes and sizes, shelter, feed and breed in varying depths from the deep ocean to the shallow zones.

Reefs such as Two Mile Reef, Stringer and Quarter Mile off Jesser Point have become famous for scuba divers and underwater photographers and for many, many thousands of tourists who delight in donning snorkel and goggles to marvel at this undersea wonderworld.

For the angler, the list of desirable game fish runs to well over 100 species. There are also some 15 shark species which occur in these waters.

In recent years game fishing (billfish) has become increasingly popular off the Sodwana coastline, with catches of large black, blue and striped marlin and sailfish. Apart from the sport involved, this new industry is of considerable economic importance.

HISTORICAL NOTES

This resort was originally proclaimed as "Sordwana" instead of "Sodwana", the Zulu name for the stream, which means "the little one on its own". This stream drains two inland lakes, Ngobozeleni and Shazibe, through an extensive reed swamp. It enters the sea north of Jesser Point, a rocky promontory which shelters the estuary and bay from southerly storms and currents. Jesser Point was named after Colonel Jesser Coope, who, with an engineer, surveyed the bay as a possible harbour for the British in 1888. Proposals to build a harbour have been made repeatedly over the years and further surveys were undertaken in 1923, 1948 and 1952. Even up until 1974, the bay was still considered for harbour development.

Sodwana was once a base for gun runners and ivory hunters who were attracted to the sheltered anchorage in the bay and its access to inland plains and forests rich in game. As the only source of fresh water between the Umfolozi river mouth in the south, and Kosi estuary in the north, it must have been a godsend to shipwrecked survivors along this desolate coast.

In 1951 only a handful of camp sites and a rough toilet were available, but without a water supply to the camp sites. In 1952, a game guard, Sgt Dlozi Nxumalo, who became a legend in his time, was transferred from Mkuzi Game Reserve to run the small camping ground. From 1956 the increase in visitor numbers required that a water supply system be installed. At this stage the development of the resort was administered by Senior Ranger Singie Denyer of Mkuzi Game Reserve. In 1963 ranger Henry Smith was appointed to extend and manage this now very well known and popular resort. During the following years development was rapid. Access to Sodwana was improved by building a new hardened road and a bridge which crossed the stream from the northern side. This replaced the maze of almost impossible to negotiate sand tracks that came in from south of Lake Ngoboseleni. The bridge was completed in May 1972, but it proved to be a disaster as it prevented sufficient inflow of salt-water. It resulted in some 80 per cent of the black mangrove *Bruguiera gymnorrhiza*, trees and saplings dying. In June 1976 construction started on a new bridge, which was completed in March 1977. To this day the mangrove community has never fully recovered and the small stream lost much of its potential and value as a breeding nursery for many forms of estuarine life. Many species of typical mangrove fauna such as snails, crabs, shrimps and small fish were exterminated.

ACCOMMODATION
Ten five-bedded and ten eight-bedded fully equipped and serviced log cabins are available. There are luxury camp sites with water and electricity in the Gwalagwala compound. Open camp sites of varying sizes are available, served by water points, showers and ablution facilities. Visitors must bring their own tents, caravans and camping equipment. Plug points for refrigerators and freezer drawers may be hired. Bait and ice are on sale and a well-stocked supermarket, from which groceries, patent medicines and beach equipment may be purchased, is situated within the park. There are privately owned dive shops, which sell a whole range of underwater equipment and who run courses and arrange diving excursions from the resort. A community hall is available for functions. Reservations for the camp should be made with the Natal Parks Board, Sodwana office.

TREES
There are several vegetation habitats to explore at Sodwana for those interested in plant life and ecology. They are the pioneer dune binding species, the coastal dune forest, thickets, open, dry and moist grass and sedge areas, riverine vegetation, swamp forest and aquatic species. A few of the plants to be found are:

Acacia karroo – sweet thorn
Balanites maughamii – green thorn
Cassine aethiopica – koo-boo berry
Cassipourea gerrardii – common onionwood
Croton gratissimus – white lavender fever-berry
Diospyros inhacaensis – Zulu jackal-berry
Diospyros rotundifolia – dune jackal-berry
Drypetes natalensis – Natal ironplum
Euclea divinorum – magic guarri
Euclea undulata – common guarri
Mimusops caffra – coastal red milkwood
Putterlickia verrucosa – false forest spike-thorn
Scolopia zeyheri – thorn pear

Sideroxylon inerme – white milkwood
Strychnos madagascariensis – black monkey orange
Tarenna littoralis – dune butterspoon bush
Vepris lanceolata – white ironwood
Ziziphus mucronata – buffalo thorn

The exotic beefwood tree *Casuarina equisetifolia* was planted in 1951 to stabilise the sand dunes.

BIRDS
Some birds of note are:

Cape cormorant
Cape gannet
coucals – black, Burchell's, green
forest weaver
frigatebird
giant petrel
louries – Knysna, purplecrested
pinkthroated longclaw

robins – brown, Natal
roseringed parakeet
Rudd's apalis
sunbirds – collared, grey, olive
terns – Caspian, swift
Woodwards' batis
yellowbellied bulbul
yellowspotted nicator

MAMMALS
Although tourists are unlikely to see many species of mammals at Sodwana, the following species occur in the various habitats and may be encountered along the approach road, and on the trails:

aardwolf
bushpig
duiker – common, red
honey badger
jackals – black-backed, side-striped
large-spotted genet
mongooses – large grey, slender,
    water, white-tailed

monkeys – samango, vervet
red squirrel
reedbuck
scrub hare
steenbok
striped polecat
suni
thick-tailed bushbaby

REPTILES
Reptile life in this region is prolific, with about 38 species having been collected, including the venomous green mamba, boomslang, vine snake, Egyptian cobra, forest cobra, common puff adder and the beautifully marked, highly venomous but seldom seen, gaboon adder. Crocodiles occur in small numbers in lakes Ngoboseleni and Shazibe, where they breed and occasionally make an appearance in the Sodwana stream. Water or Nile monitor lizards are fairly common in this area.

FISH
Notable species are:

barracuda
blacktail

bonito
elf (shad)

kingfish species
kob (salmon)
mackerel
musselcracker
Natal stumpnose
pompons
queenfish
river bream
rock cod species

roman
seventy-four
slinger
spotted grunter
steenbras
stonebream
tuna
wahoo

BAYA CAMP (LAKE SIBAYA)

Area: Part of the Maputaland marine reserve
Established: 1986

LOCATION
Maputaland coast. From the N2 take the lower Mkuzi road turn-off at Mhlosinga to Mbazwana, then follow the signs for about 20 km to Baya Camp. A 4x4 vehicle is recommended but is not essential. A second route is via Jozini. Follow the Sodwana signs from the N2 to Mbazwana. On reaching Mbazwana, take the road to the forestry station. From the airstrip the camp is well signposted.

FEATURES
The camp is a place where the visitor can relax in an area of great scenic beauty and indulge in fishing, bird watching, photography, guided boat trips, walking nature trails or enjoy the scenery and wildlife from the camp, which is sited almost at the water's edge, amid a woodland of mainly umdoni (water berry) trees.

There are two hides for bird viewing, situated close to small pans and within walking distance of the camp. Boats are available for hire. Access to a picnic site on the beach at Nine Mile can be arranged.

DESCRIPTION
The name "Sibaya" is derived from the Zulu word "isibayo" – a cattle kraal, a circle or enclosure with no visible outlet – as is the case with this lake. Sibaya, the largest freshwater body in South Africa, covers between 60-77 sq km, depending on water levels. It has an average depth of 13 m, an average length of nearly 18 km and is some 17 km in width. The maximum depth is 43 m and it is about 20 m above mean sea level. The lake is separated from the sea by a forested dune formation up to 165 m high, and the camp is situated on the eastern shore of the south-west basin.

There are a variety of habitats to explore and interesting vegetation, reptiles, birds and animals to be looked for. Around the lake are large moist grasslands, rolling, sandy, dry grasslands, open woodland, thickets and coastal dune forest. There are numerous sheltered, tongue-like creeks, some open, others overhung by trees, casting colourful reflections, yet others partially choked by papyrus beds.

ACCOMMODATION
There is a small camp of four two-bedded and four three-bedded huts, equipped with handbasins and cold running water. Bedding is supplied. A communal lounge-dining area is serviced by a fully equipped communal kitchen. Ablution blocks with hot and cold running water are provided. Hot water is obtained from solar panels and cannot be guaranteed during cold, overcast weather. Battery-powered lights are available in each hut and a deep-freeze is available for use in the kitchen. Make reservations with the KwaZulu Department of Nature Conservation, Pietermaritzburg.

TREES
Many of the trees and shrubs to be found on the Maputaland coastal plain are of great botanical interest. Some of the trees and shrubs include:
Aloe barberiae (A. bainesii) – tree aloe
Bridelia cathartica – blue sweet-berry
Canthium setiflorum – rough-leaved rock alder
Carissa bispinosa – forest num-num
Catunaregam spinosa – thorny bone-apple
Commiphora neglecta – green-stem corkwood
Crotalaria capensis – Cape rattle-pod
Croton gratissimus – lavender fever-berry
Dovyalis longispina – Natal apricot
Ephippiocarpa orientalis – dwarf toad tree
Erythrococca berberidea – prickly red-berry
Ficus bubu – Swazi fig
Ficus burtt-davyi – veld fig
Ficus verruculosa – water fig
Lagynias lasiantha – Natal medlar
Manilkara concolor – Zulu milkberry
Morus mesozygia – African mulberry
Pancovia golungensis – false soap-berry
Rhus gueinzii – thorny karree
Sapium integerrimum – duiker berry
Strychnos decussata – Cape teak
Strychnos henningsii – red bitter-berry
Zanthoxylum capense – small knobwood

There are also numerous climbers and scandent shrubs of interest, and the grassland flowers are lovely.

BIRDS (296 species)

The moist grasslands are particularly good for yellowthroated and pink-throated longclaws, the shallow vleis and creeks for species such as dabchick, moorhen, jacana, little bittern and the rare greatcrested grebe. Some of the local birds to be seen are:

brown robin

bulbuls – sombre, terrestrial, yellowbellied

gorgeous bush shrike

green twinspot

grey waxbill

greyrumped swallows

hawks – bat, cuckoo

herons – blackcrowned night, greenbacked, rufousbellied, squacco

narina trogon

Natal nightjar

sunbirds – grey, purplebanded

terns – Caspian, whiskered, whitewinged

Woodwards' batis

yellow white-eye

yellowspotted nicator

MAMMALS

Lake Sibaya supports quite a large hippo population but is not noted for a diversity of animal species. Visitors may encounter the following:

African wild cat

civet

duiker – common, red

four-toed elephant shrew

greater canerat

honey badger

large-spotted genet

mongooses – banded, slender, water, white-tailed

monkeys – samango, vervet

red squirrel

reedbuck

scrub hare

shrews – black, grey, lesser red musk

side-striped jackal

thick-tailed bushbaby

Wahlberg's epauletted fruit bat

REPTILES

Crocodiles are not abundant but nevertheless care must be taken any-where near the water's edge. There are also some highly venomous snakes. Forest cobra, Egyptian cobra, green mamba, puff adder, and in the coastal dune forest, gaboon adders, occur. Pythons and water monitor lizards are not uncommon. For those interested in frogs, some 22 species, many of them very colourful, may be found.

FISH

Although the lake is huge, it is very poor in nutrients and fish life is disap-pointing. Of the 18 species recorded, tilapia and the sharptooth catfish or barbel, are the only species caught in any numbers. The tilapia seldom exceed 1,5 kg but barbel reach very large sizes.

MABIBI COASTAL CAMP

Area: Within the Maputaland coastal reserve
Established: 1986

LOCATION
Maputaland coast. From the N2 take the Jozini turn-off and follow the Sodwana signboards to Mbazwana. From Mbazwana take the Mseleni-Pelindaba road to the Manzengwenya turn-off on the right. Follow this road through forestry plantations periodically marked by the KwaZulu Department of Nature Conservation signs. On reaching the sign to Manzengwenya offices, keep right and follow the main track in a south-easterly direction to Mabibi camp. From the south, the approach is via the Mhlosinga turn-off to Sodwana from the N2. Follow the signs to Sodwana as far as Mbazwana, then take the Mseleni-Pelindaba road, and proceed as described. A 4x4 vehicle or one with a high clearance is essential.

FEATURES
A secluded camp site, a stretch of unspoilt beach, well known for excellent surf fishing; warm, clear water with offshore reefs incredibly rich in tropical fish and marine life and a paradise for snorkelling and underwater photography make up Mabibi. There is interesting dune vegetation and various coastal bird species. It is a wonderful, relaxing venue.

DESCRIPTION
Situated north-east of Lake Sibaya, this small, well-known camping site has been established on a plateau high up amid the luxuriant subtropical dune forest.

From Mabibi northwards to Kosi Bay, this stretch of unspoiled beach, with clear, warm water, magnificent reefs, coral reefs and sheltered bays, is regarded as one of the finest in southern Africa. Mabibi is a paradise for the scuba diver, underwater photographer, the naturalist who wants to explore the intertidal life of the rock pools and reefs, and for the holiday-maker who merely wants to relax in the sun on an unspoilt beach. Mabibi is also well known for its excellent rock and offshore angling.

Access to the beach is on foot through a tunnel of tangled coastal forest, leading to a steep wooden ladder descending to the dunes below. The return climb is not easy for small toddlers or the elderly, but if one pauses to enjoy the clear calls of olive and grey sunbirds, the scolding of square-tailed drongos, the calls of terrestrial and yellowbellied bulbuls, or the melodious songs of brown and Natal robins, the effort is soon forgotten.

ACCOMMODATION
There are 10 sheltered camping and caravan sites. An ablution block with hot and cold water and a covered, as well as an open, communal braai

209

facility is provided. Please note that generators are not permitted. Vehicles are not permitted on the beach. Reservations for camp sites are made with the KwaZulu Department of Nature Conservation, Pietermaritzburg.

TREES
The dune forest composition is typical for this area of Maputaland. Apart from the common, dominant trees, a number of climbers and shrubs are of interest. Some of these are:
Acacia kraussiana – coast climbing thorn
Acridocarpus natalitius – moth-fruit
Artabotrys monteiroae – large hook-berry
Brachylaena discolor – coast silver oak
Carissa macrocarpa – big num-num
Dalbergia armata – thorny rope
Dalbergia obovata – climbing flat-bean
Deinbollia oblongifolia – dune soap-berry
Dracaena aletriformis (D. hookeriana) – large-leaved dragon tree
Garcinia livingstonei – lowveld mangosteen
Grewia caffra – climbing raisin
Mimusops caffra – coastal red milkwood
Rhoicissus digitata – baboon grape
Strelitzia nicolai – Natal wild banana
Syzygium cordatum – water berry
Tabernaemontana elegans – toad tree
Tarenna junodii – climbing Tarenna
Urera trinervis (U. cameroonensis) – climbing nettle
Vangueria infausta – wild medlar

BIRDS
The bird life is prolific and in the dune forest proper, on the forest margins and in woodland areas, some colourful species are to be found. These are:

black cuckooshrike
blackcrowned tchagra
bluebilled firefinch
cardinal woodpecker
collared sunbird
dusky flycatcher
forest weaver
goldenbreasted bunting
goldenrumped tinker barbet
goldentailed woodpecker
bush shrikes – gorgeous, greyheaded
green coucal
green twinspot

grey waxbill
narina trogon
puffback
purplebanded sunbird
louries – Knysna,
    purplecrested
Rudd's apalis
rufousnaped lark
tambourine dove
yellow white-eye
yellowbreasted warbler
yellowspotted nicator

MAMMALS
There are not many animal species to be seen at Mabibi. Blue duiker, red squirrel, samango and vervet monkeys are the commonest with, perhaps, large-spotted genets surprised by the light of a torch at night and thick-tailed bushbabies likely to be heard. Suni, slender mongoose, steenbok, common duiker, scrub hare and porcupine have been recorded north of Lake Sibaya, at Mabibi and in the Manzengwenya forests.

REPTILES
A number of interesting, small burrowing reptiles occur in this sandy country, as well as some large, highly venomous snakes, such as gaboon adder, puff adder, green mamba, forest cobra, Egyptian cobra, boomslang, vine snake and the harmless python and water and rock monitor lizards.

LALA NEK and BLACK ROCK

Area: Part of the Maputaland coastal reserve
Established: 1986

LOCATION
Maputaland coast. From the N2 take the lower Mkuzi road turn-off at Mhlosinga to Mbazwana and then go via Mseleni to the Manzengwenya forest station. Alternatively, take the Jozini turn-off from the N2 to Mbazwana and then as above. Follow the Lala Nek, Rocktail Bay track to Black Rock. A 4x4 vehicle is essential.

FEATURES
This is the most exclusive and private beach on the entire coastline. The Maputaland Marine Reserve Number 2 extends from Black Rock, a well-known landmark, northwards to Banga Nek. No vehicles are permitted on any section of this beach. It is a prime game fishing area, with warm tropical sea, marvellous tropical fish and marine life for snorkel diving, excellent light tackle angling, interesting seabirds and dune vegetation.

Few people who have walked this desolate beach at sunrise or on a night when the moon is full, are ever likely to forget the experience.

DESCRIPTION
Lala Nek and Black Rock have always enjoyed the reputation of being prime game fishing sites by those fortunate enough to have had the privilege of visiting the area.

At Black Rock, the lower platform, whose sea-facing sides are festooned with bunches of mussels, drops straight down into very deep water. It is hardly surprising that some South African record-sized game fish have been hooked off this point. The sheltered bay to the north is excellent for underwater exploration, whether with expensive equipment or with a simple snorkel and goggles. Along this entire stretch of coastline, from Sodwana bay in the south northwards to Kosi bay estuary, the water is warm, crystal clear and richly endowed with coral platforms and seaweed, oyster and mussel covered reefs supporting every imaginable type of sea creature. There are many hundreds of colourful tropical fish that inhabit these zones, and rays, stingrays, sandsharks, sharks and well over 100 species of game fish that dwell in deeper waters.

Bouton's snake-eyed skink *Cryptoblepharus boutoni* – a remarkable small, blackish skink – is found on Black Rock, the only locality where it occurs in South Africa. These skinks live on small crabs and fish. They dive into small pools to capture fish and, to escape their main predators, large crabs and seabirds, swim underwater to hide in rock crevices. The nearest other known locality where they occur is Inhambane in Mozambique.

Five species of sea turtle occur off these beaches, the green, olive ridley, hawksbill, loggerhead and leatherback. Turtles are commonly seen in the surf off Black Rock and the latter two species nest along this section of the coast. Leatherback turtles may weigh up to 900 kg and measure 2 m in length. Whale sharks weighing up to 40 tonnes and up to 18 m in length, as well as humpback whales, pass up and down the coast.

ACCOMMODATION

At Lala Nek there is a fully equipped, three-bedroomed (eight beds), furnished lodge, which is hidden beneath the dune forest canopy and shaded by large spreading coastal red milkwood trees. It is sheltered from the wind and no more than about 20 m from the beach. This lodge is not yet open to the public.

At present a day permit is required to visit Lala Nek and Black Rock. Enquire at the KwaZulu Department of Nature Conservation offices at Manzengwenya.

BIRDS

During the winter months, seabirds such as Cape gannets, albatrosses, skuas, petrels, prions, frigatebirds, terns and Cape cormorants may be observed. In the dune forest the dawn chorus of brown and Natal robins, yellowspotted nicator, grey sunbird, forest weaver, and the mingled calls of squaretailed drongo, bulbuls, gorgeous bushshrike, puffback and southern boubou is memorable.

ROCKTAIL BAY CAMP

Area: About 10 ha
Established: 1982

LOCATION
Maputaland coast. From the N2 take the Jozini turn-off, then follow the Sodwana signboards to Mbazwana and from there via Mseleni to the Manzengwenya turn-off. Follow this road through to the KwaZulu Department of Nature Conservation offices, then past Lala Nek on the track to Rocktail bay. If you do not have a 4x4 vehicle, which is essential, you can arrange to be picked up at a point about 20 km from the camp. Alternatively, you can arrange to fly to Mkuze village and be transferred by vehicle or helicopter to Rocktail bay camp. The camp is situated just south of Black Rock, midway between Sodwana bay and Kosi estuary.

It can also be approached from the south by taking the lower Mkuze road turn-off from the N2 at Mhlosinga. Follow the route signposted Sodwana as far as Mbazwana, then continue via Mseleni on the Pelindaba-Kwangwanase road until the Manzengwenya turn-off is reached. Turn right and follow the signboards as described above.

FEATURES
There is a small, luxuriously appointed camp, built into the dune forest right on the edge of one of the finest stretches of coastline in South Africa. The sea offers superb scuba diving over inshore reefs that support an incredible variety of colourful fish and marine organisms. It is a noted surf angling beach. During the summer nights huge sea turtles come ashore to lay their eggs. There are nature walks through a variety of habitats featuring interesting vegetation, small mammals and some rare and unusual forest, grassland and marine bird species. Above all, it provides an exclusive beach for ultimate relaxation. For the visitor in search of a wilderness experience, Rocktail bay is an ideal venue.

Visitors staying at Rocktail Bay Camp may obtain a day permit from the Manzengwenya offices to visit Black Rock, about an hour's drive to the north, or to Lala Nek in the south. It is an ideal venue for exploration of Maputaland's wonderful coastline.

Rocktail Bay Camp is a joint venture between private enterprise (Wilderness Safaris) and the KwaZulu Department of Nature Conservation. In addition to employment opportunities, a percentage of the tourist revenue earned is returned to the tribal authority and this, it is hoped, will create an awareness of the benefits to be gained from tourism in wilderness areas.

DESCRIPTION
From the viewing decks of the chalets, superb views over the lower forest canopy enable one to enjoy the rich bird life and colourful butterflies of the dune forest. A wooden boardwalk takes one through the forest and over

the dunes to one of the most secluded beaches on this magnificent stretch of coastline. The name "Rocktail" comes from the shape of a reef which shelters the bay in front of the camp.

This is one of the few areas where scuba divers can enter the sea from the shore and swim out to the magnificent offshore reefs. The area is good for underwater exploration and is regarded as one of the country's prime fishing spots.

During the summer months visitors are able to see leatherback and log-gerhead sea turtles come ashore at night to excavate nests in the sand, and after laying their eggs, lumber back to the sea. This is an unforgettable experience.

There are also nature walks to nearby pans and vleis, open grass plains and palmveld, or into the dense coastal dune forest.

The reefs and offshore waters support an incredible variety of colourful fish, with numerous species of butterfly fish, angelfish, coris and damsels, parrotfish, sea goldies, triggerfish, various wrasse and surgeons, snappers and rock cod. One should also be aware that these warm, clear, tropical waters also harbour species to be wary of, such as bonefish, devil firefish, moray eels, marbled electric rays, thorntail stingrays and Zambezi sharks.

ACCOMMODATION
The camp has five two-bedroomed chalets, each bedroom with four beds. Some of these chalets have two bathrooms and the family chalets have one bathroom and a lounge area. There is a separate thatched bar and dining room, and meals are served under thatch or under the stars. There are also self-catering facilities. Each wooden chalet has a viewing deck and has been elevated to fit into and just beneath the canopy of the coastal dune forest, rather like tree houses. Reservations should be made with Wilderness Safaris, Benmore, Johannesburg.

TREES
In the dune forest and grassland areas, the dominant plants are:
Diospyros rotundifolia – dune jackal-berry
Garcinia livingstonii – lowveld mangosteen
Hyphaene coriacea – lala palm
Mimusops caffra – coastal red milkwood
Phoenix reclinata – wild date palm
Sclerocarya birrea subsp. *caffra* – marula
Sideroxylon inerme – white milkwood
Strelitzia nicolai – Natal wild banana
Syzygium cordatum – water berry
Trichilia emetica – Natal mahogany

BIRDS
The list of birds recorded in this area is most impressive and the following are some of the notable species to look for:

African goshawk
African marsh harrier
Arctic skua
blackbellied korhaan
blackcrowned tchagra
bush shrike – gorgeous, olive,
  orangebreasted
crested guineafowl
eagles – Ayres', blackbreasted snake,
  brown snake, crowned, martial
flycatchers – bluegrey, bluemantled
greater frigatebird
green coucal
grey cuckooshrike
grey waxbill
gymnogene
hornbills – crowned, trumpeter
kelp gull

louries – Knysna,
  purplecrested
narina trogon
osprey
palmnut vulture
redwinged pratincole
robins – brown, chorister,
  Natal, starred, whitethroated
Rudd's apalis
sanderling
Shelley's francolin
Stanley's bustard
sunbirds – grey, purplebanded
terns – Caspian, lesser
  crested, sooty
Woodwards' batis
woollynecked stork
yellowspotted nicator

MAMMALS

Mammals likely to be seen or heard are:
bushpig
duiker – common, red
large-spotted genet
mongooses – banded, dwarf, water
monkeys – samango, vervet

red squirrel
reedbuck
thick-tailed bushbaby
Wahlberg's epauletted
  fruit bat

REPTILES

African rock python, water or Nile monitor lizard, rock monitor lizard, southern vine snake, Egyptian cobra, forest cobra, green mamba, puff adder, Natal green snake, many-spotted bush snake, and very rarely, the beautifully marked but deadly gaboon adder.

FISH

The enthusiastic offshore angler will find the area rich in desirable species. Some of these are:
blacktail
garrick
grunters – grey, spotted
kingfish – bigeye, bluefin, brassy,
  Ferdy's giant, yellowtail
mackerels – king, queen
Natal stumpnose
pompanoes – African largespot, longfin

potato bass
queenfish
rock cod (five species)
sand steenbras
shad (elf)
snapper (five species)
stonebream

KOSI BAY NATURE RESERVE

Area: 10 961 ha
Established: 19 January 1951

LOCATION

Maputaland coast, close to the Mozambique border. From the north, turn off the N2 at Jozini, then via the Nduma road follow the signs to Sihangwane across the Pongolo river towards Kwangwanase. The camp is 12 km beyond this village. From the south, turn off the N2 at Mhlosinga via the lower Mkuzi road, proceed via Mbazwana and Mseleni to the Kwangwanase main road, then turn right towards this village, and then eastwards to Kosi.

FEATURES

A scenically beautiful system of lakes, linked by narrow reeded channels opening into the sea. One of the lakes contains shallow, fresh water, and is largely waterlily-covered. There is a salinity gradient through the lakes, allowing marine fish species to enter. Kosi is famous for its excellent fishing. On the east, the lakes are separated from the Indian Ocean by high forested dunes. The western shores are fringed by tropical vegetation with swamp forest and marsh, and a unique grove of raffia palms. Towards the lower lakes, five species of mangrove line the lake shore, the only place in South Africa where all five species occur. The main lakes are very deep and, being silt free, have exceptionally clear water. The estuary mouth and offshore shallows have superb coral reefs with several hundred species of fish recorded, including numerous brilliantly coloured tropical forms, which are wonderful to snorkel over. The beaches are unspoiled and famous for the loggerhead and leatherback turtles which nest during the summer months. The bird life includes very rare species, such as the palmnut vulture which is associated with the raffia palms. The nature trails rank with the finest.

The unique system of "fish kraals" used by local tribal people to harvest fish moving in and out of the lakes is of great interest. Their construction, positioning and the manner in which fish are removed, as well as the composition of the catches, is always interesting.

To really enjoy the natural delights of Kosi, a hiking trail is strongly recommended. It passes through the habitats described and allows one to capture the moods and sounds of this rich area. This is particularly so for birding enthusiasts, as there is no road access to some habitats, while others are out of bounds to boats as well. The trails take in the splendid coral reefs at Kosi mouth, an absolute must for the keen snorkeller. In summer, in the vicinity of the Bhanga Nek trails camp, the nesting turtles can be observed. After an evening of turtle watching and a good night's sleep, what better way to wake up than to the dawn chorus of brown robins, followed by a dip in the crystal clear sea at Bhanga Nek?

Apart from its angling potential, its fauna and flora and its outstanding scenic beauty, Kosi has a charm that draws people back again and again. It is a long way from anywhere, and it has qualities found nowhere else in South Africa.

DESCRIPTION

Kosi is not in fact a bay, but a complex of four lakes and an estuarine basin with a narrow mouth opening to the sea, situated about 2 km south of Ponta do Ouro, the South African-Mozambique border.

Tidal waters push up through the mouth and the estuarine basin, known as Enkovukeni, into Makhawulani, the first lake, then via a channel into the second, Lake Mpungwini. This lake is connected via the winding, reeded Mtando channel to Lake Nhlange, then via the Ntolweni channel into the fourth, freshwater Lake Amamzimnyama, meaning "Black Water" in Zulu. It is so named because of the dark, tea-coloured water caused by decomposing vegetation and vegetable dyes.

The other three lakes are noted for the clarity of the water, especially Lake Nhlange, which is about 30 m deep in parts.

These lakes are separated from the sea by a narrow barrier of forested coastal dunes. They stretch over nearly 20 km and cover a surface area of approximately 37 sq km. The freshwater catchment area is about 500 sq km of small pans, vleis, marshlands, swamps and forest. Two small rivers enter the system, the Sihadhla into Lake Amanzimnyana, and the small Nswamanzi stream enters from the western shores of Lake Nhlange. There is a gradual change in salinity levels from the freshwater lake to the sea and this accounts for the diverse vegetation zones. Kosi is the only locality in South Africa where five mangrove species occur. They are the white, black, red, Tonga and Indian, which support communities of mud and fiddler crabs, mudskippers, snails and whelks. It also contains the only forest of naturally occurring raffia or Kosi palms, the habitat of rare birds such as palmnut vulture, palm swifts, Pel's fishing owl, and colonies of migratory straw-coloured fruit bats. The local Tongas use the huge leaves of these palms for constructing rafts and for hut building and thatching.

Along some stretches of the lake shore the swamp forest contains incredibly lush subtropical ferns, including the climbing *Stenochlaena ternuifolia* and ground orchids in a thick carpet of leaf litter from swamp figs, wild frangipani, wild poplar, quinine, powder-puff, mitzeeri and water berry trees.

There are large marshlands of reeds, sedges, the fern *Acrostrichum aureum*, papyrus, and water lilies covering open water with semi-emergent and aquatic plants. Other habitats are the grasslands, some areas of open woodland where water berry, Natal mahogany and flat-crown predominate, and palmveld with scattered clumps of wild date and lala palms.

The coastal dune forest contains numerous tree species and the Kosi area is rich in the Tongaland cycad *Encephalartos ferox*.

HISTORICAL NOTES

This area, originally only about 125 ha on the northern shore of Lake Nhlange, was proclaimed in 1950, and was administered by the Natal Parks Board. The first resident ranger was only appointed to this station in 1955. Kosi was taken over by the KwaZulu Department of Nature Conservation by proclamation of Government Notice No 474 of 1988 and the area was then increased to 10 961 ha.

Interest in the region goes back to 1888 when a proposal by the Transvaal Boer Republic to turn Kosi into a harbour was drafted. They intended to become completely independent of the British by building a road from the Transvaal to their own port. At about the same time a British adventurer-entrepreneur, Colonel William Jesser Coope, surveyed the Kosi lakes with the intention of also building a port there, and a road into Swaziland from which to export the rich deposits of coal found there. Fortunately neither of these schemes were feasible.

The present name "Kosi" is derived from Makuza, the name of a headman who resided there many years ago. With the passage of time, by word of mouth, and from people unfamiliar with the Zulu language, the name changed from Makuza's bay to Makozi's bay and was finally shortened to Kosi's, and now to Kosi bay.

Kosi bay is famous for a conservation-research project on marine turtles initiated by Mr Peter Potter of the Natal Parks Board in 1963. It is now run from the Bhanga Nek station in collaboration with the KwaZulu/Natal authorities. The research tagging, protection of nest sites and scientific data gathering has achieved international recognition, largely through the outstanding research programme implemented by Dr George Hughes, the current executive director of the Natal Parks Board. He started on the turtle beaches of Kosi in the 1960s while still a student, and now directs the programme. Since 1971 about 5 000 loggerhead and 1 000 leatherback adult sea turtles have been tagged, as well as a total of 230 689 hatchlings. Tags from adult turtles have been recovered from Mozambique, Madagascar, Tanzania and Kenya, which indicates that the Kosi beaches are very important breeding grounds in the southern Indian ocean. The tagging of hatchlings has revealed the astonishing distances covered by them, with recoveries as far afield as Struisbaai in the southern Cape, Langebaan on the Cape west coast and at Kommetjie on the Atlantic side of the Cape peninsula.

ACCOMMODATION

There is a two-bedded cottage, a lodge with three beds and two bunks and a six-bedded lodge. These are fully furnished with all facilities provided and have staff in attendance. There is a small camping and caravan site with toilets and showers. Near the boat jetty at the water's edge, it has 15 sites. For those who have booked to go on the four day hiking trail there is a comfortable base camp, and fully equipped tented camps for each overnight stop. Reservations are made with the KwaZulu Department of Nature Conservation, Pietermaritzburg.

At the estuary mouth there is a picnic area, where rustic toilets are provided. A day permit from the nature reserve office is required to visit the estuary. Four wheel drive vehicles are essential.

TREES

A selection of some of the species from these diverse habitats is:

Albizia adianthifolia – flat-crown
Antidesma venosum – tassel berry
Apodytes dimidiata – white pear
Avicennia marina – white mangrove
Brachylaena discolor – coastal silver leaf
Bridelia micrantha – mitzeeri
Bruguiera gymnorrhiza – black mangrove
Ceriops tagal – Indian mangrove
Chaetachme aristata – thorny elm
Diospyros rotundifolia – dune jackal-berry
Dovyalis longispina – Natal apricot
Dracaena mannii (*D. usambarensis*) – small-leaved dragon tree
Euclea natalensis subsp. *rotundifolia* – Tonga guarri
Ficus natalensis – Natal fig
Ficus trichopoda – swamp fig
Garcinia livingstonei – lowveld mangosteen
Hyphaene coriacea – lala palm
Kraussia floribunda – rhino coffee
Lumnitzera racemosa – Tonga mangrove
Macaranga capensis – wild poplar
Manilkara discolor – forest milkberry
Peddiea africana – poison olive
Phoenix reclinata – wild date palm
Psychotria capensis – blackbird berry
Raphia australis – Kosi palm
Rauvolfia caffra – quinine tree
Rhizophora mucronata – red mangrove
Schefflera umbellifera – bastard cabbage tree
Sideroxylon inerme – white milkwood
Sophora inhambanensis – coast bean bush
Syzygium cordatum – water berry
Tabernaemontana elegans – toad tree
Teclea gerrardii – Zulu cherry-orange
Voacanga thouarsii – wild frangipani
Warburgia salutaris – pepperbark tree

BIRDS (more than 250 species recorded)

A number of uncommon species to be searched for in the Kosi area are:

African broadbill
African finfoot
African marsh harrier
African snipe
avocet
barthroated godwit
bat hawk
broadbilled roller
Cape shoveller
corncrake
crested guineafowl
cuckoo hawk
curlew sandpiper
ducks – black, fulvous, knobbilled,
   whitebacked, whitefaced
eagles – African fish, blackbreasted
   snake, longcrested, southern
banded snake, Wahlberg's
flamingoes – greater, lesser
green coucal
knot
korhaans – blackbellied, redcrested
lesser jacana
little stint

mangrove kingfisher
narina trogon
osprey
owls – grass, Pel's fishing,
   wood
palmnut vulture
pinkthroated longclaw
plovers – Caspian, grey,
   longtoed, ringed
plumcoloured starling
pochard
purplebanded sunbird
pygmy goose
roseringed parakeet
sanderling
Stanley's bustard
Stierling's barred warbler
storks – woollynecked,
   yellowbilled
teals – Hottentot, redbilled
Temminck's courser
turnstone
yellowbreasted apalis

MAMMALS
Mammals occurring in this area are:
black musk shrew
bushbuck
bushpig
bushveld gerbil
duiker – blue, red
four-toed elephant shrew
hippo
large-spotted genet

mongooses – water,
   white-tailed
monkeys – samango, vervet
red squirrel
scrub hare
suni (very rare)
thick-tailed bushbaby
woodland dormouse

A rare species recorded from the Sihadhla stream is the Cape clawless otter. While hippo occur in small numbers, they suffer a certain amount of stress from the sometimes poor behaviour of boat owners. It is advisable to respect their territories as they are extremely dangerous animals when provoked.

REPTILES
Crocodiles are scarce and occur mainly in Lake Amanzimnyama. Other reptiles that may be encountered are the rock and Nile monitor lizards, Egyptian and forest cobras, green mamba, southern vine snake, boom-

220

slang and several smaller species, as well as lizards, skinks and burrowing reptiles. The endangered gaboon adder inhabits these lush tropical habitats but these beautifully camouflaged snakes are rarely encountered.

FISH

It is probably the ambition of every angler in the country to fish the Kosi lakes. Until recently, before completion of the new all-weather road, only owners of 4x4 vehicles were able to negotiate the deep sand tracks to reach the camp sites. A 4x4 vehicle is still needed if the visitor wishes to visit the estuary mouth. It is essential to have one's own boat as none are available for hire.

For the keen angler, at least 150 species of estuarine and marine fish occur in these lakes. Many marine fish penetrate as far up as the very large, deep Lake Nhlange. Over the years several South African record-sized specimens have been caught from these waters. Some of the anglers' favourites are:

barracuda (three species)	mini-kob
bellnose bass	mullet (12 species)
blacktail	oxeye tarpon
bream (two species)	perch
elf (shad)	pouter
grunter (three species)	queenfish (three species)
kingfish (four species)	rock cod (four species)
kob (salmon)	stonebream
largespot pompano	stumpnose (two species)
milkfish	tenpounder

SILEZA FOREST NATURE RESERVE

Area: 2 124 ha
Established: 1992

LOCATION

Northern Maputaland. East of Sihangwana, Tembe Elephant Park and Pelandaba, then south-east, about midway between the main Mbazwana-Pelandaba road and the Majaji forestry plantation. Access is off the N2 to Jozini, Mbazwana, and then northwards to the turn-off to Manzengwenya forest station. Alternatively, off the N2 via the lower Mkuzi road to Mbazwana, then northwards to the Manzengwenya forest station. Enquiries should be made to the KwaZulu Department of Nature Conservation, Ulundi.

FEATURES
This reserve has not yet been fenced, and is not open to the public. Future plans include the building of a large lodge to accommodate 80 persons, two 20-bedded bush camps, and possibly a 20-bed theme village. Extended nature trails with bird and game viewing will be the main attractions to promote tourism and provide local employment.

DESCRIPTION
A largely untouched and uninhabited area, mainly coastal grassland and palmveld. There are deep, as well as shallow, permanent pans with a variety of aquatic and marshland vegetation, and forest patches. The forests are found in long tongues, running north to south on the higher ground, or in round patches. The soils are sandy, and the area is generally quite flat.

The grasslands include snowflake grass *Andropogon* species, lovegrass *Eragrostis* species, dropseed grass *Sporobolus* species, speargrass *Trachypogon* species, wild oatgrass *Monocymbium* species, and signal grass *Brachiara* species and the area is scattered with wild date and lala palms. On the forest margins, there are many Kosi cycads *Encephalartos ferox*.

HISTORICAL NOTES
This recently proclaimed area (Government Notice No. 9 of 1992) was initiated largely by the Tembe Tribal Authority in consultation with the KwaZulu Department of Nature Conservation. It is planned as the hub of a new multi-species park, which will be developed in conjunction with a Nguni cattle breeding project. There is a possibility that the Tembe Tribal Authority will allocate an additional area of land, which will double the size of that already proclaimed.

TREES
Some of the forest patches contain very fine specimens of common yellowwood *Podocarpus falcatus*. Species typical of this region include:
Acacia karroo – sweet thorn
Cleistanthus schlechteri – false tamboti
Coffee racemosa – Mozambique coffee
Commiphora neglecta – green-stem corkwood
Craibia zimmermannii – peawood
Croton gratissimus var. *gratissimus* – lavender fever-berry
Croton steenkampianus – marsh fever-berry
Ephippiocarpa orientalis – dwarf toad tree
Lasiodiscus mildbraedii – red-hair bush
Newtonia hildebrandtii var. *hildebrandtii* – Lebombo wattle
Ozoroa engleri – white resin tree
Strychnos henningsii – red bitter-berry
Strychnos madagascariensis – black monkey orange
Xylotheca kraussiana – African dog-rose

BIRDS

The area is of particular interest for the number of *Red Data Book* species identified just to the south, most of which almost certainly occur within the proposed Sileza park area. Species identified locally include:

African broadbill
African marsh harrier
African snipe
blackbreasted snake eagle
bluecheeked bee-eater
Cape reed warbler
Caspian tern
European bee-eater
European swallow
great crested grebe
lesser jacana

longclaws – orangethroated, pinkthroated, yellowthroated
louries – Knysna, purplecrested
orangebreasted bush shrike
pygmy goose
redbilled teal
ruff
rufousbellied heron
Stanley's bustard
Woodwards' batis
yellowbilled stork

One of the pans, Manzimhlophe, is a very important refuge for wildfowl. Pinkthroated longclaw are fairly common in the grasslands.

MAMMALS

Hippo move in and out of the deeper pans seasonally. Other species recorded in this region include:

bushveld gerbil
Cape scrub hare
duiker – common, red
Hottentot golden mole

porcupine
side-striped jackal
steenbok
suni

TEMBE ELEPHANT PARK

Area: 29 000 ha
Established: 21 October 1983

LOCATION

Maputaland, on the Mozambique border. From the N2 take the Jozini turn-off and from this village cross the dam wall and take the road to Nduma (Ndumu), then the turn-off to Sihangwane-Kwangwanase. The reserve entrance is just beyond the Sihangwane store, on the left.

FEATURES

This is a unique wilderness area consisting of a mosaic of sand forest containing unusual and rare trees and plants, woodland, grassland, and swamp. It is home to a wide variety of large and small mammals, including elephant and the rare, diminutive suni. There is a rich bird fauna, including several subtropical species at the southern limits of their distribution.

Because of the generally dense nature of the sand forests, and of the aquatic vegetation around the Mosi pans, visitors to this fascinating area require at least three or four days and preferably longer, if they wish to become acquainted with the unique fauna and flora of this remote and wild area of Maputaland. They will certainly not be disappointed in the wilderness experience. Hopefully, plans will materialise to link the Tembe Park and Ndumu Game Reserve in the west, at present separated by the Mbangweni corridor.

DESCRIPTION

A variety of habitats occur in this large park. Magnificent sand forest patches, with a canopy 10-25 m high, are found on dune ridges of poorly leached sandy soils. Some areas are extremely dense with numerous woody sub-canopy shrubs, small trees and herbs. There are large areas of open woodland and grassland. A section of the Mosi swamp, a natural drainage line extending from Mozambique to further south in Maputaland, is incorporated within the park.

This swamp of seasonally filled pans is mostly fringed by dense reed beds, bulrushes, sedges and stands of papyrus. There are also sandy areas of palm veld on the lower lying flatter terrain, dominated by the lala palm, often in clumps or associated with the wild date palm. Typical trees of the open areas are the sickle bush *Dichrostachys cinerea*, black monkey orange *Strychnos madagascariensis*, silver cluster leaf *Terminalia sericea*, black monkey thorn *Acacia burkei*, velvet bushwillow *Combretum molle* and the large-leafed false thorn *Albizia versicolor*.

The grasses, mainly tussock species, form an almost continuous layer, the dominant species being bristle grass *Aristida* species, finger grass Digitaria species, red grass *Themeda triandra*, signal grass *Urochloa* species and herringbone grass *Pogonathria* species.

HISTORICAL NOTES

Although established in 1983, this very important reserve was only officially opened to the public on 9 September 1991. The park was proclaimed to protect the last remaining herds of free-ranging elephants in South Africa. These elephants once moved seasonally between Mozambique and Maputaland, but in recent years have sought refuge in the dense sand forest to escape continuous harassment across the border. Many of the elephants bear the old wounds and scars of attempts by poachers to either trap or shoot them. The opening of the reserve to the public was delayed in order to allow these animals to settle down and become used to their newfound protection.

A significant event in the planning and development of this park by the KwaZulu Department of Nature Conservation was that an agreement was reached with the local tribal authority whereby people living in parts of the

Sihangwane area, now incorporated within the boundaries of the park, would move out and establish new homesteads and fields nearby. In exchange, they would be permitted regular entry to prescribed areas in the park to harvest reeds and other materials for hut building and other purposes. This utilisation of natural resources extends to the locals receiving a percentage of the revenue earned through tourism and the park has also provided employment in the park for some of them.

ACCOMMODATION
This consists of tented camps of four two-bedded safari tents with a kitchen tent and a dining tent. All camping equipment, linen, crockery, etc. is provided. Hot and cold ablution facilities are available and a camp cook and safari guide are in attendance. Visitors must supply their own food and drink. Only closed-in 4x4 vehicles are allowed to enter the park. Reservations can be made with the KwaZulu Department of Nature Conservation, Pietermaritzburg.

TREES
The characteristic and dominant species in Tembe Park are:
Albizia forbesii – broad-pod false thorn
Balanites maughamii – green thorn
Brachylaena huillensis – lowveld silver oak
Cladostemon kirkii – three-finger bush
Cleistanthus schlechteri – false tamboti
Cola greenwayi – Zulu coshwood
Croton gratissimus – lavender fever-berry
Dialium schlechteri – Zulu podberry
Drypetes arguta – African oak
Erythroxylon emarginatum – common coca tree
Haplocoelum gallense – galla plum
Hymenocardia ulmoides – red-heart tree
Hyperacanthus amoenus – thorny gardenia
Manilkara discolor – forest milkberry
Monodora junodii – green apple
Newtonia hildebrandtii – Lebombo wattle
Pteleopsis myrtifolia – stink bushwillow
Strychnos decussata – Cape teak
Wrightia natalensis – saddlepod

The climbers, *Dioscorea* species, *Strophanthus* species and *Asparagus* species are common. The ground layer is generally sparse with *Sansevieria* species, *Gonatopus boivinii*, *Stylochiton natalense*, *Coleotrype natalensis* and *Panicum* grasses.

BIRDS
Not surprisingly in a park of this size, with its varied habitats, the bird life is rich in species diversity. There are also several that reach the southern

limit of their distribution in this subtropical region. Some of the interesting species recorded are:

African broadbill
Baillon's crake
black coucal
blackcrowned night heron
Cape parrot
crested guineafowl
cuckoo hawk
eagles – bateleur, martial,
   southern banded snake
goldenbreasted bunting
gorgeous bush shrike
green coucal
grey penduline tit
ground hornbill
harlequin quail
lemonbreasted canary
lesser blackwinged plover
lesser jacana
little bittern
longtailed shrike
narina trogon

owls – grass, marsh, Pel's
   fishing, wood
paradise whydah
pinkthroated twinspot
pygmy goose
redbilled helmetshrike
redheaded weaver
redwinged pratincole
Rudd's apalis
rufousbellied heron
Stanley's bustard
sunbirds – Neergard's,
   purplebanded
vultures – palmnut,
   whiteheaded
wattle-eyed flycatcher
white pelican
whitebrowed robin
Woodwards' batis
woollynecked stork
yellow white-eye
yellowspotted nicator

MAMMALS
A number of mammal species known to have occurred in this area in historical times, have been reintroduced and visitors may see the following:

blue wildebeest
bushpig
bushveld gerbil
duiker – common, red
eland
elephant
four-toed elephant shrew
giraffe
greater canerat
hippo
impala
kudu

large-spotted genet
mongooses – Selous', slender,
   white-tailed
nyala
red squirrel
reedbuck
suni
thick-tailed bushbaby
warthog
waterbuck
white rhino
zebra

REPTILES
Species that may be encountered include Nile crocodile, water monitor lizard, rock monitor lizard, tree agama, flap-necked chameleon, Jones' girdled lizard, olive grass snake, green mamba, Egyptian cobra, puff adder and Natal rock python.

NDUMU GAME RESERVE

Area: 10 117 ha
Established: 16 April 1924

LOCATION
Maputaland, on the Mozambique border. From the N2 take the turn-off to Jozini and then over the dam wall northwards for 80 km. The road is well signposted but care should be exercised when traversing the last 14 km stretch of rough gravel road.

FEATURES
Ndumu is undeniably one of the most scenically beautiful of all the Natal reserves. The small comfortable camp, set in spacious grounds with large shade trees, is magnificently sited, with views out over the floodplains into the distant haze of Mozambique. The camp gardens attract many species of birds over the winter months and in spring a number of species will be found nesting there. It is possible to observe, photograph and tape record over 100 species around the camp.

From an elevated hide on top of Ndumu hill there is a wonderful panoramic view over most of the reserve and its mosaic of lakes and vegetation types, the Lebombo mountains and Mozambique plains. On one of the tourist roads there is a viewing point from Redcliffs, overlooking riverine forest and the wide Usutu river towards Swaziland and Mozambique. Visitors are able to cover a large area, through many different habitats, on good tourist roads, in search of game, birds and many interesting trees. Walks through the Pongolo riverine fig forest, accompanied by a guide, are highly recommended, affording close-up views of hippo, crocodiles and African finfoot in the river below, and the chance of seeing Pel's fishing owl, narina trogon, broadbilled roller and many other forest species. A guided walk along the forested shoreline of Shokwe pan is also worthwhile.

The highlight of a trip to Ndumu is a morning or afternoon Landrover tour down to Inyamiti and Banzi pans, where wildfowl, waders and other aquatic birds are prolific, and close-up views of hippo and crocodiles of all sizes are guaranteed, especially during the winter months. The sunset over Inyamiti is unforgettable, with skeins of ducks and geese returning from distant feeding grounds to roost on the grassed flats and mudbanks against a backdrop of yellow fever trees. There are the sounds of hippo and the calls of nesting fish eagles above the whistling of ducks and waders, and, on the drive back to camp, views of elegant nyala slowly making their way up the slopes of Ndumu hill. Sitting under the stars in camp one will hear the grumblings of hippo from the floodplain below, owls and nightjars, frogs and toads, and occasionally, the distant sound of drumbeats from a homestead far across the river.

Although not noted for large numbers of animals other than nyala and

227

hippo, this small reserve is incredibly rich in the number of species of vertebrates it contains. There are 62 mammal, 420 bird, 76 reptile and chelonian, 43 fish and 45 amphibian species. The insect fauna is outstanding and 900 plant species have been recorded, including many unusual and rare species.

Ndumu is remote, fascinating and vibrant with life. It is no wonder so many visitors return again and again to savour its splendour.

DESCRIPTION

Ndumu Game Reserve is situated in Maputaland (previously known as Tongaland), on the border between South Africa and Mozambique at the southernmost extension of the Mozambique plain. The Usutu river, known as the Rio Maputo in Mozambique, is part of the international border, as well as the game reserve border in the north. The reserve is fenced on the south, east and west. The Pongolo river flows through the reserve from the south boundary to its confluence with the Usutu in the north. An old course of the Pongolo serves as a floodwater feeder channel to Lake Inyamiti and iHotwe and Sabatane pans, either directly from the Pongolo, or as feedback from the Usutu river, depending on water levels in the two rivers. There are several semi-permanent floodplain pans, Fontana, Shokwe, Bantana, Mvutsheni and Banzi on the Usutu; isiHilibindini, Mpumpununa, iPolwe, Inyamiti, iHotwe, Sabatane, Ndwanini and Bakabaka on the Pongolo, which are filled by these perennial rivers. The extensive floodplains form approximately a third of the reserve.

The highest point is Ndumu hill, which rises from the Pongolo floodplain (25 m above sea level) to a height of 160 m. The foothills of the Lebombo range rise in the extreme west of the reserve. There are flats between these two elevated areas, with extensive areas of tall thicket with scattered trees, low thicket and scrub, woodland and savanna.

There are 16 dominant soil types and numerous sub-dominant and rare soil types in this small reserve. Accordingly, vegetation habitats are diverse. The main formations are floodplain, pan-edge communities, riverine forest, fever tree forest, aquatic communities, sand forest, *Acacia tortilis* woodland, mahemane thicket, deciduous broadleaved woodland and *Acacia nigrescens* woodland. Over 900 plant species, including many not found much further south, have been identified.

With its tropical climate, diverse soil and vegetation habitats, its rich variety of plant, mammal, bird, reptile, amphibian and fish species, as well as an incredible insect fauna, all in a small area, Ndumu must rank as one of the most interesting game reserves in South Africa.

HISTORICAL NOTES

That humans have occupied the Ndumu Game Reserve area for a considerable period of time is borne out by the finding of an iron smelting furnace, complete with fragments of slag, charcoal and broken funnels into which the bellows fitted, at a site below Ndumu hill on the Pongolo floodplain. Using the radiocarbon dating method, it was established that this furnace was used some 1 400 years ago.

In the mid-1850s white hunters were attracted to this north-eastern corner of Natal by the large herds of game. These hunters, traders and explorers recorded elephant, buffalo, lion, leopard, cheetah, caracal, serval, spotted hyaena, waterbuck, steenbok, blue wildebeest, zebra, giraffe, white rhino, wild dogs and other small animals in this region. Most of these species were exterminated. The famous hunter Frederic Courtenay Selous hunted nyala in the Mahemane thicket in the reserve in 1896.

An outbreak of rinderpest, which began in 1895 and lasted till 1903, caused great loss of game in northern Zululand. In 1905, permits were issued for the destruction of animals considered to be vermin. These included monkey, baboon, lion, cheetah, hyaena, leopard, civet, jackal, warthog, bushpig, wild dog and crocodile. A reward for each animal shot was paid at the Ingwavuma magistrate's courthouse. A local trader, LC von Wissel, who settled at Ndumu in about 1896, made a lot of money shooting vermin and by poisoning crocodiles and hyaena with strychnine.

In 1923 a government proclamation listed even sterner terms for the eradication of so-called vermin and offered rewards of 20 shillings for larger animals, 1 shilling a mamba, and three pence per crocodile egg. These rewards of course attracted hunters to the area.

It was not until 16 April 1924 that Ndumu was proclaimed a game reserve, primarily for the protection of hippopotamus. This largely came about through the efforts of Cabinet Minister Deneys Reitz who visited the area on horseback in 1921 and again in 1923. Reitz was impressed by the beauty of Lake Inyamiti and its abundant wildlife. He realised that, being on the border of Mozambique and Swaziland, Ndumu was a wildlife oasis needing protection. After the proclamation of Ndumu Deneys Reitz said, "I have now done my duty to God and the hippo." Also in 1924, a campaign for the eradication of game on all Crown (state-owned) land in the Ingwavuma district was published in Provincial Notice 13. Again, numerous hunters were attracted to the area.

Initially, control of the game reserve was the responsibility of the local police sergeant. From 1947 to June 1951, ranger EB Burnett, who lived at faraway Ubombo, periodically came up to inspect the area. The first resident custodian was Sergeant Game Guard Catuane, a chief in his own right, who was outstanding in initiating the first measures for control of poaching in the reserve. However, without boundary fences, the number of people and livestock who moved into the reserve increased steadily. Capt. Harold Potter, Chief Conservator for Zululand game reserves, recorded that in 1951 there were 1 159 adults residing in 631 huts and that they grazed 916 head of cattle.

The Native Recruiting Corporation (NRC), as it was called in those days, operated from a large complex of buildings in the western area, recruiting men to work in the mines of Swaziland and all over the Witwatersrand. There was a constant stream of recruits coming and going from these offices, with wives coming to collect monies sent home to them. Later, when the offices were closed down, the South African Institute of Medical Research used the premises as a field research station for a number of years.

The first full-time white ranger, Tom Elphick, took up duties on 13 October 1951. His task was to establish and fence the reserve's boundaries, cut roads through the dense thorn scrub and enforce the conservation laws. A bachelor, he lived in a small prefab house on Ndumu hill where the camp is sited today. He retired due to ill health in early 1954. He was succeeded by Ian Player, assisted by Ken Tinley, who carried on the task of developing the reserve. In a 1954 census, Player and Tinley recorded 1 466 persons, 740 head of cattle, 1 384 goats, 8 donkeys, 3 sheep, 64 dogs and 37 cats residing in the game reserve. At this time it was rare to see game other than hippo and the occasional nyala, except for red duiker that were so common that the rangers were permitted to shoot them for rations.

A public road through the heart of the reserve, linking the Mozambican village of Catuane to the trading store at Ndumu, meant a considerable daily traffic through the reserve between the two countries. This made it virtually impossible to control poaching activities. An outbreak of foot and mouth disease in southern Mozambique in 1955 led to the Department of Veterinary Services erecting a fence from the top of the Lebombo mountains to the sea, in an effort to prevent the southward spread of the disease. All livestock was removed from the reserve so that there was a cattle-free buffer zone between Mozambique and South Africa. Many residents then voluntarily moved out with their cattle.

Boy Hancock, who arrived in March 1955, completed the fencing of the reserve along the western, southern and eastern sections. The northern border, the Usutu river, could not of course be fenced because of the annual summer flooding of the river. Once the reserve had been fenced, the Natal Parks Board reintroduced white rhino, black rhino, impala and warthog.

The rest camp was opened to visitors in late 1957 and once Ndumu became known as a mecca for ornithologists, this remote wildlife oasis began attracting an ever-increasing number of tourists who braved the incredibly bad sandy tracks of those early years.

By 1966, the last residents had moved out of the reserve and for the first time in its recent history, Ndumu was left in peace. In an incredibly short period of time, game began to emerge from hiding in the dense Mahemane thicket, the sand forest and the riverine thickets and floodplains. In that year the Natal Parks Board established a crocodile research and rearing project under the direction of Tony Pooley. Young crocodiles were reared and released back into many rivers and lakes in Zululand, to restock populations heavily depleted by hide hunters. The programme was continued until 1974.

Control of the game reserve passed from the Natal Parks Board to the newly established KwaZulu Bureau of Natural Resources (later the KwaZulu Department of Nature Conservation) in 1988. Since then, many species of game have been reintroduced. It has been a long, slow struggle, but the fauna of Ndumu, as recorded by the early hunters, is gradually being restored.

ACCOMMODATION
There are seven three-bedded huts, furnished and fully equipped including a refrigerator. A communal kitchen block, where trained staff prepare meals, serves the camp. Adjoining this are the ablution facilities. There is also a large braai-boma to the rear of the camp. There are plans to erect a tented camp on the shores of Lake Banzi in the near future. A caravan park and camp site near the entrance gate to the reserve has been built. It is managed jointly by local entrepreneurs and the KwaZulu Department of Nature Conservation. Reservations for the hutted camp are made with the KwaZulu Department of Nature Conservation, Pietermaritzburg.

Visitors must bring their own food and drink. There is a well-stocked supermarket en route to the entrance gate, where a large range of tinned food and supplies, including petrol and diesel, can be obtained.

TREES
Breonadia salicina – matumi
Cladostemum kirkii – three-finger bush
Cola greenwayi – Zulu coshwood
Craibia zimmermannii – peawood
Cussonia zuluensis – Zulu cabbage tree
Drypetes reticulata – white ironplum
Ehretia obtusifolia – sandpaper bush
Entandophragma caudatum – mountain mahogany
Faidherbia albida – ana tree
Haplocoelum gallense – galla plum
Hymenocardia ulmoides – red-heart tree
Lannea schweinfurthii – hairy false marula
Lonchocarpus capassa – apple leaf
Manilkara discolor – forest milkberry
Manilkara mochisia – lowveld milkberry
Monodora junodii – green apple
Olax dissitiflora – small sourplum
Oncoba spinosa – snuff-box tree
Pappea capensis – jacket-plum
Pavetta edentula – gland leaf tree
Pterocarpus rotundifolius – round-leaved teak
Salvadora angustifolia – Transvaal mustard tree
Sterculia rogersii – common star-chestnut
Suregada zanzibariensis – sand canary-berry
Syzygium guineense – water pear

Toddaliopsis bremekampii – wild mandarin
Vepris carringtoniana – coastal white ironwood

BIRDS (420 species recorded)

Not surprisingly, Ndumu is well known as one of South Africa's premier birding spots. The list comprises more than 85 per cent of the 472 species recorded from the whole of Maputaland. Apart from the rare subtropical and migrant species that occur seasonally, the lakes and pans are noted for the large concentrations of wildfowl that seek refuge and food over the winter months in this small reserve. Some of the notable species recorded are:

African finfoot
avocet
bat hawk
bearded robin
black egret
bluecheeked bee-eater
broadbilled roller
cuckoo hawk
dusky lark
eagles – blackbreasted snake,
   lesser spotted, southern
   banded snake
green coucal
green twinspot
grey penduline tit
helmetshrikes – chestnutfronted,
   redbilled

honey buzzard
honeyguides – scalythroated,
   sharpbilled
lesser jacana
longtoed plover
Pel's fishing owl
pygmy goose
redbilled firefinch
redwinged pratincole
Rudd's apalis
spotted flycatcher
sunbirds – bluethroated,
   marico, purplebanded
wattle-eyed flycatcher
weavers – buffalo, redheaded
whitebacked night heron
yellow warbler

MAMMALS (62 species)

aardwolf
African civet
antbear (aardvark)
black-backed jackal
blue wildebeest
buffalo
bushbuck
bushpig
duiker – common, red
giraffe
hippo
honey badger
impala
kudu
large-spotted genet
leopard

mongooses – banded, Selous',
   slender, water, white-tailed
monkeys – samango, vervet
nyala
pangolin
red squirrel
reedbuck
rhino – black, white
scrub hare
serval
spotted hyaena
striped polecat
suni
thick-tailed bushbaby
warthog
zebra

Three shrew, one mole, nine bat, one gerbil and ten rat and mouse species have been recorded in the reserve.

REPTILES AND AMPHIBIANS (76 species)
Ndumu is well represented with reptile species, with seven gecko, two agama, one chameleon, 10 skink, 10 lizard, 40 snake, one crocodile, two tortoise and three terrapin species recorded. Some of these are subtropical forms at the southern limit of their range.

Of the snakes, a number of venomous species occur and these are: boomslang, vine snake, Egyptian cobra, forest cobra, Mozambique spitting cobra, black mamba and puff adder.

FISH (43 species)
Fish are represented by three eel species, the Zambezi shark, oxeye tarpon, smalltooth sawfish and riverbream which are marine species and 36 freshwater species indigenous to the lakes, pans and river systems.

AMPHIBIANS (45 species)
Frogs and toads are particularly well represented in Ndumu, with 45 species and subspecies recorded to date, some at the southern limit of their distribution.

HLATHIKULU FOREST RESERVE (GWALIWENI)

Area: 1 213 ha
Established: 1987

LOCATION
Maputaland, Lebombo mountains. Turn off the N2 to Jozini dam. Take the road over the dam wall signposted Ingwavuma. Further directions will be supplied when applying for an entry permit.

FEATURES
A little-explored, botanically interesting tract of forest atop the ridge of the Lebombo mountain range, with a splendid view overlooking the flat country of southern Maputaland. There are no facilities as yet. A permit to visit this forest is required from the KwaZulu Department of Nature Conservation offices at Jozini.

DESCRIPTION
A variety of forest trees and shrubs of interest occur in this small reserve. It is a worthwhile destination for the botanist. The forest has not been well explored and knowledge of its fauna and flora is scanty.

HISTORICAL NOTES

The Gwaliweni forest is an area of great significance in early Zulu history. In 1840 Dingane was defeated by his brother Mpande in alliance with the Boers. Dingane fled across the Pongolo river and sought sanctuary in the Gwaliweni forest. He was found and murdered by members of the Nyawa clan that year. A local magistrate HC Lugge photographed the grave many years later.

TREES

Calpurnea aurea – Natal laburnum
Canthium inerme – common turkey berry
Celtis mildbraedii – Natal wild stinkwood
Clerodendrum glabrum – tinderwood
Cryptocarya woodii – Cape quince
Cussonia sphaerocephala – Natal forest cabbage tree
Dovyalis caffra – Kei-apple
Eugenia natalitia – common forest myrtle
Ficus natalensis – Natal fig
Ficus sur – Cape fig
Homalium dentatum – brown ironwood
Hyperacanthus amoenus – thorny gardenia
Maerua racemulosa – forest bush cherry
Margaritaria discoidea – Cape ash
Mimusops obovata – red milkwood
Notobuxus natalensis – Natal box
Olea woodiana – forest olive
Rinorea angustifolia – white violet bush
Rothmannia globosa – bell gardenia
Scolopia zeyheri – thorn pear
Strychnos mitis – yellow bitter-berry
Strychnos usambarensis – blue bitter-berry
Teclea gerrardii – Zulu cherry-orange
Turraea floribunda – honeysuckle tree
Vepris lanceolata – white ironwood

BIRDS

barbets – blackcollared, redfronted tinker
blackbellied glossy starling
Cape white-eye
chinspot batis
emerald cuckoo
forest weaver
gymnogene
hornbills – crowned, trumpeter
louries – Knysna, purplecrested
narina trogon

olive woodpecker
paradise flycatcher
puffback
robins – Cape, Natal
sombre bulbul
southern boubou
sunbirds – collared, grey
tawnyflanked prinia
yelloweyed canary
yellowspotted nicator

MAMMALS

bushbuck

bushpig

common duiker

large-spotted genet

striped polecat

vervet monkey

MAPUTALAND MEDICINAL RESOURCE AREA

Area: 100 ha

Established: 1985

LOCATION

Maputaland, adjoining the Makatini research station on the Pongolo river floodplain, in the vicinity of Mfongozi pan. Access is via the N2, turning off onto the Jozini road, then through Jozini village for approximately 20 km to the resource centre.

FEATURES

As the name indicates, a nursery has been established which specialises in the growing and distribution of medicinal plants. Several plots are established where certain species of plants are cultivated to enable the training of apprentice herb doctors in the selective use of such species and in their methods of cultivation. It is hoped that they will be motivated to establish their own medicinal resource areas. The nursery will also be a source of trees for schools and other organisations, for example, on Arbor Day.

This exciting project will be of particular interest to botanists. While there, bird watching, canoeing and fishing for tiger fish and other species in the Pongolo river, can be enjoyed.

DESCRIPTION

The developed area is situated on the east bank of the Pongolo river, approximately 20 km from Jozini and about 70 m above sea level. It is within easy walking distance of Mfongozi pan on the Pongolo floodplain, where seasonally a large number of aquatic birds may be found. Thick bush dominates the plant composition of the river banks on the western border. On higher ground one finds acacia woodlands and mixed grassveld.

HISTORICAL NOTES

A survey of the area identified suitable irrigation land and the Makatini irrigation scheme was developed, starting in 1958. It was later discovered that the land was unsuitable for irrigation and this area was redesignated as a resource area for nature conservation. In 1985, it was decided to initiate a medicinal resource area by establishing a nursery for the propagation of trees, shrubs, bulbs and other plant material in demand for their medicinal properties. It would also grow some increasingly rare species and function as a training centre for herbalists.

Several plant species, either on the point of being locally depleted, or else very scarce in other regions, have been brought in from Natal, Transvaal and the Orange Free State for propagation in this spacious, natural nursery area.

ACCOMMODATION
There are six, two-roomed four-bed housing units, accommodating 24 guests. A kitchen with gas appliances such as refrigerator, stove and hot water geyser is provided, together with cold-water showers and flush toilets, diningroom cum community hall, an outside braai and boma area. Visitors provide their own food, drink and cutlery.

Reservations are made with NPA, Community Services Branch, Pietermaritzburg.

FLORA PROPAGATED
Acacia xanthophloea – fever tree
Balanites maughamii – green thorn
Bersama tysoniana – glossy white ash
Curtisia dentata – assegai
Ficus sycomorus – sycamore fig
Garcinia livingstonei – lowveld mangosteen
Rauvolfia caffra – quinine tree
Spirostachys africana – tamboti
Trichilia emetica – Natal mahogany
Warburgia salutaris – pepperbark tree

Many species of smaller plants have also been introduced and propagated including the forest climbers *Mondia whitei*, *Boweia volubilis*, *Justicia capensis*, *Urginia* species, *Bulbine* species, *Eucomis* species, *Stangeria eriopus*, *Alepidea* species, *Gasteria* species, *Haworthia* species, *Schlechterina* species. These are all of interest to botanists and nursery owners. Plant material will in time be distributed from this centre.

BIRDS
African fish eagle
apalises – Rudd's, yellowbreasted
barbets – redfronted tinker,
  white-eared
brownheaded parrot
Burchell's coucal
European bee-eater
greenbacked bush warbler

greenspotted dove
kingfishers – giant,
  malachite, pied
nightjars – fierynecked,
  Mozambique, Natal
paradise flycatcher
puffback
redfaced mousebird

MAMMALS
four-toed elephant shrew
greater canerat

red squirrel

NATAL MIDLANDS

The region referred to as the Natal Midlands has no defined boundaries but is generally recognised as the plateau above the coastal belt from 600-1 500 m above sea level. The landscape is characterised mainly by undulating grasslands with thickly forested escarpments in some areas. The mixed *Podocarpus* mistbelt forests are often found on private property with some fine tracts near Howick, Karkloof, Balgowan, Dargle and Nottingham Road.

Situated in the mistbelt and enjoying a good summer rainfall, the Midlands is a particularly lush region, one of the few in the country with perhaps an excess of water. Compared to the coast the climate is a great deal cooler, with frost and even light snowfalls at times. It is traversed by numerous major rivers. Some of these and their tributaries are the Mgeni, Mooi, Buffalo, Tugela and Mkhomazi, and the smaller Blaaukrantz, Sundays, Mlazi and Lovu rivers. There are wetland areas and four major dams, with numerous small dams on private farms.

However, there are also areas with hot, dry summers and acacia-veld. There are arid regions such as Weenen, and in particular the Msinga district of the Tugela valley, consisting of mainly semi-deciduous valley bushveld. Msinga is one of the most densely populated and impoverished areas in Natal. Agricultural malpractices, aided by an exceptionally high density of goats, have led to serious erosion, denudation and degradation of the habitat.

The Midlands is the most productive agricultural area in the province, with a wide variety of farming practices. It is especially noted for stock, dairy and horse stud farming, sheep farms, poultry and pig farming. Extensive areas are under maize and other cereal, stockfeed and vegetable crops, with large commercial wattle, pine, eucalyptus and softwood plantations. Towns such as Pietermaritzburg, Greytown, Estcourt, Colenso, Ladysmith and some smaller centres serve the needs of the agricultural communities. Numerous major industries have developed due to an abundance of water and available labour. There are factories processimg cream, cheese, bacon, ham and beef as well as the cereal crops and a variety of timber processing and manufacturing industries.

Historically, parts of the Midlands have been occupied by humans over a long period of time, as indicated by the remains from Iron Age and San civilisations. In the recent past, from the late 1830s, extremely turbulent times were experienced with the fierce Anglo-Boer wars and the massacre of Voortrekkers by the Zulus. Numerous battlefields, monuments and museums in the vicinity of several towns commemorate these events. The presence of large armies with firearms must have been devastating to the populations of game animals during this time. However, even today there are large privately owned estates and farmlands where common species such as reedbuck, bushbuck and a variety of waterfowl and game birds are quite abundant.

The Midlands region has four major public resorts built around or adjacent to dams, with the waters stocked with indigenous and exotic fish species. These are Midmar, Albert Falls, Spioenkop and Wagendrift. Important examples of habitat types and the fauna of these areas are conserved in the Umvoti vlei, Malendeni, Weenen, Soada forest, Karkloof and Umgeni Valley nature reserves. Over recent years, the initiation of the conservancy concept has done much to improve the preservation of habitats and indigenous fauna. The creation of the Thukela Biosphere Reserve will serve a similar purpose. However, considering the large size of the Midlands region, the total conserved and well-protected land area is quite small.

Over the past twenty or so years, many species of game mammals have been reintroduced into nature reserves in areas where they occurred during historical times, but had been exterminated by hunters or declined as a result of severe habitat degradation. Weenen Nature Reserve is a fine example of land restoration and the reintroduction of important game species.

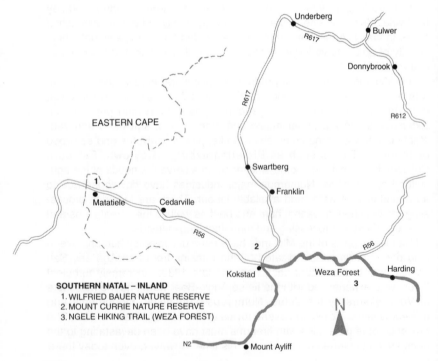

SOUTHERN NATAL – INLAND
1. WILFRIED BAUER NATURE RESERVE
2. MOUNT CURRIE NATURE RESERVE
3. NGELE HIKING TRAIL (WEZA FOREST)

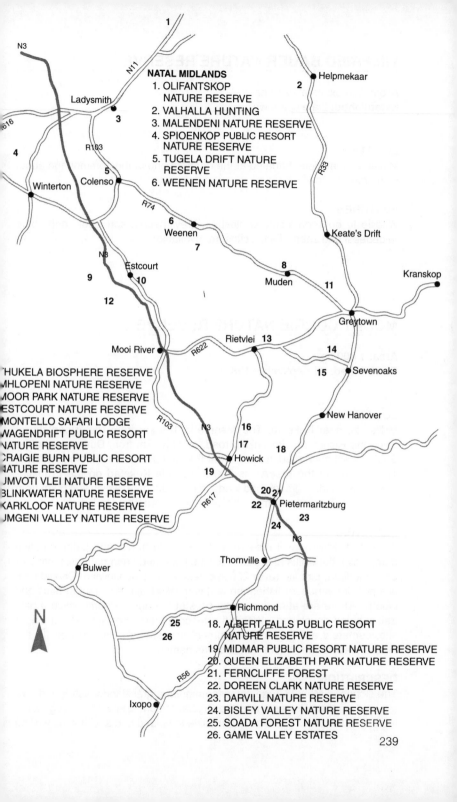

NATAL MIDLANDS

1. OLIFANTSKOP NATURE RESERVE
2. VALHALLA HUNTING
3. MALENDENI NATURE RESERVE
4. SPIOENKOP PUBLIC RESORT NATURE RESERVE
5. TUGELA DRIFT NATURE RESERVE
6. WEENEN NATURE RESERVE

THUKELA BIOSPHERE RESERVE
MHLOPENI NATURE RESERVE
MOOR PARK NATURE RESERVE
ESTCOURT NATURE RESERVE
MONTELLO SAFARI LODGE
WAGENDRIFT PUBLIC RESORT NATURE RESERVE
CRAIGIE BURN PUBLIC RESORT NATURE RESERVE
UMVOTI VLEI NATURE RESERVE
BLINKWATER NATURE RESERVE
KARKLOOF NATURE RESERVE
UMGENI VALLEY NATURE RESERVE

18. ALBERT FALLS PUBLIC RESORT NATURE RESERVE
19. MIDMAR PUBLIC RESORT NATURE RESERVE
20. QUEEN ELIZABETH PARK NATURE RESERVE
21. FERNCLIFFE FOREST
22. DOREEN CLARK NATURE RESERVE
23. DARVILL NATURE RESERVE
24. BISLEY VALLEY NATURE RESERVE
25. SOADA FOREST NATURE RESERVE
26. GAME VALLEY ESTATES

239

WILFRIED BAUER NATURE RESERVE

Area: Approximately 218 ha
Established: Date unknown

LOCATION
Midlands, Matatiele. Situated at the northern end of the commonage about 5 km from the town.

FEATURES
Wildlife to be seen includes blesbok, grey rhebok, springbok, oribi, blue wildebeest and zebra. Picnic sites are available.

MOUNT CURRIE NATURE RESERVE

Area: 1 800 ha
Established: 24 September 1981

LOCATION
Midlands, near Kokstad. The reserve is 189 km from Pietermaritzburg, using the Richmond-Umzimkulu road, and 250 km from Durban using the South Coast main road, turning off at Port Shepstone for Harding-Kokstad. The turn-off to the reserve is 200 m outside Kokstad on the Franklin-Swartberg road. A gravel road leads to the main gate, which is 4,5 km from the turn-off. The reserve may also be approached from Underberg.

FEATURES
A most attractive small reserve, with old cattle tracks and paths creating many delightful walks and climbs for the hiker and keen naturalist interested in the flora, bird life (over 220 species), and game viewing. Crystal dam is a popular venue for fishermen and is stocked with largemouth bass and bluegill. There are attractive picnic sites at the dam, around which a new trail is being developed. Within the reserve there is an interesting laager site, cemetery and national monument in memory of Adam Kok III, the Griqua leader, after whom Kokstad was named.

DESCRIPTION
The slopes of Mount Currie comprise montane grasslands, scrub and protea veld on the hillslopes, and the Crystal stream and wetland vegetation leading to the dam. The area is attractive to upland bird species, as well as

wildfowl and marsh dwellers. There are some fine trees and cover in the form of clumps of *Leucosidea* bushes.

HISTORICAL NOTES

Adam Kok III, who sold his land in the Philippolis area to the government of the OFS, trekked with 2 000 of his followers, 20 000 head of stock and some 30 wagons on an epic journey beginning in 1861. They arrived on the slopes of Mount Currie on May 12, 1863. The peak was named after Sir Walter Currie, who commanded a detachment of Frontier Armed and Mounted Police, later named the Cape Mounted Rifles, which was on hand to welcome the newcomers.

ACCOMMODATION

There are open camp sites with ablution facilities. A picnic site with braai facilities is available near Crystal dam. Reservations are made with the Natal Parks Board, Mount Currie Nature Reserve.

TREES

Buddleja salviifolia – sagewood
Canthium pauciflorum – mountain turkey-berry
Cassinopsis ilicifolia – lemon thorn
Clausena anisata – horsewood
Cliffortia nitidula – starry ricebush
Cussonia paniculata – mountain cabbage tree
Diospyros lycioides – Transvaal bluebush
Diospyros whyteana – bladder-nut
Euclea crispa – Karoo guarri
Grewia occidentalis – cross-berry
Halleria lucida – notsung
Heteromorpha trifoliata – parsley tree
Leucosidea sericea – oldwood
Myrsine africana – Cape myrtle
Olinia emarginata – mountain hard pear
Protea caffra – common sugarbush
Protea roupelliae – silver sugarbush
Rhamnus prinoides – dogwood
Scolopia mundii – red pear

BIRDS (over 221 species)

African snipe
Alpine swift
anteating chat
Baillon's crake
Barratt's warbler
black cuckoo

black harrier
blackshouldered kite
Cape eagle owl
Cape shoveller
Cape vulture

cisticolas – Ayres', cloud, fantailed,
   lazy, Levaillant's, palecrowned,
   wailing
cranes – blue, crowned
ducks – black, Maccoa, whitebacked,
   whitefaced, yellowbilled
eagles – black, longcrested, martial
Egyptian goose
finches – cuckoo, quail
flufftails – buffspotted, redchested,
   striped
francolins – greywing,
   rednecked, redwing
ground hornbill
Gurney's sugarbird
hobby falcon
kurrichane buttonquail
lammergeyer

martins – banded, brown-
   throated, house, rock, sand
mountain pipit
olive bush shrike
orangebreasted rockjumper
orangebreasted waxbill
rameron pigeon
sentinel rock thrush
South African shelduck
southern pochard
sparrowhawks – black,
   redbreasted
spurwinged goose
storks – black, white
teals – Hottentot, redbilled
wattled starling
whiskered tern

MAMMALS (24 species)
Common and larger species likely to be seen are:

black-backed jackal
blesbok
bushbuck
common duiker
mongooses – large grey, water

mountain reedbuck
oribi
reedbuck
rock dassie
scrub hare

NGELE HIKING TRAIL (WEZA STATE FOREST)

Area: 1 684 ha
Established: The original block of forest was demarcated in 1893

LOCATION
Midlands. Situated in the Weza state forest between Kokstad and Harding.
The turn-off to Weza is clearly signposted on the Harding-Kokstad road.
Take this road and proceed until the sign to Blackwater, or beyond, to one
of the alternative overnight stops as directed by the SAFCOL booking
office.

FEATURES
The Ngele trail is part of the National Hiking Way system and offers trails
of two, three and five days duration which wind their way through the

242

Weza and Ngele indigenous forests as well as through exotic plantations. The routes, which vary in duration from five to seven hours per day, follow easy gradients but there are some sections where the terrain is rugged and a reasonable degree of physical fitness is required. This area contains a fine example of mistbelt forest with beautiful trees and attractive forest glades, fine views of the surrounding countryside, waterfalls, streams and pools suitable for swimming in. There are some interesting forest birds and mammals to be seen and wonderful displays of wild flowers that bloom seasonally in the grasslands. Trout fishing is allowed but anglers require the necessary licences. A daily rod licence is available from the local forestry offices.

DESCRIPTION

The Weza forest complex includes one of the largest and finest examples of mistbelt mixed *Podocarpus* forest in Natal. It also includes the Ngele mountain, which rises to a height of 2 268 m. It is an area of heavy summer rainfall and mists which may last for several days. Heavy frosts are common in winter and snowfalls on the Ngele mountain peak are not infrequent. The forest is noteworthy for its hardwood trees such as yellowwoods, stinkwood, lemonwood and knobwood. Ferns, begonias, orchids and *streptocarpus* are found in the glades and along streams. A part of the mountain is covered by short grass and seasonally *Watsonia*, *Leonotis*, ground orchids and Christmas bells are some of the wild flowers to be seen. The noted botanists, Olive Hilliard and Bill Burtt, recorded that there are five species of plants endemic to Ngele, eight species with Ngele as their type locality (but not confined there), and six species at the northern limit of their range on Mt Ngele.

This is an important catchment area, where numerous small streams feed the Weza, Manzimnyama and Mtamvuna rivers, the latter flowing eastwards, and finally through the nature reserve of the same name, entering the Indian Ocean at Port Edward on the Natal-Transkei border. There are some attractive pools and waterfalls, in particular the Fairview falls on the trails route. For the energetic, an 880 m ascent to the Ngele peak will give fine views of East Griqualand and Transkei, down towards the sea.

HISTORICAL NOTES

The Weza forest is known to have been occupied by the Nguni peoples as far back as 1821. King Shaka held the ceremonial mourning hunt on the death of his mother Nandi in October 1827 in this region. The actual demarcation of the Weza forest occurred in 1893. Afforestation commenced on a limited scale in 1902. During the 1920s further land was acquired and in 1923 large-scale afforestation commenced. Unemployed white settlers formed the nucleus of the labour force and only left the Weza area after the end of World War II. The first Afrikaans school in Natal was established in the Weza settlement.

Nowadays the Weza forest is managed on a multiple-base land use system. This includes the production of timber and conservation of the indigenous forests, the flora and fauna of the area and the valuable water catchment area and maintenance of the trails that provide outdoor recreation and education opportunities. Sixteen species of exotic, commercially valuable trees are grown in these plantations, supplying timber for a wide variety of industrial and manufacturing purposes.

ACCOMMODATION
At overnight stops there are one or two buildings accommodating 30 persons. Each is equipped with a bunk and mattress per person, tables, benches, broom, dust pan, litterbin and lanterns. A fireplace and wood is provided. Hikers provide their own rucksacks, sleeping bags, utensils, crockery and cutlery and all food and drink, which they prepare themselves. Reservations should be made with the SAFCOL office, Weza.

TREES
Celtis africana – white stinkwood
Cryptocarya woodii – Cape quince
Curtisia dentata – assegai
Cyathea capensis – forest tree fern
Dais cotinifolia – pompon tree
Greyia sutherlandii – Natal bottlebrush
Eugenia zuluensis – forest myrtle
Ficus craterostoma – forest fig
Ilex mitis – Cape holly
Ocotea bullata – stinkwood
Podocarpus falcatus – Outeniqua yellowwood
Podocarpus henkelii – Henkel's yellowwood
Podocarpus latifolius – real yellowwood
Protea caffra – common sugarbush
Protea roupelliae – silver sugarbush
Prunus africana – red stinkwood
Rhamnus prinoides – dogwood
Rhus chirindensis – red currant
Scolopia mundii – red pear
Trichocladus ellipticus – white witch-hazel
Warburgia salutaris – pepperbark tree
Zanthoxylum davyi – knobwood

BIRDS
bluebilled firefinch	European golden oriole
bokmakierie	forest canary
Cape parrot	giant eagle owl
Cape vulture	goldenbreasted bunting
chorister robin	green twinspot
crowned eagle	ground hornbill

Knysna woodpecker
lammergeyer
malachite kingfisher
narina trogon
orangethroated longclaw
rameron pigeon

redbilled quelea
redchested cuckoo
sunbirds – greater double-
    collared, lesser doublecollared
swee waxbill
whitebellied korhaan

MAMMALS
African wild cat
black-backed jackal
bushbuck
caracal
chacma baboon
common duiker

grey rhebok
large-spotted genet
monkeys – samango, vervet
reedbuck
serval
striped polecat

REPTILES
Venomous species that may be encountered are puff adder, common night adder, berg.adder and rinkhals.

GAME VALLEY ESTATES

Area: 1 504 ha

LOCATION
Midlands, Ixopo district. To get to Game Valley from Durban, take the R56 Ixopo turn-off from the N3. Follow the road to Thornville and turn left to Richmond. Travel about 25 km to the Richmond village turn-off, take a left turn and then a right across the bridge into the village, go straight through Richmond and out the other side. About 400 m after leaving the village, take the left turn signposted Hella Hella, Eastwolds. Follow the tar for 14 km and continue down the Hella Hella pass on the dirt road (don't go left to the tea estate) and cross a few small bridges. The bridge over the Mkomazi river (22 km from Richmond) is obvious. From this point the road begins to climb. Continue for 1,8 km and turn left at the signboard for Game Valley Estates. The house is 200 m from the main road.

Coming from the Johannesburg side, bypass the off-ramps into Pietermaritzburg from the N3 and take the last one – Market Street. Yield to the left at the first intersection, then turn right at the first traffic light. Follow this road to an intersection (stop to go right or straight, yield to go left). Proceed straight on. This is the main road between Pietermaritzburg and Richmond. Turn off to Richmond and follow the instructions given above.

FEATURES

A scenically attractive reserve, with walking trails that have been laid out to allow the best views and game viewing opportunities. Popular activities include riding the rapids of the Mkomazi river with canoes or tubes and swimming in the deeper pools. For the serious ornithologist it is one of the few areas with breeding populations of the endangered blue swallow, *Hirundo atrocaerulea*, as well as an area frequented by wattled, blue and crowned cranes. It is also a popular venue for campers because of the rugged nature of the countryside and the rich fauna and flora. It has the distinction too, of having been granted South African Natural Heritage Site status for preserving its natural beauty and this type of habitat in Natal.

DESCRIPTION

A rugged mountainous area of steep hills and rock outcrops, well grassed and vegetated, with a wide variety of trees such as yellowwoods in the forest patches, aloes, tree ferns, cycads, acacias and numerous other attractive tree species. The main river that flows through Game Valley Estates is the Mkomazi (Umkomaas). The main vegetation types are Natal mistbelt and Ngongoni veld. The area is scenically spectacular with an altitude ranging from 550-1 250 m above sea level. There are some massive orange-coloured dolomite cliffs, as well as a typical lowveld valley. The area supports an interesting fauna of about 205 bird, over 40 mammal, 29 reptile (including boomslang, Mozambique spitting cobra, rinkhals and puff adder), one terrapin and 19 amphibian species.

HISTORICAL NOTES

The origin of Hella Hella, the name of the valley through which the Mkomazi river flows, is uncertain. One explanation is that Hella Hella is the corrupted version of an old Zulu expression "ihelehele", signifying an advancing crescent of flame. When a grass fire is driven by a strong wind, the leading edge of flame bulges forward and advances rapidly across the veld. This phenomenon is often witnessed by rural people and the Zulus added this word to their vocabulary to describe these events. A second theory is advanced by conservationist Ian Player, who wrote, "I thought you may be interested to know that my grandfather had a store in the Hella Hella before the Boer War. My father was born there and I believe it was my grandmother who gave the place its name because of the terrific heat." The recorded history of this district covers hardly 150 years. It has however been recorded that in earliest times a San (Bushman) by the name of Hele hunted elephants in the upper reaches of the Mkomazi and Mzimkulu rivers. Did he perhaps leave his name to this area?

ACCOMMODATION

There is a lodge with four double bedrooms sleeping 10, with bathroom, fully equipped kitchen and lounge-dining room. Visitors bring their own food, refreshments and towels. Camping sites near the river are provided with firewood, braai areas and tables. A central ablution block serves all sites. For reservations, contact the lodge manager.

TREES
Adenopodia spicata – spiny splinter bean
Brachylaena elliptica – bitter-leaf
Calodendrum capense – Cape chestnut
Combretum molle – velvet bushwillow
Cordia caffra – septee tree
Cyathea dregei – common tree fern
Dombeya tiliacea – forest wild pear
Encephalartos natalensis – Natal cycad
Euphorbia triangularis – river euphorbia
Ficus craterostoma – forest fig
Ficus ingens – red-leaved fig
Hippobromus pauciflorus – false horsewood
Maesa lanceolata – false assegai
Micrococca capensis – common bead-string
Ochna natalitia – Natal plane
Oxyanthus speciosus – wild loquat
Pittosporum viridiflorum – cheesewood
Podocarpus falcatus – common yellowwood
Podocarpus henkelii – Henkel's yellowwood
Protea caffra – common sugarbush
Protorhus longifolia – red beech
Rapanea melanophloeos – Cape beech
Seemannaralia gerrardii – wild maple
Smodingium argutum – rainbow leaf
Strychnos henningsii – red bitter-berry
Syzygium guineense – water pear
Tricalysia lanceolata – jackal-coffee
Vitex rehmannii – pipe-stem tree
Xymalos monospora – lemonwood
Zanthoxylum davyi – knobwood

BIRDS (about 205 species)
black cuckoo
blue swallow
buffy pipit
bush blackcap
Cape parrot
Cape rock thrush
Cape vulture
cinnamon dove
cranes – blue, crowned, wattled

eagles – black, booted, crowned, martial
eastern redfooted kestrel
forest canary
francolins – rednecked, Shelley's
green twinspot
Knysna lourie
longtailed wagtail
mocking chat

narina trogon
olive bush shrike
olive woodpecker
plumcoloured starling
rameron pigeon
robins – chorister, starred
southern tchagra

spotted prinia
storks – black, white
sunbirds – grey, malachite
swee waxbill
whitewinged widow
wood owl

MAMMALS (over 40 species)

The larger mammals occurring are:

aardwolf
African wild cat
antbear (aardvark)
black-backed jackal
blesbok
blue wildebeest
bushbuck
Cape clawless otter
caracal
chacma baboon
common reedbuck
duiker – blue, common
scrub hare
thick-tailed bushbaby

greater canerat
impala
large-spotted genet
mongooses – large grey,
  slender, water, white-tailed
monkeys – samango, vervet
mountain reedbuck
Natal red rock rabbit
nyala
oribi
porcupine
rock dassie
warthog
zebra

SOADA FOREST NATURE RESERVE

Area: 498 ha
Established: 7 July 1967

LOCATION

Natal Midlands. 24 km beyond Richmond, just past the Hella Hella bridge (on the road to Eastwolds) in the Mkomazi (Umkomaas) valley.

FEATURES

A well-preserved mistbelt *Podocarpus* forest, with an impressive two-stage waterfall estimated to be 90 m high. There are about 130 species of birds, including the extremely rare and endangered blue swallow. Not yet open to the public, the only access is via a private farm. Contact the Natal Parks Board, Pietermaritzburg.

NORTHERN NATAL

One of the three remote self-contained bush camps in the Itala Game Reserve wilderness area.

Grassland and bushveld habitats, typical of Itala Game Reserve.

The Ntendeka wilderness area below the Ngome State Forest.

DRAKENSBERG

Horse riding is popular at many of the Drakensberg parks. (Photo: Dr Nollie Zaloumis)

The bushmen's cave museum at Giant's Castle.
(Photo: Dr Nollie Zaloumis)

Black eagles are widespread in the Drakensberg mountains.
(Photo: Dr Nollie Zaloumis)

Indigenous forest in the valleys of the foothills of the Drakensberg mountains.
(Photo: Dr Nollie Zaloumis)

The trout dams below the hatchery at Kamberg are a favourite with fishermen.

Left: The Giant's Castle rest camp, set in indigenous gardens, commands magnificent views of the mountains.

The view from the Tendele camp in Royal Natal National Park changes continuously.

Following page: The Little Mooi river meanders through the Kamberg.

DESCRIPTION
Named after the KaSoda river, the reserve comprises a mistbelt yellow-wood (*Podocarpus*) forest on the slope of the deep Mkomazi river valley and dry bushveld in the lower valley. In addition to some giant yellow-woods, two species of cycad, the Natal cycad *Encephalartos natalensis* and *Encephalartos villosus* are found here, as well as many interesting trees. Bushbuck, common duiker, Cape clawless otter and water mongoose can be spotted.

HISTORICAL NOTES
It was declared a state forest in 1904, then proclaimed a nature reserve. Control was passed to the Natal Parks Board in 1967.

TREES
Acacia robusta – ankle thorn
Aloe barberiae (A. bainesii) – tree aloe
Azima tetracantha – needle bush
Buddleja saligna – false olive
Celtis africana – white stinkwood
Chaetachme aristata – thorny elm
Combretum molle – velvet bushwillow
Commiphora woodii – forest corkwood
Dombeya rotundifolia – common wild pear
Drypetes gerrardii – forest ironplum
Ekebergia capensis – Cape ash
Encephalartos natalensis – Natal cycad
Englerophytum (Bequaertiodendron) natalense – Natal milkplum
Euclea crispa – blue guarri
Ficus sur – broom cluster fig
Harpephyllum caffrum – wild plum
Hippobromus pauciflorus – false horsewood
Kraussia floribunda – rhino coffee
Maytenus mossambicensis – black forest spike-thorn
Rhoicissus tridentata – bushman's grape
Rhus rehmanniana – blunt-leaved currant
Vepris lanceolata – white ironwood
Zanthoxylum capense – small knobwood

BISLEY VALLEY NATURE RESERVE

Area: 250 ha
Established: 1966

LOCATION

Midlands, Pietermaritzburg. Drive along Alexandra Road towards Richmond. After passing Westgate, turn left at the Murray Road interchange. At the bottom of the hill at the crossroads, a sign indicates Bisley Valley Nature Reserve on the right.

FEATURES

A mixture of grassland and acacia-dominated thornveld with some fine trees along the three watercourses draining the higher ground. There are also some marshy areas. A series of footpaths have been laid out. This reserve harbours some interesting birds. Bird and plant lists are available from the Pietermaritzburg centre of the Wildlife Society.

QUEEN ELIZABETH PARK NATURE RESERVE

Area: 93 ha
Established: 3 June 1960

LOCATION

Midlands, Pietermaritzburg, about 8 km west of the city centre. From the city centre, travel along Commercial Road towards Howick. Keep on Commercial Road as far as the traffic circle, taking Duncan McKenzie Drive towards Montrose, over the freeway. If approaching along the N3 from Durban, take the first off-ramp into Pietermaritzburg city centre. Follow this road until it becomes Commercial Road, proceed towards Howick, via the Montrose traffic circle and along Duncan McKenzie Drive to the park. If approaching from the north, take the N3 off-ramp to Hilton, following the road through Hilton village to the Crossways hotel. Turn left into Old Howick Road and follow the road to the Queen Elizabeth Park turn-off on the left. Then follow the signs.

FEATURES

The park contains the administrative headquarters of the Natal Parks Board, including research offices and laboratories, interpretation, conservation and recreation departments, supplies and services, technical and maintenance divisions and stores and trading divisions. The central book-

250

ing office for all the board's accommodation in game reserves and resort areas is situated here. There is a curio shop and an auditorium for film shows and lectures.

The park is used as an outdoor education venue and has a small resource centre and a self-guided trail. Environmental education workshops which deal with school syllabus subjects are held from time to time.

The park has three picnic sites with toilets, braai facilities, tables and benches. Visitors can drive around the area, or walk the self-guided trails. Impala, zebra and blesbok have been introduced, while white rhino can be viewed in a large boma. Smaller indigenous species may be seen on a trail route, as well as a variety of birds. It is a most pleasant park in which to spend a leisurely day enjoying fauna and flora close to a city centre.

For the interested gardener, a small nursery propagates and sells local indigenous plants.

DESCRIPTION

A small park on a north-facing hillside, sloping down into a valley with patches of grassveld, scrub and tree-lined streams, some of which have been dammed. There are some fine indigenous trees and shrubs among numerous exotic examples.

This small park is rich in flowering indigenous plants, such as the endangered Hilton daisy. The visitor can enjoy displays of such species as *Leonotis*, *Tecomaria*, banks of *Watsonia*, *Agapanthus* and *Clivia*, arum lilies and waterlilies. There are numerous ferns along the rocky stream beds, and a fine collection of cycads.

HISTORICAL NOTES

This park, formerly a municipal park administered by the Pietermaritzburg city council, was given to the Natal Parks Board as a headquarters and wildflower reserve in 1960. The first offices were completed in June 1962, and the complex was named the Douglas Mitchell Centre, in honour of the former Administrator of Natal, Member of Parliament, and founder member of the Natal Parks Board in 1947.

BIRDS

blackcollared barbet
broadtailed warbler
Cape robin
cuckoos – Diederik, redchested
familiar chat
fiscal shrike
grassbird
Gurney's sugarbird
neddicky
olive thrush

paradise flycatcher
pintailed whydah
rameron pigeon
redcollared widow
sentinel rock thrush
sombre bulbul
southern boubou
sunbirds – black, lesser
    doublecollared
tawnyflanked prinia

MAMMALS

blesbok
bushpig
caracal
duiker – blue, common
impala
large-spotted genet

mongooses – slender,
   water, white-tailed
rock dassie
striped weasel
white rhino
zebra

FERNCLIFFE FOREST

Area: 250 ha
Established: 1973

LOCATION

Midlands, Pietermaritzburg. From the city, drive along Boshoff Street into Chatterton Road. At the circle continue in the same direction along Town Bush Road to the gates of Ferncliffe Water Works. Take the track on the right of these gates and drive about 2 km to the cottage where cars are parked; cars may also be parked at the entrance gates.

FEATURES

There are plantations of wattle, gum and pine with indigenous forest on the steep slopes, with streams and storage dams. There are spectacular views over Pietermaritzburg. Over 100 species of birds, as well as bushbuck, may be seen. Several forest trails have been established and braai and picnic sites provided. Bird and tree lists may be obtained from the city parks department. The cottage can be booked as an interpretation centre.

DARVILL NATURE RESERVE

LOCATION

Midlands, Pietermaritzburg. Take New England Road from the city with Scottsville racecourse on the left. Cross the N3, pass the Pietermaritzburg golf club on the right and continue until the entrance gate appears on the left. Carry on across the lawns until a gate is reached. Entry is by permit only, obtainable at the reception office. Telephone (0331) 961233.

FEATURES

This area has recently been taken over by Umgeni Water and will be established as a nature reserve. A series of earth dams with sedges and grasses growing to the water's edge provides habitats for warblers, herons, ducks, geese, jacanas, moorhens and grebes. An excellent hide has been built over the water for viewing the large number of waders, wildfowl and aquatic birds.

Shongweni Resources Reserve and the Wilderness Leadership School are due to take over responsibility for managing this area in the near future.

DOREEN CLARK NATURE RESERVE

Area: 5 ha
Established: 27 February 1969

LOCATION

Midlands, in the Winterskloof area of Pietermaritzburg. From the N3 north of Pietermaritzburg take the off-ramp to Hilton. Drive through Hilton village to Crossways hotel, then straight along Shepstone Road, past Cowan House, and left into Amy Wilson Drive. Continue along this road into St Michael's Road. The reserve entrance is about 200 m on the left.

FEATURES

A small but valuable piece of mixed *Podocarpus* mistbelt forest, donated to the Natal Parks Board by the Clark family. There is a small picnic site and a pleasant trail about 1,5 km long. Slender mongoose and large-spotted genet may be spotted along the trails. Although very small, this area is nevertheless a valuable site in a relatively developed area.

FLORA

Burchellia bubalina – wild pomegranate
Calodendrum capense – Cape chestnut
Celtis africana – white stinkwood
Clerodendrum glabrum – tinderwood
Combretum erythrophyllum – river bushwillow
Combretum kraussii – forest bushwillow
Cussonia sphaerocephala – Natal forest cabbage tree
Cussonia spicata – common cabbage tree
Dais cotinifolia – pompon tree
Dalbergia obovata – climbing flat-bean
Ficus natalensis – Natal fig
Gardenia thunbergia – white gardenia

Halleria lucida – notsung/tree fuchsia
Mackaya bella – forest bell bush
Nuxia floribunda – forest elder
Podocarpus henkelii – Henkel's yellowwood
Podocarpus latifolius – real yellowwood
Ptaeroxylon obliquum – sneezewood
Rinorea augustifolia – white violet bush
Xymalos monospora – lemonwood

BIRDS

African goshawk
Barratt's warbler
blackheaded oriole
bush blackcap
Cape batis
cuckoos – black, Diederik,
   emerald, Klaas's
flycatchers – bluemantled, paradise
green twinspot
lesser honeyguide
narina trogon
olive bush shrike
olive thrush
olive woodpecker
purplecrested lourie
rameron pigeon
robins – Cape, chorister,
   starred
sharpbilled honeyguide
sunbirds – black, lesser
   doublecollared, malachite
wood owl
yellowthroated warbler

These are some of the resident and summer and winter visitors to this forest.

MIDMAR PUBLIC RESORT NATURE RESERVE

Land area: 2 844 ha
Established: 21 March 1968
Surface water area: 1 822 ha

LOCATION
Midlands. 24 km from Pietermaritzburg and 7 km from Howick off the N3 freeway.

FEATURES
This is the largest and most popular inland resort in Natal, with comfortable accommodation and well-serviced camping and caravan sites. There is about 15 km of developed shoreline where attractive, shady picnic sites are available for day visitors. Adequate braai and ablution facilities are provided. There is a cafeteria and takeaway where provisions can be purchased and a large curio shop at the entrance office.

The dam is zoned for various sporting activities, such as powerboating, windsurfing, jet skiing, canoeing, yachting, fishing and bathing. The Henley-Midmar Yacht Club and the Natal Aquatic and Power Boat Club have their headquarters within this complex. Midmar has become famous for the annual Midmar Mile swim, for yachting regattas and angling competitions. Good catches of scalies, bluegill, bass and carp are recorded from these waters.

Other sporting amenities include all-weather tennis courts, squash courts and a small swimming pool available only to residents of the chalets and rustic cabins. Bicycles, windsurfers, canoes and yachts can be hired over weekends and holiday periods. Launch tours can be arranged if booked in advance, and a children's playground has been provided.

The resort incorporates a 1 000 ha game park, where entry by vehicle, bicycle or on foot is permitted. Black wildebeest, oribi, blesbok, springbok, reedbuck, zebra, red hartebeest and many smaller species may be observed. The dam harbours a variety of herons, waders and waterfowl.

The Midmar historical village is well worth visiting as a feature on its own. With minute attention to detail, it depicts the historical lifestyle and cultural past of the pioneer settlers.

A tearoom and restaurant in period style enhances a visit.

DESCRIPTION

The water surface area of Midmar averages 1 822 ha, with a large, main open area and four arms radiating out into sheltered bays and wooded creeks, some steeply banked, others verging onto gently sloped grasslands. The water level varies seasonally, exposing wide expanses of sandy beach during the dry season, low water level periods. The vegetation comprises grassland, mixed scrub and woodland, with stands of exotics – a remnant of previous farming practices. The surrounding land slopes gently down towards the water area, and the resort setting is enhanced by the magnificent backdrop of the Inhluzana hills.

HISTORICAL NOTES

The Midmar dam on the Mgeni river was opened in 1964 to supply water to the Pietermaritzburg area. It was named after the farm Midmar, which was in turn named after Midmar castle in Scotland.

ACCOMMODATION

There are 47 fully equipped, self-contained, serviced chalets with one or two bedrooms, lounge-diningroom, bathroom, toilet and kitchenette (equipped with cutlery, crockery, stove and fridge). Linen is provided. Visitors do their own cooking.

There are also 16 fully equipped rustic cabins each containing four beds. These are equipped with cutlery, crockery, hotplate and fridge. The units are serviced by a communal ablution block. Linen is provided and the cabins are serviced daily. Visitors do their own cooking and washing up.

Four separate camping areas, three along the lake shore, are served by communal ablution facilities with hot and cold running water.

Reservations are made with the Natal Parks Board, Pietermaritzburg.

BIRDS
Some of the species to be seen are:

Cape shoveller

Cape teal

ducks – Maccoa, whitefaced

fiscal flycatcher

geese – Egyptian, spurwinged

grassbird

greenspotted dove

herons – blackheaded, grey, purple

ibises – glossy, sacred

little stint

moorhen

orangebreasted waxbill

pied kingfisher

plovers – blacksmith, three-
    banded, wattled

redbacked shrike

ruff

rufousnaped lark

sandpipers – curlew, marsh

southern pochard

spotted dikkop

teals – Hottentot, redbilled

whitebellied sunbird

yellow warbler

MAMMALS
The game park supports a variety of indigenous small animals. For conservation purposes as well as visitor enjoyment, several larger mammals have been introduced. The visitor may see the following:

black wildebeest

black-backed jackal

blesbok

Cape clawless otter

caracal

springbok

striped polecat

mongooses – large grey, slender,
    water, white-tailed

oribi

red hartebeest

reedbuck

striped weasel

zebra

UMGENI VALLEY NATURE RESERVE

Area: 656 ha
Established: 1976

LOCATION
Midlands. From the N3 take the Howick turn-off. Continue through the town, turning right onto the Karkloof-Rietvlei road. The reserve sign and entrance gate are a further 1 km.

FEATURES

This small reserve has been greatly under-utilised by the public. It has interesting geological formations and the Mgeni river, its tributaries, river bed and rock pools and waterfalls with wonderful scenic vistas. The range of habitats supports over 200 species of birds and 20 indigenous and rein-troduced mammals.

Its easy access, walks along a network of trails that traverse the reserve, picnic sites and comfortable small cottages, make this reserve an idyllic retreat for those not wishing to embark on a long trip in search of a wildlife experience, or who merely want to relax in a peaceful environment.

The reserve is now well known throughout South Africa for its very fine educational centre and the excellent standards of tuition, accommodation, catering and meals provided for the pupils who enrol to do the one to five day courses.

DESCRIPTION

Umgeni Valley Nature Reserve lies in the valley of the Mgeni river, just below the well-known and impressive Howick Falls. It includes magnificent sandstone cliffs, volcanic intrusions and dolerite slabs. Waterfalls, rock pools and small streams flow from the steep plateau through well-grassed and forested valleys. From high points one has commanding views of Howick Falls, farmlands and Albert Falls dam down the Mgeni valley.

Vegetation is varied, with short grass and long grass areas on the hill-sides and plains, dry acacia-dominated thornveld, mixed open woodland and forest. There are some fine tree specimens in the different habitats, and numerous colourful veld flowers after the spring rains. Interesting cycads and ferns are abundant.

HISTORICAL NOTES

The Umgeni Valley project was launched in 1976 by the Wildlife Society of Southern Africa, with the aim of initiating an environmental conservation-education programme specifically aimed at primary and secondary school pupils between the ages of eight and 18. Courses run by trained staff cover a wide range of topics. Lectures precede field studies that take pupils along trails through widely varying habitats. A variety of subjects, such as energy flow, adaptations, natural resources, soil and water stud-ies, population explosion, mapwork, animal and plant identification and behaviour, as well as inter-relationships, are dealt with in these courses. These are geared to the different age groups of pupils.

There are also courses on careers in conservation, teachers' in-service training, general conservation awareness and a course for Guides and Scouts. These popular courses are prepared by educationists and profes-sional conservationists and are of a very high standard. From small begin-nings (only 300 in 1976), the number of children participating each year has risen to over 10 000. Not only is the experience an invaluable one educationally, but the participants enjoy camping out in beautiful surroundings and can enjoy the wide variety of fauna and flora to be found within the park.

The area was formerly inhabited by the Nguni people and the land was once terraced for the planting of crops. An old kraal site and the grave of a Zulu chief who once lived here, Chief Ngwenya, are still visible. Pottery shards have also been found in some of the caves.

ACCOMMODATION

There are two cottages with five beds each, fully equipped and self catering. Guests supply their own food and drink. School group accommodation consists of rustic wooden dormitory-type huts. Inkonka camp has 50 beds, Shelter Falls camp has 50 beds, Indulo camp has 50 beds and Cycad camp has 30 beds. Each hutted camp has a communal kitchen and ablution facilities and the individual camps are spread out within the reserve, each with a character of its own. Day visitors are welcome to do the trails or to make use of the attractive picnic sites. Pupils on courses supply their own bedding but meals are provided. Reservations should be made with Umgeni Valley Nature Reserve.

TREES

Acacia karroo – sweet thorn
Aloe candelabrum – candelabra tree
Celtis africana – white stinkwood
Combretum erythrophyllum – river bushwillow
Cussonia spicata – common cabbage tree
Cyathea dregei – common tree fern
Dalbergia obovata – climbing flat-bean
Dombeya rotundifolia – wild pear
Dracaena aletriformis (D. hookeriana) – large-leaved dragon tree
Encephalartos natalensis – Natal cycad
Erythrina caffra – coast coral tree
Ficus ingens – red-leaved fig
Halleria lucida – notsung
Syzygium cordatum – water berry
Ziziphus mucronata – buffalo thorn

BIRDS (214 species recorded)

Alpine swift
black duck
blackcrowned tchagra
Cape sugarbird
cuckoo hawk
eagles – black, booted, tawny
European roller
fairy flycatcher
green twinspot

greyheaded bush shrike
ground hornbill
ground woodpecker
hobby falcon
honeyguides – greater,
  lesser, sharpbilled
Knysna lourie
longtailed wagtail
malachite sunbird

melba finch
mocking chat
narina trogon
olive thrush
plumcoloured starling
rednecked francolin

redthroated wryneck
robins – chorister, starred
sentinel rock thrush
short-tailed pipit
wood owl
yellowthroated warbler

MAMMALS

aardvark
blesbok
blue wildebeest
bushbuck
Cape clawless otter
civet
common duiker
eland
giraffe
greater canerat
impala

large-spotted genet
mountain reedbuck
nyala
oribi
porcupine
rock dassie
vervet monkey
warthog
water mongoose
zebra

KARKLOOF NATURE RESERVE

Area: 1 700 ha
Established: 3 July 1980

LOCATION
Midlands, north of Howick on the road to Rietvlei.

FEATURES
This nature reserve is part of the Karkloof forest in the Midlands mistbelt region, extending from about 22 km north of Howick to 12 km north-east of New Hanover. There are a number of privately owned forest patches, grassland and wetland areas, mainly on the eastern side of the Karkloof range, which cover an estimated 6 000 ha. A number of uncommon plants occur in these habitats, as well as a varied bird fauna.

This reserve is not yet officially open to the public but group visits accompanied by a ranger can be arranged. Enquiries should be addressed to the Natal Parks Board, Pietermaritzburg.

DESCRIPTION
One of the largest remaining areas of mistbelt forest in Natal, the Karkloof reserve ranges in altitude from 800 m near the confluence of the Karkloof and Mgeni rivers, to 1 700 m on the upper slopes of Mt Gilboa. The grass-

259

land is classified as Ngongoni veld. The area has a number of rare ferns, a rare orchid *Neobolusia tysonii*, and the herbs *Geranium natalense* and *Plectranthus rehmannii* – known in only a few sites. The false lightning bush *Andrachne ovalis* and forest canary-berry *Suregada procera* are only found in a limited number of localities in Natal, and the black stinkwood *Ocotea bullata* is found in this reserve.

The entire Karkloof forest area is frequently subjected to hot burns along its margins and there is evidence that it is shrinking in size. The preservation of this forest and adjoining grasslands should be regarded as one of the top conservation priorities in Natal.

TREES
Allophylus africanus – black forest currant
Bersama tysoniana – common white ash
Cassine papillosa – common saffron
Celtis africana – white stinkwood
Cryptocarya myrtifolia – myrtle quince
Cussonia sphaerocephala – Natal forest cabbage tree
Diospyros whyteana – bladder-nut
Dombeya tiliacea – forest wild pear
Drypetes gerrardii – forest ironplum
Englerophytum (Bequaertiodendron) natalense – Natal milkplum
Eugenia zuluensis – paperbark myrtle
Ficus craterostoma – forest fig
Grewia occidentalis – cross-berry
Leucosidea sericea – oldwood
Nuxia floribunda – forest elder
Ocotea bullata – black stinkwood
Peddiea africana – poison olive
Podocarpus falcatus – Outeniqua yellowwood
Podocarpus henkelii – Henkel's yellowwood
Podocarpus latifolius – real yellowwood
Protorhus longifolia – red beech
Prunus africana – red stinkwood
Psydrax locuples – krantz quar
Rapanea melanophloeos – Cape beech
Rhamnus prinoides – dogwood
Scolopia zeyheri – thorn pear
Syzygium gerrardii – forest waterwood
Vepris lanceolata – white ironwood
Zanthoxylum davyi – knobwood

BIRDS
Typical birds of the Karkloof forest include:

African goshawk	buffspotted flufftail
Barratt's warbler	Cape batis

Cape parrot
Cape white-eye
cinnamon dove
crowned eagle
forest canary
forest weaver
Knysna lourie
lesser doublecollared sunbird
narina trogon

olive thrush
olive woodpecker
puffback
rameron pigeon
robins – Cape, chorister,
  starred
terrestrial bulbul
yellowthroated warbler

MAMMALS

black-backed jackal
blue duiker
Cape clawless otter
caracal

large-spotted genet
mongooses – large grey,
  water
serval

ALBERT FALLS PUBLIC RESORT NATURE RESERVE

Area: 3 090 ha
Established: 31 July 1975

LOCATION

Midlands. 24 km from Pietermaritzburg, near Cramond, on the Pietermaritzburg-Greytown road. Signposted to Albert Falls dam.

FEATURES

The Albert Falls dam is an attractive and popular venue for boating, water-skiing, sailing, canoeing and fishing. There are numerous picnic areas, squash and tennis courts, and a small swimming pool. Yachting, skiing and angling clubs operate in this resort, and canoe races are held regularly. A small game park at Notuli offers the visitor an opportunity of seeing red hartebeest, springbok, bushbuck, zebra, blesbok, reedbuck, impala and other species. About 290 species of birds have been recorded at Albert Falls. Walking and bird watching are popular pastimes.

DESCRIPTION

This resort on the Mgeni river was once privately owned land, the dam known as Peattie's Lake. Albert Falls is said to have been named after Queen Victoria's prince consort. The small land area surrounding the dam is mostly short grass to the water's edge. At low water levels the exposed areas are ideal for wading birds. There are tracts of mixed woodland, giving way to open grassland, as well as small marsh areas. In wet seasons, rank grass patches attract numerous wetland and grassland birds such as widows, weavers, waxbills and cisticolas.

ACCOMMODATION
There are two separate hutted camps, Notuli and Bon Accorde.

Notuli camp has 15 two-bedded rondavels and three six-bedded family chalets. All are fully equipped. There are 40 well-spaced camp sites at the water's edge, with hot and cold showers in the communal ablution blocks.

Bon Accorde camp has 10 five-bedded fully equipped chalets, and camp sites to accommodate 100 persons. Visitors do their own cooking and washing up at the hutted camps, but staff sweep and make beds. The chalets at Bon Accorde are being phased out.

Reservations should be made with the Natal Parks Board, Pietermaritzburg.

BIRDS
Some 290 different species have been recorded, including 12 species of heron and egret, 4 storks, 14 wildfowl, 3 cranes, 5 francolins, 5 eagles, 9 plovers, 11 waders, 4 thrushes, 10 warblers, 7 cisticolas and 9 shrikes. Some attractive and uncommon species include:

African snipe
avocet
black eagle
blackrumped buttonquail
bronzewinged courser
cisticolas – Ayres', cloud,
   croaking, fantailed, lazy,
   Levaillant's, rattling
cranes – blue, crowned, wattled
francolins – coqui, Natal,
   Shelley's, redwing, Swainson's
grey plover
ground hornbill
kurrichane thrush
little stint

longbilled crombec
pennantwinged nightjar
pinkbacked pelican
rameron pigeon
redcapped lark
ruff
sanderling
Stanley's bustard
storks – black, white,
   woollynecked, yellowbilled
thrushes – Cape rock,
   groundscraper, olive
whitebacked night heron
yellow wagtail

MAMMALS
aardwolf
African wild cat
black-backed jackal
blesbok
bushbuck
bushpig
common duiker
impala

large-spotted genet
mongooses – large grey,
   water, white-tailed
oribi
otters – Cape clawless,
   spotted-necked
red hartebeest
reedbuck

springbok   striped weasel
striped polecat   zebra

BLINKWATER NATURE RESERVE

Area: 350 ha
Proclamation: Pending

LOCATION
Midlands. The reserve is situated approximately 15 km from Sevenoaks, off the Sevenoaks-Rietvlei district road D151. Access is through private farm land.

FEATURES
The Blinkwater mountain is an important breeding area for a number of species of birds, including South Africa's most endangered bird, the blue swallow.

A system of hiking trails covering nearly 100 km was opened in March 1994. The trails traverse private timber plantations and the nature reserve. There are four overnight stops, each camp accommodating up to 12 persons. They offer a variety of styles of accommodation, from the Douglas Smith cottage to rustic camps. The distances between camps vary from 8-12 km. The trails are interlinked to create two to five day hikes and are ideal for family groups. They traverse countryside that includes *Podocarpus* mistbelt forest and upland grasslands with spring displays of wild flowers. There are waterfalls, streams, dams, lakes and superb views along the route, with an opportunity to skirt the exotic timber plantations and to see how management of this industry operates in harmony with the environment. The trail system is a joint venture between SAPPI Forests, HL & H Timber Products, the Natal Parks Board and the Umvoti centre of the Wildlife Society of Southern Africa.

DESCRIPTION
Blinkwater, or Phasiwe, as it is known to the local people, is an area of high grassland, extensive indigenous forest, and, on the lower slopes, commercial plantation. The Natal Parks Board manages 350 ha of this area. A further piece of land, previously owned by HL & H Timber Products, has been incorporated into the reserve, virtually doubling its size.

The plateau is some 1 480 m high, comprising grassland, pans and boulder-strewn veld. It is an area of high rainfall, and is the source of the Mvoti river. There are several small pockets of indigenous bush in the valleys, with extensive mistbelt forest on the southern slopes. Several small waterfalls are bordered by banks of *Begonia sutherlandii*, *Streptocarpus gardenii*, and a wealth of ferns, lichens and mosses.

HISTORICAL NOTES

Local history mentions attempts to mine coal for the railways on the northern slopes. This was abandoned because of the poor quality of the coal, but the entrance to the mine shaft is still visible. On the southern slopes a railway line was constructed early this century to remove the magnificent timber. Several saw pits are still evident in the indigenous forest. A fascinating arboretum surrounds the old homestead, which is referred to as the Old Hunting Lodge.

ACCOMMODATION

There are four rustic camps accommodating up to 12 persons each, along the trails system. Bunk beds, toilet facilities, firewood and water is provided. Visitors supply their own cutlery, crockery, cooking utensils, bedding, food and drink. Reservations are made with the Natal Parks Board, Pietermaritzburg.

Enquiries: Mrs Sue Swan, Sevenoaks. Telephone (033552) ask for 42.

TREES

Bowkeria cymosa – Natal shell-flower bush
Canthium spinosum – thorny rock alder
Clausena anisata – horsewood
Cussonia spicata – common cabbage tree
Ficus ingens – red-leaved fig
Ficus sur – broom cluster fig
Grewia monticola – silver raisin
Heteromorpha trifoliata – parsley tree
Hyperacanthus amoenus – thorny gardenia
Ilex mitis – Cape holly
Maesa lanceolata – false assegai
Maytenus acuminata – silky bark
Pachystigma macrocalyx – crowned medlar
Podocarpus latifolius – real yellowwood
Ptaeroxylon obliquum – sneezewood
Xymalos monospora – lemonwood
Zanthoxylum davyi – knobwood

BIRDS

Ayres' cisticola
bald ibis
blackwinged plover
blue swallow
buffstreaked chat
buzzards – jackal, steppe
corncrake

cranes – blue, crowned, wattled
eagles – crowned,
   longcrested, martial
longbilled pipit
orangethroated longclaw
redfooted kestrel
swifts – Alpine, horus

MAMMALS

black-backed jackal
bushbuck
caracal
Cape clawless otter
common duiker

mongooses – slender,
  white-tailed
oribi
reedbuck
samango monkey

UMVOTI VLEI NATURE RESERVE

Area: 267 ha
Established: 17 July 1975

LOCATION
Midlands. 11 km south of Greytown, 3 km west of the main road linking Greytown-Pietermaritzburg.

FEATURES
This small reserve supports a fauna and flora of considerable interest, with 116 bird species recorded. The area of reed swamp and open water is a sanctuary of major importance for wildfowl. For permission to visit this reserve, contact Mr Pat Clarence, Proud Acres, telephone (033552) ask for 1340.

DESCRIPTION
The Umvoti Vlei covers an area of about 600 ha, of which the Natal Parks Board manages a portion. Match poplar plantations have been established in the upper reaches, while arable and grazing lands adjoin the vlei proper. The extensive reedbeds and sedges are today in excellent condition.

HISTORICAL NOTES
In the late 1940s there were attempts to drain this vlei to plant match poplars, but such was the outcry that the attempt was abandoned. A spin-off of the dredging was the creation of pathways which have been inter-linked over the wetter areas by a series of boardwalks, ideal for birding. There is not yet a circular route, but an excellent hide has been built on one of the larger pans.

BIRDS (142 species)

cranes – blue, crowned
ducks – yellowbilled,
  whitefaced
eagles – African fish,
  longcrested, martial
European harrier

grass owl
little bittern
redwinged pratincole
reed cormorant
spurwinged goose
teals – Hottentot, redbilled

There are also warblers, cisticolas, weavers, queleas, widowfinches, herons and egrets.

MAMMALS

black-backed jackal

bushbuck

mongooses – large grey,
   slender, water

oribi

otters – Cape clawless,
   spotted-necked

grey duiker

large-spotted genet

porcupine

reedbuck

serval

striped weasel

MONTELLO SAFARI LODGE

Area: 100 ha

LOCATION

Midlands, near Greytown. From Pietermaritzburg take the road to Greytown. At the first robot on arriving in Greytown turn left. Travel for 10 km to the top of the hill, then right at Montello Safari Lodge sign (district road D80). Travel 4 km along a gravel road, then left at the Montello sign and proceed to large gates. The lodge is a further 6 km.

FEATURES

Regular game drives are arranged with a guide, or guests can hire a vehicle with a tracker and can then conduct their own excursions. A variety of guided walks and trails can be organised, including game spotting on horseback.

Florida bass can be fished for from two dams on Montello, adjacent to the lodges, and rainbow trout from a beautiful and well-stocked lake nearby, surrounded by tranquil forest. There is a magnificent swimming pool, leading off from the lounge and dining area, overlooking the mountains. Sundowners can be enjoyed around the pool, while watching the impressive sunsets and panoramic view.

Montello can also be booked for conferences and up to 16 people can be catered for. The lodge is also conveniently situated for visits to a number of historic Boer, British and Zulu battlefields.

Three home-style meals a day are included in the tariff, with venison a regular item on the menu. Most evening meals take the form of an outdoor braai. Champagne breakfasts and brunches in the bush can be arranged, as can bush braais.

Clay pigeon shooting facilities are available but guests must bring their own shotguns. The same applies to fishing tackle.

DESCRIPTION
It is an area with elements of thornveld, as well as woodland, thick bush, forest patches in deep valleys and rolling grassy hillsides. It is abundantly stocked with game.

ACCOMMODATION
The luxury Mgamanzi lodge, with bathrooms en suite, has its own private lounge and sleeps eight to 10 persons. For smaller groups, the Mvelase lodge sleeps six to eight, and the Ondini rondavel two to four. The latter two have separate bathroom facilities. The tariff includes all meals, tea and coffee, horse riding, bass fishing, guided trails and game drives. Reservations are made with Montello Safari Lodge.

TREES
Acacia ataxacantha – flame thorn
Acacia caffra – common hook-thorn
Acacia karroo – sweet thorn
Acacia nilotica – scented thorn
Allophylus decipiens – false currant
Carissa bispinosa – forest num-num
Clausena anisata – horsewood
Crotalaria capensis – Cape rattle pod
Cussonia spicata – common cabbage tree
Dalbergia obovata – climbing flat-bean
Diospyros lycioides – Transvaal bluebush
Dombeya tiliacea – forest wild pear
Ehretia rigida – puzzle bush
Euclea racemosa subsp. *zuluensis (E. schimperi)* – bush guarri
Heteromorpha trifoliata – parsley tree
Maerua caffra – common bush-cherry
Maytenus heterophylla – common spike-thorn
Schotia brachypetala – weeping boer-bean
Vitellariopsis dispar – Tugela milkwood
Ziziphus mucronata – buffalo thorn

BIRDS
arrowmarked babbler
batises – Cape, chinspot
blackcollared barbet
brownhooded kingfisher
Cape robin
Cape vulture
Cape wagtail
Drakensberg prinia
familiar chat
forktailed drongo
glossy starling
goldenbreasted bunting
longbilled crombec
neddicky
plumcoloured starling
shrikes – fiscal, redbacked
southern boubou
waxbills – blue, common, swee

MAMMALS

black-backed jackal	giraffe
blesbok	impala
blue wildebeest	kudu
common duiker	nyala
oribi	warthog
reedbuck	zebra
springbok	

MHLOPENI NATURE RESERVE

Area: 1 325 ha
Established: 1975

LOCATION
Midlands. Between Greytown and Muden. The turn-off to Mhlopeni is 3 km from Muden on the Greytown-Muden road. Care must be exercised on the reserve's rough gravel road after rain.

FEATURES
A wild, beautiful river valley with small waterfalls, rock pools, imposing krantzes, secluded ravines, and rolling acacia-studded grassveld with dramatic views from the plateaux. There are numerous walking trails, a wide range of game, and some 210 bird species, particularly birds of prey. There are interesting Stone Age and Iron Age sites at Mhlopeni – the reserve is an ideal venue for school groups involved in natural history projects. A brochure has been compiled as an aid to such visits.

DESCRIPTION
Mhlopeni contains some rugged terrain, with precipitous krantzes up to 400 m high. The vegetation is mainly valley bushveld, with dense thickets of *Euphorbia tirucalli* on old lands and kraal sites. There are patches of semi-deciduous bush with wild olive and shepherd's tree. Succulents such as euphorbias and aloes are common on the shallow soils.

An interior thornveld region is dominated by acacias, weeping boer bean, *Euclea* species, *Rhus* species, sickle bush, *Maytenus* species and white stinkwood near the river. The prickly dwarf shrub, *Blepharis natalensis*, is an indicator, and sometimes the only ground cover, on severely eroded areas.

As more and more of the characteristic Tugela valley bushveld is degraded and cleared to meet the demands of a growing population, the importance of Mhlopeni as a refuge area increases.

HISTORICAL NOTES

The abundance of human artefacts at Mhlopeni attests to its long history of occupation, although who the early inhabitants were, why they settled here and how they conducted their lives is unknown.

Rock art is evidence of the Bushmen (San), who lived as hunter-gatherers. The Khoi-San also lived here, as well as the first Nguni peoples, not all at the same time, but probably side by side at times. Potsherds, shell beads, iron smelting slag and associated clay artefacts suggest small industry activities for local or more distant trade.

Sites investigated by archaeologists indicate there were Early Iron Age people at Mhlopeni. At the beginning of this period the present semi-deciduous bush was probably dense thicket which was cleared and opened up by pioneering settlements. When the Voortrekkers arrived in 1838, they brought further changes to the landscape.

The present reserve was proclaimed in 1978, when a group of conservation-minded persons and businessmen made a joint bid for an insolvent estate, Huisrivier (Rem of sub 2 of Springfield). A further 517 ha of river frontage on the Mooi river was subsequently purchased, bringing the reserve to its present size.

Mhlopeni – a Zulu place name – refers to the small white stones that abound in the valley and stream.

ACCOMMODATION

A total of 20 visitors can be accommodated in the rest huts. Visitors must bring their own linen, sleeping bags, etc. Crockery, cutlery and cooking utensils are provided. There is no electricity, but gas stoves, refrigerators and lamps are provided.

Mattresses on the floor are available for school groups, but children must bring their own bedding. Food and cooking can be laid on by arrangement, but normally visitors provide their own food and beverages.

Day visitors are welcome, but prior booking is necessary. Occasionally, hunting can be arranged for groups. Make reservations and enquiries with the nature reserve itself.

TREES

Aloe arborescens – krantz aloe
Aloe barberiae (*A. bainesii*) – tree aloe
Aloe rupestris – bottlebrush aloe
Aloe spectabilis – Natal aloe
Berchemia zeyheri – red ivory
Canthium mundianum – rock alder
Commiphora harveyii – red-stem corkwood
Commiphora woodii – forest corkwood
Croton gratissimus – lavender fever-berry
Dais cotinifolia – pompon tree
Euphorbia ingens – candelabra tree

Ficus abutilifolia – large-leaved rock fig
Ficus burtt-davyi – veld fig
Ficus natalensis – Natal fig
Maerua angolensis – bead-bean
Vepris lanceolata – white ironwood
Zanthoxylum capense – small knobwood

BIRDS

About 210 species have been recorded at Mhlopeni, including 21 species of raptors such as the black, tawny, Wahlberg's, booted, longcrested, martial, crowned, and brown snake eagles. Several species common in Zululand reach their southern limit in Natal. These include:
arrowmarked babbler
pied barbet
titbabbler
whitethroated robin

Other birds of interest are:
bald ibis
black stork
blue crane
Cape vulture
crested barbet
cuckoos – black, Diederik, emerald, Jacobin, Klaas's, redchested
francolins – Natal, Shelley's, Swainson's
ground hornbill
honeyguides – lesser, scalythroated
plumcoloured starling
rameron pigeon
sentinel rock thrush
sunbirds – black, greater doublecollared, grey, lesser
    doublecollared, malachite, olive, scarletchested, whitebellied

MAMMALS

41 species have been recorded, and the visitor may encounter:

aardwolf	greater canerat
antbear (aardvark)	honey badger
black-backed jackal	impala
blesbok	klipspringer
bushbuck	kudu
bushpig	large-spotted genet
Cape clawless otter	leopard
caracal	mongooses – banded, slender, water,
chacma baboon	white-tailed
duiker – blue, common	mountain reedbuck
four-toed elephant shrew	oribi

porcupine	scrub hare
red rock rabbit	thick-tailed bushbaby
reedbuck	vervet monkey
rock dassie	zebra

CRAIGIE BURN PUBLIC RESORT NATURE RESERVE

Area: 330 ha
Established: 10 August 1978

LOCATION
Natal Midlands, midway between Greytown and Mooi River on the Rietvlei road.

FEATURES
A small recreational resort where visitors may enjoy good fishing in the dam which is stocked with rainbow trout, largemouth bass, bluegill, scalies and tilapia. Seasonally waterfowl may gather in large numbers, and boating is popular.

DESCRIPTION
The reserve encompasses the Craigie Burn dam, fed by the Mnyamvubu river, with an 11 km perimeter shoreline and a surface area of 217 ha. The land area of 113 ha is of the karoo system, Ecca series, consisting of shale, sandstone and grit at an altitude of 1 308 m. The vegetation is highland sourveld, typical of the upland moist area.

ACCOMMODATION
The camping area is limited to 50 persons. Hot and cold water and toilets are available. Reservations and enquiries: Natal Parks Board, Midmar Public Resort.

TREES
Apodytes dimidiata – white pear
Celtis africana – white stinkwood
Cussonia spicata – common cabbage tree
Heteromorpha trifoliata – parsley tree
Mimusops obovata – red milkwood
Olea europaea subsp. *africana* – wild olive
Podocarpus falcatus – common yellowwood

BIRDS (45 species)

African fish eagle
bald ibis
blackshouldered kite
giant kingfisher
grass owl
gymnogene
helmeted guineafowl

herons – purple, squacco
hobby falcon
osprey
redbilled teal
rufousnaped lark
secretarybird
yellowbilled duck

MAMMALS

aardwolf
black-backed jackal
common duiker
mongooses – slender,
   water, white-tailed

otters – Cape clawless,
   spotted-necked
porcupine
reedbuck

FISH

bluegill
largemouth bass
rainbow trout

scaly (yellowfish)
tilapia

WEENEN NATURE RESERVE

Area: 4 908 ha
Established: 1 April 1975

LOCATION

Midlands, 25 km from Estcourt and 20 km from Colenso on the Weenen road.

FEATURES

A scenically interesting reserve with spectacular views from the beacon site on one of the trails over the farmlands to the distant Weenen area. The terrain is rugged in parts and the vegetation varied. With over 230 species of birds and 25 mammal species, the reserve is a fine example of how a once severely degraded habitat can, with care, be restored to a healthy viable condition and become an area of great conservation value.

Three picnic sites with braai facilities, water points and rustic toilets are available within the reserve. There are two self-guided trails. A new bird and game viewing hide has been opened. It overlooks a large dam and offers good photographic opportunities. A small camping ground is sited near the gate.

DESCRIPTION
The Weenen reserve is situated in the heart of the Natal Midlands between Weenen and Estcourt, at altitudes of 1 000-1 240 m. It consists mainly of typical valley bushveld, characterised by several species of acacias, with woodlands and thickets, and grasslands dominated by tall stands of thatch grass *Hyparrhenia hirta* and red grass *Themeda triandra* on the shallower soils. A dolerite hill in the south and south-east is incised by a number of streams. The Bushmans river flows through a steep valley in the south and there are some dense thickets in this area.

The area preserves the fauna and flora of the central Midlands, especially animals that once roamed these hills and valleys during recent historical times. Many species wiped out by the early hunters have been restocked in small numbers.

HISTORICAL NOTES
This reserve has a long history of occupation by humans through the Stone and Iron Ages. There are still stone-walled structures to be seen that were once cattle kraals. Before the 1850s, a succession of Voortrekker farmers, and later Zulus, occupied the area. Sir Theophilus Shepstone bought the land in 1888. It was owned by the Geekie family from 1892. It was used as a labour farm until its expropriation in 1948 by the Union government. By then the land had been severely abused and the Department of Agriculture implemented reclamation and soil erosion measures over the following 25 years. Local farmers and the Weenen Town Board took steps to establish a nature reserve and in 1975 the Natal Parks Board took control of this land.

ACCOMMODATION
There are 12 camping and caravan sites near the entrance to the reserve. One big site can accommodate four caravans, another site two caravans, while the rest are single sites. Ablution facilities are nearby. Reservations are made with the officer-in-charge, Natal Parks Board.

TREES
Some trees and shrubs typical of the area:
Acacia ataxacantha – flame thorn
Acacia caffra – common hook-thorn
Acacia karroo – sweet thorn
Acacia nilotica – scented thorn
Acacia robusta – brack thorn
Acacia sieberiana – paperbark thorn
Acacia tortilis – umbrella thorn
Aloe spectabilis – Natal aloe
Boscia albitrunca – shepherd's tree
Combretum erythrophyllum – river bushwillow
Cussonia spicata – cabbage tree

Dalbergia obovata – climbing flat-bean
Dombeya rotundifolia – common wild pear
Euphorbia ingens – candelabra tree
Ficus natalensis – Natal fig
Greyia sutherlandii – Natal bottlebrush
Olea europaea subsp. *africana* – wild olive
Schotia brachypetala – weeping boer-bean
Tarchonanthus camphoratus – wild camphor bush

BIRDS (230 species, including summer visitors)
Some of the interesting birds to be seen:
arrowmarked babbler
bitterns – dwarf, little
black stork
blackthroated canary
blue crane
cuckoos – African, black, Diederik, great spotted, Jacobin,
  Klaas's, redchested, striped
eagles – martial, Wahlberg's
fierynecked nightjar
gymnogene
icterine warbler
kites – blackshouldered, yellowbilled
korhaans – blackbellied, whitebellied
lanner falcon
ostrich has been reintroduced
owls – Cape eagle, spotted eagle
redheaded finch
rock kestrel
scimitarbilled woodhoopoe
spotted dikkop
steppe buzzard
titbabbler
whitethroated robin

MAMMALS
Species that survived the early occupation of humans in and around the
area and those that have been reintroduced since 1975, are:

aardwolf	porcupine
black-backed jackal	rock dassie
bushbuck	scrub hare
Cape clawless otter	serval
common duiker	slender mongoose
klipspringer	spotted hyaena
large-spotted genet	steenbok
mountain reedbuck	

274

The more recent reintroductions are black rhino, white rhino, buffalo, giraffe, kudu, red hartebeest, reedbuck, eland, zebra and roan antelope. There is also a large variety of rodents inhabiting the grasslands – the prey of the numerous raptors to be found here.

ESTCOURT NATURE RESERVE

Area: Approximately 400 ha

LOCATION
Midlands, Estcourt. Municipal land adjoining the town's southern boundary, within easy walking distance of the town centre. Follow the old main road south and take the New Formosa turn-off to the left, where a conservancy sign is prominently displayed. Continue beyond the hospital to the parking area.

FEATURES
The reserve comprises a dry valley with steep hillsides of acacia veld, mixed scrub and grassland. There are marked walking trails, some still being laid out. Old trenches used in the Anglo-Boer war are still visible in the park. It is stocked with zebra, impala, blesbok, kudu, reedbuck, mountain reedbuck, common duiker, bushbuck and black-backed jackal. Vultures are regularly fed at one site. The bird life in the area includes some interesting species.

A furnished classroom is available at the reserve entrance for the use of school groups. This is to be developed as an interpretation centre.

WAGENDRIFT PUBLIC RESORT NATURE RESERVE

Area: 758 ha
Established: 11 October 1973

LOCATION
Midlands, Estcourt area. From the N3 take the Estcourt turn-off, travelling into town as far as the intersection of Lourne and Connor Streets, where there is a sign to Wagendrift Dam-Tabamhlophe. Proceed over the railway bridge and follow the signs. The entrance gate to the dam is about 5 km out of town on the left-hand side of the road.

FEATURES

This is principally a resort area, where popular recreational sports include motorboating, sailing, canoeing and fishing for bluegill, bass, carp, eel and the occasional trout. There is a registered boat club, the Bushmans River Boating Club. Canoes are available for hire from the Natal Parks Board, and facilities for tennis, basketball and soccer are available. Film, video and slide shows can be arranged in advance. There are numerous picnic and boat launching sites.

The Youth/Environmental Education Centre is run in conjunction with the adjacent Moor Park Nature Reserve, where educational and wildlife trails are conducted.

Game viewing drives through scenically attractive Moor Park show transitional changes in topography and vegetation from one end of Wagendrift dam to the other.

DESCRIPTION

The Wagendrift dam across the Bushmans river was completed in 1964, and lies in a valley surrounded by steeply sloping hills, with bushveld and tall grassland on the course of the Bushmans river. For a description of the fauna and flora of this resort, see the entry under Moor Park Nature Reserve.

ACCOMMODATION

There are two camping and caravan parks (36 sites) with ablution blocks equipped with hot and cold running water.

A youth centre has four 18-bed dormitories, each with a small, two-bed flat for teachers or guides. A central hall has a fully equipped kitchen. Visitors need to bring cutlery and bedding for the dormitories, as these are not serviced.

Contact the officer-in-charge, Wagendrift dam for reservations.

MOOR PARK NATURE RESERVE

Area: 264 ha
Established: 21 December 1967

LOCATION

Midlands, 12 km from Estcourt on the Dalton Bridge road. From Estcourt, take the Tabambhlophe road, and follow the signposts.

FEATURES

A scenically attractive small park on steep, sloping ground with high cliffs, broken and eroded gullies and a high plateau in the mid-eastern section. It is a predominantly dry region of three main vegetation types, valley bushveld, southern tall grassland and highveld sourveld. From the tourist roads there are spectacular views over the Bushmans river and the dam. There is an interesting self-guided trail.

Black wildebeest, blesbok, impala, zebra, mountain reedbuck, common duiker and bushbuck are some of the larger mammals reintroduced, and 190 bird species have been recorded.

Wagendrift dam is a popular fishing venue with good scaly fishing (*Barbus natalensis*). There are also introduced exotic species which include carp, largemouth bass and brown trout, as well as an indigenous eel.

The area is rich in fossils. The reptiles *Lystrosaurus* and *Glossopteris*, plant leaves and fossilised wood can be seen in shales along the trail.

DESCRIPTION

Moor Park is dominated by Makabeni hill, which is 1 549 m above sea level. The habitat zones include high slopes of sourveld grasses, bare cliffs and bluffs and southern tall grassland further down. Although there are a number of cabbage trees, Natal bottlebrush and stands of protea, the lower areas are mainly acacia-dominated thornveld. There are large areas of boulder-strewn short grass down to the water's edge, with vlei grasses and reeds along the river banks where it enters the dam.

HISTORICAL NOTES

This reserve was originally land which was donated by the Moor family on the understanding that it would be maintained in perpetuity as a nature reserve. Named after Sir Frederick Moor, Natal's last prime minister, it was proclaimed in 1967, and incorporated into the administration of Wagendrift dam in 1989.

On Makabeni hill are the remains of one of the earliest settlements in South Africa. Archaeological excavations and carbon dating of artefacts suggest the area was occupied by humans in about the 11th century.

This is the area of the 1838 three-day Battle of Veglaer, in which the Voortrekkers fought off an attack by a large force of Zulus. Details of the battle can be studied on a plaque just off the main road. Soon after the battle, the Voortrekkers moved away to settle in the Little Tugela area. On the Bushmans river is an old weir, said to have been constructed by the early settlers.

There is also an historic irrigation furrow, started by the Moor family in 1900, and completed in 1903. It was built to irrigate land which is now submerged by the dam.

Wagendrift was constructed on the Bushmans river to provide Estcourt with a water supply. The river has its source in the Giant's Castle area of the Natal Drakensberg Park, flowing through the town of Weenen before it joins the Tugela river. When the dam was completed in 1964, the narrow strip of land on its shores was controlled by the Department of Water Affairs. In 1978 it was handed over to the Natal Parks Board.

ACCOMMODATION
There is no overnight accommodation, but picnic sites and toilet facilities are available for day visitors. Visitors may camp in the nearby Wagendrift resort.

BIRDS
Some of the 190 recorded species which may be observed include:

arrowmarked babbler
bearded woodpecker
blue crane
Cape vulture
cuckoos – black, great
   spotted, Jacobin
eagles – black, martial,
   Wahlberg's
flycatchers – fiscal, spotted
greater doublecollared sunbird
lanner falcon
orangethroated longclaw

osprey
plumcoloured starling
Richard's pipit
ruff
secretarybird
South African shelduck
southern pochard
storks – black, white
whiskered tern
whitebellied korhaan
whitewinged widow
yellow warbler

MAMMALS
black wildebeest
black-backed jackal
blesbok
Burchell's zebra
bushbuck
Cape fox
caracal
common duiker
greater canerat

impala
large-spotted genet
mongooses – white-tailed,
   yellow
mountain reedbuck
otters – Cape clawless,
   spotted-necked
steenbok
striped polecat

THUKELA BIOSPHERE RESERVE

Area: 60 000 ha
Established: 1 March 1993

LOCATION
Midlands. Situated between Weenen, Colenso and Estcourt. It is bounded in the north by the Tugela river, in the west by the Colenso-Estcourt road, in the south by Estcourt and in the east, halfway along the Weenen-Muden road, by the Msinga valley. The area includes the Weenen Nature Reserve.

FEATURES
The reserve incorporates the Tugela, Blouwkrantz and Bushmans river valleys and has some of the most magnificent scenery in Natal. Visitors may enjoy horse trails, game viewing and bird watching. One of the spectacular sights is the arrival of some 2 000 and more white storks, usually in November. It is not uncommon to observe up to 500 of these migrant storks circling and wheeling in the thermals. During the summer months there is white-water rafting down the Tugela, Natal's largest river, with its stretches of rapids and deep pools. Fishing in the river is permitted. For the hunter, 12 species of antelope are available, as well as good bird shooting of guineafowl, francolin, waterfowl and pigeons. For the hiker there is some rugged country to explore, and for city children the opportunity of learning about farming practices in this integrated farming and wildlife complex.

DESCRIPTION
This area combines many habitats, including short grassed and long grassed areas, vleis, acacia-dominated valley bushveld, steep valleys, boulder beds and spectacular krantzes along the rivers, stream bed and riverine vegetation and mountains, as well as farmlands.

HISTORICAL NOTES
This exciting new concept involves 31 private landowners and farmers who, with the Natal Parks Board, have joined up and made available their properties to form this single biosphere reserve. It is likely that the area will be increased in size.

ACCOMMODATION
This comprises three luxury lodges with six beds per unit, two tented camps with 30 beds each and one tented camp with 15 beds. All camps provide crockery, cutlery, cooking utensils and are serviced. Catered and self-catering options are available. Visitors supply their own bedding for the camps. At present new camps and lodges are being developed. Reservations and enquiries for directions to individual camps should be made with the Thukela Biosphere Reserve.

TREES
Species typical of the area include:
Acacia caffra – common hook-thorn
Acacia nilotica – prickly-thorn
Acacia robusta – ankle thorn
Acacia sieberiana – paperbark thorn
Acacia tortilis – umbrella thorn
Brachylaena elliptica – bitter-leaf
Calodendrum capense – Cape chestnut
Cassine aethiopica – koo-boo berry

Celtis africana – white stinkwood
Combretum erythrophyllum – river bushwillow
Commiphora harveyi – red-stem corkwood
Croton gratissimus – lavender fever-berry
Cussonia zuluensis – Zulu cabbage tree
Dombeya cymosa – Natal wild pear
Dovyalis caffra – Kei-apple
Ehretia rigida – puzzle bush
Euphorbia grandidens – valley bush euphorbia
Ficus ingens – red-leaved fig
Maerua cafra – bead-bean tree
Nuxia oppositifolia – water elder
Ochna serrulata – small-leaved plane
Olea europaea subsp. *africana* – wild olive
Pappea capensis – jacket-plum
Premna mooiensis – skunk bush
Ptaeroxylon obliquum – sneezewood
Rhus chirindensis – red currant
Schotia brachypetala – weeping boer-bean
Vepris reflexa – bushveld white ironwood
Vitellariopsis dispar – Tugela milkwood
Vitex rehmannii – pipe-stem tree

BIRDS

African black duck
bald ibis
barbets – crested, pied
black widowfinch
blackshouldered kite
bokmakierie
brownthroated martin
brubru
eagles – black, martial
ground hornbill
Jacobin cuckoo
lanner falcon
lesser honeyguide
longbilled crombec
mocking chat
Namaqua dove

orangethroated longclaw
redbilled firefinch
rock kestrel
rock pigeon
secretarybird
shrikes – orangebreasted bush, redbacked
storks – black, white
streakyheaded canary
sunbirds – greater doublecollared, malachite
Swainson's francolin
whitethroated robin
woodhoopoe – redbilled, scimitarbilled
yellowthroated sparrow

MAMMALS (a preliminary list)

blesbok
buffalo
common duiker
elephant

giraffe
hyaenas – brown, spotted
kudu
leopard

mountain reedbuck	roan antelope
nyala	springbok
oribi	steenbok
red hartebeest	wildebeest – black, blue
reedbuck	zebra
rhinos – black, white	

There are plans to introduce other large species.

REPTILES
Crocodiles occur in small numbers in the rivers. The area is well known for African rock pythons and Nile or water monitor lizards.

TUGELA DRIFT NATURE RESERVE

Area: 41 ha
Established: 12 July 1973

LOCATION
Midlands. Situated 6 km north of the flyover bridge which spans the free-way at Colenso on the Colenso-Johannesburg route.

FEATURES
This small reserve offers good views of the Tugela river and the Colenso battlefields of the Anglo-Boer War. Picnic tables have been erected beneath some shade trees. Visitors may enjoy bird watching and the flora along the paths. There is as yet no inventory of flora and fauna.

VALHALLA HUNTING

Area: 2 500 ha
Established: 1970

LOCATION
Midlands. On the Dundee-Greytown Road. Travel 39 km from Dundee to the Helpmekaar police station, then turn right down a steep gravel road to the farm.

FEATURES
Valhalla is a working African farm, where domestic stock is integrated with wildlife in a scenically attractive area. Game viewing (over 30 mammal species) and birding (over 120 species) are popular pastimes and the vege-

tation is interesting. Fishing for black bass, tilapia, yellowfish and eels can be enjoyed in the dams. For the sport hunter, grey rhebok, bushbuck and greywing francolin may be hunted. Slaughtering facilities and a cool-room are available.

Horseriding and scenic walks are available, and caves with Bushman paintings can be viewed. There are old iron smelting sites, Zulu kraals, and adjacent to the farm, a cemetery where British soldiers, victims of the British-Zulu battles at Isandlwana and Rorke's Drift, lie buried. On the farm is a fort near Helpmekaar which the Boers erected against the advance of the British in 1890.

DESCRIPTION
Valhalla lies in a valley varying from 1 280 m at the river to 1 586 m at the highest peak. The topography is varied, with the bottom of the valley climbing away on both sides with terraces and steep inclines, giving a rolling effect to the broken rocky sections. Very good examples of weathering and fracturing of the dolerite formations are visible. There are a number of springs. Dams have been built on the high ground and in the valley. The vegetation is varied, with vleis and marshy grasslands, acacia-dominated thornveld, and residual indigenous forest along and at the foot of the krantzes. Groves of mixed wild fig trees are a feature at some elevations of the property.

HISTORICAL NOTES
Valhalla was the home of the Bushmen (San) nearly 10 000 years ago, as indicated by the carbon dating of the Sikhanyisweni Shelter. They settled here because they found food, shelter, protection, a pleasant climate and water. There is evidence of human occupation about 2 000 years ago with iron ore sites, old Zulu kraals and some cannibal dwellings. Adjoining the farm is Helpmekaar, the scene of a battle in the Anglo-Boer War of 1899-1902. On 10 May 1899, the British attacked the fort that had been built here and with their guns, silenced the Boers, suffering only five wounded and successfully driving a very strong force out of a strong position. The battle has been described as one of the neatest tactical feats of the war. From the early 1900s the area was occupied by local Zulus and later by white farmers. In 1970 it was converted into a farm-cum-tourist and hunting lodge by the present owner, Mr Danilo Pedrelli.

ACCOMMODATION
Valhalla's charm lies in its exclusivity and excellent hospitality. There is a lodge with a swimming pool and outside braai facilities leading off from a large trophy room with a fireplace. There is a separate dining room, four bedrooms, two bathrooms, and a fully equipped kitchen. Accommodation is for eight persons, but extra beds can be added. There is a separate suite with a bedroom, bathroom and lounge. This is for two persons or a family with small children. The units are fully furnished and crockery, cooking utensils, cutlery, bedding, etc. are provided. Visitors can cater for them-

selves, or be provided with full board and lodging. Farm produce can be bought, if ordered in advance.

A hunting cottage is also available on a property on top of the Normandien pass which borders the Orange Free State.

Reservations are made with Valhalla Hunting.

TREES

Acacia caffra – common hook-thorn
Acacia karroo – sweet thorn
Acacia nilotica – scented thorn
Acacia sieberiana – paperbark thorn
Apodytes dimidiata – white pear
Cussonia sphaerocephala – Natal forest cabbage tree
Dombeya rotundifolia – common wild pear
Erythrina humeana – dwarf coral tree
Erythrina latissima – broad-leaved coral tree
Ficus glumosa – mountain fig
Ficus ingens – red-leaved fig
Greyia sutherlandii – Natal bottlebrush
Olea europaea subsp. *africana* – wild olive
Trimeria grandifolia – wild mulberry

BIRDS (120 species recorded)

African snipe
bald ibis
blue crane
Cape rock thrush
Cape vulture
Drakensberg siskin
eagles – black, martial
greyheaded bush shrike
kurrichane buttonquail
lanner falcon
mocking chat

mountain chat
orangebreasted waxbill
pipits – buffy, Richard's, yellowbreasted
redbreasted sparrowhawk
redcapped lark
redheaded finch
rock bunting
sunbirds – greater doublecollared, malachite
violeteared waxbill

MAMMALS (30 species recorded)

aardwolf
African wild cat
black-backed jackal
blesbok
bushbuck
caracal
dassie
duiker – blue, common
eland
grey rhebok

impala
kudu
mongooses – water, white-tailed, yellow
mountain reedbuck
nyala
porcupine
red rock hare
reedbuck
scrub hare

steenbok	warthog
serval	wildebeest – black, blue
steenbok	zebra

REPTILES
A varied fauna, including African rock python, monitor lizards, puff adder and boomslang.

FISH
Black bass, tilapia, yellowfish (scalies) and eels in the dam.

MALENDENI NATURE RESERVE

Area: Approximately 30 ha
Established: 1986

LOCATION
Midlands, Ladysmith; 1 km east of the town.

FEATURES
Sewerage maturation ponds alongside the Klip river, with an excellent area of wetland, some grassland and a small stand of exotic trees. This is a notable wetland area where 204 species of ducks, geese and grassland, vlei and aquatic birds have been recorded, including uncommon species such as lesser gallinule, little bittern and Baillon's crake.

Permission is required for entry. The gate key is obtainable from Ken Gordon, Ladysmith, telephone (0361) 26810, during office hours.

SPIOENKOP PUBLIC RESORT NATURE RESERVE

Area: 5 400 ha
Established: 31 July 1975

LOCATION
Midlands. Situated 35 km from Ladysmith and 14 km from Winterton. From the south (Estcourt side), turn off the N3 onto the R74 signposted Winterton. 1 km past Winterton cross the Little Tugela river and turn right onto the R600 signposted Spioenkop Dam. The resort is about 13 km from the turn-off.

From the north (Harrismith side) turn off the N3 at the Bergville off-ramp

(R23). Turn left in the direction of Ladysmith and follow this route for 5 km. Turn right onto the R600 signposted Spioenkop-Winterton. The reserve is 18 km from the turn-off.

From Ladysmith the route is 2 km past the town on the R103, then turn right onto the Bergville road (R23). Travel 10 km along this road. At the Spioenkop-Winterton sign, turn left onto the R600 and travel a further 18 km until you reach the turn-off to the reserve. It is clearly signposted.

FEATURES

Spioenkop dam has been developed into a major resort with a variety of water sports, including yachting, powerboating, canoeing and fishing for carp, tilapia, bluegill and scalies. There is a game park with an impressive variety of mammals, including white rhino, zebra, giraffe, blue and black wildebeest, blesbok, red hartebeest, springbok, impala, buffalo, mountain reedbuck and eland.

There are more than 250 species of birds. Visitors can observe raptors from a hide, where feeding is done during the winter months.

Spioenkop is the site of a famous battle between the British and the Boers, and a fascinating self-guided trail leads visitors interested in history to monuments and grave sites of significance, as well as to the remains of Late Iron Age settlements.

This popular resort has a number of amenities. There are tennis courts, a swimming pool, TV lounge, recreational hall (available for hire), an interpretation centre, curio shop, children's playground, tractor rides, boat tours and horse riding.

From the summit of Spioenkop there is a panoramic view of the Drakensberg mountains. The resort is within easy reach of Drakensberg resorts, as well as local sites of historical interest.

Future plans are to develop the area more as a game reserve than as a resort. A controlled hunting area has been established where a limited number of qualified hunters may hunt in season. This will assist staff in the annual culling of certain species.

DESCRIPTION

Spioenkop reserve is a narrow strip of land surrounding the Spioenkop dam on the Tugela river. It comprises tracts of typical thornveld country, dominated by acacia trees, with many aloes on the hilly slopes. Some areas are bare and eroded through past mismanagement. It has a history of occupation going back to the Late Iron Age. The north-facing hill slopes are more densely wooded, with less grass cover, than the southern slopes. Many areas that are now thickly wooded were open grassveld at the time of the Anglo-Boer War – as is clearly depicted in old photographs.

With a variety of vegetation types, this reserve boasts 55 species of mammal, 250 species of bird, 27 reptiles, 11 fish, 10 species of amphibian and great diversity of plant life.

HISTORICAL NOTES

Spioenkop, which in Afrikaans means "spy hill", was the scene of a famous battle between the British and the Boers from 17-24 January 1900. British losses amounted to 350 dead, 1 000 wounded and 200 taken prisoner, while the Boers had 75 dead and 150 wounded. The Spioenkop battlefield lies on the far side of the dam, clearly visible from the reserve.

Humans had settled in the area long before this battle, however. In the resort are numerous stone structures constructed by Late Iron Age people. Some have been cleared for viewing. Excavations of old dwellings have turned up pieces of grinding stone, pottery, tools and even a clay pipe.

ACCOMMODATION

There are at present 25 six-bedded fully equipped chalets, as well as four two-bedded fully equipped thatched A-frame huts at the Ntenjwa rustic camp. In addition there is a caravan and camping ground with 30 sites. A new camp is planned to replace the existing old accommodation units which are being phased out.

The Ntenjwa rustic camp is situated approximately halfway between the dam wall and the headwaters of the southern shore. This camp can be reached by means of a ferry service or by visitors using their own boats. The ferry service is available only if requested when making reservations for accommodation for this camp.

A separate hunting camp can also be booked. It is recommended that enquiries for accommodation be directed to the Natal Parks Board office at Spioenkop or to Natal Parks Board reservations, Pietermaritzburg.

TREES

Acacia sieberiana – paperbark thorn
Acokanthera oppositifolia – common poison-bush
Allophylus africanus – black false currant
Aloe spectabilis – Natal aloe
Brachylaena elliptica – bitter-leaf
Buddleja saligna – false olive
Calodendrum capense – Cape chestnut
Celtis africana – white stinkwood
Coddia rudis – small bone-apple
Commiphora harveyi – red-stem corkwood
Cussonia paniculata – mountain cabbage tree
Cussonia spicata – common cabbage tree
Euclea crispa subsp. *crispa* – blue guarri
Ficus ingens – red-leaved fig
Grewia flava – velvet raisin
Greyia sutherlandii – Natal bottlebrush
Hippobromus pauciflorus – false horsewood
Kiggeleria africana – wild peach
Maytenus peduncularis – Cape blackwood

Schotia brachypetala – weeping boer-bean
Tarchonanthus camphoratus – wild camphor bush
Tricalysia lanceolata – jackal-coffee
Ziziphus mucronata – buffalo thorn

A total of seven *Acacia* and five *Rhus* species occur in this reserve.

BIRDS
Spioenkop dam is a haven for numerous aquatic birds, and wildfowl in particular. A great variety of interesting and uncommon species are to be found in the grasslands, acacia veld, dense woodland and on the koppies. These include:

African snipe
arrowmarked babbler
banded martin
black harrier
black sparrowhawk
bronzewinged courser
Cape shoveller
Cape vulture
cisticolas – Ayres', cloud,
  croaking, fantailed, lazy,
  Levaillant's, rattling, wailing
cranes – blue, crowned
cuckoo finch
ducks – African black, knobbilled,
  whitebacked, whitefaced,
  yellowbilled
eagles – African fish, black,
  booted, crowned, martial
fiscal flycatcher
francolins – Natal, Shelley's,
  Swainson's
geese – Egyptian, spurwinged
Gurney's sugarbird

korhaans – blue, whitebellied
little stint
marabou stork
peregrine falcon
pipits – longbilled, plainbacked,
  Richard's
plumcoloured starling
redbilled firefinch
ruff
sanderling
South African shelduck
southern pochard
Stanley's bustard
storks – black, white
sunbirds – black, greater
  doublecollared, malachite,
  whitebellied
teals – Hottentot, redbilled
thrushes – Cape rock, groundscraper,
  kurrichane, olive
titbabbler
whitebacked night heron
woodpeckers – bearded, olive

MAMMALS
In addition to bats, small shrews, rats and mice, the larger animals likely to be seen are:

aardwolf
African wild cat
antbear (aardvark)
black-backed jackal
blesbok
buffalo
bushbuck

Cape clawless otter
Cape fox
caracal
common duiker
eland
giraffe
greater canerat

impala	rock dassie
kudu	scrub hare
large-spotted genet	springbok
mongooses – slender, water,	springhare
white-tailed, yellow	steenbok
mountain reedbuck	striped polecat
Natal red rock rabbit	waterbuck
porcupine	white rhino
red hartebeest	wildebeest – black, blue
reedbuck	zebra

The majority of the larger species listed have been reintroduced since 1975.

OLIFANTSKOP NATURE RESERVE

Area: 2 200 ha
Established: 1983

LOCATION
Midlands, approximately 40 km north-east of Ladysmith. The reserve is located on the farm Olifantskop.

FEATURES
An as yet undeveloped nature reserve. Development plans include the building of rustic log cabins, overnight accommodation for hikers, picnic sites for day visitors and facilities for fishermen using the 50 ha dam. There has been no fauna and flora survey but the area is of importance in the conservation of valuable forest and grassland species.

DESCRIPTION
Some 40 per cent of the area consists of mountainous terrain. The altitude varies from 856-1 127 m above sea level. The Olifantskop dam, which is 50 ha in area, is fed by the perennial Sundays river. A water purifying works adjacent to the dam supplies water to a nearby settlement. The reserve is an important catchment area for this river. *Acacia* species dominate the plains while a wider variety of plant communities is found on the higher mountainous areas.

HISTORICAL NOTES
In 1983 the land was expropriated by the state to incorporate it into KwaZulu. The land had been occupied by a farmer who farmed livestock and maize crops.

ACCOMMODATION
None at present. Proposed development will consist of two-bed, four-bed and six-bed rustic log cabins, providing for a maximum of 40 tourists. The reserve will also make provision for overnight hikers and a hut to sleep a maximum of 10 persons is to be built. Enquiries to NPA Department of Community Services, Pietermaritzburg.

TREES
Acacia caffra – common hook-thorn
Acacia nilotica – scented thorn
Acacia sieberiana – paperbark thorn
Acokanthera oppositifolia – common poison-bush
Clerodendrum glabrum – tinderwood
Combretum erythrophyllum – river bushwillow
Cussonia natalensis – rock cabbage tree
Cussonia spicata – common cabbage tree
Ficus natalensis – Natal fig
Maytenus species
Rhus species
Trimeria grandifolia – wild mulberry
Ziziphus mucronata – buffalo thorn

BIRDS
blackcrowned tchagra
chinspot batis
crested barbet
familiar chat
greater doublecollared sunbird
hoopoe
rock kestrel
rock pigeon
rufousnaped lark
scimitarbilled woodhoopoe

little bee-eater
longbilled crombec
mocking chat
redbacked shrike
redfaced mousebird
robins – chorister, whitethroated
secretarybird
Shelley's francolin
sunbirds – black, whitebellied
yellowbilled duck

MAMMALS
black-backed jackal
civet
common duiker

reedbuck
rock dassie

Once the reserve is fenced, species such as zebra, kudu, impala, bush-buck, waterbuck, mountain reedbuck and red hartebeest may be intro-duced.

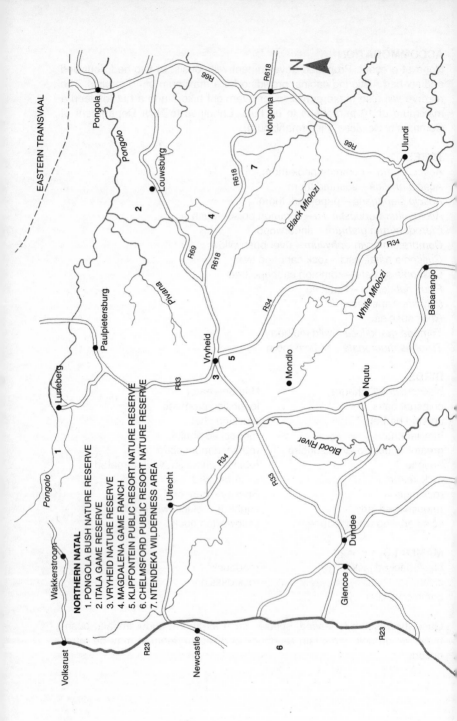

NORTHERN NATAL
1. PONGOLA BUSH NATURE RESERVE
2. ITALA GAME RESERVE
3. VRYHEID NATURE RESERVE
4. MAGDALENA GAME RANCH
5. KLIPFONTEIN PUBLIC RESORT NATURE RESERVE
6. CHELMSFORD PUBLIC RESORT NATURE RESERVE
7. NTENDEKA WILDERNESS AREA

NORTHERN NATAL

This region is mainly undulating country consisting of large plains and deep bowl-shaped valleys with outcrops of dolerite forming small koppies. Below the Drakensberg range tall grassveld predominates in parts with short sourveld grasses on the high lying plateaux. In the Pongolo river valley it varies with open savanna, tall grassland, acacia woodland and riverine thicket. There are areas of typical bushveld and of spectacular mistbelt forest and an impressive diversity of rock formations.

The principal rivers are the Buffalo, Blood, Mkuze and the Black and White Mfolozi. There are also numerous streams, many feeding the Pongolo. Farming includes pig farming, sheep and cattle ranching and maize production. The giant Iscor steel mill at Newcastle and rich local deposits of iron ore as well as vast coal seams at Dundee and Vryheid have led to the development of these major centres. Coal is exported via Richards Bay. Compared to other areas of the province this is a sparsely inhabited region. Historically there were major battles fought between the British and the Boers near Newcastle and Vryheid, the famous battle between the Boers and Zulus at Blood river, and between the British and Zulus fought at Isandlwana and Rorke's Drift.

Northern Natal has few conserved areas. There are the Klipfontein and Chelmsford Dam Public Resort nature reserves, the latter particularly rich in wildfowl, the State Forestry controlled Ngome forest and Ntendeka Wilderness Area; the small Pongola Bush and Vryheid nature reserves and Itala Game Reserve on the Transvaal border. Itala is one of the most interesting and valuable in the province with its spectacular scenery and diversity of fauna and flora. It is also a particularly fine example of restored farmlands.

CHELMSFORD PUBLIC RESORT NATURE RESERVE

Area: 6 015 ha
Established: 31 July 1975

LOCATION
North-western Natal, 26 km from Newcastle on the Ladysmith-Newcastle road. The dam is situated on the Ingangane river.

FEATURES

This is a popular recreational dam for sailing, swimming, powerboating and waterskiing. The surface area of well over 3 000 ha has been zoned for different purposes. Fishing for carp and scalies is popular. A small, well-stocked game park with a variety of birds is worth a visit. The dam is a haven for waterfowl.

DESCRIPTION

The dam is dominated by Leeukop mountain (1 240 m), which rises above the open basin of the dam. There are flat, grassy plains and occasional dolerite ridges. There are very few indigenous trees, except for paperbark thorns *Acacia sieberiana*, Natal bottlebrush *Greyia sutherlandii*, nana berry *Rhus dentata* and Drakensberg karee *Rhus montana*, but there are many exotic wattles.

ACCOMMODATION

Visitors have a choice of facilities on either the south or north bank of the Chelmsford dam.

Chelmsford park, on the northern shore, has eight fully equipped, five-bedded chalets, as well as two camping-caravan parks, Leeukop (150 persons) and Sandford (100 persons). To reach these camps, take the national road to the Normandien turn-off, 19 km south of Newcastle and turn onto district road D210. The entrance gate is 6 km along this road.

Richgate park, on the south bank of the dam, has four five-bedded fully equipped chalets, and a camping and caravan park catering for 150 persons. Playgrounds and boat-launching ramps are provided.

To reach Richgate park, turn onto district road D205 about 30 km south of Newcastle, travel 8 km, turn right onto district road D445, and then to the entrance gate.

Reservations are made with the Natal Parks Board, Pietermaritzburg.

FLORA

The area is one of tall moist grassveld, with Orange Free State affinities, supporting a variety of grass species. Some of these are: heartseed lovegrass *Eragrostis capensis*, narrow-hearted lovegrass *Eragrostis racemosa*, weeping lovegrass *Eragrostis curvula*, red grass *Themeda triandra*, purple fingergrass *Digitaria tricholaenoides*, caterpillar grass *Harpechloa falx*, large-seed setaria *Setaria nigrirostris* and blackseed grass *Alloteropsis semi-alata*. Dwarf *Erythrina*, redhot pokers, *Agapanthus*, fire lilies, wild poppies, arum lilies, pelargoniums and *Gladioli* are some of the spring flowering plants to be seen.

BIRDS (128 species recorded)

This area is particularly rich in wildfowl, cranes, waders, and wetland species, as well as a number of birds of prey. The following are some of the species to be seen:

African marsh harrier
African snipe
Baillon's crake
bald ibis
black harrier
blackcrowned night heron
blackshouldered kite
Cape shoveller
clapper lark
cranes – blue, crowned, wattled
ducks – African black, fulvous,
  whitebacked, whitefaced,
  yellowbilled
eagles – African fish, martial
francolins – greywing, Swainson's
geese – Egyptian, spurwinged
grass owl
great crested grebe

herons – goliath, purple, squacco
Hottentot teal
jackal buzzard
kestrels – eastern redfooted,
  lesser, rock
korhaan – blackbellied, blue,
  whitebellied
lanner falcon
osprey
redbilled teal
secretarybird
South African shelduck
southern pochard
spikeheeled lark
Stanley's bustard
steppe buzzard
stork – saddlebilled, white, yellowbilled

MAMMALS

The 700 ha game park has been stocked with several species. As well as smaller mammals, visitors on a drive through the park may see:

aardwolf
African wild cat
black wildebeest
black-backed jackal
blesbok
Cape clawless otter
Cape fox
hartebeest

mongooses – water,
  white-tailed, yellow
oribi
small-spotted genet
springbok
striped polecat
white rhino
zebra

FISH

The following occur in the dam:

carp
chubbyheaded barb
longfin eel

scaly
sharptooth catfish (barbel)
Tugela labeo or mudfish

PONGOLA BUSH NATURE RESERVE

Area: 858 ha
Established: 28 September 1972

LOCATION
Northern Natal, about 20 km west of Paulpietersburg on the Natal-Transvaal border. From Vryheid take the Paulpietersburg road to Luneberg, then a district road to the reserve.

DESCRIPTION
This reserve lies on the Pongolo river and contains a valuable piece of mistbelt evergreen forest with some particularly fine yellowwoods and other trees and plants. There are more than 120 species of birds. The reserve can only be visited by prior arrangement with the Natal Parks Board zone officer. Enquiries to the Pietermaritzburg office.

TREES
Canthium pauciflorum – mountain turkey-berry
Canthium spinosum – thorny rock alder
Combretum kraussii – forest bushwillow
Cryptocarya woodii – Cape quince
Cryptocarya wyliei – red quince
Cyathea dregei – common tree fern
Dais cotinifolia – pompon tree
Dovyalis rhamnoides – common sourberry
Ekebergia pterophylla – rock ash
Ficus craterostoma – forest fig
Greyia sutherlandii – Natal bottlebrush
Ochna natalitia – Natal plane
Podocarpus falcatus – Outeniqua yellowwood
Podocarpus latifolius – real yellowwood
Protea caffra – common sugarbush
Prunus africana – red stinkwood
Rhoicissus digitata – baboon grape
Trimeria grandifolia – wild mulberry
Zanthoxylum davyi – knobwood

BIRDS
bald ibis
black cuckoo
blue crane
bluemantled flycatcher
buffspotted flufftail

buffstreaked chat
bush shrikes – greyheaded, olive
bush blackcap
eagles – black, crowned, martial
forest buzzard

forest canary
helmeted guineafowl
lanner falcon
orangebreasted waxbill
pied starling
secretarybird
starred robin
storks – black, white

sunbirds – greater
  doublecollared,
  lesser doublecollared,
  malachite
thrushes – olive, orange
wood owl
woodpeckers – ground, olive
yellowthroated warbler

MAMMALS

bushbuck
Cape clawless otter
chacma baboon
common duiker

large-spotted genet
leopard
samango monkey
serval

KLIPFONTEIN PUBLIC RESORT NATURE RESERVE

Area: 4 562 ha
Proclamation: Pending

LOCATION
Northern Natal. 6 km south of Vryheid on the Vryheid-Melmoth road.

FEATURES
This resort has been developed around the shores of a large, state-owned dam on the Mfolozi river. Fishing and boating are popular activities. More than 150 bird species have been recorded. There is a camping and caravan area and picnic and braai sites have been laid out along the shore.

DESCRIPTION
The area around the inlet of the Mfolozi river into the dam is being developed as an artificial wetland and bird sanctuary. It will also act as a buffer zone between the Vryheid sewerage works and the river. The existing exotic bluegums and wattles are being removed to allow this area to return to its former diverse grassland. Indigenous trees are being established by the Vryheid branch of the Wildlife Society.

ACCOMMODATION
Ten camp sites along the shore of the Klipfontein dam. Contact the Natal Parks Board officer-in-charge to reserve camp sites.

BIRDS

African marsh harrier
francolins – coqui, Shelley's,
   Swainson's
greater flamingo
groundscraper thrush
halfcollared kingfisher
herons – blackcrowned night,
   goliath, purple
korhaans – blackbellied,
   whitebellied

larks – redcapped, rufousnaped,
   spikeheeled
orangebreasted waxbill
quail finch
redbilled quelea
ruff
snipes – African, painted
South African shelduck
southern pochard
Wahlberg's eagle

MAMMALS

aardwolf
Cape clawless otter
mongooses – slender,
   water, white-tailed, yellow

serval
steenbok

VRYHEID NATURE RESERVE

Area: 720 ha
Leased: 19 April 1985

LOCATION

Northern Natal. Situated on Lancaster hill, overlooking the northern side of Vryheid. From the town, take Kerk Street north into East Street, then right into Klip Street, proceeding along a gravel road to the entrance gate.

FEATURES

A bird-viewing hide and game-viewing trails enable the visitor to see 26 indigenous and reintroduced game species. The wild flowers are particularly attractive in spring, and some birds typical of northern Natal may be seen. Anglo-Boer War monuments are also a feature. There is a picnic site with braai facilities and toilets.

An environmental education centre is to be built in this reserve.

HISTORICAL NOTES

Lancaster hill was the scene of operations between the Boers and the British in the South African War. Vryheid (meaning "freedom"), was formerly capital of the short-lived New Republic set up by the Boers in 1884 on land granted them by the Zulu king, Dinizulu. At the conclusion of the war in 1888, Vryheid was ceded to Natal. There are historical monuments and old kraal sites within the reserve, which is leased from the Borough of Vryheid.

DESCRIPTION
The area comprises patches of grassland, wetland, mixed acacia scrub, protea veld and stands of evergreen forest.

TREES
Apart from stands of common sugarbush *Protea caffra*, and the common tree fern *Cyathea dregei*, the local trees include:

Acacia sieberiana – paperbark thorn
Aloe arborescens – krantz aloe
Burchellia bubalina – wild pomegranate
Cryptocarya woodii – Cape quince
Cussonia spicata – common cabbage tree
Dombeya rotundifolius – common wild pear
Ekebergia capensis – Cape ash
Ficus craterostoma – forest fig
Ficus sur – broom cluster fig
Greyia sutherlandii – Natal bottlebrush
Kiggelaria africana – wild peach
Ochna natalitia – Natal plane
Olinia emarginata – Transvaal hard pear
Pittosporum viridiflorum – cheesewood
Ptaeroxylon obliquum – sneezewood
Rhamnus prinoides – dogwood
Rhus dentata – nana-berry
Scutia myrtina – cat thorn
Zanthoxylum capense – small knobwood

BIRDS
Of the approximately 190 species recorded in this small reserve, the visitor may see:

bald ibis
black sparrowhawk
blackbellied korhaan
blackwinged plover
buffstreaked chat
canaries – blackthroated, bully,
  Cape, yelloweyed
Cape vulture
chorister robin
doves – cinnamon, Namaqua
eagles – crowned, Wahlberg's
grass owl

grey lourie
halfcollared kingfisher
Jacobin cuckoo
kurrichane buttonquail
larks – longbilled, redcapped,
  rufousnaped
olive woodpecker
palm swift
pipits – bushveld, plainbacked,
  Richard's, striped
rameron pigeon
rollers – lilacbreasted, European

storks – black, white
Temminck's courser

thrushes – Cape rock, groundscraper,
kurrichane, olive
whitenecked raven

MAMMALS

African wild cat
blesbok
bushbuck
caracal
common duiker
eland
greater canerat
impala
kudu
large-spotted genet
mongooses – slender, water,
white-tailed, yellow

mountain reedbuck
Natal red rock rabbit
oribi
porcupine
rock dassie
scrub hare
serval
spotted-necked otter
springbok
steenbok
vervet monkey
Wahlberg's epauletted fruit bat

MAGDALENA GAME RANCH

Area: 1 500 ha
Established: 1976

LOCATION

North-western Natal. From the north, travel via Standerton, Volksrust, Utrecht and Blood River to Vryheid. From Vryheid take the Louwsburg-Magudu-Hlobane road. After approximately 23 km pass the Hlobane crossroads and police station. After a further 1,5 km take the R618 Nongoma turn-off to the right. After 29 km, at the crest of a short steep hill, turn left. The turn-off is signposted "Magdalena Game Ranch 7 km" on the left-hand side and "D94" on the right-hand side of the road. There are two forks along this road, both of which are signposted "Magdalena". At the first, take the right fork and at the second take the left fork and continue down a steep hill to the gate on your right. The office is 5 km from the gate.

From the south, the quickest route is via the North Coast Rainbow route: Eshowe, Melmoth and Gluckstadt to Vryheid.

FEATURES

An area of unspoilt bush with interesting plants, birds and mammals and attractive scenery, where you may walk or be guided on horseback along game trails. Game drives by day or night can be arranged. Both trophy and meat hunting are on offer to hunters by prior arrangement.

DESCRIPTION
Situated in the rolling hills of north-western Natal, this reserve combines areas of highveld grassland, thornveld and riverine forest.

HISTORICAL NOTES
The present reserve was originally surveyed on 11 September 1885. It was described as the Farm Magdalena 376 and was allocated to Coenraad Scheepers on 6 February 1886. Over the years the farm changed hands many times and was eventually established as a game ranch by Mr JR van Wyk in 1976.

ACCOMMODATION
The lodge, overlooking the magnificent Msihlengeni waterfall, sleeps six persons. It is completely self-contained and serviced, with fully equipped kitchen, bathroom, pool, wood-burning sauna and choice of braai areas. Visitors provide their own food and drink. Linen is provided but not swimming towels.

A bushcamp, consisting of five comfortable rustic huts sleeping 20 people, is located on the banks of the river. A braai, kitchen and pool are provided. The bushcamp is fully equipped and serviced but visitors need to bring their own food, drink and swimming towels. This camp is only hired out to one group of friends or family at a time.

A cottage offers rustic but comfortable accommodation for two. From this unit there is a view over the entire game ranch. It is serviced and has a fully equipped kitchen, bathroom, pool and braai area. Visitors are required to bring their own food, drink and towels.

Reservations should be made with the ranch.

TREES
The vegetation of the Magdalena Game Ranch is dominated by eight *Acacia* species. The following are some of the other trees that occur:

Aloe marlothii – mountain aloe
Berchemia zeyheri – red ivory
Combretum zeyheri – velvet bushwillow
Commiphora harveyi – red-stem corkwood
Cussonia natalensis – rock cabbage tree
Dombeya rotundifolia – common wild pear
Ekebergia capensis – Cape ash
Euphorbia cooperi – Transvaal candelabra tree
Euphorbia ingens – common tree euphorbia
Heteropyxis natalensis – lavender tree
Hippobromus pauciflorus – bastard horsewood
Ormocarpum trichocarpum – caterpillar bush
Pappea capensis – jacket-plum
Rauvolfia caffra – quinine tree
Schotia brachypetala – weeping boer-bean

Vangueria infausta – wild medlar
Ximenia caffra var. *natalensis* – Natal sourplum
Zanthoxylum capense – small knobwood

BIRDS

Of the more than 160 bird species recorded, some of the typical and uncommon species are:

bald ibis
blue crane
brownthroated martin
buntings – Cape, goldenbreasted, rock
bushveld pipit
dwarf bittern
eagles – African hawk, black, brown snake, Wahlberg's
flycatchers – bluegrey, pallid
francolins – coqui, crested, Natal, Swainson's
greyheaded bush shrike
halfcollared kingfisher
honeyguides – greater, lesser, scalythroated, sharpbilled

korhaans – blackbellied, whitebellied
longbilled crombec
longtailed wagtail
melba finch
plumcoloured starling
sabota lark
Temminck's courser
thrushes – Cape rock, kurrichane, olive
white stork
whitebrowed robin
yellowbreasted apalis
yellowthroated sparrow
yellowthroated warbler

MAMMALS

blesbok
bushpig
chacma baboon
duiker – common, red
giraffe
impala
kudu
mountain reedbuck
nyala
oribi

red hartebeest
reedbuck
springbok
steenbok
thick-tailed bushbaby
warthog
waterbuck
wildebeest – black, blue
zebra

NTENDEKA WILDERNESS AREA (NGOME FOREST)

Area: 5 230 ha
Established: 2 October 1975

LOCATION

Northern Natal. Ntendeka is situated 70 km east of Vryheid and is bordered on the east by the Ngome state forest, on the north, south and east by privately owned farms and on the west, partly by HL & H forestry plantations. From Vryheid, follow the Louwsberg road for approximately 20 km. Turn right onto the Nongoma road (R618) and follow this road for approximately 50 km. Turn right at the Ngome forest signboard. The forestry office and residences are a further 600 m beyond the signboard.

From the coast, take the Nongoma road at Mtubatuba. Proceed for 40 km past Nongoma on the Vryheid road until the Ngome state forest sign is reached.

FEATURES

A fascinating area for the tree enthusiast and serious botanist, Ntendeka is of immense conservation value. While the fauna is sparse, there are interesting birds and this forest ranks among the best preserved in Natal. It is entirely undeveloped as a wilderness area but there is an extensive series of footpaths leading from the camp site through the area.

DESCRIPTION

The Ntendeka wilderness area lies within the sedimentary Ecca group of the Karoo Sequence rock formations. The approaches to the forest are very interesting geologically. The horizontal beds of the Middle Ecca sandstone are responsible for the relatively even landscape stretching towards Vryheid. Undulations in the landscape are attributable to the more resistant dolerite, which also caps the coal-bearing hills in the Vryheid area. Ntendeka is divided into two parts by the high dolerite and sandstone cliffs which follow a roughly east-west direction. These densely forested, steep valley sides are prone to landslides, particularly after heavy rains. Above the cliffs the landscape is gently undulating, while in the lower areas the numerous streams have produced a more broken sequence of valleys and ridges.

This forest contains a rare combination of coastal and inland tropical forest species not represented in any other conservation area of Natal. It contains elements of tropical and mixed *Podocarpus* forest. It is floristically exceptionally rich and has a dramatic tropical flavour, despite its distance from the coast. It is rich in epiphytic orchids, with 19 out of the 42 South African species present. The interesting plants include the Ngoya lily *Crinum moorei*, *Streptocarpus candidus*, a giant-leaved species common in the lower forest near water, and *Helichrysum spodiophyllum*. The lower forest is filled with *Clivia miniata* which create a spectacular display in season.

The forest is almost sunless due to the shade of the dense canopy of giant trees and the moist habitat creates a microclimate for a wide range of ferns. One of the most striking is *Didymochlaene truncatula* with its 2,5 m fronds, which is common in wet shady ravines.

The grassland areas are dominated by redgrass *Themeda triandra*, russet grass *Loudetia simplex*, golden setaria *Setaria sphacelata*, tussock tescue, *Festuca costata* and heartseed grass *Eragrostis capensis*. Seasonally, after burning, numerous veld flowers occur, with aloes on exposed rock outcrops. *Brachystelma ngomiense*, a rare and endemic plant, may also be found in the grassland.

Rare trees include Natal hard pear *Olinia radiata*, Transvaal stinkwood *Ocotea kenyensis*, terblanz beech *Faurea macnaughtonii* and green hazel *Trichocladus grandiflorus*.

Some 2 636 ha of Ntendeka comprises indigenous forest and the remaining 2 594 ha is covered by grasslands.

HISTORICAL NOTES
Ntendeka, "the place of precipitous heights", features in earliest Zulu history. Mzilikazi, who eventually led the Matabele to Zimbabwe after escaping the wrath of Shaka, made good use of the forest as a refuge. After the Battle of Isandlwana in 1879, Ceteswayo, the last independent king of the Zulus, who had been defeated by the British, went into hiding in this forest. He was eventually captured.

Woodcutters began to work this forest as early as 1876, during the regimes of the Transvaal Republics. The first forester was appointed in 1903 and the area has been managed by foresters ever since. At the height of the exploitation from 1876-1899, 60 woodcutters lived at Ngome. They were allowed to cut "anything, anywhere" for a tariff of three pence a month per saw. It is estimated that approximately 24 000 cubic metres of timber, particularly yellowwoods, was removed by them. Some original saw pits still remain.

ACCOMMODATION
Camp sites are available for a maximum of 24 persons. No caravans are permitted. A toilet, cold-water shower, water tank, braai grids and wood are provided. Reservations are made with the State Forester, Ngome State Forest, Vryheid.

TREES
Brachylaena discolor – forest silver oak
Combretum kraussii – forest bushwillow
Croton sylvaticus – forest fever-berry
Cryptocarya myrtifolia – myrtle quince
Cunonia capensis – red alder
Curtisia dentata – assegai
Cyathea capensis – forest tree fern

Diospyros whyteana – bladder-nut
Eugenia zuluensis – paperbark myrtle
Faurea macnaughtonii – terblanz beech
Ficus craterostoma – forest fig
Heteromorpha trifoliata – parsley tree
Kiggelaria africana – wild peach
Nuxia floribunda – forest elder
Ochna arborea – Cape plane
Ocotea kenyensis – Transvaal stinkwood
Olea capensis – ironwood
Olinia radiata – Natal hard pear
Podocarpus latifolius – real yellowwood
Prunus africana – red stinkwood
Indigofera natalensis – forest indigo
Pterocelastrus echinatus – red candlewood
Rauvolfia caffra – quinine tree
Rhus chirindensis – red currant
Rinorea angustifolia – white violet bush
Schefflera umbellifera – false cabbage tree
Syzygium gerrardii – forest waterwood
Trema orientalis – pigeonwood
Trichilia dregeana – forest mahogany
Trichocladus grandiflorus – green hazel
Xymalos monospora – lemonwood
Zanthoxylum davyi – knobwood

BIRDS (200 species)

bald ibis
blue swallow
cuckoo hawk
Delegorgue's pigeon
eagles – crowned, martial
forest buzzard
green twinspot
house martin
narina trogon
purplecrested lourie
secretarybird
trumpeter hornbill
wattled crane
white stork

MAMMALS

bushbuck
bushpig
chacma baboon
duiker – blue, common, red
porcupine
rock dassie
samango monkey

ITALA GAME RESERVE

Area: 29 653 ha
Established: 1 October 1972

LOCATION

Northern Natal. From Vryheid travel north-east on the R69 to Louwsburg. The reserve is located immediately to the north-west of this village and stretches to the Pongolo river (the Natal-Eastern Transvaal border). Visitors may also fly in to a landing strip in the reserve, where they will be collected, by prior arrangement with the camp office. This all-weather strip is 1 200 m long.

FEATURES

Itala Game Reserve has all the features a tourist could wish for. That this has been achieved in the relatively short period of 20 years, is a remarkable achievement. The main camp was recently voted as one of the top 50 landscaped camps in the world.

The accommodation caters for all tastes. The choices are: camping; exclusive and isolated bush camps; well-appointed, fully equipped and serviced chalets, either self-catering or using a modern licensed restaurant or takeaway facility. There is a luxurious lodge, a modern conference centre capable of seating and accommodating 150 delegates, a well-stocked curio shop and an interpretation centre.

Visitor activities include self-guided vehicle trails, wilderness trails during the cooler months, guided walks, conducted vehicle tours and swimming in the main camp's attractive pool, secluded among huge boulders, and in river pools at the bush camps. Fishing in the river is permitted, and attractive picnic sites have been laid out.

The views over the rugged terrain from the camps and along the roads in the reserve are memorable. With 80 mammal, 314 bird, 18 amphibian, 15 reptile and 910 plant species occurring in several habitat types, the wildlife enthusiast and photographer will not be disappointed with what Itala has to offer.

DESCRIPTION

One of the striking things about Itala is the diversity of geological features. These include formations of the Karoo Sequence, some of the oldest rocks known, which were laid down about 3 000 million years ago. The multi-coloured rocks, the sandstone cliffs with horizontal layers of white, the dark formations of dolerite, granite cliffs, banded iron stone outcrops, boulders and quartz add an immensely colourful dimension to the greens, yellows and browns of the diverse vegetation types found in this reserve. The diversity of plant life – 910 species have been identified to date – is due to the many soil types resulting from erosion of the rock formations over millions of years.

The terrain is rugged. Nine small rivers rise in or near the reserve from the high elevations of 1 400 m above sea level in the south down to 400 m above sea level in the north and all flow into the Pongolo river, the reserve's northern border. In such a well-watered area, rich in soil types, with an altitude range of 400-1 400 m and a variation in climate from sheltered valleys up to the exposed plateau, it is understandable that Itala should be rich in plant species. The vegetation types range between wetland or marsh, streambank and riverine thicket, open savanna, acacia-dominated woodland, dense thicket and tall and short grassland. It is also not surprising that Itala has such a varied fauna, with 80 mammal, 314 bird, 18 amphibian and 15 reptile species recorded. Because of its size, this reserve can carry a large mammal population. It is hoped that other species including more predators will be reintroduced in the future.

HISTORICAL NOTES
Archaeological sites discovered in Itala, dating back to the Middle Stone Age, indicate that the area has long been occupied by humans. Iron ore found locally was used in iron smelting operations. This must have involved the hewing of forest trees, particularly the hardwood species for charcoal necessary for smelting purposes, so man's influence on the environment of this area goes back many thousands of years. Examples of rock art found in a cave indicate that the Bushmen (San), who were hunter-gatherers, also occupied this area and utilised the indigenous fauna and flora.

The Zulu wars and the reigns of King Shaka and later King Dinizulu, were significant. In 1884 King Dinizulu granted land to white farmers in this area and the Boers proclaimed this land the "Nieuwe Republiek".

Historical records show that game of many species was once abundant here, before the arrival of white settlers, but intense hunting and the rinderpest epidemic of 1896 had a severe effect on game populations. As in Zululand, the anti-nagana campaign waged from 1919 to the early 1950s against the disease-carrying tsetse flies, resulted in many more thousands of animals being shot. Most of the land consisted of labour farms and was heavily populated with local blacks. The foundations of some of their dwellings and grave sites are still visible. There were only four farmhouses built on the land. The hills were overstocked and overgrazed with livestock and in the valleys whatever arable land was available was ploughed. Gold was discovered and mined at the Wonder and Ngotshe mines in the early 1900s, but these were later abandoned.

By the time the Natal Parks Board started buying up farms in 1973, overgrazing and soil erosion were widespread and very little wildlife remained. Initially, an area of 8 488 ha was acquired but from 1974-1982, a further 21 165 ha was added, making up the present reserve of 29 653 ha.

Since acquiring the land in 1973, the Natal Parks Board has implemented an extensive and effective programme of land reclamation to halt soil erosion and to heal the scars of dongas and old fields. This has included the removal of signs of past human habitation, although in some areas, traces of old fields and dwellings are still visible. Once the grasslands had been re-established and the indigenous shrubs and trees began to flourish, it was possible to reintroduce game mammals and their natural predators, species long extinct in the area.

Since 1973, 20 species have been re-established. These include white rhino, black rhino, kudu, roan antelope, eland, giraffe, cheetah, red hartebeest, tsessebe, brown hyaena, elephant and buffalo.

ACCOMMODATION
The main Ntshondwe camp has one six-bedded lodge, 25 two-bedded chalets, 12 four-bedded chalets and two six-bedded chalets. There are also 28 two-bedded non self-catering units. The chalets are fully equipped, self-contained and serviced, having one or more bedrooms, lounge-dining room, bathroom, toilet and kitchenette equipped with cutlery, crockery, stove, fridge and linen. Visitors must bring their own food and drink and do their own cooking.

The lodge, which has similar facilities and a cook, has three bedrooms en suite, is luxuriously appointed and has its own swimming pool.

The camp has a licensed restaurant with a takeaway and bar, as well as a small shop at which basic provisions may be purchased.

There are three bush camps: Thalu has four beds; Mbizo eight and Mhlangeni has 10 beds. These camps are fully equipped with cutlery, crockery, linen, cooking utensils, gas fridge and stove, and gas lights. Rustic hot and cold showers and flush toilets are provided, as are braai facilities. A game guard is resident at each bush camp to conduct visitors on game viewing walks.

There are three camp sites which have cold-water showers, flush toilets and a communal kitchen, as well as a communal lounge-diningroom shelter.

Reservations for hutted accommodation, wilderness trails and bush camps are made with the Natal Parks Board, Pietermaritzburg. Camp sites should be booked with the officer-in-charge.

TREES
Chaetachme aristata – thorny elm
Commiphora harveyi – red-stem corkwood
Cussonia zuluensis – Zulu cabbage tree
Cyathea dregei – common tree fern
Dombeya rotundifolia – common wild pear
Englerophytum magalismontanum – Transvaal milkplum
Euphorbia cooperi – Transvaal candelabra
Euphorbia ingens – common tree euphorbia
Ficus craterostoma – forest fig
Ficus sycomorus – sycamore fig
Garcinia livingstonei – lowveld mangosteen
Greyia radlkoferi – Transvaal bottlebrush
Lannea discolor – live-long

Lopholaena platyphylla
Mundulea sericea – cork bush
Pleurostylia capensis – coffee pear
Protea caffra – common sugarbush
Protea comptonii – Barberton mountain protea
Protea gaguedi – African white sugarbush
Protea roupelliae – silver sugarbush
Pterocarpus angolensis – wild teak
Rapanea melanophloeos – Cape beech
Rauvolfia caffra – quinine tree
Spirostachys africanus – tamboti
Strychnos decussata – Cape teak
Terminalia phanerophlebia – Lebombo cluster-leaf
Vepris reflexa – bushveld white ironwood
Ximenia caffra – sourplum
Ziziphus mucronata – buffalo thorn

The 12 species of acacias in Itala are: *Acacia ataxacantha, A. burkei, A. caffra, A. davyi, A. gerrardii, A. karroo, A. nigrescens, A. nilotica, A. robusta, A. senegal, A. sieberiana* and *A. tortilis.*

BIRDS (314 species recorded)

African finfoot
anteating chat
blue crane
brownheaded parrot
cuckoos – African, European
eagles – African hawk, bateleur,
   black, blackbreasted snake,
   martial
eastern redfooted kestrel
fantailed flycatcher
grassbird
ground hornbill
halfcollared kingfisher
Jameson's firefinch
lilacbreasted roller
longtailed wagtail
malachite sunbird
melba finch
mocking chat
narina trogon

neddicky
pipits – buffy, plainbacked
redbilled oxpecker
redheaded weaver
robins – bearded, Heuglin's
scimitarbilled woodhoopoe
sentinel rock thrush
shrikes – gorgeous bush,
   longtailed
storks – black, saddlebilled
Swainson's francolin
swee waxbill
white helmetshrike
whitebacked night heron
whitebacked vulture
whitebellied korhaan
woodpeckers – bearded, ground
yellow warbler
yellowspotted nicator

MAMMALS (80 species recorded)

antbear (aardvark)
aardwolf

black-backed jackal
blue wildebeest

buffalo
bushbuck
bushpig
Cape clawless otter
caracal
chacma baboon
cheetah
common duiker
eland
elephant
giraffe
greater canerat
honey badger
hyaenas – brown, spotted
impala
klipspringer
kudu
large-spotted genet
leopard
mongooses – slender,
  water, white-tailed
monkeys – samango, vervet
Natal red rock rabbit
oribi
pangolin
porcupine
red hartebeest
reedbuck
rhinos – black, white
rock dassie
scrub hare
serval
steenbok
thick-tailed bushbaby
tsessebe
warthog
waterbuck
zebra

REPTILES, AMPHIBIANS AND FISH
Nearly 100 species of reptiles, frogs and toads and 20 species of indigenous fish have been recorded.

THE DRAKENSBERG

The acquisition and development of conservation areas in the Natal Drakensberg region has extended over a period of more than 90 years. The six proclaimed Natal Parks Board reserves were established in 1903 (Giant's Castle Game Reserve), 1916 (Royal Natal National Park), 1950 (Rugged Glen Nature Reserve), 1951 (Kamberg Nature Reserve), 1953 (Loteni Nature Reserve) and in 1966 and 1967 (Vergelegen Nature Reserve).

According to Hilliard and Burtt (1987), the House of Assembly called for the state to protect the mountain catchment areas of South Africa, principally for the conservation of water supplies, in 1934. In 1946, the Soil Conservation Act was passed. This empowered the authorities to purchase or proclaim additional land in the Drakensberg catchment region. In 1948, the Drakensberg Catchment Reserve (later the Drakensberg Catchment Area) was proclaimed. In 1951 the whole of the southern Natal Drakensberg was ceded to the Department of Forestry for the implementation of water conservation measures. Various farms were subsequently purchased to increase this protected area in terms of the Forestry Act of 1968 and under the Mountain Areas Conservation Act of 1970. This permitted further acquisition of land and an action committee was established to define the areas of critical importance.

In 1973, the first Natal Drakensberg Wilderness Areas were proclaimed and included within this area were the six already proclaimed Natal Parks Board reserves. The next major development occurred in 1986 when the Department of Forestry (now part of the Department of Environment Affairs), which controlled the six state forest areas, handed these areas over to the Natal Parks Board for administration and conservation control. These areas are Cathedral Peak, Monk's Cowl, Highmoor, Mkhomazi, Cobham and Garden Castle state forests and are briefly described. According to RM Little *et al.* (1992), the Natal Drakensberg Park now consists of a complex of 12 protected areas, the six Natal parks totalling approximately 52 000 ha, and the state forests totalling about 191 000 ha. Altogether about 243 000 ha of conserved land, river catchment and wetlands in the province now comprise the Drakensberg Park.

This magnificent park is a major destination for local and international tourists because of its scenic splendour. It generates considerable revenue for the Natal Parks Board and for many local private entrepreneurs who provide a range of accommodation and tourist facilities.

The Drakensberg Park is totally surrounded by densely populated farmlands with an ever-increasing human population pressuring its borders. It is an area of immense ecological value, a reservoir of renewable natural resources and of tremendous educational value and potential for present and future generations. Preservation of this park is essential to the prosperity

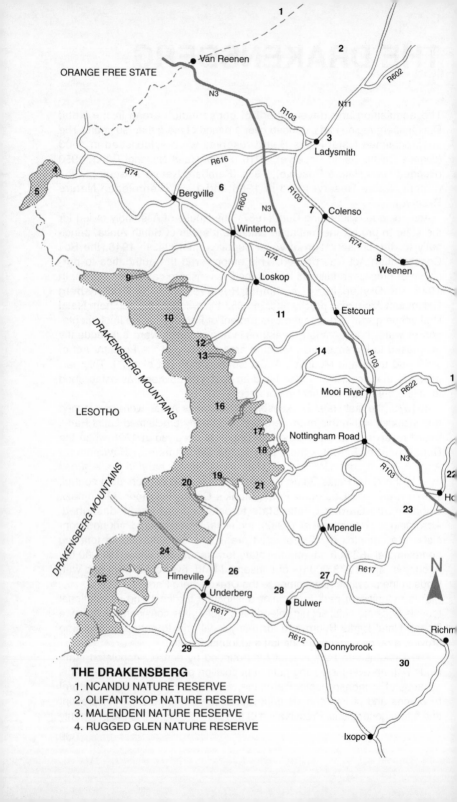

THE DRAKENSBERG

1. NCANDU NATURE RESERVE
2. OLIFANTSKOP NATURE RESERVE
3. MALENDENI NATURE RESERVE
4. RUGGED GLEN NATURE RESERVE

of an enormous population of people and their livestock, spread across the province. The park is the watershed of Natal's three largest rivers, the Mzimkulu, Mkomazi and Tugela, that carry the water upon which it is dependent for agriculture, forestry, industry, recreation and domestic purposes.

It is beyond the scope of a guide book of this nature to supply detailed descriptions of the archaeology, early history, geology and soils, climate, ecology, fauna and flora of such a vast and complex area as the Drakensberg Park. The Drakensberg has been comprehensively covered by a number of authors, photographers and scientists – some outstanding publications are listed in the bibliography. In recent years, excellent topographical maps of the area have become available.

Nature reserves which are included in this section but which are not part of the Drakensberg Park and State Forest complex, are Ncandu, Impendhle, Himeville, the Swamp and Coleford.

NCANDU NATURE RESERVE

Area: 3 520 ha
Established: 19 May 1989

LOCATION
Northern Drakensberg. 32 km south-west of Newcastle between Muller's pass and Normandien pass on the Orange Free State border.

5. ROYAL NATAL NATIONAL PARK
6. SPIOENKOP PUBLIC RESORT NATURE RESERVE
7. TUGELA DRIFT NATURE RESERVE
8. WEENEN NATURE RESERVE
9. CATHEDRAL PEAK STATE FOREST
10. MONK'S COWL STATE FOREST
11. MOOR PARK NATURE RESERVE
12. INJASUTI NATURE RESERVE
13. HILLSIDE NATURE RESERVE
14. WAGENDRIFT PUBLIC RESORT NATURE RESERVE
15. CRAIGIE BURN PUBLIC RESORT NATURE RESERVE
16. GIANT'S CASTLE GAME RESERVE
17. HIGHMOOR STATE FOREST
18. KAMBERG NATURE RESERVE
19. LOTENI NATURE RESERVE
20. VERGELEGEN NATURE RESERVE
21. MKHOMAZI STATE FOREST
22. ALBERT FALLS PUBLIC RESORT NATURE RESERVE
23. MIDMAR PUBLIC RESORT NATURE RESERVE
24. COBHAM STATE FOREST
25. GARDEN CASTLE STATE FOREST
26. HIMEVILLE NATURE RESERVE
27. IMPENDLE NATURE RESERVE
28. THE SWAMP NATURE RESERVE
29. COLEFORD NATURE RESERVE
30. SOADA FOREST NATURE RESERVE

FEATURES

The reserve is situated on the low northern Drakensberg escarpment and consists of grassland savanna and forest areas. The fauna and flora of this recently proclaimed reserve is, at present, poorly known. It is open to the public by arrangement only. Contact the camp superintendent at Royal Natal National Park.

BIRDS

African goshawk
bald ibis
Barratt's warbler
black eagle
blackeyed bulbul
boubou
Cape batis
Cape turtle dove
Cape white-eye
cinnamon dove
dusky flycatcher
forest canary
grassbird
neddicky

olive bush shrike
olive thrush
olive woodpecker
puffback
redchested cuckoo
redwinged starling
robins – Cape, chorister
spotted prinia
steppe buzzard
stonechat
sunbirds – lesser doublecollared, malachite
white stork
yellowthroated warbler

MAMMALS

bushbuck
Cape clawless otter
caracal

chacma baboon
common duiker

RUGGED GLEN NATURE RESERVE

Area: 762 ha
Established: 1 July 1950

LOCATION

Northern Drakensberg, adjoining Royal Natal National Park. Approaching from Mooi River follow the N3 northwards for 52 km, turn left onto the R615 and continue past Winterton and Bergville. At the foot of the Oliviershoek pass, turn left and follow the signposts.

FEATURES

The camping site is situated below the 1 890 m Camel's Hump mountain. It is within easy walking distance of Mont-aux-Sources hotel through a valley and several attractive bush patches. There are walks up past the Camel's Hump and on to the Ridge where, on a clear day, there is the vista of the distant peaks, including Cathkin, Cathedral and Champagne Castle, and beyond, the heights of northern Natal. These walks, though not strenuous, afford good opportunities for game viewing, bird spotting, identification of the local flora and, of course, for photographing the superb scenery.

Horse riding is a popular pastime, as is trout fishing. There are several sites to relax and enjoy a pleasant picnic.

DESCRIPTION
The geological formations, soil types, scenery, flora and fauna is similar to that of the adjacent Royal Natal National Park (see following entry).

HISTORICAL NOTES
This was originally a farming area. Two farms, Rugged Glen and Ungiyeze, were added to the adjoining Royal Natal National Park in 1950, and the area is managed and administered from there.

ACCOMMODATION
There is a camping area, set among pine trees, for 45 persons, provided with hot and cold showers and toilet facilities. Reservations must be made with the officer-in-charge, Natal Parks Board, Rugged Glen Nature Reserve.

ROYAL NATAL NATIONAL PARK

Area: 8 094 ha
Established: 19 September 1916

LOCATION
Northern Drakensberg. 46 km west of Bergville, which is 52 km from Ladysmith and 64 km from Estcourt. From the north turn off south of Ladysmith onto the Bergville road. From Bergville the road is well signpost-ed. The park is 53 km along the Bergville-Harrismith road. From the south turn off the N3 at the Winterton-Berg resorts sign and pass through Winterton and Bergville. Turn left at the Drakensberg North signpost. It is about 16 km from there to the entrance gate. The park is also accessible from Harrismith via the Bethlehem road. Travel 6 km, then turn off onto the Witsieshoek-Qwa-qwa road. Follow the signs to Oliviershoek pass, Royal Natal and Bergville.

FEATURES
This park is best known for its truly magnificent scenery. There are proba-bly more illustrated magazine articles, brochures, guide books, calendars and postcards depicting the scenery, particularly the Amphitheatre, than

have been published for any other part of the Drakensberg. It is a mecca for artists and photographers, hikers and mountaineers, and for the visitor who merely wants to relax in the mountain air, or perhaps to enjoy the scenery, plant, game and bird life. There are numerous short and long walks along the over 130 km of bridle trails and paths that have been laid out. These walks, starting from the Royal Natal National Park hotel, the main campground, Tendele camp and Rugged Glen, all afford splendid views of incomparable scenery. Roadside picnic and parking areas with braai facilities are available for day visitors.

Horse riding trails from Rugged Glen are a fine way to view game and the countryside. Trout fishing in the river, and in the dam which is open all year round, attracts anglers from far and wide. Fortunately all the berg rivers are free from bilharzia and swimming is permitted in some of the deep pools in designated areas. For those visitors who have never seen Bushman paintings, there are examples to be seen in the Sigubudu valley and at three other sites.

The park has long been extremely popular with mountaineers and there are some famous rock climbing routes. The Sentinel route, for example, was first conquered in 1910, and the Mont-aux-Sources chain ladders were constructed as far back as 1930.

Within the park, facilities include two well-stocked souvenir and gift shops – one at the visitor centre and the other at Tendele camp. Petrol and oil are obtainable at the turn-off to Tendele camp. If booked in advance, meals may be obtained by arrangement with the hotel. The visitor centre, 3 km from the entrance gate, houses a post office, a curio shop and various interpretative displays. Visitors are urged to purchase the Natal Parks Board's guide book. For the hiker and mountain climber new to the area, excellent contour maps are available. The guide book furnishes routes that can be taken for scenic drives to spectacular areas of interest in the vicinity.

DESCRIPTION

The Royal Natal National Park and the smaller adjoining Rugged Glen Nature Reserve (described separately), are administered as a single ecological unit. This complex is situated at the northern end of the high Drakensberg, adjacent to the Orange Free State border. The famous Amphitheatre virtually encloses the reserve, with the Sentinel (3 165 m), Eastern Buttress (3 048 m), the crescent-shaped wall of the Amphitheatre (averaging 2 926 m) and Mont-aux-Sources (3 282 m) dominating the scene.

Five rivers have their origins on the upper slopes of Mont-aux-Sources. The Tugela plunges over the Amphitheatre wall in a series of spectacular waterfalls, an estimated drop of over 600 m and reputed to be one of the highest waterfalls in the world. This river, joined by a tributary, the Bilanjil, flows across Natal into the Indian Ocean on the Natal-Zululand border. The Khudeda and its tributary the Khubela, join the Singu river a few kilometres south and eventually become the Orange river, flowing through

Lesotho and finally into the Atlantic ocean. The fifth river, the Elands, enters the Vaal river. The area is thus truly a "mountain of sources" as originally described and named.

The altitude ranges from 1 340-3 048 m. Different geological formations and several habitat types are found in these climatic and altitudinal belts. A wealth of plants, over 900 species, are known from this reserve. The vegetation consists of grassland, sometimes with a wide variety of wild flowers, *Protea* savanna, *Podocarpus*-dominated hardwood forests, stream and riverbank woodland, oldwood and sagewood scrub, fynbos scrub and, in the Alpine belt, *Erica-Helichrysum* heath, with short grasses and herbs able to withstand frost and snow, and numerous species of lichens, ferns and mosses growing on exposed rock faces. As with the plant communities growing at different altitudes and in different climatic conditions, so too do a majority of the birds and mammals prefer specific habitats.

No matter what terrain visitors traverse in this reserve, they cannot but be impressed by the magnificence of the scenery.

HISTORICAL NOTES
Mont-aux-Sources was discovered and named in 1836 by two French missionaries, Messrs Arbousset and Daumas.

Bushmen were known to have lived in the area as recently as 1878, and were possibly the last survivors in the Drakensberg region. The area was first surveyed in 1884, and much of what constitutes the present park was offered for sale as farms in those early years. Some of the farms were never purchased but woodcutting concessions were granted and many tons of hardwoods were felled. The forest in Rugged Glen was still being exploited in the 1930s.

Although the concept of establishing this national park goes back to 1908, it was only in 1916 that it came into being. Adjoining farms were purchased and the most recent additions were some, including Rugged Glen, purchased in 1950, increasing the size of the park to its present area of about 8 094 hectares. The area was formally handed over to the Natal Parks Board on its formation in 1947.

The first hostelry was opened in about 1913 on the farm Goodoo – land now incorporated into the reserve. Over the following years the lease rights were bought up by various owners, who each added new buildings and amenities to the old hotel. This complex burnt down in 1941, but was rebuilt in time for the British royal family visit in 1947. Thereafter, both the park and hotel acquired the title "Royal".

ACCOMMODATION
There is a range of accommodation on offer in this park. Reservations for hutted accommodation must be made with the Natal Parks Board, Pietermaritzburg.

Tendele hutted camp: A luxury lodge offers accommodation for six persons. It has three en suite bedrooms, each with two single beds, a large lounge with fireplace and an outdoor braai. Food is prepared by a cook. There are two six-bedded cottages with fully equipped kitchen; eight three-bedded bungalows and five five-bedded bungalows with communal kitchens and ablution facilities; 13 two-bedded and four-bedded chalets which are fully furnished and comprise lounge-diningroom, fully equipped kitchenette with fridge, stove, cutlery and crockery, and a veranda and outside braai. Visitors provide their own food and drink.

Mahai camp site: This caters for up to 360 campers and caravanners in open camp sites which are serviced by ablution blocks with hot and cold water. A number of electrical plug points are available. Reservations are made with the officer-in-charge, Royal Natal National Park.

Rugged Glen camp site: This is adjacent to the reserve and caters for 45 persons in open camp sites which have ablution blocks with hot and cold water, toilets and electrical plug points. Make reservations with the Natal Parks Board, Rugged Glen Nature Reserve.

The Royal Natal National Park Hotel **TYYY: A fully licensed hotel which offers its guests most amenities, including bowls, tennis, horse riding, swimming and fishing. Reservations are made with the hotel.

TREES (over 900 species recorded)
Calodendrum capense – Cape chestnut
Celtis africana – white stinkwood
Clausena anisata – horsewood
Cussonia spicata – common cabbage tree
Cyathea dregei – common tree fern
Diospyros whyteana – bladder-nut
Ekebergia capensis – Cape ash
Encephalartos ghellinckii – Drakensberg cycad
Greyia sutherlandii – Natal bottlebrush
Halleria lucida – notsung
Ilex mitis – Cape holly
Kiggelaria africana – wild peach
Leucosidea sericea – oldwood
Myrsine africana – Cape myrtle
Olinia emarginata – mountain hard pear
Pittosporum viridiflorum – cheesewood
Podocarpus falcatus – common yellowwood
Podocarpus latifolius – real yellowwood
Protea caffra – common sugarbush
Protea roupelliae – silver sugarbush
Pterocelastrus echinatus – white candlewood

Rapanea melanophloeos – Cape beech
Salix woodii – Natal willow
Scolopia mundii – red pear
Thamnocalamus tessellatus – berg bamboo

This is the only locality where *Protea nubigena* occurs.

BIRDS (about 230 species)

anteating chat
bald ibis
Barratt's warbler
black harrier
black sparrowhawk
black stork
bush blackcap
Cape eagle owl
Cape vulture
cranes – blue, crowned
cuckoo hawk
eagles – black, crowned
fairy flycatcher
francolins – greywing, Natal, rednecked, redwing, Shelley's, Swainson's
greater kestrel
grey cuckooshrike
ground hornbill

ground woodpecker
Gurney's sugarbird
halfcollared kingfisher
Jacobin cuckoo
lammergeyer
lilacbreasted roller
orangebreasted rockjumper
orangethroated longclaw
quail finch
redcapped lark
redheaded finch
sentinel rock thrush
sharpbilled honeyguide
spotted prinia
starred robin
sunbirds – greater doublecollared, lesser doublecollared, malachite
whitewinged widow
yellowthroated sparrow

MAMMALS

black-backed jackal
blesbok
bushbuck
caracal
chacma baboon
common duiker
grey rhebok
klipspringer
large-spotted genet
mongooses – large grey, small grey, water, white-tailed

mountain reedbuck
Natal red rock rabbit
oribi
otters – Cape clawless, spotted-necked
porcupine
rock dassie
serval
small-spotted genet
striped polecat
striped weasel

Small species include four shrews, one mole, two bats, four rats and five mice.

CATHEDRAL PEAK STATE FOREST (MLAMBONJA and MDEDELELO WILDERNESS AREA)

Area: 32 250 ha
Established: 1973

LOCATION
From the N3 (Pietermaritzburg), turn off to Frere, then travel 22 km to Winterton. Follow the signs for 2 km before turning right at the Cathedral Peak signboard.

From the north via Bergville, turn right just after crossing the Tugela river. From here it is well signposted.

FEATURES
Excellent trout fishing is available in the Mlambonja and Mhlwazini rivers. Spectacular scenic views of the Little Berg are obtainable from the top of Mike's Pass which is accessible by vehicle. The scenery is dramatic, with the mountain peaks of Cathedral (3 004 m), Cathkin (3 149 m), Champagne Castle (3 248 m) and Monk's Cowl (3 234 m). These are some of the most challenging climbs for keen mountaineers. The lower landscape, with its grasslands, deep gorges, forest patches and abundant spring wild flower displays is a delight. Interesting mammals and birds in this splendid area add to hikers' overall enjoyment of this true wilderness experience. For artists and hikers, the Ndedema gorge contains about 150 rock shelters, many of which have Bushman paintings.

ACCOMMODATION
The camp site has 12 sites for six persons each and an ablution block with hot and cold water. There are braai facilities, benches and tables. There are a number of caves that may be used overnight as well as the Wilderness Area itself. Reservations and enquiries should be made with the Cathedral Peak forestry office.

BIRDS
African black duck
African goshawk
arrowmarked babbler
Ayres' cisticola
Barratt's warbler
black crow
black eagle
black harrier
blackcollared barbet

blue crane
bluebilled firefinch
bokmakierie
brownthroated martin
canaries – forest,
    streakyheaded
Cape vulture
chorister robin
cinnamon dove

Drakensberg prinia
familiar chat
francolins – greywing,
 rednecked, redwing
freckled nightjar
giant kingfisher
greyheaded sparrow
gymnogene
jackal buzzard
lanner falcon
longtailed wagtail

pigeons – rameron, rock
quail finch
secretarybird
sparrowhawks – black, redbreasted
sunbirds – black, malachite
swifts – Alpine, black
thrushes – olive, sentinel rock
woodpeckers – ground, olive
yellowrumped widow
yellowthroated sparrow

MAMMALS (34 species)
African wild cat
black-backed jackal
bushbuck
caracal
chacma baboon
common duiker
common molerat
grey rhebok
Hottentot golden mole
klipspringer
large-spotted genet
mice – Brants' climbing, fat,
 multimammate, pygmy, striped,
 woodland

mongooses – small grey,
 water, white-tailed
mountain reedbuck
otters – Cape clawless,
 spotted-necked
porcupine
reedbuck
rock dassie
scrub hare
serval
shrews – forest, greater musk
striped weasel
vlei rat
woodland dormouse

MONK'S COWL STATE FOREST (MDEDELELO WILDERNESS AREA)

Area: 20 380 ha
Established: 1973

LOCATION
From the south, turn off the N3 to Loskop (opposite Estcourt). Follow this road to the end of the tar where a large information board is erected at the crossroads. Follow the route to Champagne Castle hotel, then a further 3 km along a gravel road to the Monk's Cowl forestry office.

From the north travel via Bergville to Winterton, from where the road is signposted at the crossroads.

DESCRIPTION
Monk's Cowl state forest falls within the Mdedelelo wilderness area.

ACCOMMODATION
Open camping and caravan sites accommodate 120 persons. There is an ablution block with hot and cold water. Vehicles may be parked and left at this forest station. There are a number of caves each accommodating from four to 12 persons, and tents may also be pitched for overnight stays in the wilderness area. No fires are permitted. Enquiries and reservations are made with Monk's Cowl state forestry office, Winterton.

BIRDS
African goshawk
arrowmarked babbler
bald ibis
barthroated apalis
black crow
black harrier
black saw-wing swallow
black stork
blackcollared barbet
blackshouldered kite
bluebilled firefinch
bokmakierie
bronze mannikin
buzzards – forest, jackal, steppe
canaries – Cape, forest,
 yelloweyed
Cape batis
Cape vulture
Cape wagtail
Cape white-eye
chorister robin
common quail
cuckoos – black, Diederik,
 Klaas's, redchested
Drakensberg prinia
ducks – African black,
 yellowbilled
dusky flycatcher
eagles – black, crowned, martial
familiar chat
forktailed drongo

francolins – rednecked, redwing,
 Swainson's
goldenbreasted bunting
greyheaded sparrow
gymnogene
helmeted guineafowl
hoopoe
kingfishers – brownhooded, giant
lammergeyer
lazy cisticola
neddicky
orangethroated longclaw
pigeons – rameron, rock
plainbacked pipit
rock kestrel
rock martin
secretarybird
sharpbilled honeyguide
southern black tit
speckled mousebird
stonechat
sunbirds – greater doublecollared,
 lesser doublecollared, malachite
swifts – Alpine, black, whiterumped
thrushes – Cape rock, olive
warblers – Barratt's, yellow,
 yellowthroated
waxbills – common, swee
whitenecked raven
widows – redcollared, yellowrumped
woodpeckers – cardinal, ground, olive

MAMMALS

African wild cat
black-backed jackal
caracal
chacma baboon
common duiker
eland
grey rhebok
large-spotted genet
mongooses – water, white-tailed

mountain reedbuck
otters – Cape clawless,
  spotted-necked
porcupine
reedbuck
rock dassie
serval
striped polecat

GIANT'S CASTLE GAME RESERVE

Area: 34 638 ha
Established: 27 October 1903

LOCATION

Northern Drakensberg. 70 km from the N3 at Estcourt, and 64 km from Mooi River, the reserve is well signposted.

Hillside camp can be reached via Mooi River. Travel about 46 km, turn right at Ncibidwana store, where it is signposted "Hillside". Proceed about 8 km then turn where signposted. The camp is 5 km from this turn-off. An approach can be made via Estcourt on the Wagendrift-Ntabambhlope road. After 35 km turn left at a T-junction, (opposite White Mountain resort) towards Giant's Castle. 4 km beyond this, turn right at the "Hillside camp 5 km" sign.

Injasuti hutted camp is situated in the northern area of the game reserve, between the Injasuti, or Little Tugela, and Cowl Fork rivers at the head of the Injasuti valley. There are two routes to the camp. From the north, travel via Winterton, and from the south, turn off the N3 at the Loskop interchange and follow the tarred Loskop road for 27 km, then turn left at the Injasuti signpost. The camp is a further 30 km from this point over a rough gravel road.

FEATURES

Giant's Castle, with its splendid mountain scenery and towering escarpment, is a mecca for those who love strenuous hiking trails, as well as those who prefer a leisurely stroll along a contour path to experience the peace and silence of the wilderness. From the main camp and Injasuti camp, there are 30 different routes of varying distances and duration.

This reserve is famous for its caves and shelters which are rich in Bushman paintings. A special feature is the cave museum, where visitors will enjoy seeing examples of their art. Life-like models and the tools, weapons and type of clothing they wore have been reconstructed to portray how they lived. Tours to this cave operate from the main camp twice daily. Visitors staying in the Injasuti camp should visit Battle cave to view paintings.

The reserve is well known to the fly-fishing fraternity who haunt the banks of the Bushman's river, its deeper pools and larger tributaries in search of rainbow and brown trout. Swimming is enjoyed in the streams and pools but in winter the water temperature is more than exhilarating!

Another popular attraction is Lammergeyer Hide where, during the winter months, meat and bones are put out over weekends below a comfortable, camouflaged hide built into the rock on the edge of a cliff. Lammergeyers, or bearded vultures, are rare and persecuted by some farmers, in the mistaken belief that they are predators of young lambs. The lammergeyers have learned to feed below this hide along with Cape vultures and white-necked ravens. Splendid views of black eagles, jackal buzzards and lanner falcons can also be had by patient birders and photographers.

Although Giant's Castle reserve has only about 160 bird species, there is excellent bird watching in the protea veld and particularly in the indigenous gardens of the main camp, where the attractive greater and lesser doublecollared sunbirds, malachite sunbirds and Gurney's sugarbird can be viewed at close quarters.

Horse rides are popular and a fine means of taking in the stunning scenery. For the enthusiast, there are two and three-day pony trails that pass through the wilderness areas. These operate from Hillside camp, with the nights spent in caves or mountain huts, remote from the sights, sounds and pollution of the commercial world. Pony trails should be booked in advance.

This reserve offers a wide range of accommodation options, from a luxury lodge, self-catering cottages, a range of bungalows, open-air camping grounds, to mountain huts and caves.

It is a superb reserve and is considered by many wildlife enthusiasts and lovers of the mountains to be the Natal Parks Board's premier Drakensberg reserve.

DESCRIPTION

Giant's Castle Game Reserve is situated in western Natal at the headwaters of the Bushman's and Little Tugela rivers. It borders on the Mdedelelo wilderness area in the north, onto farmlands and tribal lands on the east, the Mkhomazi wilderness area in the south and shares a common border with Lesotho in the west. It is rugged country, presided over by the Injasuti Dome of 3 410 m in the north-western area and Giant's Castle (the Giant) of 3 314 m. The altitude drops to little more than 1 300 m in the lowest lying areas. Consequently there is a variety of vegetation types governed by altitude and the effects of climate, geology, soil type, aspect, slope, drainage and fire. Most of the reserve is covered in grassland. Along the rivers there is scrub and coarse grasses. Numerous streams tumble through the many valleys and there are some fine waterfalls and spectacular high cliffs. Forest patches generally occur on south-facing slopes in protected valleys with protea savanna and mixed scrub and grasses on steep slopes and sandstone platforms. Small patches of Drakensberg fynbos with heaths and mixed herbs occur at the higher altitudes. On the plateau, Alpine grasslands predominate, with species able to withstand the harsh climatic conditions.

Over 800 species of plants have been listed as occurring in this reserve. After the spring rains, numerous ground orchids, lilies, irises and other small flowering plant species are prolific. As with the plants found in the various altitudinal zones, the distribution of game and birds is governed by their preference for distinct altitudinal habitats. This is well demonstrated by doing a transect from the low lying areas to the top of the escarpment.

HISTORICAL NOTES

It is thought that the first inhabitants of the Drakensberg were people of the Middle Stone Age, who may have occupied the area more than 20 000 years ago, but the very early history of the Drakensberg has been lost in the mists of time. From the marvellous wealth of paintings found in numerous caves and shelters in Giant's Castle, the Bushmen (San) were the undisputed masters of this magnificent mountain range. These legendary people were small in stature, nomadic in habit, and lived on herbs, roots, wild fruits and from hunting eland and other large game. They followed the seasonal movements of the animals down into the lower valleys during the harsh winter months, then returned to their caves and shelters where they recorded their activities in the many thousands of paintings that we so admire today. Some of these paintings are said to date back to 970-1370 and the most recent to 1720-1820. We will never know what ingredients they used in the manufacture of their paints, but these paintings have withstood the ravages of time, exposed to all manner of weather conditions. The Bushmen were the artists, poets and musicians of their time, master hunters and medicine men, skilled in the use of various plants and insects to manufacture the poisons for the tips of their hunting arrows.

Despite their mastery over the natural world, the Bushmen were doomed because of the spread of the Nguni peoples and later, the arrival of white settlers with their herds of cattle. The herds of eland and other big game dwindled. They could not compete with modern firearms so they resorted to stealing cattle for meat. It has been suggested that they did not understand the concept of ownership, for they tilled no soil for crops, nor farmed livestock, nor built dwellings in which to live. When conditions were harsh they had no compunction in killing the new settlers' cattle, as, after all, animals belonged to everyone. They retreated up the mountain passes into Lesotho when pursued. Several of these passes were in fact blasted during the last century to prevent this practice and the Bushmen were shot on sight when found. Several large-scale military operations were mounted against them. In addition, a series of tribal reserves were established along the foothills of the berg as a buffer zone between them and the white settlers' farms. The last recorded raid by Bushmen against white farms was in July 1869, and against black farmers in August 1872. From 1840-1872 it was recorded that the Bushmen were responsible for raids amounting to the loss of several thousand head of cattle. By this stage the Bushmen had been declared vermin.

In 1873, one of the local tribal chiefs rebelled against colonial policies. Langalibalele and his people were forced to retreat through Giant's Castle, pursued by a detachment of the Natal Carbineers. A monument in the form of a cross to those who died in battle is situated at the top of what is still called Langalibalele's Pass.

By 1903, the population of eland in the Drakensberg had been reduced from an estimated 4 000-5 000 to a few hundred because of uncontrolled hunting. The Giant's Castle area, proclaimed as a game reserve on 27 October 1903, was probably their last refuge. Sydney Barnes, the first game warden appointed, lived for many months in a mountain cave once occupied by Bushmen. His nearest supplies were at Ntambambhlope store, his nearest white neighbour 30 km distant. He was succeeded in 1906 by Roden Symons, who left in 1915. His assistant, Phillip Barnes, then assumed control, retiring in 1947. From 1947-1956 Edward Thrash continued with the development of this magnificent reserve. Then, to continue the long family association with Giant's Castle, Bill Barnes assumed control in 1956 as warden and later, because of his very extensive knowledge of the Drakensberg region, as conservator of the entire area.

A much more recent addition to the reserve was the Injasuti camp. Originally this was a cattle farm, later turned into a successful holiday resort known as Solitude, and sold to the Natal Parks Board in 1980.

The Drakensberg is known to the Zulus as "Quathlamba" or "uKhahlamba", meaning a barrier or a row of up-pointing spears, which aptly describes the pinnacles, jagged peaks and spires of this impressive mountain range. One of the names for Giant's Castle is "Ntabayikonjwa" – the mountain at which one must not point. This name is said to be associated with the legend that pointing directly at the mountain results in bad weather.

For the modern visitors enjoying the comforts and amenities available today in this popular, much loved reserve, it is perhaps worth remembering some of its turbulent early history and the hardships borne by the early pioneers in safeguarding the wildlife we so enjoy and cherish in these present times.

ACCOMMODATION
Main camp: A luxury seven-bedded lodge, comprising three bedrooms, lounge-dining room, toilet and bathrooms, fully furnished and equipped. A resident cook is in attendance.

Four six-bedded cottages, furnished, fully equipped, with their own kitchens. There is no cook but these cottages are serviced. Four five-bedded, seven three-bedded and two two-bedded bungalows, all fully equipped and furnished with lounge-dining room, bathroom and toilet.

Crockery, cutlery, a fridge and linen are provided. Food is prepared by staff in a central kitchen.

Hillside camp: This camp is situated 30 km from the main camp. An eight-bedded rustic hut is provided with crockery, cutlery and cooking utensils but contains no fridge or stove. Meals are prepared by visitors over open-hearth fires outside. No linen or towels are provided. There is a camping area with two ablution blocks and braai facilities.

Injasuti hutted camp: 17 six-bedded cabins with two bedrooms (one with a two-bunk alcove) and two eight-bedded cabins. These are fully furnished and equipped but visitors supply their own food. A cleaning service is provided but visitors cook their own food and wash their own dishes. Braai facilities are provided at each cabin. A camping site below the hutted camp accommodates 50 persons and is provided with an ablution block and braai facilities.

Mountain huts: There are three mountain huts in the reserve. Giant's hut, about 10 km from the main camp, and Bannerman's hut, about 19 km north of Giant's hut, sleep eight persons each. These huts consist of one large room with a divider. Four double bunk beds and mattresses, a two-plate gas stove, cold water and a toilet are provided. A third, Meander hut, sited about 5 km to the east of the rest camp, accommodates four persons. This has two double bunks, a gas cooker, toilet and water.

Caves: Visitors who wish to overnight in the Lower Injasuti, Junction or Fergies caves (which can accommodate eight people per cave), should reserve these shelters through the central reservations office.

Visitors supply their own food and drink when using the mountain huts and caves, and their own sleeping bags, cooking and eating utensils. Reservations for hutted camps should be made with the Natal Parks Board, Pietermaritzburg. Camp sites are booked with the officers-in-charge at Hillside and Injasuti.

TREES
Buddleja loricata – mountain sage
Celtis africana – white stinkwood
Cussonia paniculata – mountain cabbage tree
Cyathea dregei – common tree fern
Dais cotinifolia – pompon tree
Dovyalis zeyheri – wild apricot
Encephalartos ghellinckii – Drakensberg cycad
Erica caffrorum – mountain tree heath
Erythrina humeana – dwarf coral tree
Greyia sutherlandii – Natal bottlebrush

Leucosidea sericea – oldwood
Maytenus peduncularis – Cape blackwood
Olinia emarginata – red-berry tree
Pittosporum viridiflorum – cheesewood
Podocarpus falcatus – common yellowwood
Podocarpus henkelii – Henkel's yellowwood
Podocarpus latifolius – real yellowwood
Polygala myrtifolia – September bush
Protea caffra – common sugarbush
Protea roupelliae – silver sugarbush
Protea subvestita – lip-flower sugarbush
Psoralea pinnata – fountain bush
Rapanea melanophloeos – Cape beech
Rhoicissus tridentata – bushman's grape
Rhus dentata – nana-berry
Salix woodii – Natal willow
Scolopia mundii – red pear
Widdringtonia nodiflora – berg cypress

BIRDS (about 160 species)

African black duck
Alpine swift
bald ibis
Barratt's warbler
black eagle
black harrier
black stork
bush blackcap
Cape vulture
chats – buffstreaked, familiar,
   sicklewinged
cinnamon dove
Drakensberg siskin
fairy flycatcher
francolins – greywing,
   rednecked, redwing
greater doublecollared sunbird
ground woodpecker

Gurney's sugarbird
helmeted guineafowl
jackal buzzard
kingfishers – giant, malachite
lammergeyer
lanner falcon
olive thrush
orangebreasted rockjumper
orangethroated longclaw
robins – Cape, chorister
Stanley's bustard
thickbilled lark
whitenecked raven
yellow canary
yellow warbler
yellowbreasted pipit
yellowrumped widow
yellowthroated warbler

MAMMALS (50 species)

African wild cat
black-backed jackal
blesbok
bushbuck
caracal
chacma baboon

common duiker
eland
greater canerat
grey rhebok
klipspringer
large-spotted genet

mongooses – Egyptian,
  water, white-tailed
mountain reedbuck
Natal red rock rabbit
oribi
otters – Cape clawless,
  spotted-necked
porcupine

red hartebeest
reedbuck
rock dassie
scrub hare
serval
striped polecat
striped weasel
vervet monkey

There are small species including four shrews, two moles, one bat, two molerats, five rats and seven mice.

REPTILES (31 species recorded)
The reptile fauna for Giant's Castle reserve comprises the following species: one gecko, one agama, one chameleon, two skinks, nine lizards and 17 snakes. Three of the snakes, rinkhals, puff adder and berg adder, are highly venomous.

HIGHMOOR STATE FOREST (MKHOMAZI WILDERNESS AREA)

Area: 28 100 ha
Established: 1973

LOCATION
From the N3 (south) turn off at the Nottingham Road off-ramp and proceed to Rosetta, through Nottingham Road. From Rosetta take the Kamberg-Giant's Castle road for 31 km where a signboard, 200 m beyond the Kamberg sign, indicates the route to Highmoor.

Travelling from the north on the N3, turn off at Mooi River, then to Rosetta and thereafter as described.

FEATURES
There are two exceptional trout dams at Highmoor, rated among the best in Natal. They are sited at high altitude, with magnificent views of the escarpment. Angling is limited to eight rod tickets per day, which must be booked in advance by fishermen. These are obtainable from Natal Parks Board offices in the area.

DESCRIPTION
This reserve falls within the Mkhomazi Wilderness Area, as does the Mpofana Nature Reserve. In the southern Drakensberg the Mkhomazi

Wilderness Area runs south from the border of Giant's Castle Game Reserve to Kokotabagi Ridge, the northern watershed of the Mkhomazana, in whose valley Sani Pass runs. Loteni and Vergelegen nature reserves form enclaves within it.

ACCOMMODATION
Visitors may pitch their tents in the camping area. One ablution block with cold water only is provided. There are three caves in each of which four persons are permitted to camp overnight.

BIRDS
African snipe
bald ibis
black crow
black eagle
black harrier
black swift
blackeyed bulbul
blackheaded heron
blackshouldered kite
bokmakierie
buffstreaked chat
Cape canary
Cape robin
Cape turtle dove
Cape vulture
Cape wagtail
Cape white-eye
cisticolas – Levaillant's, wailing
common waxbill
dabchick
francolins – greywing, redwing
greyheaded sparrow

ground woodpecker
hamerkop
jackal buzzard
malachite sunbird
orangethroated longclaw
quail finch
redknobbed coot
redwinged starling
rock kestrel
rock martin
rock pigeon
secretarybird
southern pochard
Stanley's bustard
stonechat
thrushes – Cape rock, olive
wattled crane
whitebreasted cormorant
whitenecked raven
widows – longtailed, redcollared, yellowrumped
yellowbilled duck

MAMMALS (16 species)
aardwolf
black-backed jackal
Cape clawless otter
caracal
chacma baboon
common duiker
eland
grey rhebok

mongooses – water, white-tailed
mountain reedbuck
oribi
porcupine
red hartebeest
reedbuck
serval

KAMBERG NATURE RESERVE

Area: 2 232 ha
Established: 1 June 1951

LOCATION
Drakensberg foothills. From the N3 south take the Nottingham Road turn-off, and travel for 42 km via Rosetta.

From the north, turn off at the second interchange at Mooi River, take the first left turn to Rosetta, and then travel on to Kamberg.

FEATURES
An attractive and spaciously laid out small camp, set against the rugged scenery of the Drakensberg foothills. Kamberg is renowned for the excellent trout fishing in the Mooi river which flows through the reserve. There are also several dams, stocked with brown or rainbow trout, which can be fished all year round. A guided tour of the trout hatchery is an interesting experience.

There are many pleasant walks and self-guided trails of varying distances, which pass through wooded gullies with streams and waterfalls, across boulder-strewn hillsides, wetlands and grasslands, up to the highest points which command spectacular views of the distant peaks of Giant's Castle.

Some 200 bird species occur in this secluded small reserve. The visitor may also encounter reedbuck, mountain reedbuck, blesbok, black wildebeest, grey rhebok, eland, red hartebeest and oribi.

The 4 km Mooi river trail, specifically designed for the handicapped, can also be enjoyed by the less energetic. The trail is level and easily negotiated by wheelchair.

DESCRIPTION
The landscape of the Kamberg Nature Reserve has been considerably modified by past farming practices. Parts of the hill slopes have been eroded by the grazing of cattle, sheep, goats and horses. Some of the original forest was felled for building timber, and some destroyed in order to open up grassland areas for grazing. Exotic trees such as blue gums, black wattles, plane trees and willows were introduced.

The present landscape is varied. Although comprising mostly grass-covered hill slopes, there are also jagged sandstone rock outcrops, cliffs, crags, gullies and valleys with moist, low-lying grass and wetland areas. From Gladstone's Nose peak, at 2 265 m, down to the placid waters of the Mooi river, there is a considerable variation in topography.

Although not noted for the diversity of its vegetation, apart from numerous grass species, Kamberg has some fine specimens of real yellowwood *Podocarpus latifolius*, stands of silver sugarbush *Protea roupelliae*, the tree fern *Cyathea dregei* and the oldwood or mtshitshi bush *Leucosidea sericea*, which forms an important part of the diet of eland. In the shade of its canopy it shelters ferns, arum lilies and other plants. In spring, like most Drakensberg grasslands and wetlands, Kamberg's wild flowers are a delight.

HISTORICAL NOTES
The first inhabitants of the Drakensberg were the Bushmen (San), and evidence of their occupation can be seen in the beautiful paintings that adorn the rock faces of numerous caves and shelters at Kamberg. The Bushmen were succeeded by the Nguni, who were essentially pastoralists. In 1838 the first white settlers arrived. The present hutted camp was the site of the homestead of Mr "Chummy" Potterill, an early settler, and it was only in 1951 that this small part of the valley was proclaimed a nature reserve. The first settlers named prominent peaks and features of the landscape after people famous at that time. Hence "Gladstone's Nose" – a sandstone peak which presumably bore a resemblance to Gladstone, an early British prime minister. The name "Kamberg", however, is derived from the Afrikaans word for comb, which was used to describe the dominant ridge at Kamberg, a spine-shaped formation which resembles a cockerel's comb.

ACCOMMODATION
There are five three-bedded huts and a six-bedded cottage, all fully furnished and serviced. In addition, about 8 km from the camp, there is a rustic cottage, Stillerust, with 10 beds. Visitors supply their own linen and do their own cooking at Stillerust. Reservations should be made with the Natal Parks Board, Pietermaritzburg.

BIRDS
The endangered wattled crane breeds in the wetland areas of this nature reserve. Other species include:

African snipe
bald ibis
black harrier
blackrumped buttonquail
Cape vulture
chats – anteating,
  buffstreaked, familiar
corncrake
cranes – blue, crowned
eagles – black, martial
great spotted cuckoo
ground hornbill
Gurney's sugarbird
lammergeyer
orangebreasted rockjumper

owls – Cape eagle, grass
quail finch
rameron pigeon
redcapped lark
rock bunting
Stanley's bustard
storks – black, white
striped flufftail
sunbirds – lesser doublecollared,
  malachite
Swainson's francolin
thrushes – Cape rock, groundscraper,
  olive, sentinel rock
whitenecked raven
woodpeckers – ground, olive

MAMMALS

African wild cat	large-spotted genet
black wildebeest	mountain reedbuck
black-backed jackal	oribi
blesbok	porcupine
bushbuck	red hartebeest
caracal	reedbuck
chacma baboon	rock dassie
common duiker	serval
eland	striped polecat
grey rhebok	striped weasel

IMPENDLE NATURE RESERVE

Area: 8 000 ha
Established: 1985

LOCATION
Drakensberg. The reserve is 75 km west of Pietermaritzburg on the southern Drakensberg route, between Boston, Bulwer and Impendle.

FEATURES
Impendle Nature Reserve's biggest attraction is its rich biological diversity and location. It is surrounded mainly by tribal lands. High populations of humans and domestic stock are creating social and biological demands which these environments are no longer able to meet. This area can function as a biosphere reserve for some of the local people, a reservoir to supply firewood, building poles, thatch, herbal medicines and other renewable resources. The scope for environmental education, with the emphasis on correct land use and resource management, is a major consideration for the future conservation of the area.

There are plans for wilderness areas with strictly controlled human impact, hiking trails and vehicular access to vantage points for game viewing, etc. There is also scope for professional hunting, hunting camps, horse trails and photographic safaris.

The magnificent closed forests, pools, waterfalls, open grassed hills, valleys, gorges and plateaux, with distant views of the Drakensberg, as well as the interesting fauna, should be enough to satisfy the casual and professional visitor.

This reserve has the potential to become an extremely important multi-use conservation centre.

DESCRIPTION

This reserve falls within the southern borders of the Natal Midlands and uplands, with the Mkhomazi river forming part of its southern boundary. It is surrounded on two sides by the former KwaZulu, with plantations and private cattle farms bordering the remaining eastern areas. It is situated in the mistbelt and altitude ranges from 940 m along the Mkomazi river, to 1 586 m, the highest point, Twaleyakhe, near the central entrance gate.

The area comprises ancient plateaux of weathered dolerite. The Mkhomazi river has gouged a deep scar through the plateau from west to east. A steep and picturesque escarpment with gradients up to 90 degrees has developed, with varying densities of mixed *Podocarpus* forests. Perennial and annual rivers and streams, primarily from the north, criss-cross the higher grassy areas where valleys and rocky outcrops of varying size bisect this plateau. Deep gorges cut through the escarpment where cataracts, waterfalls and rocky pools abound below the filtered sunlight of the forest canopy. Numerous species of lilies, irises and orchids can be seen on the rocky hills and grasslands, as well as along the stream banks. There are nine perennial earth dams and a number of springs and seepage areas.

HISTORICAL NOTES

Stone Age middens have been found in the surrounding areas but no archaeological research has been undertaken in the reserve itself. Since the mid-19th century farmers have settled here to breed livestock for beef and dairy products. Parts of the forest were vigorously exploited for building materials, primarily the yellowwoods *Podocarpus* species. On the lower slopes and flats along the Mkhomazi river, maize and vegetable crops were grown.

This reserve, originally called Seven Mile Bush, was officially sanctioned for conservation use by NAKOR in 1985. The whole area is comprised of portions of 11 farms. Alien wattle infestation, erosion and past mismanagement of both forests and grasslands are evident as a result of past farming activities.

ACCOMMODATION

None at present. Plans to accommodate visitors in luxurious chalets and more basic bush or wilderness camps, as well as camping, are proposed. One of the entrance gates, an office, environmental centre and a workshop and storeroom have already been built. Enquiries should be addressed to the NPA Department of Community Services, Pietermaritzburg.

TREES

Cassine peragua – Cape saffron
Cassinopsis ilicifolia – lemon thorn
Celtis africana – white stinkwood
Cephalanthus natalensis – strawberry bush

Clausena anisata – horsewood
Combretum edwardsii – Natal creeper
Cryptocarya woodii – Cape quince
Dalbergia armata – thorny rope
Diospyros whyteana – bladder-nut
Encephalartos ghellinckii – Drakensberg cycad
Olea capensis subsp. *macrocarpa* – ironwood
Olea europaea subsp. *africana* – wild olive
Podocarpus falcatus – common yellowwood
Podocarpus henkelii – Henkel's yellowwood
Podocarpus latifolius – real yellowwood
Protea caffra – common sugarbush
Protea roupelliae – silver sugarbush
Ptaeroxylon obliquum – sneezewood
Rapanea melanophloeos – Cape beech
Rhamnus prinoides – dogwood
Rothmannia capensis – Cape gardenia
Xymalos monospora – lemonwood
Zanthoxylum capense – small knobwood
Zanthoxylum davyi – knobwood

The two main vegetation types are highland sourveld and southern tall grassveld, the latter classified as a threatened veld type.

BIRDS

bald ibis	Knysna lourie
Cape batis	olive bush shrike
Cape canary	rameron pigeon
Cape white-eye	robins – Cape, chorister
collared sunbird	secretarybird
eagles – crowned, martial	sombre bulbul
ground hornbill	southern boubou
gymnogene	Stanley's bustard
jackal buzzard	wattled crane

MAMMALS

bushbuck	oribi
Cape clawless otter	reedbuck
caracal	rock dassie
duiker – blue, common	serval
large-spotted genet	Smith's red rock rabbit

Species reintroduced are springbok, blesbok, black wildebeest and red hartebeest. It is also planned to introduce eland, grey rhebok, mountain reedbuck, klipspringer and zebra.

LOTENI NATURE RESERVE

Area: 3 984 ha
Established: 2 April 1953

LOCATION
Southern Drakensberg. 14 km north-west from the Loteni store. Approximately 76 km from Nottingham Road on the Nottingham Road-Himeville road, it is well signposted. From the south, travel via Underberg and Himeville, which is about 47 km from the camp.

FEATURES
Visitors to Loteni cannot fail to be impressed by the splendid views of the mountains. It is situated in the foothills of the high Drakensberg. Loteni is known among anglers for its brown trout fishing. Enthusiasts return again and again to enjoy the many walks, trails and climbs, the reedbuck, grey rhebok, eland, oribi and other smaller mammals, the wild flowers in spring, and local bird species such as lammergeyer, black and martial eagles, lanner falcon, black stork, and the bright, metallic green malachite sunbirds on silver protea bushes. The accommodation is comfortable, the mountain air invigorating. There are pleasant picnic sites, and for those brave enough, swimming in the somewhat cool waters of the river.

DESCRIPTION
The whole area is generally similar in its geology, fauna and flora to the adjacent Giant's Castle Game Reserve, and consists mainly of open grassveld, with deep valleys and boulder outcrops. The south-eastern slopes and valleys have bush and forest patches, and there are impressive rock formations. From river bed to mountain top, the geological formations of the Drakensberg can be clearly seen, beginning with the upper Beaufort beds in the valley, to Molteno beds, then red beds, which stand out as alternate beds of red shale and sandstone; the creamy white cliffs of cave sandstone and, at the summit, basaltic lavas, eroded over 50-200 million years.

The forests were once heavily exploited for the timber of trees such as the yellowwoods *Podocarpus*. Human influence on this environment can also be seen in the alien wattles present in the reserve, as well as the Australian blackwoods, pines, and undesirable shrubs such as brambles.

Nevertheless, roaming the hillsides of this attractive landscape, one is rewarded by views of protea woodland, with silver sugarbush *Protea roupelliae*, common sugarbush *Protea caffra*, some fine tree ferns *Cyathea dregei*, the Natal bottlebrush *Greyia sutherlandii*, numerous oldwoods or mtshitshi *Leucosidea sericea* and patches of the rare berg bamboo *Thamnocalamus tessellatus*. After the spring burns and first showers, the bloom of wild flowers, too numerous to list by species, is spectacular. The ifafa lily *Cyrtanthus falcatus*, however, is particularly noteworthy.

HISTORICAL NOTES
Like some of the other Drakensberg reserves, Loteni was formerly farm land. The farms were first surveyed in 1897 and 1901, and settlers took occupation of the land early this century. Because of the rugged nature of the terrain, stockfarming was the main activity, with crops cultivated only on the level ground along the river course.

Part of the present reserve originally belonged to William and Catherine Root, and their old homestead has been restored and refurnished as a settler museum. Another building of historical interest is Symes cottage, the home of bachelor farmer Symes who lived on the land for 43 years.

The remainder of the farm lands that comprise the present reserve were acquired by the Natal Parks Board between 1953 and 1966.

The reserve is named for the Lotheni river which flows through the valley. "Lotheni" is derived from the Zulu word for ash, "umlotha", and means, literally, the place of ashes. Some believe the name originated in the colour of the shale found in the valley, others believe it was a description of the grey-black ash-like colour reflected by the water.

ACCOMMODATION
The reserve has 12 fully equipped, four-bedded bungalows with lounge-diningroom, bathroom, toilet and fridge. Crockery, cutlery, cooking utensils and linen are provided. They are served by two kitchen blocks. There are two self-contained cottages which have the services of a cook.

Symes cottage, a rustic cottage next to a small trout dam, is also available for bookings. It accommodates 10 persons and is provided with crockery, cutlery, cooking utensils, fridge and stove. Visitors supply their own linen and cook for themselves.

About 2 km from the main camp is a camping ground with 10 camp sites and an ablution block with hot and cold running water.

Reservations for hutted accommodation should be made with the Natal Parks Board, Pietermaritzburg. Book camp sites with the camp superintendent, Loteni Nature Reserve.

BIRDS (140 species recorded)
The montane bird fauna is interesting, and some of the species are:

black harrier	grassbird
black stork	ground woodpecker
Cape rock thrush	Gurney's sugarbird
Cape vulture	jackal buzzard
cranes – blue, crowned	lammergeyer
eagles – black, martial	lanner falcon
familiar chat	olive thrush
giant kingfisher	orangethroated longclaw

Stanley's bustard
redwing francolin
pigeons – rameron, rock
stonechat

sunbirds – greater doublecollared,
malachite
wailing cisticola

MAMMALS

Apart from the very small rodents, the most common species to be seen in Loteni include:

African wild cat
black-backed jackal
bushbuck
chacma baboon
common duiker
eland
grey rhebok

large-spotted genet
mountain reedbuck
oribi
reedbuck
striped polecat
striped weasel

VERGELEGEN NATURE RESERVE

Area: 1 159 ha
Established: 14 December 1967

LOCATION

Drakensberg. The reserve is 19 km from the main Underberg-Nottingham Road road, with the turn-off 16 km north of Himeville.

FEATURES

This is a small, secluded reserve, noted for its excellent brown trout fishing. There are a number of short, pleasant walks within the park. It is open to day visitors for picnics. It is planned to provide a number of camp sites within the park. Vergelegen is the gateway to some of the most remote wilderness in the Cobham and Mkhomazi areas. It is a starting point for a number of mountain hikes. Thaba Ntlenyana, southern Africa's highest mountain, can be viewed from this reserve. Game such as reedbuck, mountain reedbuck, grey rhebok, eland, oribi and common duiker are readily seen.

DESCRIPTION

A reserve of deep valleys, steep hillsides and highveld sourveld grassland in similar highland country to that of the nearby Loteni Nature Reserve. It is situated at an altitude of over 1 500 m along the Mkhomazi river at its confluence with the Mlahlangulo river. The flora is similar to that of the Loteni Nature Reserve.

HISTORICAL NOTES

Originally the farm Vergelegen, it was first occupied in October 1905 by a Mr JJ Bronkhorst, who had permission to graze his stock throughout the present-day park and over what is now the Mkhomazi wilderness area. The area, as it stands today, was donated to the Natal Parks Board by the Rissik family of the Transvaal. By then much of the area had been extensively planted with pine trees.

ACCOMMODATION

There are two five-bedded, self-contained cottages. Visitors must provide their own food and drink. Make reservations with the Natal Parks Board, Pietermaritzburg.

BIRDS (98 species recorded)

bishops – golden, red
buzzards – forest, jackal
Cape vulture
cuckoos – black, Jacobin
eagles – black, martial
familiar chat
francolins – rednecked, redwing
Gurney's sugarbird
horus swift
lammergeyer
lanner falcon

longbilled pipit
rameron pigeon
streakyheaded canary
sunbirds – greater doublecollared,
    lesser doublecollared, malachite
thrushes – Cape rock,
    groundscraper, olive
white stork
whitenecked raven
woodpeckers – ground, olive
yellow warbler

MAMMALS (11 species recorded)

black-backed jackal
Cape clawless otter
chacma baboon
common duiker
eland

grey rhebok
mongooses – water, white-tailed
mountain reedbuck
oribi
reedbuck

MKHOMAZI and MZIMKULU WILDERNESS AREAS and MZIMKULWANA NATURE RESERVE

Area: 49 150 ha
Established: 1973

LOCATION

Turn off the N3 at the Nottingham Road off-ramp. From Nottingham Road follow the route signposted to Loteni-Sani pass. Continue for 44 km, the last 14 km of which is a gravel road. At the Mzinga river bridge there is a signboard indicating Mkhomazi state forest on the right. Proceed a further 2 km. The Mkhomazi Wilderness Area may be entered from one of the other forest stations in the region, or indirectly via Giant's Castle, Kamberg, Vergelegen and Loteni nature reserves to the east. Permits are required.

FEATURES
The main attractions are the spectacular scenery and the rugged mountains, in particular the Sani pass, Rhino's Horn (3 051 m) and Hodgson's Peaks (3 244 m and 3 229 m). In this region stands Thaba Ntlenyana (3 482 m) in Lesotho, southern Africa's highest mountain.

DESCRIPTION
This area contains a part of the Mkhomazi Wilderness Area and the Kwamehlenyati Nature Reserve. Giant's Castle is its northern boundary and it extends southwards to the Sani pass. The Mzimkulu Wilderness Area and the Mzimkulwana Nature Reserve stretch southwards from Sani pass to Bushman's Nek and contain the Loteni and Vergelegen nature reserves. This is the catchment area of the Mkhomazi (Umkomaas) river into which the smaller Lotheni, KaNtuba and Mkomazana rivers flow. It was named by the Zulus as "the place of cow whales", because it flows into the Indian Ocean on the northern border of the upper South Coast town of Umkomaas where, in former times, whales and their calves apparently used to shelter off the mouth of the river.

HISTORICAL NOTES
The forest station was established in March 1975. The farm Cyprus on the Izinga river was purchased in 1974, and the Mkhomazi forest station moved there at the end of 1980.

ACCOMMODATION
Basic camping is available in three caves for up to 16 people. One cave can accommodate four people and the other two six each. Enquiries should be directed to the Mkhomazi state forest office, Nottingham Road.

BIRDS

black swift	Cape wagtail
blackshouldered kite	Cape white-eye
bokmakierie	cisticolas – Ayres', Levaillant's
brownthroated martin	common waxbill
buzzards – jackal, steppe	crows – black, pied
Cape canary	Drakensberg prinia
Cape robin	fiscal shrike
Cape turtle dove	forktailed drongo
Cape vulture	goldenbreasted bunting

338

greyheaded sparrow
ground woodpecker
hadeda ibis
hamerkop
helmeted guineafowl
hoopoe
longtailed widow
orangebreasted rockjumper
orangethroated longclaw
paradise flycatcher
pintailed whydah

quail finch
redwing francolin
rock pigeon
southern boubou
speckled mousebird
starlings – pied, redwinged
stonechat
streakyheaded canary
sunbirds – greater doublecollared,
    malachite

MAMMALS (18 species)

aardwolf
African wild cat
black-backed jackal
caracal
chacma baboon
common duiker
eland
grey rhebok
mongooses – water, white-tailed

mountain reedbuck
otters – Cape clawless,
   spotted-necked
porcupine
reedbuck
rock dassie
serval
striped polecat
vervet monkey

COBHAM STATE FOREST
(MZIMKULU WILDERNESS AREA)

Area: 30 500 ha
Established: 1973

LOCATION

From the N3 at Howick take the R617 to Underberg, then turn off to Himeville, which is 5 km further on. From Himeville take the D7 and travel for 13 km on a gravel road to reach the Cobham office. This reserve is approximately 150 km from Pietermaritzburg. From the South Coast take the R612 via Umzinto, Ixopo, Donnybrook onto the R617, turning left at the sign to Himeville, then as above.

DESCRIPTION

The Mzimkhulu river and its tributaries which rise in this catchment area near the Lesotho border, flow south-east past Underberg and the Transkei border to enter the Indian Ocean on the northern border of Port Shepstone on the lower Natal South Coast. The Mzimkhulu is the largest river south of the Tugela river.

This catchment area is one of true wilderness, with rugged mountainous country and deep forested gorges sheltering giant yellowwood and other hardwood tree species. There are steep, grassed hillsides, heath and scrub, thicket and streambank vegetation. There are rock pools where small waterfalls tumble from sheer krantzes along the courses of the rivers and streams. For the hiker, there is the chance of encountering some 21 species of mammals, numerous interesting and rare bird species and many attractive trees, shrubs and colourful smaller flowering plants along the trails. Trout fishing is available in the Pholela river.

HISTORICAL NOTES
Cobham forest station was established on a farm of that name, purchased in 1963. This state forest is part of the Mzimkhulu Wilderness Area, which embraces part of Cobham and Garden Castle state forests and stretches to the Sehlabathebe National Park in Lesotho to the south.

ACCOMMODATION
There are 10 camping and caravan sites for six persons each. Four caves accommodate 12 persons per cave and one cave accommodates six persons. The Pholela biosphere reserve complex houses 30 persons per night. Reservations and entry permits are obtainable from the Cobham forestry office.

BIRDS

black cuckoo
black stork
black swift
blackheaded heron
blackheaded oriole
blackshouldered kite
bokmakierie
brownthroated martin
Cape batis
Cape robin
Cape vulture
chats – familiar, mountain
cranes – blue, crowned
Drakensberg prinia
ducks – African black,
   yellowbilled
dusky flycatcher
eagles – black, crowned,
   longcrested
francolins – greywing, Swainson's
grassbird

greater honeyguide
ground woodpecker
Gurney's sugarbird
gymnogene
hoopoe
jackal buzzard
lanner falcon
longbilled pipit
neddicky
olive thrush
orangebreasted rockjumper
orangethroated longclaw
owls – grass, spotted eagle
pied starling
redthroated wryneck
Richard's pipit
secretarybird
southern black tit
speckled mousebird
thrushes – Cape rock, kurrichane

MAMMALS (21 species)

African wild cat
black-backed jackal
caracal
chacma baboon
common duiker
eland
greater musk shrew
grey rhebok
ice rat
large-spotted genet

mongooses – water, white-tailed
mountain reedbuck
otters – Cape clawless,
   spotted-necked
porcupine
reddish-grey musk shrew
reedbuck
rock dassie
serval
striped polecat

HIMEVILLE NATURE RESERVE

Area: 105 ha
Established: 1 February 1956

LOCATION
Southern Drakensberg. 130 km east of Pietermaritzburg, adjoining Himeville village.

FEATURES
There are two dams noted for trout fishing and an attractive, shady picnic site with braai facilities alongside one of the dams. Rowing boats are available for hire. Blesbok occur in this small park, and the dam attracts flocks of wildfowl at times.

DESCRIPTION
Situated in the foothills of the Drakensberg, on the Himeville commonage, the reserve comprises a well-grassed valley in a scenically attractive setting. The two large dams constructed across the valley take up much of the reserve area.

HISTORICAL NOTES
The village of Himeville was named after Sir Albert Henry Hime, Prime Minister of Natal from 1899-1903. It was proclaimed a township in 1905.

ACCOMMODATION
There are 10 camp sites with ablution facilities. Reservations should be made with the Natal Parks Board, Himeville Nature Reserve.

MAMMALS
blesbok
mongooses – water, white-tailed
otters – Cape clawless, spotted-necked

GARDEN CASTLE STATE FOREST
(MZIMKULU WILDERNESS AREA)

Area: 30 766 ha
Established: 1971

LOCATION
From the N3 take the R617 to Bulwer, Underberg, Himeville and the Drakensberg Gardens route for 39 km, continue through the hotel grounds for a further 3 km to the Garden Castle forestry office. From the South Coast, take the R612 via Umzinto, Ixopo and Donnybrook to Himeville. Then follow the Drakensberg Gardens route as above.

FEATURES
Spectacular scenery, good rainbow trout fishing, and as in all of the Drakensberg reserves, true wilderness and many delightful walks are available. Compared to other regions, the bird life is rather poor but 27 mammal species occur and the larger species, such as eland, grey rhebok, mountain reedbuck and reedbuck, are likely to be encountered.

DESCRIPTION
Garden Castle forest station was established in 1971. The southern watershed of the Mkhomazana river is the northern boundary of the Mzimkhulu Wilderness Area, which embraces parts of Cobham and Garden Castle state forests and stretches to the Natal-Lesotho border above Bushman's Nek, where it adjoins Sehlabathebe National Park in Lesotho.

ACCOMMODATION
There are 12 caves, accommodating a maximum of 12 persons each, along the trails system. Make enquiries to Garden Castle state forest office, Underberg.

BIRDS
black crow
black eagle
bokmakierie

Cape canary
Cape rock thrush
Drakensberg prinia
fiscal shrike

forktailed drongo
giant kingfisher
goldenbreasted bunting
hadeda ibis
jackal buzzard
malachite sunbird
redwinged starling

rock pigeon
secretarybird
stonechat
wailing cisticola
widow – longtailed, yellowrumped
yellowbilled duck

MAMMALS (27 species)

African wild cat
bats – Geoffroy's horseshoe,
   yellow house
black-backed jackal
bushbuck
caracal
chacma baboon
common duiker
common molerat
eland
golden moles – Hottentot,
   Sclater's
grey rhebok

large-spotted genet
mongooses – water, white-tailed
mountain reedbuck
otters – Cape clawless,
   spotted-necked
porcupine
reddish-grey musk shrew
reedbuck
rock dassie
striped mouse
striped polecat
striped weasel
vlei rat

THE SWAMP NATURE RESERVE

Area: 220 ha
Established: 21 June 1984

LOCATION
Drakensberg. 14 km east of Himeville on the Pevensey road. Take the Marievale-Bulwer road from the N3 about 20 km from Pietermaritzburg. Pass through the village of Bulwer, then take the Pevensey road on the right about 18 km further on.

FEATURES
Approximately 60 ha consist of wetland, which is an important refuge for wattled and crowned cranes and wildfowl. It is open to day visitors.

DESCRIPTION
The Polela river flows for about 3 km along the southern boundary of this wetland area of reedbeds, sedges, marsh grasses, channels and pools.

BIRDS

African marsh harrier
African snipe
bishops – golden, red
blackshouldered kite
cisticolas – fantailed,
    Levaillant's, wailing
cranes – crowned, wattled
eastern redfooted kestrel
Egyptian goose

grass owl
orangebreasted waxbill
orangethroated longclaw
quail finch
redknobbed coot
spurwinged goose
white stork
yellowbilled duck

MAMMALS

mongooses – large grey, slender, water, white-tailed
otters – Cape clawless, spotted-necked
reedbuck

COLEFORD NATURE RESERVE

Area: 1 272 ha
Established: 24 February 1948

LOCATION
Southern Drakensberg. 27 km from Underberg on the Swartberg road.

FEATURES
This is one of South Africa's premier rainbow trout fishing areas. The
Ngwangwana and Ndawana rivers are famous among fly fishermen.
Casual visitors can purchase a licence to fish on a daily basis. Trout fishing tackle can be hired. Braai and picnic sites are provided. Horse riding
and guided horse trails through game country can be arranged. A small
game and bird viewing hide has been built for visitors. Facilities for tennis,
deck quoits and croquet are available, and equipment for these sports can
be hired.

There are magnificent walks through aloes and proteas, grassland and
scrub, with a chance of seeing black wildebeest, oribi, mountain reedbuck,
blesbok, grey rhebok, red hartebeest and smaller species, as well as some
interesting birds. One does not have to be a trout fisherman to enjoy this
scenically attractive small reserve.

DESCRIPTION
The reserve is situated in hilly, sourveld grassland at the junction of the
Ngwangwana and Ndawana rivers, adjacent to the Cape province border.

344

The reserve was formerly the farms Coleford and Sunnyside, and is named after James Cole, a previous landowner.

The Ngwangwana was first stocked with trout by local farmers in about 1914. Its tributary, the Ndawana, rises near the Lesotho border, west of Mount Sutherland, and flows east-southeast to the confluence of the two rivers.

ACCOMMODATION

The hutted camp has six three-bedded rest huts, two three-bedded bungalows, three five-bedded bungalows, and two six-bedded cottages, with kitchen, ablution blocks and communal lounge. About 5 km from the main camp is Sunnyside cottage, with two bedrooms and an outside rondavel catering for a total of seven persons. Visitors must supply their own food and drink. Reservations are made with the Natal Parks Board, Pietermaritzburg.

BIRDS

blackheaded heron
bokmakierie
Cape canary
Cape robin
cisticolas – Ayres',
    Levaillant's, wailing
crowned crane

ducks – black, yellowbilled
Egyptian goose
malachite sunbird
orangethroated longclaw
pied starling
Stanley's bustard

MAMMALS

Some of the larger species are:

African wild cat
black wildebeest
black-backed jackal
blesbok
grey rhebok
large-spotted genet
mongooses – large grey, water,
    white-tailed

mountain reedbuck
oribi
otters – Cape clawless,
    spotted-necked
red hartebeest
serval
striped polecat

NAMES, ADDRESSES, TELEPHONE NUMBERS AND BOOKING DETAILS

KEY TO THE SYMBOLS

SC Self-catering accommodation   ➤ Fishing

FC Fully-catered accommodation   ⚓ Swimming (sea/river)

▲ Campsite   🚤 Boating

R Restaurant   ⚔ Mountaineering

⊼ Picnic site   🐎 Horseriding

🜷 Walking trails   🚙 Game drives

🏃🏃 Guided walks

For changes in telephone numbers, phone enquiries on 1023/5.

ABU MADI GAME RANCH

SC ▲ 🜷 🏃🏃 ⚓ 🚙   Hides

Enquiries: The Manager, PO Mkuze, Zululand 3965
Accommodation: Telephone: (035) 5731233

ALBERT FALLS PUBLIC RESORT

SC ▲ ⊼ 🜷 ➤ ⚓ 🚤   Sailing   Canoeing

Accommodation: The Reservations Officer, Natal Parks Board,
  Telephone: (0331) 471981
Camping: Camp Superintendent, Albert Falls Public, Resort, PO Box 31,
  Cramond 3420, Telephone: (03393) 202/203

AMATIKULU NATURE RESERVE

▲ 🜷 ➤   Canoeing

Enquiries: KwaZulu Department of Nature Conservation, P/Bag X23, Ulundi 3838,
  Telephone: (0358) 700552

ASSAGAY NATURE RESERVE
Enquiries: Assagay Health Committee, PO Box 196, Hillcrest 3650,
  Telephone: (031) 752997

346

BABANANGO VALLEY LODGE

FC 🕴 🕴🕴 ～～

Enquiries: The Manager, Babanango Valley Lodge, PO Box 10, Babanango 3850
Reservations: Telephone: (0358) 350062

BAYA CAMP (LAKE SIBAYA)

SC ⛺ 🕴 ～🐟 ～🚤 Hides

Accommodation: The Reservations Officer, KwaZulu Department of Nature
Conservation (KDNC), 367 Loop Street, Pietermaritzburg 3201,
Telephone: (0331) 946698
Written enquiries: The Conservator, Baya Camp, KDNC, P/Bag X22, Jozini 3969

BEACHWOOD MANGROVES NATURE RESERVE

🕴 Resource centre Bird hide

Enquiries: Natal Parks Board, Durban office, Telephone: (031) 251271

BISLEY VALLEY NATURE RESERVE

🕴

Enquiries: The Pietermaritzburg City Council, PO Box 321, Pietermaritzburg 3200
(Parks & Recreation Dept), Telephone: (0331) 422970

BLACK ROCK and LALA NEK

 Scuba diving

Enquiries: KwaZulu Department of Nature Conservation, P/Bag X23, Ulundi 3838,
Telephone: (0358) 700552 or Manzengwenya office
Permit enquiries: Telephone: (035) 5920142

BLINKWATER NATURE RESERVE

SC 🕴

Accommodation: Natal Parks Board, Pietermaritzburg, Telephone: (0331) 471981
Enquiries: Mrs Sue Swan, Telephone: (033552) ask for 42

BLUFF NATURE RESERVE

⛺ Hides

Enquiries: Natal Parks Board, Durban office, Telephone: (031) 427030 or
(031) 251271

BONAMANZI GAME PARK

SC FC 🕴 ～～ Hunting Conference centre

Accommodation: Bonamanzi Game Park, PO Box 408, Hluhluwe 3960,
Telephone: (03562) 3530, Fax: (03562) 131
Enquiries hunting: Bonamanzi Safaris, PO Box 58, Hluhluwe 3960,
Telephone: (03562) ask for 143 or 1704

347

BURMAN BUSH NATURE RESERVE

⛩ 𝗑 Resource centre

Enquiries: Durban Parks, Recreation & Beaches Department, PO Box 3740, Durban 4000, Telephone: (031) 234466

BUSHLANDS GAME LODGE

FC R ～🐟～ 🚙

Accommodation: The Manager, PO Box 79, Hluhluwe 3960
Enquiries: Telephone/Fax: (035) 5620144/5620205

CAPE VIDAL

SC ▲ ⛩ 𝗑 𝗑𝗑 🐟 ～🐟～ 🚤 Scuba diving

Accommodation: The Reservations Officer, Natal Parks Board
Trail bookings: Telephone: (0331) 471981
Camping/Enquiries: The Officer-in-Charge, Cape Vidal, P/Bag
St Lucia Estuary 3936, Telephone: St Lucia Estuary (035) 5901404

CATHEDRAL PEAK STATE FOREST

▲ ⛩ 𝗑 🐟 ✕

Camping/Wilderness: The Officer-in-Charge, Cathedral Peak
State trails: Forest, P/Bag X1, Winterton 3340, Telephone: (0364) 881880

CHARTER'S CREEK CAMP

SC ⛩ 𝗑 🐟 ～🐟～ 🚤

Accommodation: The Reservations Officer, Natal Parks Board,
Telephone: (0331) 471981
Enquiries: The Officer-in-Charge, Charter's Creek, P/Bag 7205, Mtubatuba 3935,
Telephone: Mtubatuba (035) 5501513

CHELMSFORD PUBLIC RESORT NATURE RESERVE

SC ▲ 🐟 ～🐟～ 🚤 Canoeing

Accommodation: The Reservations Officer, Natal Parks Board,
Telephone: (0331) 471981
Camping: The Officer-in-Charge, Chelmsford Public Resort, PO Box 3,
Ballengeich 2942, Telephone: Newcastle (03431) 77205

CLIVE CHEESMAN NATURE RESERVE

SC ⛩ 𝗑

Enquiries: The Wildlife Society, 100 Brand Road, Durban 4001,
Telephone: (031) 213126

COBHAM STATE FOREST

Λ ⚸ ⥤ ⥥

Enquiries: The Officer-in-Charge, Cobham State Forest, P/Bag X116,
  Himeville 4585, Telephone: (033722) 1831

COLEFORD NATURE RESERVE

SC ⊼ ⚸ ⥤ ⛊ Hide

Accommodation: The Reservations Officer, Natal Parks Board,
  Telephone: (0331) 471981
Enquiries: The Senior Ranger, PO Box 128, Underberg 4590,
  Telephone: (033712) 2140 or (0331) 471961

CRAIGIE BURN PUBLIC RESORT NATURE RESERVE

Λ ⥤ ⥥

Accommodation: The Reservations Officer, Natal Parks Board,
  Telephone: (0331) 471981
Camping/Enquiries: The Camp Superintendent, Midmar Public Resort,
  P/Bag Howick 3290, Telephone: Howick (0334) 71182

CRESTHOLME NATURE RESERVE

⚸

Enquiries: The Wildlife Society, 100 Brand Road, Durban 4001,
  Telephone: (031) 213126

DARVILL NATURE RESERVE

Hide

Enquiries: Umgeni Water, Telephone: (0331) 961233 or Wilderness Leadership
  School, Durban, Telephone: (031) 428642

DLINZA FOREST NATURE RESERVE

⊼ ⚸

Enquiries: KwaZulu Department of Nature Conservation, P/Bag X23, Ulundi 3838,
  Telephone: (0358) 700552

DOREEN CLARK NATURE RESERVE

⊼ ⚸

Enquiries: Natal Parks Board, Telephone: (0331) 471961

EASTERN SHORES STATE FOREST AND NATURE RESERVE
Enquiries: Natal Parks Board, Telephone: (0331) 471961 or
  St Lucia Estuary (035) 5901233

EMPISINI NATURE RESERVE

SC ⛩ 🏃   Resource centre

Accommodation: The Town Clerk, Umkomaas 4170
Enquiries: Telephone: (0323) 30090/31073

ENSELENI NATURE RESERVE

⛩ 🏃

Enquiries: Natal Parks Board, Telephone: (0331) 471961, The Officer-in-Charge,
Enseleni Reserve, Telephone: (0351) 923732

ENTUMENI NATURE RESERVE
Enquiries: Natal Parks Board, Telephone: (0331) 471961 or Eshowe (0354) 42473

ESTCOURT NATURE RESERVE

🏃

Enquiries: The Estcourt Municipality, PO Box 15, Estcourt 3310,
Telephone: (0363) 23000/7

FALSE BAY PARK

SC ⛰ ⛩ 🏃 🐟 🚤

Accommodation: The Reservations Officer, Natal Parks Board,
Telephone: (0331) 471981
Camping: The Officer-in-Charge, False Bay Park, PO Box 222, Hluhluwe 3960,
Telephone: (03562) 2911

FANIE'S ISLAND CAMP

SC ⛰ 🏃 🐟 🚤   Resource centre

Accommodation: The Reservations Officer, Natal Parks Board,
Telephone: (0331) 471981
Camping: The Officer-in-Charge, Fanie's Island, PO Box 201, Mtubatuba 3935,
Telephone: Mtubatuba (035) 5501631

FERNCLIFFE FOREST

⛩ 🏃

Enquiries: The Pietermaritzburg City Council, Parks and Recreation Department,
PO Box 321, Pietermaritzburg 3200, Telephone: (0331) 422970

FREDERIKA NATURE RESERVE
Enquiries: The Southbroom Health Committee, P/Bag X02, Southbroom 4277,
Telephone: (03931) 6125

FUNDIMVELO NATURE RESERVE
Enquiries: Natal Provincial Administration, Community Services Branch, P/Bag
  X9078, Pietermaritzburg 3200, Telephone: (0331) 952996, Fax: (0331) 952584

GAME VALLEY ESTATES
SC ▲ 🕺 🏊 🚤

Accommodation: The Manager, Game Valley Estates
Enquiries: PO Box 70, Richmond 3780, Telephone: Richmond (03322) 3171

GARDEN CASTLE STATE FOREST
▲ 🕺 🏊

Enquiries: The Officer-in-Charge, Garden Castle State Forest, P/Bag X312,
  Underberg 4590, Telephone: Himeville (033712) ask for 1722

GIANT'S CASTLE GAME RESERVE
SC ▲ 🕺 🐟 🏊 🐎 Hide Pony trails Bushman exhibit

Accommodation: The Reservations Officer, Natal Parks Board,
  Telephone: (0331) 471981
Giant's Lodge: The Director's secretary, Telephone: (0331) 471961
Camping: Hillside camp. The Officer-in-Charge, Hillside Camp, PO Box 288,
  Estcourt 3310, Telephone: (0363) 24435
  Injasuti hutted camp: The Officer-in-Charge, Injasuti, P/Bag X7010,
  Estcourt 3310, Telephone: 0020 ask for Loskop 1311

GLENHOLME NATURE RESERVE
🏕 🕺 Trail for disabled

Enquiries: The Wildlife Society, 100 Brand Road, Durban 4001,
  Telephone: (031) 213126

GOEDETROUW PUBLIC RESORT
🏕 🐟

Enquiries: Natal Parks Board, Telephone (0331) 471961 or Eshowe (0354) 42473

GREATER ST LUCIA WETLAND PARK
Enquiries: The Conservator, Natal Parks Board, St Lucia Estuary,
  Telephone: (035) 5901130

HAROLD JOHNSON NATURE RESERVE
▲ 🏕 🕺 Historical sites

Camping: The Officer-in-Charge, Natal Parks Board, Harold Johnson Nature
  Reserve, PO Box 148, Darnall 4480, Telephone: Darnall (0324) 61574

HAWAAN FOREST RESERVE

Enquiries: (A private reserve and permission is required for entry.) Contact
Municipality of Umhlanga,Telephone: (031) 5611101

HAZELMERE PUBLIC RESORT NATURE RESERVE

 Canoeing

Camping: The Officer-in-Charge, Natal Parks Board, Hazelmere Public Resort,
PO Box 1013, Verulam 4340, Telephone: (0322) 332315

HIGHMOOR STATE FOREST

Enquiries/Camping: The Officer-in-Charge, Highmoor State Forest
Trails: PO Box 51, Rosetta 3301, Telephone: Rosetta (0333) ask for 37240

HIMEVILLE NATURE RESERVE

Camp sites: The Officer-in-Charge, Natal Parks Board, Himeville Nature Reserve,
PO Box 115, Himeville 4585, Telephone: Himeville (033622) ask for 36

HLATHIKULU FOREST RESERVE
Enquiries: KwaZulu Department of Nature Conservation, Telephone: Jozini
035672 – ask for KDNC on 11

HLUHLUWE GAME RESERVE

SC FC R ⛺ 🚶 👫 Scenic drives   Hides   Interpretation centre

Accommodation: The Reservations Officer, Natal Parks Board,
Telephone: (0331) 471981
Enquiries: The Camp Superintendent, Hluhluwe Game Reserve, Telephone:
(035) 5620255

ILANDA WILDS NATURE RESERVE

Enquiries: The Municipality of Amanzimtoti, PO Box 26, Amanzimtoti 4126,
Telephone: (031) 9032121 or The Wildlife Society, Durban (031) 213126

ILLOVO LAGOON NATURE RESERVE

Enquiries: The Borough of Kingsburgh, PO Box 30, Winklespruit 4145,
Telephone: (031) 963340 or The Wildlife Society, Durban (031) 213126

IMPENDLE NATURE RESERVE

Enquiries: Impendle Nature Reserve, PO Boston 3211, Telephone: (03394) 613 or NPA Department of Community Services, Telephone (0331) 952996

INGWENYA NATURE RESERVE

🪑 🚶

Enquiries: The Mandini centre of the Wildlife Society, Telephone: (03245) 2397

ITALA GAME RESERVE

SC △ R 🪑 🚶🚶 🐟 ⚊ 🚙

Accommodation: The Reservations Officer, Natal Parks Board, for Ntshondwe Camp, bush camps and overnight trails only, Telephone: (0331) 471981
Camp site bookings: The Officer-in-Charge, Itala Game Reserve, PO Box 42, Louwsburg 3150, Telephone: (0388) 75239
Conference centre bookings: Telephone: (0388) 75105

KAMBERG NATURE RESERVE

SC 🚶 🐟

Accommodation: The Reservations Officer, Natal Parks Board, Telephone: (0331) 471981
Enquiries: Telephone: (0331) 471961

KARKLOOF NATURE RESERVE

Enquiries: Natal Parks Board, Telephone: (0331) 471961

KENNETH STAINBANK NATURE RESERVE

🪑 🚶 Trail for disabled

Enquiries: The Officer-in-Charge, Natal Parks Board, Telephone: (031) 427030 or Senior Ranger/Naturalist (031) 421125

KLIPFONTEIN PUBLIC RESORT NATURE RESERVE

△ 🪑 🐟 🛥

Camping/Enquiries: The Officer-in-Charge, Natal Parks Board, Klipfontein Public Resort, PO Box 1744, Vryheid 3100, Telephone: Vryheid (0381) 4383

KOSI BAY NATURE RESERVE

SC △ 🪑 🚶 🚶🚶 🐟 🛥 Scuba diving Wilderness trails

Accommodation: The Reservations Officer, KwaZulu Department of Nature Conservation, 367 Loop Street, Pietermaritzburg 3201, Telephone: (0331) 946698
Camping: The Officer-in-Charge, KDNC, PO Box 01, Kwangwanase 5973

KRANTZKLOOF NATURE RESERVE

⛱ 🚶 Interpretation centre

Enquiries: The Officer-in-Charge, Natal Parks Board, PO Box 228, Kloof 3640, Telephone: (031) 7643515

LAKE ETEZA NATURE RESERVE

Enquiries: The Regional Scientist, Natal Parks Board, St Lucia Estuary 3936, Telephone: St Lucia (035) 5901342

LEEUKOP GAME RANCH

SC 🚶 👫 🛶 🚤 🐎 🚙

Accommodation: The Manager, PO Box 12, Golela 3990
Enquiries: Telephone: (03843) 51123

LOTENI NATURE RESERVE

SC ⛰ 🚶 🐟 ✗ 🏊

Accommodation: The Reservations Officer, Natal Parks Board, Telephone: (0331) 471981
Camping/Enquiries: The Camp Superintendent, Loteni Nature Reserve, PO Box 14, Himeville 4585, Telephone: Himeville 033622 ask for 1540

MABIBI COASTAL CAMP

⛰ 🐟 🚤 Scuba diving

Accommodation: KwaZulu Department of Nature Conservation
Enquiries: 367 Loop Street, Pietermaritzburg 3201, Telephone: (0331) 946698

MAGDALENA GAME RANCH

SC 👫 🛶 🐎 Hunting

Accommodation: The Manager, PO Box 476, Vryheid 3100
Enquiries: Telephone: Hlobane (0386) 71865

MALENDENI NATURE RESERVE

Enquiries: Mr Ken Gordon, Ladysmith, Telephone: (0361) 26810

MAPELANE NATURE RESERVE

SC ⛰ 🐟 🏊 🚤

Accommodation: The Reservations Officer, Natal Parks Board (Log cabins), Telephone: (0331) 471981
Camping (5 sites) The Officer-in-Charge, Mapelane, P/Bag St Lucia Estuary 3936, Telephone: St Lucia Estuary (035) 5901407

MAPUTALAND MEDICINAL RESOURCE AREA

SC ➤ Canoeing Nursery

Enquiries: Natal Provincial Administration, Community Services Branch,
P/Bag X9078, Pietermaritzburg 3200, Telephone: (0331) 952996

MARIANNWOOD NATURE RESERVE

卅

Enquiries: Pinetown Parks Department, PO Box 49, Pinetown 3600
(Officer-in-Charge Natural Areas), Telephone: (031) 7192215

MBUMBAZI NATURE RESERVE

Environmental education centre

Enquiries: Mbumbazi Nature Reserve, PO Box 85, Paddock 4244,
Telephone: (0397) 91738 or NPA Department of Community Services
(0331) 952996

MFULI GAME RANCH

SC R 🏃 ➤ 🚙 Hunting Sports facilities

Accommodation: The Manager, Mfuli Game Ranch, PO Box 17, Nkwalini 3816
Enquiries: Telephone: (03546) 620

MHLOPENI NATURE RESERVE

SC 🏃 Hunting

Accommodation: The Manager, Mhlopeni Nature Reserve
Enquiries: PO Box 386, Greytown 3500, Telephone: Muden (03346) 722 or
Durban (031) 839655

MIDMAR PUBLIC RESORT NATURE RESERVE

SC Δ R 卅 🏃 ➤ ➤ Launch tours Sailing Sports facilities
Historical village

Accommodation: The Reservations Officer, Natal Parks Board,
Telephone: (0331) 471981
Camping: The Officer-in-Charge, Midmar Public Resort, P/Bag Howick 3290,
Telephone: (0332) 302667/8/9

MISSION ROCKS OUTPOST and MOUNT TABOR

卅 🏃 ➤ Wilderness trails

Enquiries: Natal Parks Board, Telephone: St Lucia Estuary (035) 5901233

MKHOMAZI and MZIMKULU WILDERNESS AREAS and MZIMKULWANA
NATURE RESERVE (MKHOMAZI STATE FOREST)

Camping/Enquiries: The Officer-in-Charge, Mkhomazi State Forest, PO Box 105,
Nottingham Road 3280, Telephone: (0333) ask for 36444

MKUZI GAME RESERVE

SC Hides Hunting Ethnic village

Accommodation: The Reservations Officer, Natal Parks Board,
Telephone: (0331) 471981
Camping: The Camp Superintendent, Mkuzi Game Reserve, P/Bag X550,
Mkuze 3965, Telephone: Mkuze (035) 5731001
Hunting enquiries: The Conservator, Hunting, Natal Parks Board,
Telephone: (0331) 471961

MOLWENI NATURE RESERVE

Enquiries: PO Box 1024, Linkhills 3652, Telephone: (0331) 773659 or NPA
Department of Community Services (0331) 952996

MONK'S COWL STATE FOREST

Camp site enquiries: The Officer-in-Charge, Monk's Cowl State Forest, P/Bag X2,
Winterton 3340, Telephone: (0364) 681103

MONTELLO SAFARI LODGE

FC

Enquiries: Montello Safari Lodge, PO Box 267, Greytown 3500
Reservations: Telephone:(0334) 33344, After hours: (0334) 31465

MOOR PARK NATURE RESERVE

Enquiries: The Warden, Natal Parks Board, Wagendrift Nature Reserve,
Telephone: (0363) 532736

MOUNT CURRIE NATURE RESERVE

 National monument

Camp sites: The Officer-in-Charge, Natal Parks Board, Mount Currie Nature
Reserve, PO Box 378, Kokstad 4700, Telephone: Kokstad (0372) 3844

MPENJATI PUBLIC RESORT NATURE RESERVE

Enquiries: The Zone Officer, Natal Parks Board, Telephone: (03931) 30447

NCANDU NATURE RESERVE

Enquiries: Natal Parks Board, Telephone: (0331) 471961 or (0364) 38103
Permission to visit: Royal Natal National Park (0364) 3801051

NDUMU GAME RESERVE

SC ▲ ⛢ 👫 🚙 Hides

Accommodation: The Reservations Officer, KwaZulu Department of Nature
  Conservation, 367 Loop Street, Pietermaritzburg 3201, Telephone: (0331) 946698
Enquiries: Telephone: Ndumu (038482) ask for 32

NEW GERMANY NATURE RESERVE

▲ ⛢ 🚶 Hide Interpretation centre

Enquiries: The Borough of New Germany Parks Department, PO Box 2,
  New Germany 3620, Telephone: (031) 7054360 (Open Wednesday-Sunday)

NGELE HIKING TRAIL

SC 🚶 🐟 🐟

Enquiries: SAFCOL, P/Bag 1, Weza, 4685
Reservations: Telephone: (039452) ask for 24 (office hrs 8h00-13h00)

NGOYE FOREST RESERVE

Enquiries: (Permit required for entry) KwaZulu Department of Nature
  Conservation, 367 Loop Street, Pietermaritzburg 3201, Telephone: (0331) 946698
Permits: Contact Head, Communications Conservator – Ulundi,
  Telephone: (0358) 700552, specifying date of intended visit – allow 30 days for
  reply.

NKANDLA FOREST RESERVE

Enquiries: (Permit required for entry) KwaZulu Department of Nature
  Conservation, Ulundi, Telephone: (0358) 700552
Permits: Contact Head, Communications Conservator – Ulundi,
  Telephone: (0358) 700552 specifying date of intended visit – allow 30 days for
  reply.

NORTH PARK NATURE RESERVE

⛢

Enquiries: The Officer-in-Charge, Natal Parks Board, North Park Nature Reserve,
  PO Box 288, Kloof 3640, Telephone: (031) 7643515 or NPB Durban office,
  Telephone: (031) 251271

NTENDEKA WILDERNESS AREA

▲ 🚶

Camp sites/Enquiries: The State Forester, Ngome State Forest, P/Bag X9306,
  Vryheid 3100, Telephone: (0386) 71883

NYALA GAME RANCH

SC 🌲 🚶‍♂️ 🏊 🐎 🚙 Scenic drives

Accommodation: PO Box 647, Empangeni 3880
Enquiries: Telephone: (0351) 924095 or (0351) 24543

OCEAN VIEW GAME PARK

🌲

Enquiries: Natal Parks Board, Telephone: Eshowe (0354) 42473

OLIFANTSKOP NATURE RESERVE
Enquiries: Natal Provincial Administration, Community Services Branch,
P/Bag X9078, Pietermaritzburg 3200, Telephone: (0331) 952996

OPATHE GAME RESERVE
Enquiries: KwaZulu Department of Nature Conservation, Ulundi,
Telephone: (0358) 700552

ORIBI GORGE NATURE RESERVE

SC 🌲 🚶 🐟 ✗ Scenic drives

Accommodation: The Reservations Officer, Natal Parks Board,
Telephone: (0331) 471981
Enquiries: Oribi Reserve, Paddock, Telephone: (0397) 91962

PALMIET NATURE RESERVE

🌲 🚶 🚶‍♂️

Enquiries: Westville Municipality, Environmental Officer, PO Box 39,
Westville 3630, Telephone: (031) 861331

PARADISE VALLEY NATURE RESERVE

🌲 🚶

Enquiries: Pinetown Parks Department, PO Box 49, Pinetown 3600
Contact Officer-in-Charge, Paradise Valley Nature Reserve, Telephone: (031) 723443

PHINDA RESOURCE RESERVE

FC 🚶‍♂️ 🏊 🚙 Airstrip Launch tours Flights arranged

Accommodation: Phinda Holdings (Pty) Ltd, PO Box 1211, Sunninghill 2157,
Telephone: (011) 8038421, Fax: (011) 8031810
Zululand: Telephone: (035562) 0271 or 0088

PIGEON VALLEY PARK

🌲 🚶

Enquiries: Durban Parks, Recreation & Beaches Department, PO Box 3740,
Durban 4000, Telephone: (031) 234466

PONGOLA BUSH NATURE RESERVE
Enquiries: The Officer-in-Charge, Natal Parks Board, Telephone: (0381) 4383

PONGOLAPOORT PUBLIC RESORT NATURE RESERVE

Enquiries: Natal Parks Board, Telephone: (0331) 471961

PONGOLWANE PRIVATE NATURE RESERVE
SC ➤ ➤ ➤
Accommodation: The Manager, PO Box 12, Golela 3990
Enquiries: Telephone/Fax: (03843) 51123

PUMALANGA NATURE RESERVE
SC ⋔ ➤ ➤ ➤
Accommodation: The Manager, PO Box 169, Hluhluwe 3960,
  Telephone: (03562) 1912, Fax: (035) 5620210

QUDENI NATURE RESERVE
Enquiries: KwaZulu Department of Nature Conservation, P/Bag X23, Ulundi 3838,
  Telephone: (0358) 700552 or Chief Nature Conservator – Head Communications
  Eshowe (0354) 74634/42487

QUEEN ELIZABETH PARK NATURE RESERVE
⍋ ⋔   Resource centre   Nursery
Enquiries: The Officer-in-Charge, Queen Elizabeth Park Nature Reserve, Natal
  Parks Board, PO Box 662, Pietermaritzburg 3200, Telephone: (0331) 471961

RICHARDS BAY GAME RESERVE
➤
Enquiries: The Officer-in-Charge, Natal Parks Board, Richards Bay,
  Telephone:(0351) 32330

ROCKTAIL BAY CAMP
SC   FC   ⋔ ➤ Scuba diving
Accommodation/Enquiries: Wilderness Safaris, PO Box 651171, Benmore 2010 or
  180 Helen Road, Strathavon, Sandton 2199, Telephone: (011) 8841458/4633,
  Fax: (011) 8836255, Telex: 428642 WILD SA

ROOSFONTEIN NATURE RESERVE
⍋ ⋔
Enquiries: The Westville Municipality, PO Box 39, Westville 3630,
  Telephone: (031) 861331

ROYAL NATAL NATIONAL PARK

SC FC Δ R ⊼ ⋀⋀ ⤙ ⤜ ⤢ 🐎

Accommodation: The Reservations Officer, Natal Parks Board,
  Telephone: (0331) 471981
Camp sites/enquiries: The Officer-in-Charge, Mahai camp sites,
  PO Mont-aux-Sources, 3353, Telephone: (0364) 381803
Royal Natal The Lessee, Royal Natal National Park Hotel,
  PO Mont-aux-Sources, 3353, Telephone: (0364) 381051

RUGGED GLEN NATURE RESERVE

Δ ⊼ ⋀ ⤙ 🐎

Camping/Enquiries: The Officer-in-Charge, Natal Parks Board, Rugged Glen
  Nature Reserve, PO Mont-aux-Sources 3353, Telephone: (0364) 381803

SEATON PARK

⋀

Enquiries: Durban Parks, Recreation & Beaches Department, PO Box 3740,
  Durban 4000, Telephone: (031) 234466

SHONGWENI RESOURCES RESERVE

⊼ ⋀ ⤙ ⤢ 🐎   Scenic drives

Enquiries: Wilderness Leadership School, PO Box 53058, Yellowwood Park 4011,
  Telephone: (031) 428375 (Msinsi Holdings)

SILEZA FOREST NATURE RESERVE
Enquiries: KwaZulu Department of Nature Conservation,
  Telephone: Ulundi (0358) 700552

SILVERGLEN NATURE RESERVE

⊼ ⋀ ⋀⋀ Nursery

Enquiries: Durban Parks, Recreation & Beaches Department, PO Box 3740,
  Durban 4000, Telephone: (031) 433608

SKYLINE (ARBORETUM) NATURE RESERVE

⋀ Herbarium Library

Enquiries: The Zone Officer, Natal Parks Board,
  Telephone: (03931) 50112

SOADA FOREST NATURE RESERVE
Enquiries: Natal Parks Board, Telephone: (0331) 471961

360

SODWANA BAY NATIONAL PARK

SC ▲ 🕴 🐟 ⛵ 🚤

Accommodation: The Reservations Officer, Natal Parks Board (Chalets),
  Telephone: (0331) 471981
Camp sites only: The Officer-in-Charge, Sodwana Bay National Park, P/Bag 310,
  Mbazwana 3974, Telephone: Mbazwana (035682) 51

SPIOENKOP PUBLIC RESORT NATURE RESERVE

SC ▲ 🕴 🐟 🚤 🐴   Hide Sailing Canoeing Sports facilities

Accommodation: The Reservations Officer, Natal Parks Board,
  Telephone: (0331) 471961
Camp sites/enquiries: The Camp Superintendent, Spioenkop Public Resort,
  PO Box 140, Winterton 3340, Telephone: Winterton 03682 ask for Spioenkop
  Public Resort
Hunting enquiries: The Conservator, Hunting, Natal Parks Board,
  Pietermaritzburg, Telephone: (0331) 471961

SPRINGSIDE NATURE RESERVE

🕴

Enquiries: Hillcrest Town Board, PO Box 38, Hillcrest 3650,
  Telephone: (031) 751222 or Wildlife Society, 100 Brand Road, Durban 4001,
  Telephone: (031) 213126

ST LUCIA CROCODILE CENTRE and GAME PARK

🕴   Educational centre

Enquiries: The Warden, Natal Parks Board, St Lucia Crocodile Centre, P/Bag X01,
  St Lucia Estuary 3936, Telephone: (035) 5901386

ST LUCIA PUBLIC RESORT and ESTUARY

SC ▲ R 🕴 🐟 ⛵ 🚤   Crocodile interpretation centre Launch tours

Accommodation: The Officer-in-Charge, Natal Parks Board
Enquiries: St Lucia Resort, P/Bag St Lucia Estuary 3936,
  Telephone: St Lucia (035) 5901340

SUNGULWANE GAME LODGE

FC 👥 ⛵ 🚙 Hides Hunting

Accommodation: PO Bayala, Zululand 3966
Enquiries: Telephone: (03562) 2831, Fax: (03562) 138, Central reservations
  (Travel Africa), Telephone: (011) 8834345/6/7, Fax: (011) 8832556

SWAMP NATURE RESERVE

SC FC 🕺 🐟 🐴   Hunting

Enquiries: Natal Parks Board, Telephone: (0331) 471961

TC ROBERTSON NATURE RESERVE

🎋 🕺

Enquiries: The Town Clerk, Scottburgh, Telephone: (0323) 21202

TEMBE ELEPHANT PARK

SC Δ

Accommodation: KwaZulu Department of Nature Conservation
Enquiries: 367 Loop Street, Pietermaritzburg 3201, Telephone: (0331) 946698 or
 The Officer-in-Charge, Tembe Elephant Park, KDNC, P/Bag 356,
 Nkwangwanase 3973, Telephone: (0355) 920001

THUKELA BIOSPHERE RESERVE
Accommodation: No central booking office as yet
Enquiries: Telephone: (0363) 41938 or (03346) 777 after hours

TRAFALGAR MARINE RESERVE

🦆 🐟 🚤

Enquiries: The Zone Officer, Natal Parks Board, Telephone: (03931) 30447

TREASURE BEACH ENVIRONMENTAL EDUCATION CENTRE

Environmental centre

Enquiries: The Wildlife Society, Treasure Beach Project, 835 Marine Drive,
 Brighton Beach 4052, Telephone: (031) 478507/8

TUGELA DRIFT NATURE RESERVE

🎋 🕺

Enquiries: Natal Parks Board, Telephone: (0331) 471961

UBIZANE GAME RANCH

SC FC 🕺🕺 🚙

Accommodation: The Manager, Ubizane Game Ranch
Enquiries: PO Box 102, Hluhluwe 3960, Telephone: (03562) 3602,
 Fax: (03562) 193

UMBOGOVANGO "THE UMDONI DAMS"

⛱ 🚶 Environmental centre   Hides

Enquiries: (A private nature reserve – an appointment to visit is required.) Owned by AECI (Ltd), Telephone: (031) 9492081

UMDONI PARK

⛱ 🚶 ⚲ Golf course

Enquiries: The Manager, Telephone:(0323) 51227

UMFOLOZI GAME RESERVE

SC ▲ ⛱ 🚶 👥 🚙 Scenic drives   Hides

Accommodation: The Reservations Officer, Natal Parks Board
Wilderness Trails: Telephone: (0331) 471981
Enquiries: Umfolozi Game Reserve, Telephone: (035) 5620287

UMGENI VALLEY NATURE RESERVE

SC ⛱ 🚶 Educational courses

Accommodation: The Manager, Umgeni Valley Nature Reserve
Enquiries: PO Box 394, Howick 3290, Telephone: (0332) 303931

UMGENI VLEI NATURE RESERVE

Enquiries: Natal Parks Board, Telephone: (0331) 471961

UMHLANGA BUSH NATURE RESERVE

🚶

Enquiries: (Privately owned – permission for entry must be obtained.) Borough of Umhlanga, Telephone: (031) 5611101

UMHLANGA LAGOON NATURE RESERVE

⛱ 🚶

Enquiries: Natal Parks Board, Durban Office.
Telephone: (031) 251271

UMHLANGA PONDS

Bird hides

UMLALAZI NATURE RESERVE

SC ▲ 🏕 🧍 🐟 🏊 🛶

Accommodation: The Reservations Officer, Natal Parks Board,
  Telephone: (0331) 471981
Camping/Enquiries: The Officer-in-Charge, Umlalazi Nature Reserve, PO Box 234,
  Mtunzini 3867, Telephone: Mtunzini (0353) 401836

UMTAMVUNA NATURE RESERVE

🏕 🧍 Herbarium

Enquiries: The Officer-in-Charge, Natal Parks Board, PO Box 25,
  Port Edward 4295, Telephone: (03930) 32383

UMVOTI VLEI NATURE RESERVE

🧍 Hide

Enquiries: (A permit is required for entry) Contact Mr Pat Clarence, "Proud Acres",
  Telephone: (035552) 1340 or Zone Officer, Natal Parks Board, Sevenoaks,
  Telephone: (035552) 1511 or (0334) 32329

UMZIKI GAME RANCH

SC 🧍🧍 🐟 🏊 🚙 Hunting

Accommodation: Telephone: Empangeni (0351) 26756
Enquiries: After hours (0351) 26054 Theo Zietsman or Hlobane (0381) 3541

UVONGO RIVER NATURE RESERVE

🏕 🧍

Enquiries: The Town Clerk, PO Box 13, Uvongo 4270, Telephone: (03931) 51222

VALHALLA HUNTING

SC FC 🧍 🐟 🏊 🐎 Hunting

Accommodation: The Manager, Valhalla, PO Box 790, Dundee 3000
Enquiries: Telephone/Fax: (03425) 790 or the Wildlife Society, Vryheid Zone
  (0381) 812271

VERGELEGEN NATURE RESERVE

SC 🏕 🧍 🐟

Accommodation: The Reservations Officer, Natal Parks Board
Enquiries: Telephone: (0331) 471981

VERNON CROOKES NATURE RESERVE

SC 🏕 🧍 🐟 Scenic drives

Accommodation: The Officer-in-Charge, Natal Parks Board
Enquiries: Telephone: Umzinto (0323) 42222

VIRGINIA BUSH NATURE RESERVE

ᛉ ᛉᛉ   Resource centre

Enquiries: Durban Parks, Recreation & Beaches Department, PO Box 3740,
  Durban 4000, Telephone: (031) 234466

VRYHEID NATURE RESERVE

ᛒ ᛉ Hides

Enquiries: Natal Parks Board, Telephone: (0331) 471961

WAGENDRIFT PUBLIC RESORT NATURE RESERVE

▲ ᛒ ➤ ➤   Canoeing Sailing Sports facilities Educational youth centre

Camping/Enquiries: The Officer-in-Charge, Natal Parks Board, Wagendrift Public
  Resort, PO Box 316, Estcourt 3310, Telephone: (0363) 22550
Bookings for Education Centre: Telephone: (0331) 471981

WEENEN NATURE RESERVE

▲ ᛒ ᛉ   Hide

Camping: The Officer-in-Charge, Natal Parks Board, Weenen Nature Reserve,
  PO Box 122, Weenen 3325, Telephone: Weenen (0363) 41809

WILFRIED BAUER NATURE RESERVE

ᛒ

Enquiries: The Municipality of Matatiele, Telephone: (0373) 3135/6

WINDY RIDGE GAME PARK

SC ᛒ ᛉᛉ 🚙   Scenic drives Airstrip Hunting

Accommodation: Windy Ridge Game Park, PO Heatonville, Zululand 3881,
  Telephone: (0351) 23465

ZULU NYALA SAFARIS

FC ᛉᛉ ➤ ➤ ➤ 🐎 🚙   Sports facilities

Accommodation: Zulu Nyala Safaris, PO Box 1775, Johannesburg 2000
Enquiries: Telephone: (011) 3332919, Fax: (011) 3332319

BIBLIOGRAPHY

Abbott, AT and Nicholson, HB. 1985. Some indigenous plants of southern Natal. *Veld and Flora*, Vol. 71, No. 1, March, pp. 4-9.

Anon. Undated. *Uvongo River Reserve. A wildlife handbook.* Compiled by Uvongo-Shelley Beach Business Club, pp. 1-31.

Anon. January 1993. *The environmental impact assessment for the eastern shores of Lake St Lucia (Kingsa Tojan Lease Area)* 3 vols: Vol. 1, part 1, Specialists' reports; Vol. 1, part 2, Comments on the specialists' reports; Vol. 2, Reports on the key issues; Vol. 3, Environmental impact report. Published by the CSIR Environmental Services, Pretoria.

Anon. August 1993. *Environmental impact assessments, eastern shores of Lake St Lucia (Kingsa Tojan Lease Area)* Vol. 4, part 1, Final report (response to comments received); Vol. 4, part 2, Comments on the environmental impact assessment. Published by the CSIR Environmental Services, Pretoria.

Baldwin, WC. 1863. *African hunting from Natal to the Zambezi (1852-1860).* Richard Bentley, London.

Bartholomew, R. 1989. *The Ntendeka wilderness area.* Pamphlet 423, Department of Forestry and Environmental Affairs. August, pp. 1-20.

Begg, George. 1978. *The estuaries of Natal.* Natal Town and Regional Planning Report, Vol. 41, pp. 1-657.

Begg, George. 1984. *The estuaries of Natal part 2.* Supplement to Natal Town and Regional Planning Report, Vol. 41, pp. 1-631.

Begg, George. 1982. Kosi Bay – a wonderful aquarium and the most gorgeous aviary. *African Wildlife*, Vol. 36, pp. 178-180.

Begg, George. 1985. *Policy proposals for the estuaries of Natal.* Natal Town and Regional Planning Report, Vol. 43, pp. 1-37.

Begg, George. 1991. The Natal coastline. *Veld and Flora*, Vol. 77(4), December, pp. 111-113.

Bennett, Gordon. 1989. *Where to see birds in Natal.* Natal Bird Club, pp. 1-48.

Berjak, P, Campbell, GK, Huckett, BI and Parmenter, NW. 1977. *In the mangroves of southern Africa.* Natal Branch of the Wildlife Society of Southern Africa, pp. 1-66.

Berruti, A and Sinclair, JC. 1983. *Where to watch birds in southern Africa.* Struik Publishers, Cape Town, pp. 302.

Bond, Creina. 1977. Nxwala. *African Wildlife*, Vol. 31, No. 3, pp. 6-8.

Boon, Richard. 1992. Vernon Crookes Nature Reserve. *Birding in Southern Africa*, Vol. 44, No. 1, March, pp. 12-14.

Bourquin, O, Vincent, J and Hitchins, PM. 1971. The vertebrates of the Hluhluwe Game Reserve – Corridor (state land) – Umfolozi Game Reserve. *The Lammergeyer*, No. 14, December, pp. 5-58.

Bourquin, O and Mathias, I. 1984. The vertebrates of Oribi Gorge Nature Reserve. *The Lammergeyer*, No. 33, pp. 35-44.

366

Braadvedt, HP. 1949. *Roaming Zululand with a native commissioner*. Shuter & Shooter, Pietermaritzburg, Natal.

Branch, Bill. 1988. *Field guide to the snakes and other reptiles of southern Africa*. Struik Publishers, Cape Town.

Bronner, GN and Meester, JAJ. 1987. Mammals of Bluff Nature Reserve. *The Lammergeyer*, No. 38, December, pp. 1-7.

Brooks, Shirley J. 1990. Playing the game. The struggle for wildlife protection in Zululand, 1910-1930. Unpublished MA thesis, Queens University, Kingston, Ontario, Canada.

Brown, CJ and Barnes, PR. 1984. Birds of the Natal Alpine belt. *The Lammergeyer*, No. 33, pp. 1-13.

Browning, Jane and Getliffe-Norris, Fiona. 1989. *Trees (some shrubs/climbers). Vernon Crookes Nature Reserve, Natal*. Cyclostyled Report, Natal Parks Board, Pietermaritzburg, Natal, pp. 1-126.

Bruton, MN and Cooper, KH (Editors). 1980. *Studies on the ecology of Maputaland*. Rhodes University and the Natal branch of the Wildlife Society of Southern Africa.

Bryant, AT. 1929. *Olden times in Zululand and Natal*. Longman Green, London.

Bulpin, TV. 1952. *Shaka's country. A book of Zululand*. Howard Timmins, Cape Town.

Chittenden, Hugh (Editor). 1992. *Top birding spots in southern Africa*. Southern, Halfway House.

Cooper, KH. 1982. Maputaland – an ecological approach to land use. *African Wildlife*, Vol. 36, p. 189.

Cooper, KH. 1985. *The conservation status of indigenous forests in Transvaal, Natal and OFS, South Africa*. The Wildlife Society of Southern Africa, Conservation Division, 100 Brand Road, Durban, pp. 1-108.

Cornish-Bowden, ME. 1967. Dad's story. Extracts from the diary of LC von Wissel, compiled 1895-1910. Unpublished.

Coles, Ramond B. 1959. *Zulu journal. Field notes of a naturalist in South Africa*. University of California Press, Berkeley.

Crass, RS. 1964. *Freshwater fishes of Natal*. Shuter & Shooter, Pietermaritzburg, pp. 1-167.

Cunningham, Tony. 1982. Making the most of Maputaland plants. *African Wildlife*, Vol. 31, No. 6, pp. 190-191.

Cyrus, Digby and Robson, Nigel. 1980. *Bird atlas of Natal*. University of Natal Press, Pietermaritzburg.

Delegorgue, Adulphe. 1990. *Travels in South Africa Vol. I*. Translated by Fleur Webb. Introduced and indexed by Stephanie J Alexander and Colin de B Webb. Killie Campbell Africana Library and University of Natal Press Publication No. 5, Pietermaritzburg.

De Moor, Phillip (Editor). 1990-1993. *Albatross*. Newsletter of the Natal Bird Club. Nos 304-313.

Dodds, David A. 1975. *A cradle of rivers. The Natal Drakensberg*. Purnell, Cape Town.

Downing, BH. 1980. Relationships between rock substrata, landform and soil in Umfolozi Game Reserve, as explained for conservation purposes. *The Lammergeyer*, No. 30, pp. 32-48.

Dutton, TP. 1970. Iron smelting furnace in the Ndumu Game Reserve. *The Lammergeyer*, No. 12, November, pp. 37-39.

Edwards, Denzil. 1967. A plant ecological survey of the Tugela river basin. Botany survey of SA memoir No. 36. Town and Regional Planning Commission, Natal, pp. 1-285.

Ellis, Bev. 1975. Game conservation in Zululand 1824-1947. Unpublished BA (Hons) thesis, Department of History and Political Science, University of Natal, Pietermaritzburg.

Feely, J. 1974. *Background to the natural history of Zululand*. Wilderness School, Durban.

Hall, Martin. 1979. The Umfolozi, Hluhluwe and Corridor Reserves during the Iron Age. *The Lammergeyer*, No. 27, October, pp. 28-40.

Harrison, ER. 1989. *Memories of early Mtubatuba and district*. Limited edition: Zululand Stationers and Printers, Mtubatuba. Published by ER Harrison, Mtubatuba, pp. 1-103.

Heeg, J and Breen, CM. 1982. Man and the Pongola floodplain. SA Natural Sciences Programmes Report No. 56, CSIR, Pretoria, p. 117.

Hilliard, OM and Burtt, BL. 1987. *The botany of the southern Natal Drakensberg*. Annals of Kirstenbosch Botanic Gardens, Vol. 15, pp. 1-253.

Hocking, Anthony. 1992. *Renishaw. The story of Crookes Bros*. Hollards, South Africa, pp. 1-320.

Hocking, Anthony, Johnson-Barker, Brian, Keegan, Marilyn and Tingay, Paul. 1983. *Reader's Digest illustrated guide to the game parks and nature reserves of southern Africa*. Reader's Digest, Cape Town.

Irwin, Dave and Irwin, Pat. 1992. *A field guide to the Natal Drakensberg*. 2nd revised ed. Rhodes University, Grahamstown.

Issacs, Nathaniel. 1949. *Travels and adventures in eastern Africa*. Vol. 1. Edward Churton, London.

Jobes, Gertrude. 1962. *Dictionary of mythology, folklore and symbols*. Parts 1 and 2. The Scarecrow Press, New York.

Junkin, Elizabeth Darby (Editor). 1989. *South African passage. Diaries of the Wilderness Leadership School*. Fulcrum, Golden, Colorado.

Junod, HA. 1927. *The life of a South African tribe*. 2 vols. Longman, London.

Killick, Donald. 1990. *A field guide to the flora of the Natal Drakensberg*. Jonathan Ball and AD Donker, Johannesburg.

King, Lester. 1982. *The Natal monocline. Explaining the origin and scenery of Natal, South Africa*. 2nd ed. University of Natal, Pietermaritzburg.

Krauss, Ferdinand. 1973. *Travel journal – Cape to Zululand*. (Edited by OH Spohr) AA Balkema, Cape Town.

Kriel, JP (Editor). 1966. *Report of the Commission of Enquiry into the alleged threat to animal and plant life in the St Lucia Lake*. Government Printer, Pretoria.

Lawson, D. 1987. A preliminary checklist of the plants of the closed canopy communities of False Bay Park, Zululand. *The Lammergeyer*, No. 38, December, pp. 20-27.

Levy, Jaynee. 1987. *The complete guide to walks and trails in southern Africa.* Struik, Cape Town, pp. 1-352.

Little, Robin M and Bainbridge, William R. 1992. *Birds of the Natal Drakensberg Park. A wildlife handbook.* Illustrated by Tony Clarkson. The Wildlife Society of Southern Africa, Natal branch, pp. 1-159.

Ludlow, Capt. WR. 1822. *Zululand and Ceteswayo.* Simkin and Marshall, London.

Lugg, HC. 1970. *A Natal family looks back.* Griggs, Durban.

MacDevette, DR, MacDevette, DK, Gordon, IG and Bartholomew, RLC. 1989. The floristics of the Natal indigenous forest. Natal Parks Board report, January, pp. 1-20.

Mackeurtan, G. 1931. *The cradle days of Natal.* Longman Green, London.

Maclean, Gordon Lindsay. 1985. *Roberts' birds of southern Africa.* The Trustees of the John Voelcker Bird Book Fund, Cape Town.

Maddock, AH and Zaloumis, G. 1987. Additional and continuing records of the vertebrates at Vernon Crookes Nature Reserve, with indications of rodent and ungulate abundances. *The Lammergeyer,* No. 38, December, pp. 40-54.

Meintjies, Johannes. 1973. *The Voortrekkers. The story of the Great Trek and the making of South Africa.* Cassell, London.

Moll, EJ. 1968. Some notes on the vegetation of Mkuzi Game Reserve, Natal. *The Lammergeyer,* No. 8, March, pp. 25-30.

Morris, Donald R. 1965. *The washing of the spears.* Simon & Schuster, New York.

Mountain, Alan G. 1990. *Paradise under pressure.* Southern, Halfway House.

Nicholls, Geoff and Fairall, Monica. 1992. *Day walks in and around Durban and Pietermaritzburg.* Struik, Cape Town, pp. 1-128.

Nicholson, HB and Nicholls, GR. 1991. Skyline Arboretum. *Journal of Dendrology,* No. 13, pp. 1-8.

Ntombela, Magqubu. Unpublished papers collated by Ian Player.

O'Keefe, JH (Editor). 1986. The conservation of South African rivers. SA National Scientific Programmes Report No. 131. CSIR, Pretoria, pp. 1-117.

Osborn, Robert F. 1964. *Valiant harvest. The founding of the South African sugar industry 1848-1926.* SA Sugar Association, pp. 1-343.

Palgrove, KC. 1988. *Trees of Southern Africa.* 2nd ed. Struik, Cape Town.

Pearse, RO. 1973. *Barrier of spears. Drama of the Drakensberg.* Howard Timmins, Cape Town.

Player, FHA. Unpublished personal tape transcriptions, 1917 game drive in Zululand.

Player, Ian. 1964. *Men, rivers and canoes.* Simondium, Cape Town.

Player, Ian. 1972. *The white rhino saga.* Collins, London.

Pooley, AC and Michener, C. 1969. Observations on nests of stingless honey bees in Natal (Hymenoptera: Apidae). *Journal of the Entomology Society of SA,* Vol. 32, No. 2, pp. 423-430.

Pooley, AC, Hadley, ES, Pooley, ES and Gans, Carl. 1973. *Ecological aspects of the distribution of subsoil herpetofauna in Ndumu Game Reserve.* Annals of the Carnegie Museum, No. 44, pp. 103-115.

Pooley, AC. 1982. *Discoveries of a crocodile man.* William Collins & Sons, London.

369

Pooley, AC. 1982. The ecology of the Nile crocodile *Crocodylus niloticus* in Zululand. Unpublished MSc thesis, University of Natal, Pietermaritzburg, pp. 1-333.

Pooley, AC. 1992. *Mashesha, the making of a game ranger*. Southern, Halfway House.

Pooley, ES. 1978. A checklist of the plants of Ndumu Game Reserve, north-eastern Zululand. *Journal of SA Botany*. 44(1), pp. 1-54.

Pooley, ES. 1993. *The complete field guide to trees of Natal, Zululand and Transkei*. Natal Flora Publications Trust, Natal Herbarium, Durban.

Potter, Capt. HB. 1935. Letter to Provincial Secretary, Pietermaritzburg, ref CCZ/696 dated 6 September 1935 re: Ndumu Game Reserve.

Poynton, JA. 1964. *The amphibia of South Africa*. Annals of the Natal Museum. Vol. 17, pp. 1-334.

Pringle, John A, assisted by Bond, Creina and Clark, John. 1982. *The conservationists and the killers*. TV Bulpin and Books of Africa, Cape Town.

Raper, PE. 1987. *Dictionary of southern African place names*. Lowry, Johannesburg, pp. 1-368.

Rautenbach, IL, Nel, JAJ and Root, GA. 1981. Mammals of Itala Nature Reserve, Natal. *The Lammergeyer*, No. 31, pp. 21-37.

Reitz, D. 1943. *No outspan*. Faber & Faber, London.

Roberts, A. 1936. *Report upon a survey of the higher vertebrates of NE Zululand*. Annals of the Transvaal Museum, 18(3), pp. 163-222.

Rose, Mary. 1977-8. The oldest game reserves in Africa. *African Wildlife*, Vol. 31, No. 6, pp. 16-21.

Ross, JH. 1972. The flora of Natal. Botanical Survey memoir No. 39, Department of Agricultural Technical Services, Botanical Research Institute.

Ross, JH and Moll, EJ. 1972. *A list of Natal trees*. The Wildlife Society of Southern Africa, Natal branch.

Rowe-Rowe, DT. 1991. *The ungulates of Natal*. Natal Parks Board, Pietermaritzburg, pp. 1-36.

Rowe-Rowe, DT. 1992. *The carnivores of Natal*. Natal Parks Board, Pietermaritzburg, pp. 1-31.

Rowe-Rowe, DT. 1993. *Mammals recorded in Natal Parks Board game reserves*. Natal Parks Board, Pietermaritzburg, pp. 1-12.

Ryan, PG, Cooper, J, Hockey, PAR and Berruti, A. 1986. Waders (*Charadrii*) and other water birds on the coast and adjacent wetlands of Natal, 1980-1981. *The Lammergeyer*, No. 36, pp. 1-33.

Scotcher, JB, Wright, MG, Wright, CW and Collinson, RFH. 1978. An evaluation of veld condition in Moor Park Nature Reserve. *The Lammergeyer*, No. 26, pp. 7-18.

Shepherd, Olive. 1989. *Wild places of Natal. Nature reserves, resorts and parks.* The Wildlife Society of Southern Africa, Natal branch.

Smithers, Reay HN. 1983. *The mammals of the southern African sub-region*. University of Pretoria, Pretoria.

Steele, Nick. 1971. *Take a horse to the wilderness*. TV Bulpin and Books of Africa, Cape Town.

Steele, Nick. 1979. *Bush life of a game warden*. TV Bulpin, Cape Town.

Steele, Nick. 1992. *Poachers in the hills*. Nick Steele, PO Box 355, Melmoth 3835.

Stuart, CT and Stuart, MD. 1992. *Guide to southern African game and nature reserves*. 2nd ed. Struik, Cape Town.

Tait, BC. 1961. *The Durban story*. Knox Printing, Durban.

Taylor, RH (Editor). 1993. *Proceedings of the workshop on water requirements for Lake St Lucia*. Department of Environment Affairs, Pretoria, pp. 1-83.

Tinley, KL. 1976. *The ecology of Tongaland*. The Wildlife Society of Southern Africa, Natal branch.

Vincent, Jack. 1988. *Web of experience. An autobiography*. Privately published. ISBN 0-620-13383-X, pp. 1-365.

Von Breitenbach, F and von Breitenbach, J. 1990. *National list of indigenous trees*. 2nd revised ed. Dendrological Foundation, Pretoria.

Von Wissel, LC. Undated. Unpublished manuscript, compiled from the notes of LC von Wissel by ME Cornish-Bowden and ML Heaton, pp. 1-43.

Wager, Vincent A. 1976. *Dwindling forests of the Natal Coast*. The Wildlife Society of Southern Africa, Umhlanga Centre, Natal branch, pp. 1-33.

Whateley, A and Brooks, PM. 1985. The carnivores of the Hluhluwe and Umfolozi game reserves 1973-1982. *The Lammergeyer*, No. 35, June, pp. 1-27.

Wirminghaus, JO. 1990. A checklist of the plants of the Karkloof forest, Natal Midlands. *Bothalia*, 20. 2, pp. 159-165.

Wiseman, G and Garland, I. 1978. Mapelane. Unpublished report. The fieldwork section. The Wildlife Society of Southern Africa, Natal branch, pp. 1-8.

INDEX